Energy Law in Taiwan

Energy Law in Taiwan

Second Edition

Anton Ming-Zhi Gao

This book was originally published as a monograph in the International Encyclopaedia of Laws/Energy Law.

Founding Editor: Roger Blanpain
General Editor: Frank Hendrickx
Volume Editors: Kurt Deketelaere & Bram Delvaux

Wolters Kluwer

Published by:
Kluwer Law International B.V.
PO Box 316
2400 AH Alphen aan den Rijn
The Netherlands
E-mail: international-sales@wolterskluwer.com
Website: lrus.wolterskluwer.com

Sold and distributed by:
Wolters Kluwer Legal & Regulatory U.S.
7201 McKinney Circle
Frederick, MD 21704
United States of America
Email: customer.service@wolterskluwer.com

ISBN 978-94-035-3320-9

e-Book: ISBN 978-94-035-3321-6
web-PDF: ISBN 978-94-035-3322-3

The Author

Prof. Gao received a master's degree (M.A.) from National Taiwan University, and a second master's degree in energy and environmental law (LL.M.) from the Institute of Environmental and Energy Law of KU Leuven, Belgium. He also received a Ph.D. in Law from KU Leuven. Since then, he has devoted himself to energy and climate legal research and projects in Taiwan. He has published books and articles, hosted local and international energy law conferences, and has participated in international events. Prof. Gao envisions making the National Tsing Hua University one of the leading research institutes for energy law in East Asia. His main research interests lie in energy and environmental law and their interactions. Over the past few years, he has been very active in international publications centered on investigations of global legal issues, as well as European, Asian, and Taiwanese energy laws. He remains one of the most productive scholars in the field of energy law in Taiwan, publishing articles in international energy and environmental law journals (e.g., *European Environmental Law Review*, *International Energy Law Review*, *Renewable Energy Law and Policy*, *Carbon and Climate Law Review*), as well as in science-oriented energy journals (*Energy Policy, Renewable Energy and Sustainable Energy Review*).

In addition to international journals, Prof. Gao has also been devoted to studying and investigating energy law and policy development in Taiwan. He has participated in the formation of several legislations, such as the draft of the Nuclear-Free Homeland Act, the Nuclear Phase-out Act, the Basic Law for Sustainable Energy, as well as amendments to the Electricity Act and to the Renewable Energy Development Act, among others. His recent publications also include "100 questions regarding amendments to the Electricity Act" and "100 questions regarding amendments to the Renewable Energy Development Act." He has also written opinion pieces on issues concerning energy transition, such as the Nuclear-Free Homeland Policy and offshore wind farms.

The Author

Table of Contents

List of Abbreviations

AEC	Atomic Energy Council
BIPV	Building-Integrated Photovoltaic
BOM	Bureau of Mines
CCS	Carbon Capture and Storage
CECER	Committee on Energy Conservation and Emission Reduction
CGS	Central Geological Survey
CHP	Combined Heat and Power
CPC	Chinese Petroleum Corporation
CPNE	Committee on the Promotion of New Energy
DPP	Democratic Progressive Party
EEZ	Exclusive Economic Zone
EHS	Environment, Health and Safety
EIA	Environmental Impact Assessment
EPA	Environmental Protection Administration
FIT	Feed-in Tariff
FPCC	Formosa Petrochemical Corporation
FTC	Fair Trade Commission
GHG	Greenhouse Gas
GHGEPS	GHG Emission Performance Standard
GOMO	GO (Greenhouse Office)-MOEA
IC	Integrated Circuit
IDB	Industrial Development Bureau
IEA	International Energy Agency
INER	Institute of Nuclear Energy Research
IPP	Independent Power Producer
ITRI	Industrial Technology Research Institute
kl	kiloliter
KMT	Kuomintang
LCYCIC	Lee Chang Yung Chemical Industry Corporation

List of Abbreviations

LED	Light-Emitting Diode
LNG	Liquefied Natural Gas
MOEA	Ministry of Economic Affairs
MOEABOE	Bureau of Energy, Ministry of Economic Affairs
MOEAEC	Energy Commission, Ministry of Economic Affairs
MP	Member of Parliament
NAMAs	Nationally Appropriate Mitigation Actions
NGO	Non-governmental Organization
NTD	New Taiwan Dollar
NTPA	Negotiated Third Party Access
OECD	Organisation for Economic Co-operation and Development
PV	Photovoltaic
R&D	Research and Development
RTPA	Regulated Third Party Access
ROC	Republic of China
SEA	Strategic Environmental Assessment
SEC	State Enterprise Commission
TIGO	Industrial Greenhouse Office
TPA	Third Party Access
TPBOM	Taiwan Provincial Bureau of Mines
UNFCCC	United Nations Framework Convention on Climate Change
VAT	Value Added Tax

Acknowledgment

This manuscript owes its completion to the research funding of the National Science Council of Taiwan (Project number: NSC 109-2410-H-007 -038 -MY2; 109-2627-M-011-001-) and the book publication incentive provided by the Research Center for Humanities and Social Sciences, National Tsing Hua University.

Acknowledgment

General Introduction

Chapter 1. General Background

§1. Geography and Population

1. The Republic of China (ROC (Taiwan)) is an oceanic nation of 23.59 million (2018) people located off the southeastern corner of Eurasia. With a combined area of approximately 36,000 square kilometers, it comprises the main island of Taiwan, the archipelagoes of Penghu, Kinmen, and Matsu, and a number of other islands. The main island is blessed with climatic zones ranging from the tropical to the temperate, resulting in a wealth of animal and plant species, many of them endemic to Taiwan. Among the myriad mountains that give the island its varied topography, over 200 peaks tower higher than 3,000 meters above sea level. While average annual rainfall is high, Taiwan also enjoys plenty of sunshine. The smaller islands have their own unique natural features, such as the basalt columns on the Penghu Islands and the marine hot springs on Green Island; the Kinmen Islands and Taiping Island of the Nansha Islands are located at positions of considerable strategic significance.[1]

2. These geographical features along with the condition of its population are very important in terms of Taiwan's energy development. As a young island, Taiwan lacks indigenous energy resources and relies heavily on imports. Yet, due to its isolated island nature, Taiwan finds it hard to develop more secure oil and gas pipeline supplies, relying on shipping instead. The lack of an interconnected transmission system also makes electricity trade impossible. All of these factors contribute to the importance of nuclear power in Taiwan. The lack of proper sites for building liquefied natural gas (LNG) terminals and for storage has also led to limited supplies of gas and concerns about gas security. LNG vessels may not be able to unload natural gas because of the impacts of typhoon. This may lead to concerns around gas security, as well. In sum, the concerns about energy security have engendered the attitude toward energy liberalization. The general perception is that without a sufficient upstream energy supply, it is difficult to introduce competition. Therefore,

1. Ministry of Foreign Affairs, 2019-2020 Taiwan: at a Glance, available at: http://multilingual.mofa.gov.tw/web/web_UTF-8/MOFA/glance2019-2020/English.pdf. *See also*, BBC, Taiwan country profile, Feb. 1, 2019, available at: http://news.bbc.co.uk/2/hi/asia-pacific/country_profiles/1285915.stm; CIA, East Asia/Southeast Asia: Taiwan, available at: https://www.cia.gov/library/publications/the-world-factbook/geos/tw.html.

electricity liberalization, which has progressed for decades, has adopted a very limited version of the liberalized green electricity market in recent times.[2] Gas liberalization has not been introduced yet.

3. There are also other geographical features that affect the use of energy. For instance, due to Taiwan's being located in an earthquake zone, the use of gas pipelines is not widespread, which leads to reliance on LPG for cooking. Its location in a quake zone has also necessitated the use of concrete and steel as house building materials, which may consume a lot of energy during building or after building. The large number of air conditioning units present on the island is due to its subtropical and tropical location. The emphasis on adequate ventilation, instead of on insulation, to prevent heat waves is also related to this location factor.

4. Finally, the population has also influenced the energy situation. Due to the high population density, the best way to accommodate citizens is in housing complexes, which also leads to wasteful energy use from public electricity sources and other energy guzzlers, such as elevators.

§2. Legal and Political Structure

I. Legal Structure

5. Taiwan adopted the civil law system of Continental Europe, instead of the common law system. In this regard, all legislations, including constitutional law and detailed implementation Ordinances, are codified in what is called "the Six Codes," including the Constitution,[3] the Civil Code,[4] the Code of Civil Procedure[5] and associated laws, the Criminal Code,[6] the Code of Criminal Procedure (刑事訴訟法)[7] and associated laws, and the administrative and administrative procedure laws. However, this does not mean that Taiwan has only these six codes. With the need to regulate complex social lives and technology development, many new laws and regulations are being developed, such as the Copyright Act,[8] Patent

2. Anton Ming-Zhi Gao, Chien-Te Fan and Chao-Ning Liao, Application of German energy transition in Taiwan: A critical review of unique electricity liberalisation as a core strategy to achieve renewable energy growth, Energy Policy, 2018, vol. 120, issue C, 644-654.
3. MOJ, Constitution of the Republic of China (Taiwan), 1947-01-01, available at: https://law.moj.gov.tw/ENG/LawClass/LawAll.aspx?pcode=A0000001.
4. MOJ, Civil Code, Amended Date: 2019-06-19, available at: https://law.moj.gov.tw/ENG/LawClass/LawAll.aspx?pcode=B0000001.
5. MOJ, the Code of Civil Procedure, Amended Date: 2018-11-28, available at: https://law.moj.gov.tw/ENG/LawClass/LawAll.aspx?pcode=B0010001.
6. MOJ, Criminal Code of the Republic of China, Amended Date: 2020-01-15, available at: https://law.moj.gov.tw/ENG/LawClass/LawAll.aspx?pcode=C0000001.
7. MOJ, Code of Criminal Procedure, Amended Date: 2020-01-15, available at: https://law.moj.gov.tw/ENG/LawClass/LawAll.aspx?pcode=C0010001.
8. MOJ, Copyright Act, Amended Date: 2019-05-01, available at: https://law.moj.gov.tw/ENG/LawClass/LawAll.aspx?pcode=J0070017.

Act,[9] Air Pollution Act,[10] etc. In addition, the energy law can be considered one of these types of "new-generation" regulations. Yet, in the existing six codes, certain energy issues are dealt with. For instance, the Criminal Code deals with electricity theft,[11] while the Civil Code is relevant to the contract of purchasing cylinders of LPG. Many new-generation energy laws, such as the Renewable Energy Act[12] and the Energy Management Act,[13] can also be classified and considered to be some sort of administrative regulation.

6. There is another aspect to Taiwan's legal system. Taiwan has embraced the public/private law system. Public law involves constitutional law, the criminal code, and administrative law, whereas the private law includes mainly the civil code and other associated legislations. Key energy legislation, including the Energy Management Act, Electricity Business Act, Renewable Energy Act, and Petroleum Management Act, can all be considered public law.

7. The development of related laws is greatly influenced by the Western world and Japan. For instance, the Constitutional law was influenced by the German constitution (Grundgesetz für die Bundesrepublik Deutschland) and French constitutional law.[14] In civil code, there is a mixture of German, Japanese, and traditional Chinese civil code elements. Taiwanese intellectual property laws are heavily influenced by those of the US. The promulgation of law is often done by legal scholars with different foreign education backgrounds. Drafting Energy Law involves an international component. As energy laws and amendments are usually made by energy economics or engineering think tanks, a unique mixture of different countries' legal regimes can be found. How does this fact affect energy law? For instance, as in the case of France and Germany, Taiwan's constitutional law emphasizes the public utility's public service obligation duty, which position makes it difficult for the government to push through the idea of privatization and liberalization. The feed-in tariff (FIT) scheme in the Renewable Energy Act of 2009 was influenced by the German Renewable Energy Act of 2000,[15] whereas the renewable (and storage) obligation imposed on large electricity users in the recent Renewable Energy Act of 2019 was inspired by the renewable portfolio standards (RPS) scheme in the US and UK. This combination of the Anglo-Saxon style RPS scheme and the German FIT in one country is very unique. There are People's Republic of

---

9. MOJ, Patent Act, Amended Date: 2019-05-01, available at: https://law.moj.gov.tw/ENG/LawClass/LawAll.aspx?pcode=J0070007.
10. MOJ, Air Pollution Control Act, Amended Date: 2018-08-01, available at: https://law.moj.gov.tw/ENG/LawClass/LawAll.aspx?pcode=O0020001.
11. Article 323 of the Criminal Code: "Electricity, thermo-energy, and other energies shall be considered a movable property within the meaning of this Chapter." *See also*, Art. 320 of the Criminal Code.
12. MOJ, Renewable Energy Development Act, Amended Date: 2019-05-01, available at: https://law.moj.gov.tw/ENG/LawClass/LawAll.aspx?pcode=J0130032.
13. MOJ, Energy Administration Act, Amended Date: 2018-08-01, available at: https://law.moj.gov.tw/ENG/LawClass/LawAll.aspx?pcode=J0130002.
14. Yu-chung Shen, Semi-presidentialism in Taiwan A Shadow of the Constitution of the Weimar Republic, Taiwan Journal of Democracy, Vol. 7, No. 1: 135-152.
15. BMWI, Das Erneuerbare-Energien Gesetz, abrufbar unter: https://www.erneuerbare-energien.de/EE/Redaktion/DE/Dossier/eeg.html?cms_docId=71110.

China (PRC) elements in Taiwan's Renewable Energy Act of 2009. As there are usually no special renewable energy funds created in countries adopting the FIT scheme, the existence of a Renewable Energy Fund in the Renewable Energy Act of 2009 is highly likely to be influenced by PRC's Renewable Energy Act of 2005.[16]

II. Political Structure

8. The ROC was established in 1911 after a successful revolution overthrew the corrupt Qing Empire and the dynasty by Doctor Sun Yat-sen. At that time, the ruling territory covered only mainland China and several islands. Yet, during that period, Taiwan was not a part of the ROC, but a colony of Japan. After World War II, the ruling party—Kuomintang (KMT)—won the battle with Japan and acquired Taiwan. Yet, it lost the battle with the Communist Party and escaped to Taiwan and initiated a new ruling status in 1949.[17]

9. The constitutional law of Taiwan upholds the concept of "separation of powers" and "checks and balances" when designing governmental institutions. The Taiwanese government is mainly composed of five "Yuan." Borrowing from the concept of the three main branches of government, the Executive Yuan and The Examination Yuan exercise administrative power; the Judicial Yuan exercises judicial power; the Legislative Yuan (the Parliament) and the Control Yuan exercise legislative and auditing power. Even though the President was not a very important player in the original version of the constitutional law, the office has gained importance in the latest addition of the constitutional law in 2005.[18] The whole constitutional system of Taiwan leans toward the presidential system, in spite of the preference for a Cabinet in the original version. The presidential power to influence legislation cannot be ignored. For instance, the President's support for the adoption of the Renewable Energy Act of 2009 was very influential. In 2016, strong support for energy transition and renewable energy in the new elected President Tsai's inaugural address triggered a series of energy policy and legislative reforms, especially the long-awaited electricity liberalization that unfolded in 2017, and the ambitious promotion of offshore wind power.

10. Different ministries are created under the Executive Yuan. The energy authority belongs to the Ministry of Economic Affairs (MOEA), which is in charge of setting energy tariffs, regulating the state-owned energy enterprises, and conducting energy research and development (R&D), etc. Yet, this power of the MOEA is neither absolute nor exclusive. For instance, the Executive Yuan has a long history of intervening in the energy tariff set by the MOEA.

---

16. lawinfochina, Renewable Energy Law of the People's Republic of China, Amended Date: 2009-12-26, available at: http://www.lawinfochina.com/display.aspx?lib=law&id=3942.
17. Taiwan.gov.tw, History, available at: https://www.taiwan.gov.tw/content_3.php.
18. MOJ, Additional Articles of the Constitution of the Republic China, Amended Date: 2005-06-10, available at: https://law.moj.gov.tw/ENG/LawClass/LawAll.aspx?pcode=A0000002.

11. After escaping to Taiwan, the KMT introduced martial law for several decades until the middle of the 1980s. The KMT remained the dominant ruling party during the terms of five Yuan and the Presidency. There was no alternation of power at that time. The right to freedom of speech and to organize parties did not exist. Yet, since the abolition of martial law, many political parties have sprung up. After freedom of speech and of organization was restored, civil society began to launch large-scale demonstrations over the development of electricity power plants, nuclear power, and other similar environmental issues. In spite of Taiwan's multi-party system, there are only two main parties, no more than five small parties, and numerous tiny parties in Taiwan. In 2000, the chief opposition party, the Democratic Progressive Party (DPP), won the presidential election and became the ruling party. Because of its "green" background, it began to launch the nuclear phase-out scheme under the "Nuclear-free Homeland" slogan but failed to complete this initiative after losing the election in 2008. The KMT returned to and remained in power until 2016. In spite of having been labeled as a pro-nuclear party for a long time, the KMT government passed a milestone renewable energy legislation in 2009 and set up the FIT scheme. After the Fukushima accident, the KMT government also launched a program to promote the construction of 1000 wind turbines and 1 million solar roofs.[19] The construction of the controversial fourth nuclear power plant was frozen in 2014.[20] Therefore, the pro-nuclear KMT seemed to play a key role in contributing to the legal and policy infrastructure. In 2016, the DPP government was back on the political stage again, stronger and more powerful than before. This was the first time in Taiwanese history that the DPP had won both the presidential elections and a majority in the Parliament. In addition to the goal of establishing a nuclear-free homeland by 2025, the DPP government invested a lot of effort in promoting energy transition and setting up the very ambitious 20% renewable energy by 2025 agenda (from only around 5% in 2016).[21] The thrust of offshore wind power development from 8 MW in 2016 to 5.7 GW in 2025 was scheduled. Therefore, it seemed like both main parties had treated renewable energy as a priority in their works.

12. Finally, it is worth noting that Taiwan has to a certain extent been at enmity with mainland China PRC since 1945. Even though there is a free trade agreement called the Economic Cooperation Framework Agreement (ECFA) signed by the two sides on June 29, 2010, the cross-strait tension has not lessened. This situation seems merely a "military" and "diplomatic" issue and is less relevant to "energy" affairs. However, it does have some import for "energy." For instance, the governmental reasoning behind the development of nuclear power has been that if mainland China PRC launches a measure to blockade Taiwan, nuclear power plants can keep supplying electricity for several months and thus win some time for Taiwan.

---

19. Bureau of Energy Ministry of Economic Affairs, Taiwan, Policy for Promoting Renewable Energy & Current Status in Taiwan, March 2013, available at: https://www.mofa.gov.tw/Upload/RelFile/2508/111035/2e9e6ebe-d594-4d46-822b-1110f07f8482.pdf.
20. Reuters, Taiwan to halt construction of fourth nuclear power plant, Apr. 27, 2020, available at: https://jp.reuters.com/article/instant-article/idUSL3N0NJ08C20140427.
21. Energypedia, Energy Transition in Taiwan, last modified on Oct. 31, 2020, available at: https://energypedia.info/wiki/Energy_Transition_in_Taiwan.

Furthermore, as Japan's oil and LNG tankers use the Taiwan Strait as the most economical, viable route to transport fuel to Japan, the tension between Taiwan and PRC also triggers diplomatic concerns in Japan. The development of offshore wind power may be relevant for such cross-strait sentiments. Some supporters have argued that such offshore wind power development can reinforce Taiwan's energy security as more and more electricity would be produced locally. However, opponents have contended that these offshore wind turbines would be very easy for PRC missiles to target and maybe vulnerable during wartime. Such cross-strait concerns may affect the realization of the "super-Asia grid" proposed by a rich Japanese businessman.[22] Taiwan is very concerned about the interconnection issues with mainland China.

§3. Economic Characteristics

13. In terms of economic development, Taiwan amazes the world. Taiwan evolved successfully from an agriculture-based society to a high-tech society within less than fifty years. Since 1945, the main export was agricultural products, such as bananas. Then the government started to develop labor-intensive manufacturing industries, such as the clothes industry. Afterward, other energy intensive industries, including petrochemical, steel, and cement, came into play. So far, Taiwan is one of the world's most dynamic economies and an essential partner in a number of high-tech fields. Taiwan was the 18th largest exporter and the 17th largest importer of merchandise in 2018. It was also one of the largest holders of foreign exchange reserves as of December 2018.[23]

14. Taiwan occupies an important position in the global economy. It is a top player in the world's information and communication technology industry and a major supplier of goods across the industrial spectrum. Its gross domestic product (GDP) per capita reached USD 25,004 in 2018. Taiwan ranks close to Argentina and Sweden in terms of nominal GDP, while its GDP per capita expressed as purchasing power parity is similar to those of Austria and Denmark.[24]

15. However, there remain certain weaknesses in the Taiwan economy, particularly from the energy consumption perspective. Even though the government always describes Taiwan's industry as a high-tech industry, these high-tech industries whose margin is based on Original Equipment Manufacturer and Original Design Manufacturer remain energy, water, and pollution intensive industries. The recent development priority of "green energy industry," such as photovoltaic (PV) or light-emitting diode (LED), is also not as green as its name implies. The PV manufacturing process is also energy intensive and with high pollution. Taiwan has become a manufacturing base of PV cells and exports them for use in Europe. The greener the industry is, the more energy it consumes. A similar situation will unfold in the

22. REI, Asia Super Grid, available at: https://www.renewable-ei.org/en/asg/about/.
23. Taiwan.gov.tw, Economy, available at: https://www.taiwan.gov.tw/content_7.php.
24. Taiwan.gov.tw, Economy, available at: https://www.taiwan.gov.tw/content_7.php.

context of the recent promotion of the 5+2 innovative industries plan, including smart machinery, IoT, Green energy, the Biotech pharmaceutical industry, and the Defense industry,[25] and can lead to more energy consumption in the manufacturing process. Finally, whether the development of a service sector and sustainable tourism industry can bring new hope for Taiwan remains to be seen. This "third" sector remains an energy guzzler as witnessed by the frightening energy bills and electricity consumption in shopping malls and department stores.

§4. Social and Cultural Characteristics

16. Taiwan is a multi-ethnic and multi-cultural society. About 4,000 years ago, there were Taiwan aborigines settled in Taiwan. Long before the Qing Empire of the Ming Dynasty, the Dutch and Spanish occupied parts of Taiwan in the early 1600s. Many people fled mainland China to escape the cruel control of the Ming Empire. Then, during the early Qing Empire, the Qing invaded Taiwan and set up an official government in Taiwan. They started to develop Taiwan, but lost it to Japan in a battle. After fifty years of Japanese colonization, Taiwan then became a part of China. The arrival of the KMT in Taiwan further heightened Taiwan's multicultural character. Taiwan was also under the influence of the US and receiving military support from it at that time, which means US culture had begun to take root in Taiwan. The integration and the fusion of these multiple cultures created a very special "Taiwan culture."[26]

17. These cultural elements affect energy use habits. For instance, Taiwan has a food culture involving its world-famous night markets. This night market culture results in the popular use of cylinder LPG and diesel generators. The popular use of neon lights as shop signs may also be relevant. The tea culture also leads to the habit of drinking warm water only and leads to the unique appliance of warm water suppliers. Furthermore, the influence of Japanese culture has led to the use of geothermal baths, the popular use of auto bikes for commuting, the popular use of Japanese autos, which are relatively smaller and more fuel efficient than those made in the US/Europe, and the popular use of Japanese electronic appliances, such as refrigerators and air conditioners, as well as the development of large department stores. Yet, the influence of Western society can also be seen, for instance, in the invasion of supermarket malls, such as Carrefour and Costco, and the construction of large shopping malls.

---

25. Executive Yuan Taiwan, 5+2 innovative industries plan-Introduction, available at: https://english.ey.gov.tw/iip/B0C195AE54832FAD.
26. LSE, Taiwan in comparative perspective, Dec. 2008, vol. 2, available at: http://eprints.lse.ac.uk/50977/1/__libfile_REPOSITORY_Content_Taiwan%20Culture%20Research%20Programme_Taiwan%20in%20Comparative%20Perspective_Taiwan%20in%20Comparative%20Perspective_vol%202.pdf.

Chapter 2. Basic Principles of Energy Law

18. The basic principles of energy law are not currently provided in a legal document, but are rather placed in a policy document and in environmental/climate legislation. Taiwan's energy policy and law have long been guided by a very important policy document called the 1996 Taiwan Energy Policy and Measures, which was approved by the Executive Yuan.[27] Despite being of the nature of a policy guideline, the document uses the wording of energy policy "provisions." This also reflects the ambiguous nature of this document, straddling as it does the nexus between policy and law. The six policy principles proposed in this document involve "stabilizing the energy supply," "increasing energy efficiency," "deregulating the energy market," "emphasizing energy security and environmental protection," "enhancing energy R&D," and "promoting energy education."

19. Apart from these principles, environmental legal principles, which can be used to supplement the environmental protection direction noted above, are also applicable, such as the polluter pays principle,[28] prevention, precautionary measures,[29] cooperation, and sustainable development,[30] under the Environmental Basic Act.

20. After the adoption of the GHG Reduction Act of 2015, a wide range of climate, energy, economics, and environmental principles were introduced. The Act provides for many policies and legal principles to support the functioning of the government and the industry in approaching a low-carbon future. The provisions can be divided into two categories: (1) cross-cutting, which covers broad issues in economic, energy, and environmental policies, and (2) climate change.[31] Article 5 of the GHG Act provides a number of general principles that address the former, which are listed in Table 1.

27. Bureau of Energy Taiwan, Taiwan Energy Policy and Measures 1996, Jul. 25, 1996, available at: http://www.moeaboe.gov.tw/Policy/PoMain.aspx?PageId=executepolicy.
28. Article 28 of the Environmental Basic Act.
29. For example, Arts 6, 19, 22, 24 of the Environmental Basic Act.
30. For example, Arts 6˜8 of the Environmental Basic Act.
31. Anton Ming-Zhi Gao, A Critical Review of the Role of Taiwan's 2015 Emission Reduction Act in the Energy Sector's Mitigation and Adaptation Initiatives, June 2019, The Taiwan Law Review, at 73–105 (2019).

Table 1 General Principles of the GHG Reduction Act of 2015

Aspects	*Legal Provisions*
Overall	The national government shall ensure the sustainable utilization of the nation's resources, maintain balanced energy supply and demand, mitigate and respond to the impacts of climate change, and place balanced emphasis on environmental protection, economic development, and social justice.—Article 5 All levels of government shall encourage technological innovation, research, and development, enhance financial mechanisms, spur economic momentum, encourage competition, promote low-carbon green growth, create employment opportunities, and boost national competitiveness.—Article 5
Energy	To ensure the nation's energy security, the government shall draft mid- to long-term strategies for gradually reducing dependence on fossil fuels with a mid- to long-term aim of renewable energy policies, and the gradual realization of a nuclear-free homeland.—Article 5(1) To respond to the impact of climate change, under the principle of equality and social welfare promotion, the government should implement tax mechanisms on imported fossil fuels based on carbon dioxide equivalent.—Article 5(3) To lessen environmental pollution and GHG emissions, the government should promote resource and energy use efficiency, and resource recycling.—Article 5(5)
Climate	In line with the "user charge" principle of environmental justice, the free allowances allocation method will be gradually replaced by allowances sold at a fixed price.—Article 5(2) To respond to the impact of climate change, under the principle of equality and social welfare promotion, the government should implement tax mechanisms on imported fossil fuels based on carbon dioxide equivalent.—Article 5(3) To lessen environmental pollution and GHG emissions, the government should promote resource and energy use efficiency, and resource recycling.—Article 5(5)
Economy and industrial policy	The government should actively help traditional industries achieve energy conservation and carbon reduction or transition, develop green technology and green industry, create new employment opportunities and green economies, and promote a low-carbon, green growth plan for the nation's infrastructure.—Article 5(4)
Environment	To lessen environmental pollution and GHG emissions, the government should promote resource and energy use efficiency, and resource recycling.—Article 5(5)

Source: Anton Ming-Zhi Gao, A Critical Review of the Role of Taiwan's 2015 Emission Reduction Act in the Energy Sector's Mitigation and Adaptation Initiatives, June 2019, The Taiwan Law Review, at 73–105 (2019).

21. Furthermore, the past energy policy focused only on the application of foreign technology, but there has been a recent trend to develop a domestic green energy industry that could tackle the energy challenges resulting from climate change or energy security. The principle of *supporting the domestic energy industry* as an export-oriented industry and a competitive industry is well established. There has been discussion recently about developing the nuclear power industry into an export-oriented industry. The introduction of the local content requirement in mid-2017 as the main criteria for the allocation of the offshore wind power development right can be seen as the latest application of this principle.[32]

22. Finally, the principle of *national responsibility for the energy supply* is affecting the design of the Taiwan energy market. Unlike the liberalization of the telecommunications and bank sector that triggered privatization, the energy market in Taiwan is less liberalized and privatized. For instance, in spite of oil liberalization, the government remains the main shareholder of state-owned oil company Chinese Petroleum Corporation (CPC). The gas sector is not liberalized or privatized, except for the local gas distribution and supply companies. Compared with large-scale electricity liberalization in both wholesale and retail sectors in Europe, the US, and Japan, only a limited extent of the green electricity market has been liberalized in Taiwan. This idea is also rooted in Article 144 of the Constitutional law: Public utilities and other enterprises of a monopolistic nature, in principle, should be under public operation. In cases permitted by law, they may be operated by private citizens.

23. In order to establish legal principles governing energy policy and law, the idea of a "Sustainable Energy Basic Bill" was proposed, discussed, and concluded in the National Energy Conference of 2009. The importance of this Bill was confirmed again under the First Program of the 2010 Master Plan on Energy Conservation and Emission Reduction. The completion of the drafting process of this bill is considered to be a very important step in developing a legal framework for Energy Conservation and Emission Reduction. It is expected that the above-mentioned important legal principles will be incorporated into this bill, which is being drafted by the MOEABOE. Yet, unfortunately, this bill did not progress as expected. It may have influenced the legal principles concerning energy in the GHG

32. Peter Gill, Taiwan Offshore Wind Supply Chain Localization: Challenges & Opportunities, Apr. 25, 2019, available at: https://gwec.net/wp-content/uploads/2019/05/GOWST-Peter-Gill-Northland-Power.pdf.

Reduction Act in 2015. Moreover, a Sustainable Development Bill is also being discussed under the purview of the Environmental Protection Agency (EPA) in 2010.[33] The legal principles in this bill may also be relevant to the energy sector, yet may not be so direct and powerful.

24. Apparently, these principles are inevitably conflictive. Thus, in practice, certain principles take precedence over others when implementing energy law. In general, the principles of energy security and national responsibility take precedence over those related to the environment and efficiency. For instance, the government is very keen on subsidizing and maintaining a low energy price, to accommodate the electricity needs of energy intensive industries. For this reason, an Energy Taxation Bill, which would benefit the environment, remains unlikely to be presented to the Executive Yuan in the near future despite intense discussions on the matter over the past few years. Furthermore, due to the heavy involvement of national enterprises in the electricity and gas sector, a gas and electricity liberalization bill has been promoted for decades. As noted above, there has been no planning for gas liberalization in recent times, and the scale of electricity liberalization in 2017 was highly restrained.

25. A similar situation also applies to energy policy. The energy security principle overrides other principles. For instance, in spite of emission concerns and radioactive waste concerns with regard to coal and nuclear power plants, respectively, energy security concerns have led to a high proportion of coal and nuclear use in the Taiwan electricity mix. Although coal and nuclear fuel rods are also imported, their relatively stable and diverse supply sources make them more secure than oil and gas. Under the policy agenda of achieving a nuclear-free homeland by 2025, the main focus is to use the renewable energy and fossil fuel plants to replace the role of nuclear power, in spite of the climate change and emission concerns around the use of coal-fired and/or gas-fired power plants.

---

33. Environmental Protection Administration, Public Discussion for Sustainable Development Bill, Jun. 29, 2010, available at: https://enews.epa.gov.tw/Page/3B3C62C78849F32F/a1d5cc02-31c6-4715-9a64-08d2fe79e1d1.

Chapter 3. Historical Background and Development of Energy Law

26. The development of energy law is closely related to the creation of an energy authority. Before the creation of a competent energy authority—the Energy Commission—in 1979, there were few energy legislations in place and the energy legislative framework was less organized. This stage is considered to have been the "underdeveloped stage." On May 26, 1930, the Mining Act was promulgated. Another related law dealing with energy matters is the Act on Monitoring Private-Owned Utilities (December 21, 1929), which allows private companies to conduct a utility business. In general, a utility business should be conducted by state-owned or local-owned companies. However, several businesses, including road lighting, electricity, coal gas, transportation, water, local telecommunications, trams, etc., are exceptions.[34] Later, an Electricity Business Act (December 10, 1947) and an Ordinance on the Management of Coal Gas Business (April 23, 1968) were enacted. In sum, at the beginning of the last century, most energy businesses were mainly conducted by state or local government; hence, the laws seemed less necessary. Therefore, only the "private" elements substantiated the need for enacting legislations. For instance, several provisions of the Electricity Act regulated the private-owned self-generators. The Ordinance on the Management of Coal Gas Businesses is closely tied to regulating the business of liquefied petroleum gas (LPG) and gas.

27. The development of Taiwan's energy law and policy was greatly influenced by the international energy situation.

§1. The First Wave of Energy Law Development in the 1970s

28. After the first oil crisis in 1973, the Energy Policy of Taiwan was created; whereas a comprehensive energy law—the Energy Management Act—was enacted in 1980 after the second oil crisis of 1979. It should be noted that the creation of an Energy Commission was also in reaction to the oil shocks and this Commission played a very important role in drafting the Energy Management Act. Similar to the energy rationalization and efficiency efforts of many countries around the globe after the oil crisis, the main purpose of the Energy Management Act in Taiwan is to improve the efficiency of energy use and deal with the demand-side energy use. This Act was supposed to be demand-side legislation. However, as there was a deficiency of other laws, such as oil laws, to tackle the emergency or energy-shortage situation at that time, a special Chapter 2—Energy Supply—was integrated into this Act to require "safety stocks" by energy supply businesses (e.g., electricity, oil, and gas businesses).[35] This "two-sided" feature also made this Act a very fundamental energy act in Taiwan before the enacting of other supply-side laws (e.g., the Petroleum Business Act of 2001).

---

34. Article 2, Act on Monitoring Private-Owned Utilities.
35. Article 7, Energy Management Act.

29. In addition, as a result of Taiwan's close ties with the US, Taiwan's policy was also affected by the idea of peaceful use of nuclear energy, which was promoted by the US government after World War II. Due to the oil crisis shock, Taiwan sought to diversify its electricity supply from reliance on oil by developing nuclear power plants. The Atomic Energy Law was enacted in 1968. A nuclear regulator was created under the Organization Act of the Atomic Energy Council of the Executive Yuan of 1970, and a Nuclear Damage Compensation Act was promulgated and went into effect on July 26, 1971. However, the main efforts to develop a more detailed legal framework for the nuclear energy sector started at the beginning of 2000. This took place with the first change in the ruling party of Taiwan within fifty years. The new ruling party promoted the idea of a "nuclear-free homeland" and the need to tighten nuclear regulations. This led to the promulgation of the Ionizing Radiation Protection Act of 2002, Nuclear Reactor Facilities Regulation Act of 2003, Nuclear Emergency Response Act of 2003, Nuclear Materials and Radioactive Waste Management Act of 2002, Act on Sites for Establishment of Low Level Radioactive Waste Final Disposal Facility of 2006, and their Ordinances.[36]

§2. The Second Wave of Energy Law Development Influenced by Global Warming

30. The second wave of reform was greatly influenced by the environmental movement and the concerns over climate change, and by the wave of regulatory reform around the globe. The Energy Management Act was revised several times (in 1992, 2000, 2002, 2009, 2016) to improve the supply-side and demand-side management. Furthermore, the electricity, gas, and oil liberalization bills were proposed from the early 1990s. The Petroleum Business Act and Electricity Liberalization Act were promulgated in 2001 and 2017, respectively.

31. Over the past twenty years, Taiwan's energy policy and laws were greatly influenced by developments in Germany. Between 2000 and 2008, the (greener and more anti-nuclear) ruling party of Taiwan sought to follow Germany's approach and phase out nuclear power plants. In this regard, a Nuclear-Free Homeland Bill, a Bill on Early Phase-out of Nuclear Power Plants, and a Renewable Energy Bill were

---

36. The related Ordinances, such as Enforcement Rules for the Ionizing Radiation Protection Act, Classification of High Level Radiation Facilities and Administrative Regulations for Their Operators (Chinese Only), Regulations Governing Radiation Protection and Control for Military Institutions (Chinese Only), Standards for Exemption from Regulation for Radiation Sources (Chinese Only), Standards for Collection of Regulation Fees for Ionizing Radiation Protection (Chinese Only), Regulations on the Prevention and Management of Incidents of Radioactive Contaminated Buildings (Chinese Only), Administrative Regulations on the Establishment of Medical Exposure Quality Assurance Teams and Assignment of Specialists and Commissioning of Jobs to Relevant Organizations (Chinese Only), etc. *See* Atomic Energy Council Taiwan, available at: http://www.aec.gov.tw/www/english/index.html.

proposed, while a policy instrument of an "Action Plan for a Nuclear-free Homeland" was approved by the Executive Yuan after the important National Nuclear-Free Homeland Conference. Yet, these bills were quite controversial and were shelved after the government again changed hands in 2008.

32. After the Kyoto Protocol took effect in 2005, Taiwan also sought to propose a comprehensive legislative package of "Four Bills of Energy Saving and Emission Reduction." These four important bills include three new bills, namely, the Renewable Energy Bill, Emission Reduction Bill, and Energy (Carbon) Taxation Bill, and the revision of the existing Energy Management Act. After a long debate, the Renewable Energy Act and the Amendment to the Energy Management Act were adopted in 2009. Yet, the main instrument to introduce an emissions trading system in Taiwan—the Emission Reduction Bill—and the important economic incentive to internalize the environmental and carbon costs of energy use (Energy Taxation Bill) have been very controversial. However, the GHG Reduction Act, which provides a legal basis for the emissions trading scheme (ETS) was passed and adopted in 2015.

33. In 2016, the pro-green and anti-nuclear party returned to power. The main energy legislation reform focused on the revision of the Electricity Act to introduce liberalization and the revision of the Renewable Energy Act of 2009. Unexpectedly, the revision of the Referendum Act in 2018 affected energy development. After the revision, the referendum was held at the end of 2018. Three of the ten issues in the referendum related to energy:[37]

– No. 7: "Do you agree that the electricity output of thermal power plants should be lowered by at least 1 percent per year on average?"
– No. 8: "Do you agree that Taiwan should establish an energy policy that undertakes not to construct any new coal-fired power plants or generators or expand existing facilities (including the expansion of the Shen'ao Power Plant)?"
– No. 16: "Do you agree with abolishing the first paragraph of Article 95 of the Electricity Act, which means abolishing the provision that 'all nuclear-energy-based power-generating facilities shall cease to operate by 2025'?"

34. From the foregoing, the prospect of the development of energy law seems quite positive. However, this author would like to provide certain caveats. First, as energy laws often have a great impact on the national economy, it usually takes a long time to move from legislative proposal to proclaimed Act. For instance, the Renewable Energy Bill was proposed in 2001, yet enacted in 2009. It also took a lot of time to shift the Petroleum Business Act/Electricity Liberalization Bill from a bill to a law. The amendment of the Renewable Energy Act, whose main purpose is to supplement the implementation of the Electricity Liberalization Act that was passed in January 2017, took over two years to be passed in the Parliament. Second, the implementation of energy legislation often faced delays. Aside from the lack of accompanying revisions as seen in the Electricity Act of 2017, the ETS

37. Focus Taiwan, The 10 referendum questions Taiwanese are voting on, Nov. 24, 2018, available at: https://focustaiwan.tw/politics/201811240010.

embedded in the 2015 GHG Reduction Act has not been implemented thus far. The renewable and/or storage obligation on large electricity users introduced by the Renewable Energy Act of 2019 in April 2019 is not expected to be implemented until the end of 2020, because of opposition from the industries.

35. In this regard, even after the development of an energy legal regime beginning in 1980, the most important legal instrument remains the first-generation energy act, the Energy Management Act, which coordinates the demand- and supply-side regulation. With regard to sectoral legislations, the Electricity Act, the Renewable Energy Act, and the Petroleum Business Act would play key roles.

36. Apart from the issue of inadequate energy legislations, the substantive content of these energy Acts and Bills is unsatisfying as well. Generally speaking, the provisions in these Acts and Bills are quite vague and abstract and leave a lot of discretion to government to formulate further Ordinances, which may trigger the concerns about a "constitutional state (Rechtsstaat)." For instance, Article 34 of the Petroleum Business Act requires that oil exploration or import companies and petrochemical feedstock manufacturers that produce petroleum by-product and sell it to oil refinery operators contribute to the Petroleum Fund, whose function is similar to a universal service or public benefit fund. Even though this Article provided further instruction on the setting of different rates for light oil, crude oil, gasoline, coal oil, diesel, LPG, etc.,[38] it is unclear if the rate is based on the carbon contents or environmental effects of these fuels. In general, the root of this problem results from the fact that most energy legislations are proposed and drafted by energy economics think tanks. Thus, the legal language in these Acts and Bills is not very precise and there is much room for improvement.

37. However, there are several warning signs indicating a digression from the rule of law in the energy sector. For instance, the legal provisions addressing the recent controversial renewable and/or storage obligation on large electricity users may violate the legal principle of clear legal designation and may result in legal uncertainty during implementation. From the language of Article 12(3) of the Renewable Energy Act of 2019, it is unclear how "the aforesaid chartered capacity, certain installed capacity, certain amount, categories of the renewable energy power generation facilities installed, categories of storage facilities, payment of monetary substitution" should be defined.

> "When the chartered capacity on electricity consumption agreements signed by the user of electricity exceeds a certain capacity, the user shall install on their own or provide space to install renewable energy power generation and storage facilities with certain installed capacity or purchase a certain amount of electricity generated from renewable energy and a certificate; If the user fails

38. Article 34(2) of the Petroleum Management Act: "The rates mentioned in the preceding paragraphs will be charged by volume and based on the average import price of oil. The central competent authority will announce the amounts collected for the fund."

to take actions according to the aforesaid regulations, the user shall pay monetary substitution to the competent authority for the purpose of the development of renewable energy." (Article 12(3) of the Renewable Energy Act of 2019)

38. Another example can be found in the abuse of administrative (internal) orders in their application to offshore wind power sectors. According to Taiwan's constitution and law,[39] any stipulation that "concerns the rights or obligations of the people" shall be provided for by a statute. As the development of renewable energy is related to the reallocation of state-wide resources to subsidize renewable energy development and also relates to the increase in electricity prices for all citizens, it is necessary to pass the Renewable Energy Act to deal with the subsidy scheme. In 2009, Taiwan followed the German Renewable Energy Sources Act of 2000 (Erneuerbare-Energien-Gesetz, EEG) and introduced the FIT scheme in the Renewable Energy Development Act of 2009. As a result of the insufficient offshore wind power FIT in the early stage of implementation, Taiwan introduced the Demonstration Subsidy Ordinance under the authorization of the Renewable Energy Act in 2012. However, unlike the use of 39 provisions in the German EEG to provide a legal basis for tendering, Taiwan simply relied on legal non-authorized administrative internal rules to change the FIT to a selection/tendering scheme in January 2018[40] This sudden change from the no-development-cap/no-price competition FIT in the 2009 Renewable Energy Act to the selection/tendering scheme can affect investment security seriously.

39. Article 23 of the ROC Constitution: "All the freedoms and rights enumerated in the preceding Articles shall not be restricted by law except by such as may be necessary to prevent infringement upon the freedoms of other persons, to avert an imminent crisis, to maintain social order or to advance public welfare."
Art. 5 of Central Regulation Standard Act:

> The following objects shall be stipulated by a statute: ...
> 2. Stipulation concerns the rights or obligations of the people. ...
> 4. Other objects with substantial importance shall be stipulated by a statute.

40. Directions for Allocating Installed Capacity of Offshore Wind Potential Zones Jan. 18, 2018, https://www.moeaboe.gov.tw/ECW/populace/news/wHandNews_File.ashx?file_id=12616.

Chapter 4. Role of Government Institutions in the Shaping and Administration of Energy Law and Policy

39. The following governmental authorities are very relevant to the development of Taiwan's energy law and policy. Further, the role of the national electricity, oil, and gas companies should not be underestimated either.

§1. Energy Authority, MOEA

40. The creation of a "formal" energy authority came about quite late in Taiwan. At the beginning, there was only an "Energy Development Group," which became subordinate to the International Economic Cooperation and Development Council of the Executive Yuan in July 1968. This group was renamed the "Energy Policy Deliberation Group" and came under the aegis of the MOEA in January 1970. Later, the Energy Policy of the Taiwan Area of January 11, 1979, provided some policy suggestions to create a more competent energy authority under the MOEA. On November 1, 1979, the Energy Commission (EC) under the MOEA was established. However, this Commission remained an informal authority inside the government, as no Act was passed by the Parliament to legalize its establishment. The creation of this Commission reflected the need to have a more competent authority to develop energy policy and laws and deal with oil crises. Finally, on January 20, 1994, the Act of the Organization of the Bureau of Energy (BOE) was promulgated by the President's order. On July 1 of the same year, the BOE was formally established.

41. According to the "Act of the Organization of the Bureau of Energy," the functions of this Bureau include the following:[41]

(1) formulating energy policies and energy related-regulations;
(2) evaluating and planning energy supply and demand;
(3) granting permission for the exploration, production, transport, storage, transformation, distribution, marketing, and utilization of energy;
(4) reviewing natural gas and electricity prices;
(5) granting establishment permits, and undertaking matters concerning the registration, administration, counseling, and oversight of energy enterprises;
(6) undertaking matters concerning the registration and oversight of energy technical personnel;
(7) establishing an energy database system;
(8) promoting energy conservation programs and education, and providing technical assistance;
(9) promoting R&D of new and renewable energy technology and energy conservation technology;

41. MOJ, Organization Act of Bureau of Energy, Ministry of Economic Affairs, 2004-01-20, available at: https://law.moj.gov.tw/LawClass/LawAll.aspx?pcode=J0000087.

(10) promoting international energy cooperation;
(11) other energy-related matters.

42. Over the past few years, the MOEABOE and MOEAEC have been very active in developing energy policies and proposing energy-related bills. As noted above, "the Energy Policy and Implementation Measures of Taiwan" developed by the MOEAEC, became a very fundamental policy guide for Taiwan's energy law and policy. Recently, in order to tackle the challenge of climate change, the MOEA-BOE developed a series of policy frameworks, including the "Sustainable Energy Policy Framework," the 2007 Energy Technology R&D White Paper, and the 2010 Energy Industry Technology White Paper. After the 2009 amendment to the Energy Management Act, the MOEABOE became authorized by law to adopt the Energy Development Guidelines to ensure the stable and safe supply of energy, while also taking the environmental impact and economic development into consideration.[42] The latest Guidelines on Energy Development was approved by the Executive Yuan and was published in April 2017.[43] In the past few decades, important renewable energy programs were published by the MOEABOE as well, such as the 1000 onshore and offshore wind power program and the million solar roof program in 2011,[44] and the current Four-year Wind Power Promotion[45] and Two-year Solar PV Promotion Plans.[46]

43. Besides, numerous legislative proposals and administrative ordinances have been proposed and drafted, which were then adopted by the MOEAEC and MOEA-BOE. For instance, the MOEAEC proposed the first generation of electricity, oil, and gas liberalization bills in the 1990s. The MOEABOE proposed several important legislations, such as the Renewable Energy Bill and Nuclear-Free Homeland Bill in the 2000s. The recent key energy law amendments, i.e., Renewable Energy Act of 2019 and Electricity Liberalization Act of 2017, and Energy Management Bill, were all proposed by the MOEABOE.

44. After oil and electricity liberalization, the MOEABOE began to play the roles of both an energy policymaker and an oil/electricity market regulator. Originally, there was a discussion on whether to create an independent electricity regulator in the course of the deliberations on the Electricity Liberalization Bill in 2016. However, because of opposition from the BOE, the electricity regulator became non-independent and unclear. The unclear nature is the result of a provision that

---

42. Article 1(2) of the Energy Management Act.
43. Guidelines on Energy Development, April 2017, available at: https://www.moeaboe.gov.tw/ECW/main/content/wHandMenuFile.ashx?file_id=559.
44. Bureau of Energy, Policy for Promoting Renewable Energy & Current Status in Taiwan, March 2013, available at: https://www.mofa.gov.tw/Upload/RelFile/2508/111035/2e9e6ebe-d594-4d46-822b-1110f07f8482.pdf.
45. Executive Yuan, Four-year Wind Power Promotion Plan, Jun. 14, 2019, available at: https://english.ey.gov.tw/News3/9E5540D592A5FECD/d603a1bf-9963-4e53-a92b-e6520a3d93ff.
46. Executive Yuan, Promotion of solar energy, Oct. 29, 2019, available at: https://english.ey.gov.tw/News3/9E5540D592A5FECD/777fcee7-90db-4b72-9927-573eecf9ea9e.

requires the designation of the MOEA to become the electricity regulator: "The central competent authority shall designate the electricity industry regulatory authority to deal with the following matters: ... "[47] This requirement made acting independently impossible. The MOEA designated its subdivision BOE to carry out its regulatory functions. This rendered the office of an electricity regulator meaningless. The provision establishing an electricity regulator also becomes unique in terms of administrative agency design.

45. Since 2008, there has been a new wave of reform known as "Governmental Reorganization." The new Organizational Act of the Executive Yuan has passed and came into force on January 1, 2012. Under this wave of reform, the role of the energy authority gained importance and a new authority, the Ministry of Economic and Energy Affairs, was being created. The role of energy affairs was enhanced from the third level of government (The Executive Yuan- MOEABOE) to the second level. This new authority is expected to have greater competence and influence on energy law and policy. However, because of the slow progress of legislative negotiations, the Act has not been passed in the Parliament thus far. The latest version of this draft Act can be found on the website of the Executive Yuan.[48]

46. Another central competent authority is the MOEA, with its BOE and the Industrial Development Bureau (IDB) in charge of aligning the nation's energy and industrial sectors with the United Nations Framework Convention on Climate Change (UNFCCC) and other international trends. In 2006, the MOEA opened a specialized Industrial Greenhouse Office to help Taiwanese industries adjust to green production and develop a low-carbon economy. This office was renamed the GO (Greenhouse Office)-MOEA (GOMO) in 2008 and the Office of Carbon Mitigation and Energy Conservation (influenced by the 2010 Master Plan on Energy Conservation and Emission Reduction) in 2011.[49] Compared to the Greenhouse Gas Reduction Management Office under the EPA, this office is more industry-oriented and focuses on helping industrial players tackle climate change.

47. Yet, such "offices" in charge of certain energy or emission reduction affairs may not be "official" under the law. For instance, the special office to promote the 1000 onshore/offshore wind turbines program was founded in 2011, and was later renamed as the "One-stop Shop Office for Wind Power."[50] A similar situation was also applied to the Special Office for A Million Solar Roofs and the One-stop Shop Office for Solar PV.[51] The green energy industry promotion center is also of this

---

47. Article 3(4) of the Electricity Act of 2017.
48. Executive Yuan, Organization Act for Ministry of Economic and Energy Affairs, May 3, 2018, available at: https://www.ey.gov.tw/Page/AE106A22FAE592FD/5510ce33-8ad1-416f-ae31-681cb94cdd30.
49. Greenhouse Gas Reduction Information Web, Minister of Economic set up energy saving and carbon reduction office, Apr. 24, 2018, available at: https://www.go-moea.tw/about-01.php.
50. TWTP, Thousand Wind Turbines Promotion Project, available at: https://www.twtpo.org.tw/eng/Home/.
51. MRPV, The Single Service Window for Solar PV, available at: https://www.mrpv.org.tw/index.aspx.

kind.[52] These offices or centers are usually project-based and are run by energy think tanks. Their role is to help the MOEA or MOEABOE carry out administrative work. No authority has been conferred on these offices, although it appears as though they are public authorities, going by their official names. For example, the One-stop Shop Office for Wind Power is run by researchers from the Industrial Technology Research Institute (ITRI), a leading energy think tank in Taiwan. The One-stop Shop Office has neither the authority to issue a permit nor to coordinate different ministries. The applicants for offshore wind power may still have to apply to different ministries for different permits, such as the Ministry of Interior Affairs, Fishery Agency, EPA, etc.

§2. Bureau of Mines (BOM), MOEA

48. Currently, Taiwan imports almost 99% of its energy supplies from abroad. Yet, domestic coal production played a major role in Taiwan's energy supply system in the 1940s. The Mining Authority is mainly in charge of the safety and environmental conditions of coal, oil, and gas mine production in Taiwan.

49. In order to streamline the administration of mines and relevant mine safety, the Taiwan Provincial Government integrated the Coal Industry Regulatory Committee, the Second Section of the Reconstruction Department governing mine safety, and the Second Division of the Industry and Mine Inspection Committee overseeing inspection of mine safety into the "Taiwan Provincial Bureau of Mines" (TPBOM) on February 11, 1970, under the direct jurisdiction of the Reconstruction Department. Thereafter, to accommodate environmental changes and downsize the Taiwan Provincial Government, the TPBOM was added to the MOEA as the Bureau of Mines (BOM) on July 1, 1999. In order to adapt to the changing mining industrial environment, this Bureau was reorganized on March 13, 2004.[53]

50. However, with the depletion of coal and the closure of coal mines in the 1990s as well as the reduction in domestic production of oil and gas, the role of the TPBOM and BOM in the energy supply has decreased. With increasing imports of natural resources from abroad, the current focus of the BOM is on debris for construction sites.[54] After the Governmental Reorganization, the BOM was expected to become a sub-section of the new EPA, the Ministry of Environment and Resources. The new arrangement is scheduled to come into effect in 2012. Again, the merger did not take place because of the delayed legislative proceedings at the Organization Act for the Ministry of Environment and Resources.[55]

---

52. Green Energy Industry Promotion Center, available at: http://www.geipc.tw/
53. MINE, Profile, available at: https://www.mine.gov.tw/english/.
54. MINE, mission, available at: http://www.mine.gov.tw/intro/will.asp.
55. Organization Act for Environmental Protection Agency, available at: https://www.ey.gov.tw/Page/AE106A22FAE592FD/dedb1006-a1b8-4676-be99-5e51ff80b06e.

51. Recently, there has been discussion about the exploration of oil fields near the Diaoyu Islands, in the northeast part of Taiwan. Currently, Japan and China have signed an agreement to explore the oil fields. Yet, as the islands are a major foreign relations issue between Japan and the PRC and between Japan and the ROC, Taiwan is unlikely to explore that area in the short term.

§3. Atomic Energy Council, the Executive Yuan

52. Taiwan followed the trend in the US in developing its nuclear power plants: it separated the nuclear energy developer and the nuclear regulator, and created an independent nuclear energy regulator—the Atomic Energy Council (AEC)—under the Executive Yuan at the ministerial level in 1955. Its original mission was to foster peaceful applications of atomic energy, and to coordinate international cooperation on nuclear energy.[56] A formal Organization Act of the Atomic Energy Council of the Executive Yuan of 1970 confirmed the status of this Commission. The AEC has played an important and successful role in ensuring the safe operation of six commercial nuclear power reactors in Taiwan since then.

53. As noted above, the AEC is very important in the development of a nuclear energy regulatory regime. In the late 1960s, two important laws were established,[57] while a series of legislations and ordinances have been adopted since 2000.[58] Apart from its regulatory function, the AEC's policy function is to focus on R&D. The Institute of Nuclear Energy Research (INER) was founded in 1968. After the governmental reorganization, the AEC was scheduled to be merged with the Ministries of Technology and Economics and Energy Affairs. The merger was also delayed because of the delay in the legislative process pertaining to the Organization Act.

§4. EPA, the Executive Yuan

54. In general, the EPA is responsible for the environmental aspect of energy laws. The EPA plays the important role of assessment, evaluation, and monitoring of environmental effects resulting from energy use. The related legal instruments include the Air Pollution Control Act, Water Pollution Control Act, Environmental Impact Assessment (EIA) Act, etc.

55. In addition to enforcing environmental regulations, the EPA is also very active in promoting the use of renewable energy, even though the main competent authority for renewable energy is the MOEABOE. For instance, since the EPA is

56. Atomic Energy Council, Homepage, available at: http://www.aec.gov.tw/www/english/index.html.
57. For example, Atomic Energy Law of 1968 and Nuclear Damage Compensation Act of 1971.
58. For example, Ionizing Radiation Protection Act of 2002, Nuclear Reactor Facilities Regulation Act of 2003, Nuclear Emergency Response Act of 2003, Nuclear Materials and Radioactive Waste Management Act of 2002, Act on Sites for the Establishment of Low-Level Radioactive Waste Final Disposal Facility of 2006, and their Ordinances, etc.

responsible for waste management, it began in 1999 to encourage the use of methane for power production by providing a FIT. The EPA has also developed a policy to encourage the use of waste incinerators (subject to similar incentive scheme as cogenerators (combined heat and power (CHP))) to promote the creation of electricity from solid municipal waste.

56. Long before the promulgation of the GHG Reduction Act in 2015, the EPA already was the main authority responsible for dealing with climate change. In order to curb the emissions from energy production and use, the EPA developed a series of policy measures and legal instruments. Recently, the development of a general legal regime for carbon capture and storage (CCS) was also being considered by the EPA.

57. The central Environmental Protection Administration (EPA) opened its first greenhouse gas (GHG) reduction department in 2008. After an organizational restructuring, the Greenhouse Gas Reduction Management Office comprises a Reduction Planning Division, Trade Examination Division, and Adaption Advocacy Division, with a Greenhouse Gas Reduction Guidance Commission offering advice and assistance in GHG reduction management.[59]

§5. Role of the SEC and State-Owned Energy Enterprises

58. In order to manage and supervise state-owned enterprises supervised by the MOEA, a special committee—the State Enterprise Commission (SEC)—was created under the MOEA in 1969. The state-owned enterprises managed by the SEC include energy companies (the CPC and Tai-Power), and those manufacturing steel, sugar, salt, etc. In addition to companies directly owned by the MOEA, the SEC also regulates those companies invested in by the MOEA and those companies invested in by the above state-owned enterprises. Unlike the focus on energy security of the MOEABOE, the SEC mainly focuses on the operational performance of these state "investments."

59. State-owned enterprises are supposed to be regulated by the government. How then is it that these enterprises have become rule makers or regulators themselves? Due to the technical nature of energy-related affairs, it is impossible for the government to promulgate detailed rules to regulate the energy market. Hence, in certain technical fields, the government establishes only basic rules and standards and leaves the formulating of detailed rules to the professional energy companies. For instance, in spite of the competent authority's authorization to set up rules on interconnection and electricity purchase for connecting CHP power plants to Tai-Power under the Energy Management Act,[60] the authority has merely established

59. The information concerning Greenhouse Gas Reduction Management Office, available at: https://www.epa.gov.tw/Page/CEFA13EC80406D10.

60. Article 10(3) of the Energy Management Act: "Measures regarding the rates for the purchase of excess power ... as well as measures regarding the *interconnection* between the systems of the

basic principles in its Ordinance on the Promotion of CHP of 1988, and has left the formulating of technical rules regarding interconnection and electricity sales to Tai-Power.[61] A similar regime was also applied to the Renewable Energy Acts of 2009[62] and 2019. For instance, the power purchase agreement (PPA) on the FIT was stipulated by Tai-Power, instead of MOEA, in accordance with Article 9(4) of the Renewable Energy Act of 2019.[63]

§6. Climate Change and Energy Committee/Office under the Executive Yuan

60. In order to comply with the Copenhagen Accord, particularly the implementation of Nationally Appropriate Mitigation Actions (NAMAs), as well as to deal with cross-ministerial and comprehensive affairs regarding climate change and energy issues, Taiwan determined to set up a committee, the *Committee on Energy Conservation and Emission Reduction (CECER)* and the *Committee on the Promotion of New Energy (CPNE)*, which were established in 2010. The function of the CECER is to coordinate the climate and energy affairs distributed among numerous ministries and to provide advice and a comprehensive strategy. The main organizer of this Committee is the Minister without portfolio who has professional competence in energy and climate-related issues. Yet, it should be noted that in spite of the CECER's cross-ministerial nature, its website is under the sub-net of the MOEA-BOE.[64] This situation also shows the weakness of this Committee. Due to not having its own complement of staffs, this Committee remains under the direction of the existing authorities. The structure of this Committee and related ministries is illustrated in Figure 1.

---

energy user and the vertical integrated utilities, the method of purchasing electrical energy, the rates for power and backup power purchased, and the duration of the obligation to purchase excess power by the vertical integrated utilities shall be stipulated by *the central competent authority*."

61. *See, e.g.*, Key Points of Interconnection Between Tai-Power and CHP Operators (Tai-Power), available at: https://www.taipower.com.tw/upload/169/2017110811514440559.pdf; Ordinance on Electricity Purchase between Tai-Power and CHP Operators (Tai-Power), available at: http://www.rootlaw.com.tw/LawArticle.aspx?LawID=A040100051002900-0911002.
62. *See, e.g.*, Key Points of Interconnection Between Tai-Power and Renewable Electricity Generators, available at: https://www.taipower.com.tw/upload/228/2018120409203473289.pdf; Tai-Power Feed-in Tariff Ordinance, available at: https://www.taipower.com.tw/upload/228/2018011615421434129.pdf.
63. Article 9(4) of the Renewable Energy Act of 2019: "When the electricity retailing utility enterprise purchases electricity generated from renewable energy at wholesale according to the preceding paragraph, the enterprise shall sign a contract with the installers of renewable energy power generation facilities, and the contract shall be submitted to the central competent authority for future reference."
64. MOEABOE, Website of Committee on Energy Conservation and Emission Reduction, The Executive Yuan., available at: www.moeaboe.gov.tw/Policy/ReduceCO2Emission/default.html (visited on Oct. 10, 2020).

Figure 1 The Structure of Committee on Energy Conservation and Emission Reduction

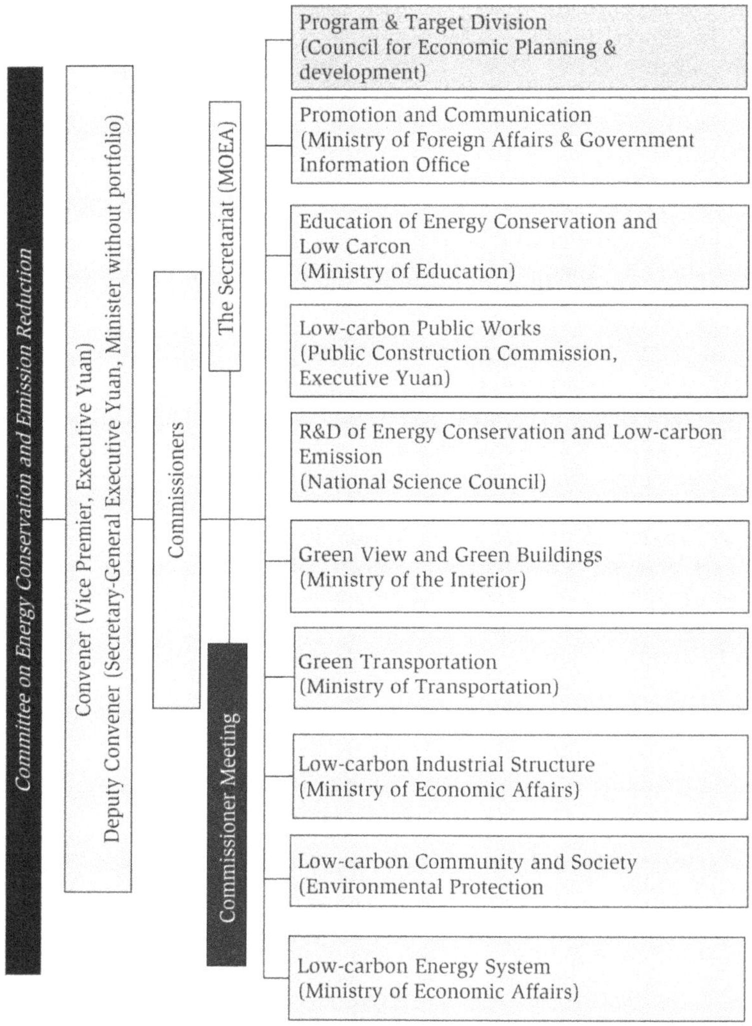

Source: Compiled by the author.

61. At the same time, a similar Committee—the CPNE—was also created to promote the development of renewable energy. In the first meeting on March 26, 2009, and the second meeting on August 16 of that same year, the main discussion was on the renewable energy road map and vision for 2030. A recent discussion focused on sectoral measures to realize these goals. For instance, a Special Strategic Group on Offshore Wind Farming was established under this Committee, and measures to provide investment subsidies of 50% are under consideration, with a view to achieving 4200 MW installed capacity by 2030.

62. Apart from the changes to the EPA and MOEA under the Governmental Reorganization Act of February 2010, an additional parliamentary decision was notably taken along with this Act. This decision urges the Executive Yuan to realize the cross-ministerial nature of climate change affairs and encourage the creation of a *cross-ministerial climate change competent authority* to implement climate change policy and measures. This design was inspired by the UK's Department of Energy and Climate Change.[65] This new authority was scheduled to be formally established in January 2012. If such an initiative is realized, this authority could replace the existing weak temporary committee with a more powerful and resourceful formal authority. However, there have been a few discussions on this new climate authority since then. It seems the missionary climate change and energy committee will remain for the present.

63. After the ruling party rotation in 2016, the new government merged the existing committees and created the Office of Energy and Carbon Reduction under the Executive Yuan.[66] The main mission of this office was to achieve the realization of four policy initiatives and visions including a nuclear-free homeland, energy security, a green economy, and environmental sustainability.[67]

§7. Local Government

64. The role of local governments in energy, climate change, and related affairs is gaining importance. First, the laws of the central government continue to reinforce the authority of the local government in energy affairs. For instance, the recent Renewable Energy Act of 2019 gives the local government authority to issue a permit to renewable installations below 2 MW,[68] which is only 500 kW under the Renewable Energy Act of 2009. Local governments continue to use their "environmental" autonomy to intervene in energy affairs. For instance, the Yunlin government passed a local law banning the burning of coal in 2015.[69] The local government of Tainan promulgated the Tainan City Self-Government Ordinance for

65. GOV.UK, Department of Energy & Climate Change, available at: https://www.gov.uk/government/organisations/department-of-energy-climate-change.
66. Executive Yuan, Executive Yuan to set up energy and carbon office, Jun. 16, 2016, available at: https://english.ey.gov.tw/Page/61BF20C3E89B856/f5e3677e-a7df-4b99-b850-319482c49b8f.
67. Office of Energy and Carbon Reduction EY, Vision, available at: https://www.ey.gov.tw/oecr/C2CB1A9BE5491FEA.
68. Article 4(2) of the Renewable Energy Act of 2019.
69. Focus Taiwan, Yunlin county councilors pass bylaw to ban coal burning, May 15, 2015, available at: https://focustaiwan.tw/business/201505150038.

a Low-Carbon City in 2012 and required a user with a power usage contract capacity of 800 kW or above to select a suitable site in the city to set up a solar photovoltaic system to generate at least 10% of the contract capacity.[70]

70. Tainan City Government, Tainan City Self-Government Ordinance for a Low-Carbon City, Apr. 17, 2017, available at: http://law01.tainan.gov.tw/glrsnewsout/EngLawContent.aspx?lan=E&id=15.

Chapter 5. Sources of Energy Law

65. Taiwan's energy law is derived from diverse legal sources. According to the tradition of legal precedence, international law and other related national law are the sources of energy law. With regard to international law, in spite of Taiwan's ambiguous position as a sovereign state, Taiwan is very keen on participating in the drafting of international laws. For instance, Taiwan became a formal member of the World Trade Organization in 2002. In this regard, its tariff scheme for oil and gas imports should follow the normal rules under the General Agreement on Tariffs and Trade. Apart from Taiwan's compliance with international law as a member of international organizations, in the many cases where it is excluded from international treaties, Taiwan voluntarily complies with several of them and joins in discussions on their formulation. For instance, Taiwan has participated in the Conference of Parties under the United Nations UNFCCC from the very beginning, and drafted rules to achieve the emission reduction targets. The adoption of the Renewable Energy Act in 2009 may have been related to the Conference of Parties (COP) meeting in Copenhagen the same year. The adoption of the GHG Reduction Act in 2015 may be relevant to the COP meetings that took place in Paris in 2015.

66. In addition to international legal sources, the most important sources of energy law are domestic law. Constitutional law creates a state-owned energy company structure for regularizing the domestic energy market.[71] Moreover, the laws that pertain the most to energy "regulation" are administrative ones, including, generally, the Administrative Procedural Act, Information Disclosure Act, Act on State-Owned Enterprises, Land Act, Urban Planning Act, Fair Trade Act, and, specifically, the Energy Management Act, Renewable Energy Act, etc.

67. The so-called economic law, while being an independent legal discipline, is also the legal source of energy law. It includes the Electricity Business Act, Natural Gas Business Act, and Petroleum Management Act. Certain Acts may also be related to energy affairs. For instance, the Act on Facilitating the Upgrade of Traditional Industries might have been helpful in encouraging the purchasing of energy saving and high efficiency installations. This Act was replaced by the Act on Innovative Industries, which plays a similar role in providing tax incentives to encourage R&D activities by domestic industries.

68. As energy laws are usually very technical in nature, the reliance on secondary legislation, such as administrative ordinances, is necessary. Article 150 of the Administrative Procedure Act defines such ordinance as "an abstract prescription with external legal effects, established by an administrative authority as enabled by

71. Article 144 of the Constitutional Law: "Public utilities and other enterprises of a monopolistic nature shall, in principle, be under public operation. In cases permitted by law, they may be operated by private citizens."

law in respect of general matters and applicable to a multiple number of non-specified persons."[72] Such an ordinance shall specify the authority conferred by law based on which it is established, and shall not transgress the scope of such authority or diverge from the legislative purposes of the enabling law.[73] Most secondary energy legislation meets these criteria. Yet, the recent rules concerning offshore wind power may not do so. For instance, there are no laws conferring the IDB with power to promulgate rules addressing the local content requirement of offshore wind power.[74] Thus, the administrative internal order, which was not supposed to have legal effects under the Administrative Procedure Act,[75] can become an emerging source of energy law while promoting energy transition in Taiwan.

69. Finally, the traditional laws, such as the Civil Code or Criminal Code, can also become the source of energy law. For instance, the "road right" for laying electricity underground cables is provided for under the civil code.[76] The stealing of electricity, heat, and other energy is considered to be the stealing of "movable property" under Article 320 of the Criminal Code. The impediment of the operation of electricity and gas businesses may be considered a criminal act of endangering public safety and be punished by a fine or up to five years in prison.

---

72. MOJ, Administrative Procedure Act, Amended Date: 2015-12-30, available at: https://law.moj.gov.tw/ENG/LawClass/LawAll.aspx?pcode=A0030055.
73. Article 150(2) of the Administrative Procedure Act.
74. IDB, Regulations on Offshore Windpower Industries, Nov. 13, 2018, available at: https://www.moeaidb.gov.tw/ctlr?PRO=policy.rwdPolicyView&id=6474.
75. Article 159 of the Administrative Procedure Act:

> The term "administrative rules" used in this Act means generalized and abstract provisions issued by a superior authority to its lower units or by a superior officer to his subordinate officers, by virtue of its or his powers, for the purpose of regulating the internal order and operation of the authority, with no direct external effects as legal norms.
>
> Administrative rules include the following provisions:
>
> 1. General provisions relating to the organization, allotment of affairs, the manner in which business is conducted, personnel management, and other internal matters of the authority; and
> 2. Provisions of an interpretation nature and guidelines on the exercise of discretion, issued to assist lower units or subordinate officers in making unified interpretation of laws and regulations, finding the facts and exercising the power of discretion."

76. Article 786 of Civil Code: "Where electric wires, water pipes, gas pipes or other pipes cannot be constructed without making use of the land of another or where they can only be constructed through the incurring of excessive expenses, the landowner is entitled to construct the said wires or pipes on, over, or under the land of another person, provided that the place and method chosen of constructing such wires or pipes will cause the least injury to such other land and provided that compensation shall be made.

    If, following the construction of electric wires, water pipes, gas pipes, or other pipes in accordance with the provision of the preceding paragraph, there is a change of circumstances, the owner of such other land is entitled to demand a change to the aforesaid construction.

    The expenses of the change of such construction shall be borne by the landowner. However, if the statutes or customs provide otherwise, such statutes or customs shall be followed."

Part I. Regulatory Framework for Coal

Chapter 1. General Introduction

§1. Coal Supply and Demand Situation

70. Currently, Taiwan imports 100% of its coal. The total coal supply was 44,303.8 10^3 KLOE in 2019,[77] of which 76.03% of domestic consumption was consumed by power generation plants, and 12.69% by the industrial sector.[78] The total coal supply grew from 37.17 million metric tons in 1998 to 66.51 million metric tons in 2018, depicting an average annual increase of 2.95%.[79] Australia (50.3%) and Indonesia (25.6%) are the largest coal exporters to Taiwan.[80]

§2. Coal Policy

71. Coal is one of the few fuels that Taiwan has produced indigenously in large quantities in the past. Domestic Coal has played an important role in the energy mix of Taiwan from around the 1950s, by which time the coal industry was quite developed. In this regard, at that time, the main policy focus was on the "safety of coal mines," the "health of mine workers," and the control of supplies. However, with the depletion of coal,[81] problems occurred including the high cost of digging deeper into the mines, the shortage of mine workers, the competition from imported coal, and the three coal mine incidents in 1984.[82] Taiwan's self-sufficiency rate with regard to coal diminished from 76.9% in 1977 to 0.3% in 1997,[83] and is currently 0%.

72. Therefore, the coal policy began to shift from domestic production to coal use and imports. The main policy issues of coal are elaborated as follows:

---

77. Energy Supply, available at: https://www.moeaboe.gov.tw/ECW/main/content/wHandMenuFile.ashx?file_id=1403.
78. Bureau of Energy, About, http://www.moeaboe.gov.tw/About/webpage/book_en3/page7.htm.
79. MOEA, Energy Statistics Handbook 2018, October 2019, available at: https://www.moeaboe.gov.tw/ECW_WEBPAGE/FlipBook/2018EnergyStaHandBook/2018EnergyStaHandBook.pdf.
80. MOEA, Energy Statistics Handbook 2018 Revised, October 2019, available at: https://www.moeaboe.gov.tw/ECW_WEBPAGE/FlipBook/2018EnergyStaHandBook/index.html#p=53.
81. MOEAEC, Energy White Paper of 1998 80 (1998).
82. *Id.*, at 86.
83. *Id.*, at 96.

I. Reduction of Coal-Fired Power Plants in the Electricity Mix

73. Coal-fired power plants are not very popular among the public. In 2018, two questions in the referendum pertained to a reduction in the coal-fired power plants (Table 2). These were: "Do you agree with the reduction in the electricity production of thermal power plants at 1% each year?" and "Do you agree with the establishment of an energy policy to 'Stop the construction and expansion of any coal-fired thermal power plant or generator units (including the Shen Ao Power Plant currently under construction)'?" A vast majority was against the development of coal-fired power plants.

Table 2 Results for the Two Referendums on the Fate of Future Coal-Fired Power Plants in 2018

Question	*For*		*Against*		*Invalid/Blank*	*Total*	*Registered Voters*	*Turnout*	*Outcome*
	Votes	*%*	*Votes*	*%*					
Reducing output from thermal power plants	7,955,753	79.04	2,109,157	20.96	715,140	10,780,050	19,757,067	54.56	Adopted
Ceasing expansion of coal power plants	7,599,267	76.41	2,346,316	23.59	823,945	10,769,528		54.51	Adopted

Source: Central Election Commission, 2018 Referendum Results, http://referendum.2018.nat.gov.tw/pc/en/00/m00000000000000000.html; https://web.archive.org/web/20181124220825/http://referendum.2018.nat.gov.tw/pc/en/00/m00000000000000000.html.

74. Compared with the coal phase-out agenda in Germany and the UK,[84] there are very few discussions on the coal phase-out in Taiwan. Over the past ten years, coal-fired power has occupied the ratio between 49.36% and 45%.[85] Therefore, it is unlikely to reduce the ratio to 0 within a very short period. In spite of this, according to the New Energy Policy by MOEA in 2016, the government intended to reduce the coal in the electricity mix to 30%.[86] However, as there were only less than five years to achieve that goal and all nuclear power (around 10%) is expected to phase out, it poses great challenges to achieve that goal.

II. Supply Security of Coal

75. There is some concern over the supply security of coal, which is similar to other fossil fuel energy as an imported fuel. In Taiwan's 1996 Energy Policy and Measures, the diversification of country sources for imported coal, oil, gas, and nuclear fuel is mentioned. Further, the development of sufficient coal-related facilities is also a concern of this policy. For instance, as coal is mainly used as electricity fuel, Tai-Power has participated in coal exploration and exploitation, and recently secured a coal mine in Bengalla, Australia.

III. Climate Change Concerns: Clean Coal and CCS

76. As coal is a relatively secure form of energy for Taiwan, Taiwan relies on it. Improving the environmental quality of coal has been a main concern of the energy policy. As far back as the 1996 Taiwan Energy Policy and Measures, the facilitation of RD&D in pursuit of "clean coal" technology has been mentioned. (1996 policy)

77. Recently, the role of CCS has also been highlighted in climate change and energy policy packages. The 2008 Sustainable Energy Development Framework serves to "Introduce clean coal technology and CCS technology through international cooperation to reduce the CO2 emission of power-generating systems."[87] A similar indication can also be found in the 2010 Master Plan on Energy Conservation and Emission Reduction. In the recent Guidelines on Energy Development (April 2017), the clean coal technology is mentioned in the following: "Introduce clean coal and carbon reduction related technologies based on technological

84. CLEW, Spelling out the coal exit—Germany's phase-out plan, Jul. 3, 2020, available at: https://www.cleanenergywire.org/factsheets/spelling-out-coal-phase-out-germanys-exit-law-draft. NS Energy, Coal phase-out: From Canada to UK, which countries are ditching the fuel, Mar. 3, 2020, available at: https://www.nsenergybusiness.com/features/coal-phase-out/.
85. Bureau of Energy Taiwan, Energy Statistics, available at: https://www.moeaboe.gov.tw/wesnq/Views/B01/wFrmB0102.aspx.
86. Evan A. Feigenbaum, Jen-yi Hou, Overcoming Taiwan's Energy Trilemma, April 2020, available at: https://carnegieendowment.org/2020/04/27/overcoming-taiwan-s-energy-trilemma-pub-81645.
87. MOEA, Framework of Taiwan's Sustainable Energy Policy, 2008.06.05, available at: www.epa.gov.tw/FileLink/FileHandler.ashx?file=11942.

progress assessment, and enhance the efficiency of coal-fired power generation in order to reduce the carbon emissions from coal consumption."

78. As Taiwan's energy sufficiency rate is below 1%, coal has always been considered a very important source of energy security. However, in the light of the environmental and climate change concerns generated by coal-fired power plants, the use of coal has come under attack from many environmental NGOs. Currently, cleaner fossil fuel, i.e., LNG, seems to be favored under the current national climate change program. For example, to reduce emissions from electricity generation, the use of natural gas was promoted in the 2010 Master Plan on Energy Conservation and Emission Reduction and in the Energy Policy of 2016, which set 50% gas-fired plants as a target to be achieved by 2025. However, this does not mean coal is no longer important in Taiwan's electricity supply. In recognition of the double-edged sword that coal energy represents and to strike a balance between energy security and emission reduction, there is a move to develop coal power plants meeting higher efficiency and less emission requirements, such as supercritical or ultra-supercritical steam generators. This direction also reflects the rule under the 2017 Guidelines on Energy Development: "Improve the efficiency of power plants, and regulate new power plants to adopt the commercialized best available technology."

IV. Efficiency of Coal Use

79. Apart from the two purposes (environmental and energy security) noted above, there are also certain policy measures intended to improve the efficiency of coal use. In the 1996 Taiwan Energy Policy and Measures, CHP is promoted under the energy efficiency measures. So far, around 75% of CHP are coal-fired. By this means, the waste heat during the coal burning process can be recycled and reused. In addition, under the 2010 Master Plan on Energy Conservation and Emission Reduction, the main measures seek "to improve thermal efficiency via replacing or replenishing the existing fossil-fuel [mainly coal-fired] power plants" in keeping with the policy direction of "reduction of emission from power generators."[88]

80. As a result of the low reserve margin situation in recent times, the CHP also handles electricity security. Its important role was also highlighted in the 2017 Guidelines on Energy Development in the following words: "Make good use of the potential of the cogeneration system in terms of compliance with power dispatching in order to stabilize power supply and to ensure power quality."

88. Executive Yuan, National Plan of Energy Saving and Carbon Reduction, May 2002, available at: https://www.google.com/url?sa=i&url=https%3A%2F%2Fgrb-topics.stpi.narl.org.tw%2Ffile%2Fdownload%3FflsId%3D4b1141c264eef5760164eef862d200c0&psig=AOvVaw30i2i_DkhGOd4m6Rz4KWqy&ust=1597452969569000&source=images&cd=vfe&ved=2ahUKEwi9oNKXvpnrAhUDNKYKHVHfB5QQr4kDegUIARClAQ.

§3. AUTHORITY

81. During the era of coal mine exploitation and exploration, the Mining Act and BOM played a central role. However, with the exhaustion of coal mines; oil; and gas, the function of the Mining Act and BOM changed to administrating, overseeing, and monitoring non-energy minerals, such as jade, sand stone, etc.

82. Currently, the main regulatory authority for coal focuses mainly on the ship transportation, storage, sales, and environment, health and safety (EHS) concerns arising from the use of coal. The main authorities involved are the Department of Transportation, the EPA, the Fair Trade Commission (FTC), and the MOEA.

Chapter 2. Mining Act and the Exploitation of Coal, Petroleum, and Gas

83. The law governing the production of more than 61 types[89] of minerals, including coal,[90] is the Mining Act, which was promulgated on May 26, 1930, enforced on December 1, 1930, and recently amended on December 31, 2003. The purpose of the Mining Act is "to utilize effectively national mineral resources for promoting sustained economic development and boosting social welfare." Briefly, it intends to regulate the related EHS concerns arising from exploration and mining activities, including soil and water conservation, environmental protection (the impact of exploration or mining activities on the environment), mine safety measures, and mining hazard prevention for sustained operations.[91] As this Act is also applied to oil,[92] gas,[93] and uranium,[94] the introduction in this section will also apply to these natural resources as well. (More oil-specific and gas-specific regulations will be provided later.)

84. According to Article 2 of the Mining Act, all minerals within the territory, exclusive of the economic marine zone and continental shelf of Taiwan, are state-owned. Exploitation without a mineral right acquired pursuant to this Act is prohibited. Thus, before beginning exploitation activities, businesses must acquire a mineral right from the MOEA.[95] The mineral right is further divided into two types: exploration right and mining right.[96]

§1. Mineral Right

85. The main regulations concerning mineral rights are further stipulated in Chapter 2 (Mineral Right) (Articles 8–42) and Chapter 4 of this Act dealing with the Mineral Right Fee and Mineral Royalty (Articles 53–56). These two Chapters

89. Article 3-I of the Mining Act: "The minerals referred hereunder include the following: 1. Gold minerals 2. Silver minerals 3. Copper minerals 4. Iron minerals 5. Tin minerals 6. Lead minerals 7. Antimony minerals 8. Nickel minerals 9. Cobalt minerals 10. Zinc minerals 11. Aluminum minerals 12. Mercury minerals 13. Bismuth minerals 14. Molybdenum minerals 15. Platinum minerals 16. Iridium minerals 17. Chromium minerals 18. Uranium minerals 19. Radium minerals 20. Tungsten minerals 21. Manganese minerals 22. Vanadium minerals 23. Potassium minerals 24. Thorium minerals 25. Zirconium minerals 26. Titanium minerals 27. Strontium minerals 28. Sulfur and Pyrite 29. Phosphate minerals 30. Arsenic minerals 31. Quartz crystal 32. Asbestos 33. Mica 34. Gypsum 35. Salt 36. Aluminite 37. Diamond minerals 38. Natural Alkali 39. Baryte 40. Chile saltpeter 41. Glauber's salt 42. Borax 43. Graphite 44. Beryl 45. Fluorspar 46. Fireclay 47. Talc 48. Feldspar 49. Kaolin 50. Marble & Calcite 51. Magnesium & Dolomite 52. Coal 53. Petroleum & Oil Shale 54. Natural Gas 55. Gem & Jade 56. Abrasives 57. Mineral Pigments 58. Limestone 59. Serpentine 60. Silica Sand 61. Other minerals designated by the Executive Yuan."
90. Article 3-I(52), Mining Act.
91. Article 15(2), Mining Act.
92. Article 15 (1) (53), Petroleum & Oil Shale, Mining Act.
93. Article 3(1) (54), Mining Act.
94. Article 3(1)(18), Mining Act.
95. The authority under this Act is the MOEA. *See* Art. 5, Mining Act.
96. Article 4I (7), Mining Act.

comprising 40 Articles constitute the main part of this Act (80 Articles). In Chapter 2, there are further sections, including Section 1 dealing with the Nature and Validity of the Mineral Right; Section 2, the Establishment and Renewal of a Mineral Right; Section 3, the Change, Transfer, and Extinction of a Mineral Right; Section 4, the Mortgage of a Mineral Right.

86. Section 1 provides the following regulations for mineral rights:

- The mineral right is also subject to the provisions of the Civil Code relating to real estate (Article 8)[97]
- The duration of exploration rights including the first-time application and extension is limited to four years (Article 12). The duration of an exploration right shall not exceed a period of two years. An application shall be submitted to the MOEA for approval of an extension ranging from six months to a year before expiration and only once. The extension shall not exceed a period of two years.
- The duration of the mining right (Article 13): The duration of a mining right shall not exceed a period of twenty years. An application for extension shall be submitted to the MOEA for approval from six months to a year before expiration. The extension duration shall not exceed a period of twenty years each time.

87. Section 2 governing the application procedure for a mineral right: According to Article 15, when applying for the establishment of an exploration right, an applicant shall submit an application form, application fee, mineral concession map, and conceptualized exploration plan. In seeking to establish a mineral right, an applicant shall submit an application form, application fee, mineral concession map, ore deposit description, conceptualized mining plan, and its drawing explanation. Due to the concerns over national security or environmental effects, the following areas are prohibited from application for mineral rights: (Article 27)

- Within the forbidden areas of fortresses, military ports, garrison areas, and military facilities and premises, where permissions from the related governing agencies have not been secured.
- Within one kilometer from the border of a commercial district or market place, where permissions from the related governing agencies have not been secured.
- Within conserved forests, watershed areas of a reservoir, designated scenic areas and national parks, where permissions from the related governing agencies have not been secured.
- Within 150 meters from public buildings, national cemeteries, railroads, national highways, provincial highways, important factory sites, and unmovable famous relics, where permissions from the related governing agencies have not been secured.
- Within the areas where exploration or mining is prohibited without permission from the governing agency as designated by other Acts, where permissions from the related governing agencies have not been secured.

97. Article 8, Mining Act: "A mineral right is deemed as a real right, to which, unless otherwise specified herein, the provisions of the Civil Code on real estate shall be applicable."

– Within the areas where exploration or mining is prohibited by other Acts.

88. Nevertheless, the MOEA enjoys much freedom to determine whether an application should be allowed. According to Article 28, the authority is allowed to reject an application out of concerns that it may be "detrimental to the public interest."

89. Furthermore, Section 3 provides regulations relating to the Change, Transfer, and Extinction of Mineral Rights. In general, changes (increasing, decreasing, combining, or severing of the approved mineral concession area (Article 34) and the transfers of mineral rights due to inheritance, assignment, compulsory execution, or entrustment (Article 36)) are subject to the approval of the MOEA.

90. With regard to the Mineral Right Fee and Mineral Royalty:

- Mineral right fee: A mineral right holder shall pay a mineral right fee based on the kind of minerals, the area of concession, and the rate of exploration right or mining right.[98] This may be applied to a reduction in mineral royalties paid of up to 80%.[99] Further regulations are provided in the Ordinance on Mineral Right Fees.[100] The exploration fee for coal is 150 NTD per hectare,[101] while the mining fee for coal is 450 NTD per hectare.[102]
- Mineral royalty: The mineral right holder for coal shall pay mineral royalty based on the mineral price at the rate of 2% to 10%.[103] Further stipulations are given in the Ordinance on Mineral Royalty.[104] The formula for mineral royalties is as follows: the amount of production of minerals*mineral price*rate.[105] The amount of mineral production is based on the data provided to the MOEA by miners each year;[106] the mineral price is calculated by the weighted average price of each exploration and mining site.[107] The ratio is set at 2% for coal.[108]

---

98. Article 53, Mining Act.
99. Article 53(3), Mining Act: "The mineral right holder under Paragraph 1 may apply to have the business tax or mineral royalty paid for the mineral production reduced on the basis of the mineral right fee paid for the same type of mineral; however, the reduction due to the mineral right fee shall be limited to 80%."
100. Bureau of Mines, available at: http://www.mine.gov.tw/Download/Law/%C4q%B7˜%C5v%B6O%A6%AC%B6O%BF%EC%AAk.pdf.
101. Article 2(1)(1), Mining Act.
102. Article 2(1)(2), Mining Act.
103. Article 54I, Mining Act. The mineral rights holders of petroleum and natural gas mines should pay 2% to 50% of the mineral product price; the mineral rights holders of metal mines should pay 2% to 20% of the mineral price; others; The owner of the mineral rights shall pay the mineral royalties at 2% to 10% of the price of the minerals. The price and payment rate of mineral products in the preceding paragraph shall be determined by the competent authority.
104. MOEA, Ordinance on Mineral Royalty, available at: http://www.mine.gov.tw/Download/Law/%C4q%B2%A3%C5v%A7Q%AA%F7%A6%AC%B6O%BF%EC%AAk.pdf.
105. Article 2, Ordinance on Mineral Royalty.
106. Article 3I, Ordinance on Mineral Royalty.
107. Article 3II, Ordinance on Mineral Royalty.
108. Article 4I(3), Ordinance on Mineral Royalty.

– The fee should be paid on an annual basis.[109]

91. Finally, it should be noted that similar to the MOEA in determining whether to grant a mineral right, the MOEA likewise enjoys great power in setting or adjusting mineral fees: "In order to cope with a special situation related to the domestic or overseas economy and to ensure the rational operation of the industry, the governing agency may adjust the mineral royalty as necessary." Apparently, this introduces uncertainties into the exploration and mining activities in Taiwan. The government can change the fee on the basis of an abstract reason such as the "domestic or overseas economy and rational operation of the industry."

§2. Supervision of Mining Industry

92. Articles 57–64 of Chapter 5 provide regulations for regulating the mining industry.

- Mining work: (Article 57) Mining work should not be detrimental to the public interest. Otherwise, the governing agency can instruct the mineral right holder to take remedial measures within a designated time period, or suspend the work temporarily.
- The issuing of a mine registration certificate: (Article 58) After registration of a mineral right, the holder shall file with the governing agency for commencement of work by submitting a mine commencement application, mine office photos, construction plan and drawing, detailed list of mining equipment and facilities inside and outside the mine portal, as well as the certificates of appointment for the person responsible for supervising the mine, key technicians, and documents pertaining to the purchasing or leasing of the mining land. The government agency will then issue a mine registration certificate after inspection and approval of the documents.
- The requirement of keeping related documents: (Article 59) A mineral right holder shall keep a mining survey map and a mining logbook at the mine office.
- The requirement of filing: (Article 60) A mineral right holder shall file with the governing agency a detailed list of the mining operation of the previous year and the construction and operation plan of the current year every January.
- Selling permission: (Article 61) The mineral obtained from exploration shall not be sold without the permission of the governing agency.
- The related documents issued by the professional mining engineer: (Article 62) The conceptualized exploration plan and its drawing, the conceptualized mining plan and its drawing, the mining and construction plan and its drawing, and the annual construction plan and its drawing attached to the application for a mineral right shall be issued by a professional mining engineer registered under the professional engineering Act.

---

109. Article 55I of Mining Act: "A mineral right holder shall pay a mineral right fee and mineral royalty on an annual basis."

- Inspected by authority: (Article 63) The governing agency may dispatch personnel to inspect the mining-related mining logbook, records or equipment, and the mineral right holder shall not evade, obstruct, or refuse such inspection.

§3. Promotion of Mining

93. There are certain provisions in place to promote mining activities. Of four provisions (Articles 65–68), two promotional measures are potentially relevant for the development of coal.

- To explore an area for mineral deposits, the governing agency may set up an exploration institute or commission other related parties to conduct the exploration. (Article 65)
- In order to assist in mining operations, the governing agency may provide assistance in land acquisition, fund raising, equipment procurement, human resources training, and technique development. (Article 66)

Chapter 3. Other Regulations Concerning Coal

§1. Sale or Use of Coal

94. The sale of coal is subject to several legal regimes. For instance, the FTC may intervene in the sale of coal if there is anti-competitive behavior by the coal importer on the market. There is a special subdivision within the FTC to deal with the mine or coal industry.[110] In addition, as coal may cause air pollution problems during use, there is a permission regime for the sale of coal and other potential air polluting materials.[111] The local government has the authority to issue permissions for coal use, which can then be used by the local government to affect or intervene in the operation of coal-fired power plants in Taichung City.[112]

§2. Coal Mine Disaster

95. Mine disasters, including those at coal mines, come under the supervision of the MOEA under the Disaster Act.[113] The MOEA is responsible for drafting a Plan for Dealing with Mine Disasters.[114] For high-risk mining sites, the related information should be disclosed in advance.[115]

96. At the time of a serious mine disaster, a Central Emergency Response Center for the mine disaster should be established.[116] The BOM and the MOEA should set up a Special Emergency Response Taskforce to tackle the emergency situation.[117]

110. MOJ, Art. 9 of Ordinance on Organizational Structure of Fair Trade Commission. Yet, this Ordinance has been revoked in 2012.
111. Permission Ordinance on the use of substance prone to cause air pollution, 2003-06-25, Amended on: 2020-03-23, available at: https://oaout.epa.gov.tw/law/LawContent.aspx?id=FL025346.
112. TaiChung Local Government Law on the Regulation of use of coal and prohibition the use of Petroleum coke in public and private domain, 2016-01-26, available at: http://lawsearch.taichung.gov.tw/GLRSout/LawContent.aspx?id=GL002466.
113. Article 3(1) of the Disaster Act.
114. The plan in Chinese is available at: https://cdprc.ey.gov.tw/Upload/UserFiles/%E7%A4%A6%E7%81%BD%E7%81%BD%E5%AE%B3%E9%98%B2%E6%95%91%E6%A5%AD%E5%8B%99%E8%A8%88%E7%95%AB(%E6%A0%B8%E5%AE%9A%E7%89%88).pdf.
115. MOJ, Ordinance on Mine Disaster Information Disclosure, 2008-10-27, available at: https://law.moj.gov.tw/LawClass/LawAll.aspx?pcode=J0020050.
116. Ordinance on the Establishment of Central Emergency Response Center for Mine Disaster. https://www.mine.gov.tw/Download/Service/S000263.pdf.
117. Ordinance on Establishment of Special Taskforce for Mine Disaster, available at: https://www.mine.gov.tw/Download/Service/S000127.pdf.

97. In order to facilitate the reconstruction and emergency response work, burdensome administrative procedural red tape must also be simplified.[118] After a mine disaster, victims may be awarded certain compensation.[119]

§3. Labor Safety and Other Safety Concerns

98. Certain mine safety rules focus on the safety of labor in the coal mine. Of course, this regulatory regime is no longer applicable, as there is no domestic coal production. Under the old regime, the Mine Right Owner should adopt safety measures to prevent the explosion of coal dust.[120] Detailed safety measures were further defined in the Ordinance,[121] such as the hiring of Mine Safety Management Personnel in coal mines,[122] the installation of a water spray system,[123] the avoidance of fire and smoke at coal selection sites and coal dust places,[124] the adoption of anti-explosive and anti-dust measures for the lighting and electrical installations of the mine site,[125] etc. Other ordinances, such as the Ordinance on the Prevention of Hypoxia and the Prevention Ordinance on Harm from Specific Chemical Substances, are also related to labor safety. The coal storage site is considered to be a Hypoxia-danger zone[126] and several measures were to be adopted under this Ordinance.

99. To prevent laborers from being harmed by the pollution emanating from the coke oven when coal is injected, the opening and closing of the coal oven cover should be operated with a remote control device.[127]

100. Apart from safety rules onshore, there are also rules concerning the shipping of coal. For instance, the Ordinance on Shipping Dangerous Goods prohibits the placing of pressurized air containers and organic peroxides right on the top of coal tanks or cabins.[128] In general, the ship is obliged to install fire extinguishers. However, for those ships specially designed for transporting coal or having steel

---

118. Ordinance on Simplifying Administrative Procedure Rules during Mine Disaster. https://law.moj.gov.tw/LawClass/LawAll.aspx?pcode=J0020051.
119. Ordinance on Compensation after Mine Disaster, https://law.moj.gov.tw/LawClass/LawAll.aspx?pcode=J0020049#:˜:text=%E7%81%BD%E5%AE%B3%E6%95%91%E5%8A%A9%E7%A8%AE%E9%A1%9E%E5%A6%82%E4%B8%8B%EF%BC%9A,%E9%87%8D%E5%82%B7%E6%95%91%E5%8A%A9%E9%87%91%E9%87%91%E9%A1%8D%E8%80%85%E3%80%82.
120. Article 10 of Mine Safety Act.
121. *See, e.g.*, Arts 10, 15, 19, 24, 26, 28, 38, 70, 71, 72, 78, 89, 90, 91, 92, 93, 94, 96, 108, 112, 114, 121, 126, 127, 131, 142, 208, 214 of Ordinance on Mine Safety Act.
122. Article 10 of Ordinance on Mine Safety Act.
123. Article 19 of Ordinance on Mine Safety Act.
124. Article 24 of Ordinance on Mine Safety Act.
125. Article 38 of Ordinance on Mine Safety Act.
126. Article 2 of Ordinance on the Prevention of Hypoxia.
127. Article 45 of Prevention Ordinance on the Harm from Specific Chemical Substances.
128. Articles 68 and 78 of Ordinance on Shipping Dangerous Goods.

hatch covers or other closure installations, which can be used to close all ventilation tubes, the installation requirement is waived under Article 135 of the Ordinance on Shipping Facilities.

§4. Environmental Concerns

101. The coal in Taiwan is mainly used in electricity generators and other boilers, in regard to which activities there are intensive regulations, such as the Air Pollution Act, the Ordinance on Air Pollution Act, the Emission Standard for Power Installations, the Ordinance on Environmental Impact Assessment, the Ordinance on the Installation of Air Quality Monitor Facilities, and the Permission Fee Ordinance on Air Pollution from Stationary Sources.

102. In addition to regulating the coal-using installations noted above, in Taiwan, the environmental concerns about the coal supply chain are mainly in relation to the "coal storage site." The water quality of effluents from firms and sewage systems, and the building of sewage treatment facilities near to coal storage sites are regulated under the Ordinance on Effluent Standards. The limit value for Biochemical oxygen demand, Chemical Oxygen Demand, and Suspended Solid materials has been established.[129]

129. Article 2 of Ordinance on Effluent Standards.

Part II. Regulatory Framework for Electricity

Chapter 1. General Introduction

§1. Electricity Demand and Supply

103. On the demand side, electricity and petroleum are two major energy sources in Taiwan. In 1991, the consumption of petroleum products and electricity was 43.8% and 43.7%, respectively, of the overall energy supply. Yet, after 1996, the consumption of electricity exceeded that of petroleum products. Since then, electricity has become the main energy source in terms of energy consumption. In 2018, the consumption of electricity was 29.17% of the total energy.[130]

104. On the supply side, the electricity mainly came from coal (47.62%), gas (33.54%), nuclear power (10.05%), renewable sources (4.59%), oil (2.99%), and pumped hydro (1.22%) in 2018.[131] Yet the role of renewable electricity is emerging and is expected to become more important in the future. The scheduled 2025 renewable target (20%) is next to gas-fired (50%) and coal-fired (30%) power plants in electricity mix.

§2. Energy Policy on Electricity

105. As electricity plays a major role in Taiwan's economic development and energy supply, electricity policy has been a very vital part of its energy policies; such policies include the Energy Policy Provision of 1996, the Energy White Paper of 2005, the Sustainable Energy Policy Framework of 2008, the National Comprehensive Program for Energy Conservation and Emission Reduction of 2010, etc. The general policy direction outlined in these policies is as summarized below. As there are special parts for renewable energy and nuclear energy, this author will exclude them and focus on the electricity policy only:

130. MOEA, Energy Statistics Handbook 2018, October 2019, available at: https://www.moeaboe.gov.tw/ECW_WEBPAGE/FlipBook/2018EnergyStaHandBook/2018EnergyStaHandBook.pdf.
131. MOEA, Energy Statistics Handbook 2018, October 2019, available at: https://www.moeaboe.gov.tw/ECW_WEBPAGE/FlipBook/2018EnergyStaHandBook/2018EnergyStaHandBook.pdf.

- The promotion of **low-carbon** electricity: On the one hand, the use of natural gas is encouraged and scheduled to account for more than 25% of power generated in 2025.[132] On the other hand, it is hoped that the share of low-carbon energy in electricity could increase generation systems from the current 40% to 55% in 2025.[133]
- Improvement of the **efficiency** of electricity supply: At the upstream level, the government wishes to enhance the thermal efficiency standards of newly established and renewed coal-fired plants and of combined power-cycle gas-fired plants from 35% to 40% and from 45% in 2004 to 53%, respectively.[134] This enhancement will mostly be effected by the replacement of existing power plants or by developing power plant efficiency improvement programs.[135] The promotion of CHP installations from 8 million kilowatts in 2010 to 10 million kilowatts installed capacity in 2020, would lead to the enhancement of efficiency. At the same time, the development of CHP would also lead to a more distributed generation electricity system before electricity liberalization. At the transmission and distribution level, line loss is expected to be less than 5%.
- Electricity **liberalization** and deregulation of electricity market: The policy direction wishes to speed up the amendment of the Electricity Business Act.[136] During the deliberation on the electricity liberalization bill in the Parliament, the government also launched a program to attract the establishment of independent power plants under the Current Bidding Program for Independent Power Producers (IPPs)[137] and the Fourth Phase of the Bidding Program for IPPs.[138] Even though the electricity produced by these IPPs continues to be sold to Tai-Power, Tai-Power has become less dominant and is no longer as powerful in the electricity generation sector.
- Ensuring electricity **supply security**: First of all, the government urged Tai-Power to diversify its fuel sources, including coal, nuclear power fuel, and gas, to avoid the risk of relying on too few import sources.[139] Sometimes, these measures can move more upstream to encourage the investment in exploring and exploiting foreign energy mines and acquiring the mining rights to these.[140]

106. Since 2016, the new ruling government began to promote the energy transition and nuclear-free homeland 2025 agenda, which sought to bring in vast

132. MOEA, Framework of Taiwan's Sustainable Energy Policy, 2008.06.05, available at: https://www.ey.gov.tw/Page/9277F759E41CCD91/6f0faa1c-9406-48d0-97aa-78ccea4f3f02.
133. EPA, UNFCC, available at: http://unfccc.epa.gov.tw/unfccc/english/04_our_efforts/061_policy.html.
134. Bureau of Energy, About, available at: http://www.moeaboe.gov.tw/About/webpage/book_en3/page3.htm.
135. IEEJ, Chinese Taipei, available at: www.ieej.or.jp/aperc/PREE/PREE_Chinese_Taipei.pdf.
136. 1996 Taiwan Energy Policy and Measures, available at: http://www.moeaboe.gov.tw/Policy/PoMain.aspx?PageId=executepolicy
137. The Current Bidding Program for Independent Power Producers.
138. The Fourth Phase of the Bidding Program for Independent Power Producers.
139. 1996 Taiwan Energy Policy and Measures, available at: http://www.moeaboe.gov.tw/Policy/PoMain.aspx?PageId=executepolicy.
140. 1996 Taiwan Energy Policy and Measures, available at: http://www.moeaboe.gov.tw/Policy/PoMain.aspx?PageId=executepolicy (visited on Oct. 10, 2020).

changes to the electricity policy. Apart from the aforementioned 50-30-20 electricity mix target for 2025 under the new energy policy that was announced on May 25, 2016,[141] a lot of new policy planning paved the way for the promotion of liberalization, and smart grid, and renewable energy expansion. For instance, in the 2017 Guidelines on Energy Development, the electricity market reform idea was mentioned in the following words: "Promote the domestic power industry reform by phases under the premise of stable power supply with the goal of 'Diversified Supply, Equity in Usage, and Freedom of Choice,' facilitate fair, competitive and reasonable operation of power industry, and adjust the performance indicators of state-owned business following the direction of energy transition in order to protect the users' rights and interests while increasing social well-being." The "Problem-solving-oriented" smart grid master plan (amendment) was approved by the Executive Yuan of Taiwan in 2019.[142] Finally, the following detailed policy initiatives were set to give impetus to the development of renewable electricity:

- The Forward-looking Infrastructure Development Program: Green energy,[143]
- The Four-year Wind Power Promotion Plan,[144] and
- The Two-year Solar PV Promotion Plan.[145]

107. In order to achieve the above measures in support of liberalization, low-carbon electricity, and supply security, energy law is supposed to play an important role. The original intention of the Electricity Bill before 2016 was to set up a comprehensive legal framework to support full-scale liberalization. However, the Electricity Liberalization Act passed in 2017 changed the goal and introduced liberalization only in the green electricity market. Therefore, to promote renewable electricity under the energy transition initiative, the Renewable Energy Acts of 2009 and 2019 continue to play key roles in contributing to low-carbon electricity supply, while certain energy security measures can be helpful in improving electricity supply security. Finally, the original purpose of the GHG Reduction Act of 2015 was to gradually develop the emission trading scheme to contribute toward emission reduction. Yet, because of the slow implementation of the ETS scheme, the scheme has not been put into practice yet. Therefore, the role of energy law is far more limited because of its original design or implementation.

108. However, as Taiwan adopts a more centralized regime of electricity supply, state-owned enterprises are expected to play a major role in implementing these

141. Tze-Luen Alan Lin, Energy Transition and Democracy in Taiwan, Feb. 9, 2019, available at: https://www.isep.or.jp/wp/wp-content/uploads/2019/01/Lin_rev.pdf.
142. Bureau of Energy, The Smart Grid Master Plan, Oct. 21, 2020, available at: https://www.moeaboe.gov.tw/ECW/english/content/Content.aspx?menu_id=9950.
143. Executive Yuan, Forward-looking Infrastructure Development Program: Green energy, Mar. 27, 2019, available at: https://english.ey.gov.tw/News3/9E5540D592A5FECD/9c3a795e-3a4b-4c28-8e1f-838960716e06.
144. Executive Yuan, Four-year Wind Power Promotion Plan, Jun. 14, 2019, available at: https://english.ey.gov.tw/News3/9E5540D592A5FECD/d603a1bf-9963-4e53-a92b-e6520a3d93ff.
145. Executive Yuan, Promotion of solar energy, Oct. 29, 2019, available at: https://english.ey.gov.tw/News3/9E5540D592A5FECD/777fcee7-90db-4b72-9927-573eecf9ea9e.

policies. For instance, the improvement of the thermal efficiency of existing combustion plants depends greatly on the investment and operation plans of Tai-Power. Similarly, the development of low-carbon electricity, such as gas-fired power plants, is also dependent on the initiatives of Tai-Power. Furthermore, in order to improve electricity security, the development of prospective power plants and major infrastructure by Tai-Power under the Long-Term Electricity Development Program (2009–2018)[146] and the Sixth and Seventh Major Transmission Lines and Substation Project is necessary. In order to reflect the three energy referendums at the end of 2018, the Long-Term Electricity Development Program become a very important document in designing the 2025 electricity mix.[147]

§3. Authorities and Regulators in the Electricity Sector

109. As noted above, it took a long time for Taiwan to establish a "formal" policy maker and competent energy authority in the energy sector. Although there were discussions around setting up a US-style "Public Utility Commission" or a UK-style "Energy Regulator" while formulating and drafting the Electricity Liberalization Bill in 2016, the MOEABOE's insistence made it impossible. In spite of establishing the authority called the "Electricity Business Regulatory Authority,"[148] the MOEA finally designated the original electricity policy authority as the one responsible for conducting the function of the electricity regulator. According to the new law, certain regulatory works were authorized to certain expert committees. For instance, the central competent authority can invite government agencies, scholars, experts, and related civil society organizations to form the Electricity Reliability Commission and the Electricity Industry Mediation Commission to carry out responsibilities of regulation.[149] The Electricity Tariff Examination Council was to be created in accordance with Article 49(4) of the Electricity Liberalization Act of 2017, to review and determine the price of electricity, rates, and charges, and other related matters. This raised a very interesting question as to why the Electricity Liberalization Act of 2017 creates such an authority with unique non-independent, and non-fixed institutional design, and lack of key regulatory function of electricity price setting. Thus, for electricity regulator, there remains simply a special division in the MOEAEC and MOEABOE to take care of electricity matters. Thus, the MOEABOE plays the role of both electricity authority and regulator. The work to control and supervise Tai-Power can also be done by the State-owned Enterprise Commission.

110. Tai-Power can also be a very important rule maker when implementing government policy. As electricity matters are often very technical, making it difficult for the competent authority to set up detailed rules, Tai-Power has become more

146. Taipower, Previous Power Plans, Feb. 17, 2020, available at: https://www.taipower.com.tw/tc/page.aspx?mid=212&cid=116&cchk=1bed6e6a-f219-45b6-827c-f405e08dee53.
147. Taipower, Plan for Power, available at: https://www.taipower.com.tw/tc/page.aspx?mid=212&cid=122&cchk=260a432c-fc0e-47e0-a90e-2bc0cc52cb61.
148. Article 3(4) of the Electricity Liberalization Act of 2017.
149. Article 3(7) of the Electricity Liberalization Act of 2017.

active in formulating game rules to realize the government policies of promoting CHP (qualified facilities) and IPPs, and to facilitate renewable electricity. For instance, under the Energy Management Act, the government started to promote CHP by the net-metering mechanism, following the enactment of the Ordinance on the Promotion of CHP of 1988.[150] Originally, the Energy Management Act authorized the competent authority to enact further rules concerning the grid connection issues of the CHP in order to avoid these issues becoming an obstacle. Yet, in reality, due to the technical and complex nature of these interconnection rules, Tai-Power first set these rules and notified the authority, and then asked the authority's permission for further revision under the Key Points of Interconnection Between Tai-Power and CHP Operators.[151] Similarly, an abstract rule concerning power purchasing between Tai-Power and qualified CHP operators is also mentioned in the Ordinance on the Promotion of CHP of 1988, but detailed rules are provided in the Ordinance on Electricity Purchase between Tai-Power and CHP Operators.[152] Furthermore, in keeping with governmental policy to encourage the development of renewable electricity during the transitional period for deliberating the Renewable Energy Bill in Parliament, Tai-Power also established a preliminary "FIT" scheme, and promulgated an "Ordinance" on the Purchase of Renewable Electricity by Tai-Power on November 4, 2003.[153]

111. In spite of the introduction of electricity liberalization in 2017, the "authority function" remains. For instance, the development right of offshore wind power can be changed by Tai-Power on the grounds of feasibility, steadiness of transmission, and layout of cables.[154] Tai-Power is also free to use its system security reasoning to curtail the renewable electricity feed-in without paying compensation under Article 9 of the FIT power purchase agreement. In spite of the continuing opposition to this clause from banks and offshore wind power developers, Tai-Power insists on retaining the clause. From the foregoing, we realize that Tai-Power has some rule-making power in practice.

112. Other authorities that may be relevant for electricity matters include the *EPA*, which is responsible for environmental concerns related to the development and operation of electricity installations; the Consumer Protection Commission of the Executive Yuan, which is responsible for the electricity contracts such as the

150. Ordinance on the Promotion of CHP of 1988.
151. Key Points of Interconnection Between Tai-Power and CHP Operators of 1989, Jan. 13, 1989, available at: https://www.taipower.com.tw/upload/169/2017110811514440559.pdf.
152. Ordinance on Electricity Purchase between Tai-Power and CHP Operators of 1988, abrogated on Oct. 2, 2002, available at: http://www.rootlaw.com.tw/LawArticle.aspx?LawID=A040100051002900-0911002.
153. Tai-Power, "Ordinance" on the Purchase of Renewable Electricity by Tai-Power on Nov. 4, 2003, amended on Jul. 5, 2011, available at: https://www.taipower.com.tw/upload/228/2018011615421434129.pdf.
154. Article 18(5) of Directions for Allocating Installed Capacity of Offshore Wind Potential Zones.

Standard Contract for Electricity Supply Service;[155] and the Atomic Energy Council, which is responsible for the regulation of nuclear power plants, etc. Finally, following the expanding role of FTC after petroleum liberalization, the role of the FTC is likely to gain importance, as well. However, it remains to be seen whether the renewable energy developers would be inclined to sell to the free market after the 2017 Electricity Liberalization Act or not. There is almost no room for the FTC to intervene for developers selling to Tai-Power under the FIT scheme.

§4. Main Players in the Electricity Market

113. As electricity liberalization was introduced only recently, this book will elaborate on the players before and after liberalization.

I. Single-Buyer Model Before Liberalization in 2017

114. Taiwan's electricity had not been liberalized before 2017. Yet, the Electricity Business Act does not exclude an operator from building its own power plant for the production of electricity for its own use. Chapter 7 of the Electricity Business Act regulates the establishment of self-generators. The establishment of self-generators is allowed only on the grounds presented below.[156] Further, registration and a license are also required.[157] Finally, the surplus electricity produced by a self-generator can also be sold to Tai-Power at the discretion of the latter.

(1) Subject limitation: Industrial mining companies, farmland irrigation facilities, government institutions or schools, and hospitals.
(2) Use limitation: The power is produced mainly for its own exclusive use.
(3) One of the following criteria must be met:
   - Where local electricity is absent or in short supply and where an increase in electricity supply within one year is considered unlikely.
   - Where no by-products can be utilized.
   - Where the steam used for production can be used for power generation.
   - Where power supply cannot be interrupted.
   - Where the cost for procurement exceeds that of self-generation to the extent that business development may be hampered.

115. In addition, in order to encourage the use of waste heat during the industrial production process, the development of CHP is facilitated under the Energy

155. Tai-Power, Standard Contract for Electricity Supply Service, available at: https://www.ey.gov.tw/Page/AABD2F12D8A6D561/7ab79e02-c4f0-42c1-a401-de037f07a600.
156. Article 97 of the Old Electricity Business Act.
157. Articles 101 and 102 of the Old Electricity Business Act.

Management Act and its CHP Ordinance.[158] Operators of qualified and high-efficiency CHP facilities receive incentives and are allowed to sell surplus electricity to Tai-Power to earn extra profit. With Taiwan's industrial policy of encouraging the development of energy intensive industries (such as petrochemical and cement) over the past few decades, the use of electricity from CHP has been increasing over the years and has become a very important electricity source for Tai-Power and Taiwan.

116. Further, in view of the difficulty Tai-Power faces in developing new power generators, public participation in the electricity industry is being encouraged, and the development of IPPs via the bidding process is a policy priority to improve energy security. The first phase of the "IPPs Program"[159] was published on January 21, 1999. Several IPPs were selected through the bidding process, and secured a twenty-five-year PPA with Tai-Power. The IPPs' role has recently outpaced that of the CHP in Taiwan's electricity system. Yet, it should be noted that the main bidder for this process is a traditional fossil fuel power plant. With the development of the fourth phase of the "IPPs Program,"[160] their role in the electricity mix should become more significant. Even after liberalization in 2017, they were obliged to sell their electricity to an Electricity Retailing Utility Enterprise or an Electricity Transmission and Distribution Enterprise, as an auxiliary service,[161] both of which are operated by Tai-Power.

117. Finally, another important emerging electricity source and player in Taiwan is the renewable electricity facility installer. With the adoption of the Renewable Energy Act in 2009, a lot of new capacity was installed. The government set an ultimate target ranging from 6.5 million MW to 10 million MW installed capacity at the time. This was increased to 27,000,000 kilowatts under Article 6 of the 2019 Renewable Energy Act.

118. In spite of the existence of many electricity generators in Taiwan, Tai-Power remains the dominant operator in the transmission, distribution, and supply sectors. The generators are not allowed to supply the end customers directly. They act as "satellite factories" of Tai-Power and are required to sell to Tai-Power, which then resells the electricity to the final consumer via its own transmission and distribution network. The power supply structure of Taiwan is illustrated in Figure 2.

158. CHP Ordinance I, available at: http://www.cogen.org.tw/doc/new%20service/4-2%A8T%B9q%A6@%A5%CD%A8t%B2%CE%B1%C0%BCs%BF%EC%AAk.htm; CHP Ordinance II, available at: http://law.moj.gov.tw/LawClass/LawContent.aspx?PCODE=J0130014.
159. IPPs Program, Jan. 21, 1999.
160. IPPs Program, the fourth phase.
161. Article 45(1) of the Electricity Liberalization Act of 2017.

Figure 2 Power Supply Structure of Taiwan

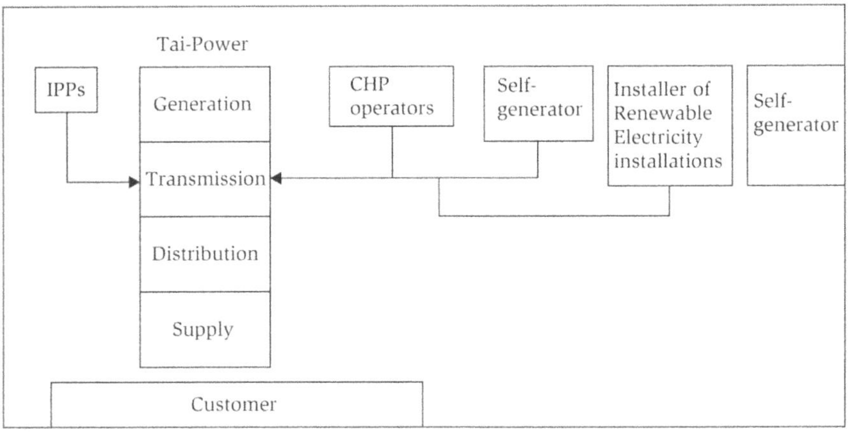

Source: compiled by this author.

119. The state-owned Tai-Power remains the main supplier of installed electricity generator capacity in the market, accounting for two-thirds of the overall installed capacity in 2009. However, Tai-Power's role in electricity generation has decreased over the past twenty years from 96.2% in 1989 to 67.3% in 2009, and has continued to decrease thus far, because of the slow progress in constructing renewables (Table 3).

Table 3 Installed Electricity Capacity in Taiwan

Unit: MW	*2004*	*2009*	*2010*	*2011*	*2012*	*2015*	*2016*	*2017*	*2018*	*2019*
Taiwan Power Company	**27,591.1**	**32,311.0**	**32,944.2**	**32,758.4**	**32,205.0**	**31,669.1**	**32,466.8**	**31,750.0**	**33,414.8**	**35,386.0**
Hydro	4,501.0	4,500.0	4,540.5	4,603.8	4,644.4	4,652.4	4,652.4	4,652.4	4,652.4	4,652.4
Conventional[1]	1,899.0	1,898.0	1,938.5	2,001.8	2,042.4	2,050.4	2,050.4	2,050.4	2,050.4	2,050.4
Pumped Storage	2,602.0	2,602.0	2,602.0	2,602.0	2,602.0	2,602.0	2,602.0	2,602.0	2,602.0	2,602.0
Thermal	17,943.7	22,487.2	23,010.0	22,717.7	22,119.7	21,560.5	22,358.2	21,641.4	23,933.0	26,425.6
Coal-Fired	8,100.0	8,800.0	8,800.0	8,800.0	8,200.0	7,600.0	8,400.0	9,200.0	10,000.0	11,600.0
Oil-Fired	3,571.1	3,610.2	3,625.6	3,324.6	3,326.6	3,325.4	3,323.1	2,570.1	2,569.1	2,569.1
LNG-Fired	6,272.6	10,077.0	10,584.4	10,593.1	10,593.1	10,635.1	10,635.1	9,871.3	11,363.9	12,256.5
Nuclear	5,144.0	5,144.0	5,144.0	5,144.0	5,144.0	5,144.0	5,144.0	5,144.0	4,508.0	3,872.0
Geothermal	-	-	-	-	-	-	-	-	-	-
Solar	-	-	0.5	6.1	10.1	18.2	18.2	18.2	18.2	123.6
Wind	2.4	179.8	249.2	286.8	286.8	294.0	294.0	294.0	303.2	312.4
IPPs	**7,230.7**	**7,939.0**	**7,971.2**	**7,980.4**	**8,028.8**	**8,119.2**	**8,162.8**	**8,196.3**	**8,505.8**	**8,671.8**
Hydro	10.7	38.9	38.9	38.9	39.0	39.0	39.0	39.0	41.2	42.2
Thermal	7,220.0	7,710.0	7,710.0	7,710.0	7,710.0	7,710.0	7,710.0	7,710.0	7,992.5	7,992.5
Solar	-	-	-	-	-	21.8	30.1	53.3	66.6	109.2
Wind	-	190.1	222.3	231.5	279.8	348.3	383.7	394.0	405.5	527.8
Cogeneration	**7,114.7**	**7,670.9**	**7,928.1**	**8,014.3**	**8,145.4**	**8,877.3**	**8,949.9**	**9,339.7**	**10,521.6**	**11,857.1**

										Unit: MW
2004	*2009*	*2010*	*2011*	*2012*	*2015*	*2016*	*2017*	*2018*	*2019*	
6,468.6	6,947.8	7,180.4	7,180.4	7,209.4	7,319.6	7,039.6	6,930.0	7,151.2	7,226.6	Thermal
-	-	-	-	-	-	-	-	0.0	0.3	Geothermal
0.6	9.5	34.1	123.8	221.2	844.2	1,196.7	1,696.2	2,653.3	3,916.7	Solar
6.1	4.4	4.4	4.4	4.4	4.4	4.4	4.4	4.5	5.0	Wind
97.6	86.8	86.8	81.3	81.3	80.0	80.0	80.0	80.6	76.6	Biomass
541.8	622.5	622.5	624.4	629.1	629.1	629.1	629.1	631.9	631.9	Waste
41,936.5	**47,921.0**	**48,843.5**	**48,753.2**	**48,379.3**	**48,665.7**	**49,579.6**	**49,286.1**	**52,442.2**	**55,914.9**	**Total**[2]
2,602.0	**2,602.0**	**2,602.0**	**2,602.0**	**2,602.0**	**2,602.0**	**2,602.0**	**2,602.0**	**2,602.0**	**2,602.0**	Hydro
5,144.0	**5,144.0**	**5,144.0**	**5,144.0**	**5,144.0**	**5,144.0**	**5,144.0**	**5,144.0**	**4,508.0**	**3,872.0**	Nuclear
31,632.3	**37,145.0**	**37,900.4**	**37,608.1**	**37,039.1**	**36,590.1**	**37,107.8**	**36,281.4**	**39,076.7**	**41,644.7**	Thermal
2,558.2	**3,030.0**	**3,197.1**	**3,399.1**	**3,594.2**	**4,329.5**	**4,725.7**	**5,258.7**	**6,255.5**	**7,796.2**	Renewable Energy[3]

Source: Installed Capacity https://www.moeaboe.gov.tw/ECW/main/content/wHandMenuFile.ashx?file_id=1464.

Notes:

1. Conventional hydro-power of Taiwan Power Company includes self-owned and commissioned hydro-power units.

2. The total installed capacity is the summation of installed capacity of Taiwan Power Company, IPPs, and cogeneration generators, which include non-utility power generators. It is different from the installed capacity of the Tai-Power grid system released by the Taiwan Power Company.

3. Renewable energy in this table refers to geothermal, solar, wind, biomass, and waste.

II. Green Electricity Model After Liberalization in 2017

120. Unlike the main scheme of liberalization that has been implemented world over, Taiwan adopted a very unique scheme to liberalize its renewable electricity sector. There is no gradual schedule to liberalize the general market from the wholesale to the retail market. The wholesale and retail renewable electricity market was liberalized simultaneously by implementing the 2017 Electricity Liberalization Act.

121. In the new market, the renewable electricity generators that were obliged to sell to Tai-Power under the FIT scheme of the Renewable Energy Act of 2009 or the earlier single-buyer model were allowed to freely choose to sell to the free market as well.[162] Renewable-Energy-Based Electricity Generating Enterprises with powerlines connecting to the power grids were free to supply electric power to users through power grids, or by installing powerlines connecting directly to their users. Therefore, the Electricity Liberalization Act had the potential to make the PPA between renewable electricity generators and electricity users possible.

122. Aside from this, new licenses were created in the retail market. Tai-Power's dominance in the retail market has been abolished but it retains its license of "Electricity Retailing Utility Enterprise" and plays the role of a public utility that purchases electricity in order to resell it to the users.[163] A new form of license, called "Renewable-Energy-Based Electricity Retailing Enterprise" (a non-public utility that purchases electricity generated from renewable energy to resell it to users) has been created. Therefore, the renewable electricity retailer would be the "real" new market player in the electricity market after electricity liberalization.

123. Would these new market players, particularly the "Renewable-Energy-Based Electricity Retailing Enterprise" depend on incentives under the FIT scheme of the Renewable Energy Act? Thus far, most renewable electricity that has been developed after liberalization has been inclined toward sale to Tai-Power under the very favorable FIT regime for twenty years. Only those renewable projects that have relatively low purchase prices can benefit from a green liberalized electricity market. For instance, Orsted decided to sell renewable electricity from its tendering offshore wind power projects that tendered a price of only 2.5 NTD/kWh below the average electricity price in Taiwan to TSMC, the biggest semiconductor manufacturer in the world, in July 2020.[164]

162. Article 45(2) and (3) of the Electricity Liberalization Act of 2017.
163. Article 2 of the Electricity Liberalization Act of 2017.
164. Taiwan News, Taiwan chip giant TSMC places world's largest wind power order with Ørsted, Jul. 8, 2020, available at: https://www.taiwannews.com.tw/en/news/3962736.

Chapter 2. Statutory Structure and Legal Regime

124. Compared with the late development of gas and oil law, the development of a legal regime for the electricity industry commenced quite early. The Electricity Business Act was adopted in 1929 and developed a comprehensive legal regime to deal with the electricity sector. Further, the Energy Management Act is also relevant to the regulation of the electricity sector, as the electricity industry is treated as both an "energy user" and an "energy supplier" under this Act.

125. Other related legislations and measures relating to the electricity sector are the CHP Ordinance, the Renewable Energy Act of 2009, the measures to introduce IPPs, the original electricity liberalization bill, and 2017 Electricity Liberalization Act, apart from the introduction of renewable energy. This author will elaborate on these respective electricity sector-related legislations and measures.

§1. Management of the Electricity Industry Before Liberalization

126. The single-buyer model before liberalization in 2017 contributed toward the stable supply of electricity that served as the backbone of Taiwan's economic growth and industrial development after World War II.

I. Electricity Business Act and Its Ordinances

127. The Electricity Business Act developed a comprehensive regulatory framework for the electricity business. In Chapter 1, the General Clause of this Act provides a legislative definition of this Act and other general regulations, such as the duty to have a Chief Technical Personnel in place,[165] the general prohibition on engaging in other business,[166] and the responsibility of the electricity utility's "Responsible Person."[167]

128. Chapter 2, on the "Rights of an Electricity Business," deals with the licensing regime pertaining to the running of an electricity business. For instance, conforming to the application procedure and submitting the essential application

165. Article 13 of the Electricity Business Act. The qualification of this personnel is further provided in the Ordinance on Hiring Chief Technical Personnel.
166. Article 14 of the Electricity Business Act: "Unless the competent authority has granted approval, electricity enterprises shall not engage in other businesses.
Where the enterprise is engaged concurrently in electricity and other businesses, said enterprise shall establish separate accounting records for the electricity business.
The central competent authority will stipulate the accounting titles and the depreciation rates for fixed assets thereof for the electricity business."
167. Article 16 of the Electricity Business Act: "In the event that the responsible person of an electricity enterprise is in violation of the Act in his or her handling of the electricity business, which has caused damage to others, the responsible person shall bear joint and several liabilities with the electricity enterprise concerned for the compensation to the party suffering said damage."

document are required.[168] The license is valid for between twenty and thirty years, and a request for extension is permissible.[169] Under certain circumstances, the license may be revoked by the central authority.[170] The license fee and other fees in this Act are also detailed in an Ordinance.[171] The franchised electricity supply area should be approved by the MOEABOE and cannot be changed without consent.[172] Finally, special rules were developed for issuing a generation license, and a comprehensive test should be done before the issuing of a formal generation license.[173] For example, a wind turbine has to run a continual test for twenty-four hours.

129. Chapter 3 on Electricity Works is the longest chapter in this Act. Around twenty-three provisions provide the very technical details concerning the construction and operation of electricity installations. Most of the provisions seek to ensure the safety and security of the electricity supply. For instance, the standardization of electricity installations[174] and supply voltage, and standards for the alternating current[175] are measures to ensure supply security. In addition, certain safety measures,

---

168. Articles 18, 19, and 20 of the Electricity Business Act.
169. Article 34 of the Electricity Business Act.
170. Article 32 of the Electricity Business Act: "Under one of the following circumstances, the central competent authority or the local competent authority, after reporting to the central competent authority and having been granted approval, may revoke the electricity business right of the relevant electricity enterprise. The local government or private sector at the place of said industry may raise the needed funds to purchase the electricity equipment of the original electricity enterprise for continued operation:

    1. Where the business operation term has expired and no extension application has been filed pursuant to Art. 24.
    2. Where the electricity supply has been suspended for more than three months due to force majeure.
    3. Where the electricity enterprise has failed to perform its electricity supply obligations within the operation region for reasons other than particular obstacles.
    4. Where the electricity enterprise is in violation of the Act and has failed to make rectification within the period specified by the central or local competent authority."

171. Ordinance on License Fee and Other Related Fee under the Electricity Business Act.
172. Article 17 of the Electricity Business Act.
173. Ordinance on Inspecting and Testing before Issuing Generation License.
174. Article 34 of the Electricity Business Act: "Electricity equipment shall be standardized whenever possible, and the methods, specifications, and the installation rules thereof shall be provided by the central competent authority."
175. Article 35 of the Electricity Business Act: "The standard for the voltage of electricity supply and the frequency of the alternating current (AC) shall be specified by the central competent authority."

    The Ordinance on Frequency of Supply Voltage is enacted under this Provision. *See also*, Art. 36 of the Electricity Business Act: "The fluctuation rate of the voltage of electricity supply in principle shall not exceed the following percentages: 1. For lighting devices, the voltage fluctuation shall be limited to plus and minus five per cent (+/-5%) relative to the specified voltage.

    2. For energy and heat supply, the voltage fluctuation shall be limited to plus and minus ten per cent (+/-10%) relative to the specified voltage. Where the lighting devices, energy, and heat supplies share the same electricity line, the standard for the lighting device voltage shall prevail."

such as safety equipment[176] and regular inspections,[177] are required to ensure a safe power supply. The construction work of certain large projects, such as pipeline works for electricity power plants and electricity towers carrying a voltage of 11,000 or more, should be supervised by a professional technician.[178] In addition, "high-voltage electrical equipment" should be tested by qualified institutes, whose qualification process is detailed in one Ordinance.[179] Once a safety-related accident occurs, there is a duty to report it.[180] Finally, several provisions (Articles 50–56) deal with the "right of way" granted for the prerogative granted electricity installations. Generally, these provisions are quite preferential to electricity businesses. For example, electricity businesses are generally allowed the use of public land during construction works.[181] A Special Ordinance concerning the acquisition of land for public infrastructure purposes[182] and the settlement of disputes between landowners and electricity businesses[183] is further provided.

130. Chapter 4 provides operational rules for the electricity business. First, a universal service obligation is stipulated.[184] The core clauses in this chapter relate to the electricity rate scheme. The rate scheme for "normal" electricity businesses is

176. Article 41 of the Electricity Business Act: "Electricity enterprises shall install security equipment in places where it is necessary."
177. Article 42 of the Electricity Business Act: "Electricity enterprises shall inspect the machines and power lines and record the inspection results at least once a year."
178. Article 34-1(2) of the Electricity Business Act and Ordinance on Supervising Construction Work and Design by Professional Technician.
179. Ordinance on Qualification of Professional Institutes concerning Conducting Testing of "High-Voltage Electrical Equipment."
180. Article 47 of the Electricity Business Act: "In the event of an electric shock or an accident with electricity equipment that has resulted in casualties, the relevant electricity enterprise shall report to the local competent authority at the place of incident."
181. Article 50 of the Electricity Business Act: "Where necessary for construction, electricity enterprises may use rivers, ditches, bridges, embankments, roads, public woodlands, and other public lands, provided that the original function of said property is not affected and that a prior notice to the competent authority of said property has been made."
182. Ordinance on Acquiring Land for Private-Participation Public Infrastructure.
183. Ordinance on Settlement Principles over Land Dispute between Electricity Business and Land Owners.
184. Article 57 of the Electricity Business Act: "Electricity enterprises shall not reject any electricity supply request within the operation region without proper justification."

different from that of the state-owned enterprise: the former is approved by the central authority,[185] whereas the latter relies on a formula over which Parliament frequently has a say.[186] The general rule for the revenue of electricity business is cost-plus-reasonable-profit.[187] With regard to the tariff charged for different users, a "preferential" (discount) rate below the regular rate should be provided when supplying electricity to public utility businesses such as domestic water supply companies, electric cars and electric rail systems,[188] and local government street lighting units.[189] However, under certain circumstances, a rate higher than the regular rate may be allowed for supplying electricity to rural users,[190] in spite of the obligation of universal service. Finally Article 73[191] and its Ordinance deal with penalties for those found stealing electricity.[192]

131. Chapter 5 makes provision for supervision and monitoring by the authority. In fact, many monitoring issues were already dealt with in the previous chapters, such as works regulations, licenses, and the tariff scheme, etc. Hence, this chapter deals only with some remaining details and the supervisory power of the authority. For instance, with regard to the reporting duty, electricity businesses are

185. Article 59(1) of the Electricity Business Act: "Electricity enterprises shall submit newly formulated and revised operation regulations, electricity prices, and the rates of various charges to the local competent authority or the in-charge authority of the business that said industry is engaged in for comments and suggestions before forwarding the documents to the central competent authority for approval. The approved documents shall be posted for the local public."

186. Article 59(2) of the Electricity Business Act: "The electricity rate charging standards of government-owned electricity enterprises shall comply with the provisions set forth under Art. 20 of the Regulation on the Management of Government-Owned Business Enterprises [whose tariff formula is reviewed by the Parliament]."

187. Article 60 of the Electricity Business Act: "Electricity prices shall be set at a level commensurate with the necessary cost plus a reasonable profit. Said reasonable profit shall be calculated on the basis of the present value of the replacement cost for the fixed assets in effective use and the amount of working capital, and shall take into account the local practices of margin setting."

188. Article 65 of the Electricity Business Act.

189. Article 66 of the Electricity Business Act.

190. Articles 67 and 68 of the Electricity Business Act:

> Art. 67: "For the small number of remote users for whom electricity supply requires placement of separate power lines, the relevant electricity enterprise may charge a premium for line placement and maintenance, of which the charging standard and fee collection method shall be formulated by the electricity enterprise and submitted to the central competent authority for approval."
>
> Art. 68: "For electricity supply to remote users, the relevant electricity enterprise may raise the electricity rate and the base kilowatt/hour consumption, and shall specify the electricity charging standard in the operation regulations."

191. Article 73 of the Electricity Business Act: "In regard to users or non-users stealing electricity, the relevant electricity enterprise may, on the basis of the type of electricity use equipment installed, calculate the amount of watts or horsepower consumed according to the set time and rate of electricity of said industry and claim a reimbursement amount of not less than three months but not more than one year of the electricity fees owed. The governing rules on electricity theft shall be provided by the central competent authority."

192. MOJ, Ordinance on Dealing with Stealing Electricity, Amended on Aug. 2, 2017, available at: https://law.moj.gov.tw/LawClass/LawAll.aspx?pcode=J0030020.

required to produce and submit a monthly summary report of business operations and an annual business report within three months of the end of each business operation year to the central and the local competent authority, respectively, for record-keeping.[193] The competent authority enjoys administrative inspection power to verify compliance with the regulations in this Act.[194] Finally, the competent authority also has the power to approve capital increase or decrease, or bond issuance or external (foreign) debt acceptance.[195]

132. Finally, in Chapters 6 and 7, special regulations are developed for small electricity business and self-generators. Chapter 8 provides administrative and criminal penalties for non-compliance with the legal obligations in this Act. At the end, there are also a group of Ordinances relating to the details of registration, installation management, and the qualifications of Professional and Technical Personnel. They are illustrated in Table 4.

Table 4 Ordinance Concerning Registration, Installation Management, and the Qualification of Professional and Technical Personnel

Direction	*Related Ordinance*
Registration and licensing rules	– Ordinance on Registration and License of Electricity Business– Ordinance on Registration of Self-Generators
Technical installation rules	– Ordinance on The Governing Rules for User Premise Power Line Placement – Ordinance on The Governing Rules for Outdoor Power Line Placement – Placement Ordinance on Transformer Station – Placement Ordinance on Control Installation of Electricity Business – The Ordinance on the Interleaved Parallel between Transmission Line of Electricity Business and Telecommunication Line
Qualification of professional and technical personnel	Ordinance on Electricity Contractor Ordinance on Professional Electricity Technical Personnel and Inspection and Maintenance Personnel for Electricity Installations

Source: Compiled by the author.

193. Article 80 of the Electricity Business Act.
194. Article 82 of the Electricity Business Act: "The central or local competent authority may carry out inspection of the equipment of electricity enterprises at any time. In the event of nonconformity, a time period may be specified for repair or replacement; where a danger is likely to occur due to said nonconformity, a suspension of operation or use of equipment may be imposed."
195. Article 85 of the Electricity Business Act.

II. Energy Management Act

133. The focus of the Energy Management Act is on the "thermal power" generators, instead of on transmission, distribution, and retailing. In this regard, the generation branch of Tai-Power and IPPs may be subject to the control of the Energy Management Act. A thermal power generator is subject to both the provisions of Chapter 2 for the control of "energy supplying businesses" and those of Chapter 3 for "energy users" under the Energy Management Act.

134. As energy suppliers, electricity supply businesses with generation installation capacity over 500 MW[196] are required to follow the two requirements under Article 7 of the Energy Management Act, namely, the submission of monthly operations data to the energy authority and the establishment of energy storage facilities. If the supplier is a coal-fired power plant, then it has to have stored a supply of at least thirty days of the average daily coal fuel, calculated on the basis of the previous year's usage. Only large (more than 500 MW) coal-fired power plants run by Tai-Power and IPPs or gas-fired plants run by Tai-Power are subject to this regulation.

135. Also, electricity generators may be considered big energy users under the Energy Management Act, if they are "coal users whose annual use exceeds 6,000 tons," "fuel oil users whose annual use exceeds 6,000 kiloliters," or "gas users whose annual use exceeds 10,000,000 m3."[197] Once those conditions are met, they are required to comply with the following requirements, which are the submission of energy data annually, the establishment of an energy auditing scheme, energy conservation goals and an implementation plan, the retaining of energy management personnel, and the submission of requests for the approval of new construction or for expansion of energy-using infrastructure.[198] This requirement may be applied not only to electricity generators of "thermal power plants," but also to CHP operators. The scope of the energy user regulations is greater than that of the energy supply business regulations. A special format to comply with these requirements is also provided in the Ordinance.[199,200]

---

196. Ordinance on Energy User Using Large Amount of Energy., 1993-10-22, Amended on 2018-03-09, available at: https://www.moeaboe.gov.tw/ECW/populace/Law/Content.aspx?menu_id=615.
197. Ordinance on Annual Energy Data Submission, 2010-01-08, Amended on 2019-12-24, available at: https://www.moeaboe.gov.tw/ECW/populace/Law/Content.aspx?menu_id=618.
198. Articles 9, 11, 12, 16 of the Energy Management Act.
199. Ordinance on Annual Energy Data Submission, 2010-01-08, Amended on 2019-12-24, available at: http://www.moeaboe.gov.tw/opengovinfo/Laws/all/LAllMain.aspx?PageId=l_all_06; https://www.moeaboe.gov.tw/ECW/populace/Law/Content.aspx?menu_id=618
200. Annex Table 2 for CHP Plants and Thermal Power Plants, available at: https://www.moeaboe.gov.tw/ECW/main/Law/wHandEditorFile.ashx?file_id=5713.

§2. PROMOTION OF CHP DEVELOPMENT SINCE THE LATE 1980S

136. The promotion of CHP development is a governmental policy priority in response to the energy crisis. Taiwan adopted a carrot-and-stick approach in promoting CHP installations. From the stick side, there is a technology mandate for those that produce steam above a certain threshold to establish CHP installations under the Energy Management Act.[201] Yet, there is also a carrot incentive provided in that CHP operators can profit from the selling of surplus electricity back to Tai-Power. As noted above, self-generators may be allowed to sell the surplus electricity to Tai-Power but it is not a guaranteed right. However, under this Act, CHP installers have an absolute right to sell surplus electricity to Tai-Power, as long as the CHP installations meet certain thermal efficiency requirements.[202]

137. The Ordinance on CHP Promotion was further promulgated on July 15, 1988.[203] Then it was replaced by a new CHP Ordinance in 2002.[204] This CHP ordinance has been subject to several revisions that have taken place nearly once or twice each year, so far. The twenty-fifth version was published on December 24, 2019.[205]

138. This Ordinance provided a general framework for promoting CHP. First, the most important issue is the substantive qualification requirement and the procedural qualification rules. Chapter 2 defines the former as being that the effective heat rate is not less than 20% and the percentage of the total thermal efficiency not less than 52%.[206] Yet, there is no threshold for waste incinerators, which is also encouraged under this CHP scheme. On the other hand, Chapter 3 regulates the application, licensing, and qualification procedure of a qualified CHP. A detailed Ordinance on inspection to determine compliance is also provided.[207]

139. On becoming a qualified CHP, the operator can enjoy the benefit of selling surplus electricity to Tai-Power. Two Chapters (Chapters 4 and 5) outline the function of this net-metering scheme. The buy-back price is determined by two factors: whether it is possible to provide guaranteed capacity at peak hours[208] and whether the CHP operator is old, new, or large.[209] New installations that can provide guaranteed capacity during peak hours at summertime receive the highest rate. The MOEABOE regularly publishes the latest rates.[210] Moreover, in order to run this

201. Article 10(1) of the Energy Management Act.
202. Article 10(2) of the Energy Management Act.
203. CHP Ordinance I.
204. CHP Ordinance II.
205. MOJ, CHP Ordinance II, 2002-09-04, Amended on 2019-12-24, available at: https://law.moj.gov.tw/LawClass/LawHistory.aspx?pcode=J0130014.
206. Article 5 of the CHP Ordinance II.
207. Ordinance on Inspection of Qualified CHP.
208. Article 13 of the CHP Ordinance II.
209. Article 14 of the CHP Ordinance II.
210. Rate Scheme for CHP, available at: http://www.cogen.org.tw/cogeninfo/Attfile/%E8%83%BD%E6%BA%90%E5%B1%8011.4.19%E5%85%AC%E5%91%8A.docx.

net-metering scheme, Tai-Power also enacted company rules in regard to buying CHP electricity[211] and created a standard contract format.[212]

140. Apart from the regulations on net-metering, this net-metering scheme also has necessary supplementary provisions The development of interconnection rules and grid access rules are indispensable for selling electricity back to Tai-Power. Chapter 7 of this CHP Ordinance provides the interconnection duty of Tai-Power. Tai-Power also enacted its own Technical Ordinance to implement the interconnection duty.[213] Besides, CHP operators may face the need for regular inspection of the installation or to maintain their CHP installations. In case Tai-Power overcharges, the rules concerning the tariff for this backup power are also provided in Chapter 6 of the CHP Ordinance. Tai-Power also regularly notifies the MOEA about its rate for backup power from CHP generators.[214]

141. In terms of emission reduction, a CHP has certain environmental advantages in reducing the pollution from waste heat and facilitating the effective use of resources. However, as most of the fuels used by CHP installations in Taiwan come from fossil fuel—mainly coal, oil, and municipal waste—air pollution from the combustion process has attracted clean air regulations. First, the CHP operators are required to pay a Special Levy for Air Pollution Prevention under the Ordinance on Special Levy for Air Pollution Prevention.[215] Second, emission standards are also provided for electricity installations and[216] non-mobile fixed air pollution sources.[217]

142. Under this scheme, qualified CHP operators are found throughout all industrial sectors. The petrochemical industry accounts for almost half of the installed CHP capacity, followed by plastic, chemical fiber, government, refinery, steel, and paper.

143. Similar to Europe's and other countries' considering CHP as an "emission mitigation technology," Taiwan's 2010 Master Plan on Energy Conservation and Emission Reduction and the 2011 Energy Development Framework also highlight CHP. The CHP development target under the latter is scheduled to be 100,000,000 MW in 2020. However, because of the emphasis on renewable electricity after the government's energy transition initiative in 2016, the CHP's role is mentioned only

---

211. Ordinance of Tai-Power on Buying of Electricity from Qualified CHP Operators.
212. The Standard Contract Form of Buying Electricity from Qualified CHP Operators.
213. Technical Ordinance on Interconnection between Tai-Power and CHP Operators.
214. Tai-Power's Rate for Backup Power to CHP Operators.
215. Ordinance on Special Levy of Air Pollution Prevention, 1995-03-23, Amended on 2010-09-06, available at: https://oaout.epa.gov.tw/law/LawContent.aspx?id=FL015371.
216. MOJ, Ordinance on Emission Standard of Air Pollutants for Electricity Installations, Amended on 2014-12-01, available at: https://law.moj.gov.tw/LawClass/LawAll.aspx?pcode=O0020026.
217. MOJ, Ordinance on Emission Standard for Non-mobile Fixed Source of Air Pollutants, 2000-04-10, Amended on 2013-04-25, available at: https://oaout.epa.gov.tw/law/LawContent.aspx?id=FL0 15350.

among the qualitative directions in the draft version of Taiwan's Energy Transition White Paper (which supports the development of CHP).[218] No quantitative target has been set in recent times.

144. Yet, a closer look reveals that 90% of qualified CHP so far in Taiwan are coal-fired or oil-fired. It is certain that coal-fired CHP would be better than coal-fired power plants. Yet, the development of gas-fired CHP would bring more environmental benefits than do oil and coal-fired CHP. In this regard, this author urges the government to re-think this "quantitative-only" approach and consider developing a more high quality gas-fired or biomass CHP.

§3. The Evolution of Electricity Regulatory Reform and Liberalization

I. From the 1990s to the 2010s

145. In the 1990s, Taiwan, affected by the trend of electricity liberalization and restructuring under the Public Utility Regulatory Policies Act (PURPA) of 1978 in the US, the Electricity Act of 1989 in the UK, and other Organisation for Economic Co-operation and Development (OECD) countries, began to promote the idea of electricity liberalization and privatization. The policy of electricity regulatory reform has been mentioned in governmental energy policy since then. For example, in the 1996 Taiwan Energy Policy and Measures, both electricity liberalization and privatization are mentioned. Furthermore, unlike the unclear restructuring of the gas and petroleum industry, a detailed electricity restructuring plan was mentioned in the 1998 Energy White Paper and 2005 Energy White Paper.[219]

146. In fact, the electricity liberalization bill was proposed to Parliament in the mid-1990s for review. The list below gives the essential elements of this bill in 2007.[220] Subsequently, generators were expected to be able to sell power to consumers directly, which means the market structure would no longer be monopolistic. In addition, a competitive mechanism would be established to improve the performance of utilities. The bill proposes as follows:[221]

– Promoting the liberalization of the power industry.

---

218. Bureau of Energy, Energy White Paper, Dec. 29, 2017, available at: https://energywhitepaper.tw/upload/201712/151418632798726.pdf.

219. *See* MOEA, Energy Policy White Paper, December 2005.

220. iReadeBooks, Liberalization of Power Market in Taiwan, 2008, available at: https://www.airitibooks.com/Detail/Detail?PublicationID=P20100203097&DetailSourceType=0 MOEA-BOE, Liberalization of Power Market in Taiwan, 2007, available at: http://www.moeaboe.gov.tw/About/webpage/book_en4/page2.htm (visited on Oct. 10, 2020).

221. iReadeBooks, Liberalization of Power Market in Taiwan, 2008, available at: https://www.airitibooks.com/Detail/Detail?PublicationID=P20100203097&DetailSourceType=0 MOEABOE, Liberalization of Power Market in Taiwan, 2007, available at: http://www.moeaboe.gov.tw/About/webpage/book_en4/page2.htm (visited on Oct. 10, 2020).

- Encouraging the development of renewable energy by setting up a renewable obligation scheme.
- Removing the obstacles to install power infrastructure.
- Strengthening the management of the power industry.
- Maintaining the stability and safety of the power supply.
- Integrating the management of industry and industry-related associations.
- Relaxing the limitations on Tai-Power's operation.

Step-by-Step Approach of Electricity Liberalization

147. In order not to affect the existing electricity industry too dramatically and thus jeopardize electricity supply security, this bill adopts a step-by-step approach to introducing liberalization.[222] At the preparation phase (six months after the amendment passes), the MOEABOE would enact and review the related regulations to implement the Act. Then, power companies shall renew their licenses and revise the operation regulations in accordance with the Act. Afterward, at the second phase, the liberalization begins. Within six months to two years after the passing of the amendment, the private sector's application to operate a vertically integrated utility, a generator, transmission utility, and a distribution utility would be allowed. Other measures include the following:

- Involving users in the power market by allowing power purchase options to users whose electricity voltage is not less than 69 kV.
- Entrusting Tai-Power with the responsibility for power dispatch and for maintenance of the power system's safety.
- Forming an "Electricity Tariff and Rate Review Committee" to review the power tariff and rate of public utilities.
- Establishing an "End Operation for Nuclear Power Plant Fund" to deal with the retirement of nuclear power plants.
- Establishing an "Electricity Fund" for promoting the usage of renewable energy and implementing the R&D of energy.

148. In the third phase, middle-term measures would be adopted for a period of two years to five years after the amendment passes. They are:

- Putting an Independent System Operator (ISO) in charge of dispatching business prior to the privatization of Tai-Power.
- Involving users in the power market by allowing power purchase options to users whose electricity voltage is not less than 11.4 kV.
- Establishing an "Electricity Research and Testing Laboratory" for researching power technology regulations and improving the reliability of the power system.
- Conducting the specified technical examination for power engineering technicians to secure the rights of present employees.

222. MOEABOE, Energy White Paper, available at: http://web2.moeaboe.gov.tw/ECW/Policy/EnergyWhitePaper/94/main/main.html.

149. Finally, long-term measures would be phased within five years after the amendment passes. The government would assist the utilities and enterprises to establish a voluntary power pool and permit a bilateral contract model. Besides, the government would review the implementing of user's power purchase options to enable more users to get involved in the market.

150. The important issues under the Electricity Business Bill of 2008 will be elaborated as follows.

Unbundling Measures

151. In the first phase of liberalization, account unbundling is to be adopted. In this regard, the vertical integrated electricity companies are required to establish separate accounts for their generation, transmission, distribution, and retail businesses. Cross-subsidizing is generally prohibited.[223] However, the requirement for vertically integrated electricity companies to split their original bundled service into different and unbundled services is not expressly mentioned in this bill. Hence, whether there is a duty of service unbundling is uncertain. However, it is expected that with the introduction of consumers' right to choose their own electricity supply, the service unbundling scheme would accompany it. Furthermore, functional unbundling requirements, such as the requirement to have separate brand images for network and non-network sectors, separate office locations for network and non-network businesses, separate staffs for network and non-network businesses, the establishment of codes of conduct, etc., are also missing in this bill. Therefore, unlike the combination of account unbundling, service unbundling, and functional unbundling in the first phase of electricity liberalization in Europe and the US, the unbundling regime in this bill is quite unsound and defective.

152. The bill itself seems to identify and realize the weakness of this unbundling measure. A much more rigid unbundling regime, i.e., the ISO, would be introduced in the second phase of liberalization. According to Article 8 of the Electricity Business Bill, an ISO would be set up to conduct the system operation function of Tai-Power subsequent to the passing of this bill.[224] The ISO will be responsible for dispatching power in compliance with the grid code regulated by the central competent authority, and ISO's implementation and arbitration would be supervised by the central competent authority.[225] Article 9 to Article 15 of this bill provides further regulations for the function, organization, duty of financial guarantee, and duty of report, etc. In this regard, the safe, fair, and transparent dispatch and operation of "common carrier" networks would be ensured under this ISO regime.[226] The ISO regime would also facilitate the implementation of third party access (TPA) regimes.

TPA Regime

---

223. Article 6 of the Electricity Business Bill in 2007.
224. Article 8 of the Electricity Business Bill in 2007.
225. Article 9 of the Electricity Business Bill in 2007.
226. Article 7 of the Electricity Business Bill in 2007.

153. The removal of barriers to new entrants is key to encouraging market competition. To help new entrants compete with existing vertically integrated companies and enter the market, their access to existing transmission and distribution networks should be regulated under the liberalization bill. In this bill, the owner of the electricity network of a vertically integrated company,[227] the transmission line of the transmission company,[228] and the distribution network of the distribution company[229] should follow the principles of *fairness, transparency, and non-discrimination*, by opening the network for use by all other electricity businesses. Refusal of access should be approved by the central competent authority and should be based on justifiable and legitimate reasons. The rate for open access will be set by the competent authority.[230] In this regard, a regulated third party access (RTPA) regime should be set up under this bill.

Market Opening Schedule

154. The ultimate purpose of the above two measures is to give consumers the option to purchase electricity from different utilities or generators. Yet, in order to open the market gradually, and avoid jeopardizing electricity supply security, a step-by-step approach would be adopted. In the Energy Policy White Paper of 2005, the consumers' option would be gradually introduced to super-high-voltage (≥69 kV) customers within two years of the bill's passage, high-voltage (≥11.41 kV) customers after two to five years, and all other customers after five years.[231] In this regard, the power generators can wholesale the electricity they generate to integrated utilities, distribution utilities, and other power generators, which can also sell electricity directly to eligible customers through the grid or through their own power lines.

155. However, the Electricity Business Bill does not adopt this schedule for opening the market. To give the competent authority more flexibility in determining the market opening schedule, the eligibility of the customers will be determined by the authority gradually in accordance with the development of related interface technology.[232]

Evaluation

156. In spite of the detailed design and the bill on electricity regulatory reform as noted above, the proposal for electricity liberalization in Taiwan over the last two decades has still faced much opposition, particularly from the labor union that is concerned about job losses at Tai-Power. The first reason for the delay may be the

---

227. Article 52(1) of the Electricity Business Bill in 2007.
228. Article 53(2) of the Electricity Business Bill in 2007.
229. Article 54(5) of the Electricity Business Bill in 2007.
230. Article 59 (1), (2) of the Electricity Business Bill.
231. iReadeBooks, Liberalization of Power Market in Taiwan, 2008, available at: https://www.airitibooks.com/Detail/Detail?PublicationID=P20100203097&DetailSourceType=0; MOEA-BOE, Liberalization of Power Market in Taiwan, 2007, available at: http://www.moeaboe.gov.tw/About/webpage/book_en4/index.htm (visited on Oct. 10, 2020).
232. Article 55(3) of the Electricity Business Bill.

institutional design, particularly the existence of a state-owned company. The second reason may be related to the international situation and isolated geographical features of Taiwan. Several electricity outages resulting from the defective liberalization drives in California and in Victoria State (Australia) have been used to discourage the authority's efforts at liberalization. Furthermore, there is usually a policy discussion in Taiwan over whether a liberalization regime is suitable for an isolated island electricity system like Taiwan's. For this reason, since the early 2000s, the government has implicitly postponed the schedule of liberalization (and even stopped the plan for liberalization), in spite of the attractive picture painted in the 2005 Energy Policy White Paper and 2006 Electricity Business Bill.

157. Whether the above two reasons are justifiable and reasonable requires further deliberation. First, the electricity crisis in California may have more to do with the defective design of its liberalization regime, which defect was not found in other countries. Second, if being an isolated island would definitely trigger concerns over electricity security, why has Taiwan, an oil importing country without domestic sources, been able to introduce oil liberalization and to function without oil supply security concerns so far? It appears, therefore, that the main reason behind the failure of efforts at electricity liberalization may be political. A lack of a powerful lobby group, like the oil sector's Formosa Petrochemical Corporation (FPCC), in the electricity sector may be the main reason.

158. Without electricity liberalization, Taiwan will find it more challenging to achieve "carbon mitigation" and the "development of renewable electricity." In terms of climate change and energy policy, energy liberalization and the internal energy market have long been considered important in Europe. Yet, these do not play a role in Taiwan most of the time. Moreover, the European experience of promoting renewable electricity in the 1990s has demonstrated that the existence of a giant state-owned or vertically integrated enterprise under a non-liberalization regime would impede and discourage the development of renewable electricity. These enterprises tended to treat distributed renewable electricity generation as a threat and a headache to their system and they threw up many administrative barriers or grid access barriers to impede its development.

II. Partial Liberalization: IPP Policy and Implementation and Renewable Energy Development

159. As noted above, Taiwan's original intention was to introduce certain IPPs and to pave the way for full liberalization. However, as the liberalization process stalled, the government changed its focus on liberalization to that of promoting the introduction of IPPs to contribute to the electricity generation system.

160. Under two Ordinances,[233] the MOEA has promoted the opening of the market to IPPs in four stages: the first in January 1995, the second in August 1995, the third in January 1999, and the fourth in June 2006.[234] Originally, foreign investment in the electricity business was restricted in Taiwan. However, since January 2002, under this new scheme, foreign investors have been permitted to own up to 100% of an IPP.[235]

161. As with the CHP regime, Tai-Power developed further detailed rules. For example, the dispatch rules and the legal relationship between Tai-Power and IPPs are dealt with under the twenty-five-year Standard Contract.[236] The interconnection between an IPP and Tai-Power is expected to follow the Ordinance on Interconnection with Generators.[237] The important power purchase rate is determined by the competitive bidding process among different generators.

162. As a result, five IPPs have been completed and started commercial operation during the first and second stages, accounting for the total installed capacity of 5,270 MW. For the third stage, three private power plants were completed and have started commercial operation. In June 2006, the MOEA announced the "Fourth Phase of the Bidding Program for Independent Power Producers" as a guideline for the addition of 1,980 MW of IPP-generated power between 2011 and 2013.[238]

163. Finally, renewable energy also played an important role in contributing to Taiwan's electricity system before liberalization in 2017. Since 2003, private onshore wind power developers, particularly Infravest, had benefited from the power purchase scheme that was introduced by Tai-Power,[239] not to mention the large development of PV and wind power after the implementation of the Renewable Energy Act of 2009.

III. The Introduction of Liberalization since 2017

164. Once the anti-nuclear party came into power, a series of reforms were promoted in the energy sector. In spite of the significant development of renewables after 2009, the new government blamed the slow development on the absence of liberalization. Therefore, the promotion of electricity liberalization became their first priority in their policy agenda to promote renewable energy development.

---

233. The Current Bidding Program for Independent Power Producers; The Fourth Phase of Bidding Program for Independent Power Producers.
234. iReadeBooks, Liberalization of Power Market in Taiwan, 2008, available at: https://www.airitibooks.com/Detail/Detail?PublicationID=P20100203097&DetailSourceType=0.
235. Yun-Hsun Huang, Jung-Hua Wu, Energy Policy on Taiwan: Historical Developments, Current Status and Potential Improvements, Energies, 2009, vol. 2, 623-645, available at: www.mdpi.com/1996-1073/2/3/623/pdf.
236. Standard Contract of Tai-Power and IPPs.
237. Tai-Power, Technical Ordinance on Interconnection with Generator's power plants of 1990.
238. MOEABOE, Energy Situation, available at: http://web2.moeaboe.gov.tw/ecw/About/energy%20situation/main/en_11.html.
239. Tai-Power, "Ordinance" on the Purchase of Renewable Electricity by Tai-Power on Nov. 4, 2003.

165. Taiwan's electricity market is dominated by the state-owned electricity company Tai-Power. Even if a few players, such as IPPs, cogeneration generators, and renewable electricity producers exist in the wholesale market, they are obliged to sell at a fixed price to Tai-Power. Thus, there is no competition in the market.

166. The Electricity Act of 2017 intends to set three milestones in the history of global liberalization in terms of its relationship with RE:[240]

(1) All customers will be eligible to choose only renewable electricity generators and retailers (instead of only large customers being eligible for traditional electricity generators).
(2) All renewable electricity generators will be allowed direct access or wheeling to end customers, while traditional electricity generators will continue to be subject to the single-buyer scheme, that is, selling to a vertically integrated company, instead of traditional electricity generators benefiting from direct access or wheeling (TPA).
(3) There will be freedom to set up renewable electricity retail companies (instead of energy retailers running both traditional and renewable electricity businesses).

167. The three privileges provided to RE in the first phase of liberalization may be unique in the world. We provide an overview of these three privileges below.

Green Privilege I: Direct Selling/TPA for Renewable Electricity Generation Businesses

168. Instead of selling all RE to Tai-Power under the existing FIT scheme after the Renewable Energy Act of 2009 came into force, the RE generation business gained the freedom to sell directly to end customers either through its own (direct access) or Tai-Power's grid (TPA, wheeling), within 1–2.5 years of the EA coming into effect. In addition to this freedom, additional incentives were given to encourage the adoption of the direct selling scheme, including:[241]

(1) Priority dispatch: Under the precondition of electricity system security, the transmission and distribution company is required to prior-dispatch RE.[242] This was already in practice under the current FIT scheme of the Renewable Energy Act of 2009.

---

240. Anton Ming-Zhi Gao, Chien-Te Fan, Chao-NingLiao, Application of German energy transition in Taiwan: A critical review of unique electricity liberalisation as a core strategy to achieve renewable energy growth, Energy Policy, vol. 120 (2018) 650.
241. Anton Ming-Zhi Gao, Chien-Te Fan, Chao-NingLiao, Application of German energy transition in Taiwan: A critical review of unique electricity liberalisation as a core strategy to achieve renewable energy growth, Energy Policy, vol. 120 (2018) 650.
242. Article 8 of Electricity Act of 2017: "The Electricity Transmission and Distribution Enterprise is responsible for managing the electric power dispatching by giving priority to the grid connections that allow access to the renewable energy on the condition that the power systems remain safe and stable."

(2) Favorable reduction rate for the use of the transmission and distribution grid's dispatch service and ancillary service during the direct access process:[243] The setting of such fees for RE generation while providing direct selling services should take "GHG emission factors" of the RE into account. Thus, low emission RE, such as onshore and offshore wind power and PV, may be subject to a preferential rate.

(3) Exemption of electricity reserve capacity obligations for small-scale RE generation: To maintain a stable and secure supply of electricity, all electricity suppliers and RE generators (direct selling) should set aside a certain amount of electricity reserve capacity. However, RE generation businesses below a certain installation capacity may be exempted from this obligation. Such a duty can be fulfilled by contracts with other generation resources, IPPs, and/or demand response aggregators.[244]

169. Apart from such a preference for RE, there is also an additional burden for all generation businesses, including RE generation. Traditional and RE generation businesses, especially wind power and a certain scale of PVs, are required to contribute to a community support fund in accordance with the electricity they generate or transmit/distribute.[245]

Privilege II: Opening Renewable Retail Businesses

170. Apart from direct selling to end customers through RE generators, the Electricity Act (EA) 2017 allows sale through RE retail businesses.[246] The reason behind this may be related to the lack of power exchange in the initial stages. Thus, RE

243. Article 9 of Electricity Act of 2017: "To ensure the supply safe and stable of the power system, the Electricity Transmission and Distribution Enterprise shall provide necessary ancillary services according to the needs of the electric power dispatching and the application of the Electricity Generation Enterprise and Self-Use Power Generation Equipment."

Art. 10 of the Electricity Act of 2017: "A Renewable-Energy-Based Electricity Generating Enterprise or Retailing Enterprise that requires the power grids to distribute the power generated or purchased for sale may request the service of the Electricity Transmission and Distribution Enterprise for electric power dispatching and pay the electricity dispatching service fee based on the total amount of electricity dispatched."

244. Anton Ming-Zhi Gao, Chien-Te Fan, Chao-NingLiao, Application of German energy transition in Taiwan: A critical review of unique electricity liberalisation as a core strategy to achieve renewable energy growth, Energy Policy, vol. 120 (2018) 650.

245. Article 65 of the Electricity Act of 2017: "To facilitate the development and operation of the electric power, to develop the areas in the proximity of the Electricity Generation, Transformation and Distribution Facilities, and to bring welfare to the residents thereof, the Electricity Generating Enterprise and Electricity Transmission and distribution Enterprise shall allocate assistance fund to facilitate the development of electric power to assist the competent authority at the level of the municipal government or county (city) government in promoting development of electricity and harmony with the communities. The given assistance fund is on the basis of a certain percentage of the kilowatts of electricity generated or transmitted."

246. Article 47 of Electricity Act of 2017.

suppliers and brokers would be very useful in reducing the transaction cost, which is a barrier for direct selling by RE generators. This makes the idea of a green electricity company possible.[247]

Privilege III: Customer Eligibility for All for Renewable Electricity

171. Unlike the approach in most countries wherein only large industrial customers are eligible to choose electricity generation sources (often cheap/gray electricity) freely in the early phase of liberalization, Taiwan's EA adopted the novel idea of opening up eligibility to all customers for RE alone.[248]

Other Supplementary Measures to Facilitate Direct Selling of RE

172. To facilitate the entrance of RE retailers and to encourage the direct selling of RE generation, some supplementary measures are provided below:[249]

(1) Unbundling: In addition to account unbundling, the existing vertically integrated company, Tai-Power, is obliged to adopt either ownership or legal unbundling.[250] Such a scheme can reduce its dominance and help supplement the implementation of TPA scheme.
(2) Procedural rules for setting related tariffs: RE-friendly rates, such as dispatch, grid access/usage, and ancillary service rates, play a key role in facilitating renewable electricity in the market. The EA provides very detailed and transparent procedural rules for rate-setting.[251]

Summary

173. The liberalization of the green electricity market alone is the most unique approach to liberalization world over. From a general perspective, it would be a lot easier to liberalize cheaper gray electricity, which is also the norm in all countries that have pursued liberalization thus far. For expensive renewables, these countries set up a special regulated market such as the FIT scheme, to provide a stable environment for the development of renewables. Thus far, only cheap renewables are likely to be sold in the free market. However, to sell freely in the market in large volumes, sellers have to bear the obligation of reserve margins.[252] Owing to the tight

247. Anton Ming-Zhi Gao, Chien-Te Fan, Chao-NingLiao, Application of German energy transition in Taiwan: A critical review of unique electricity liberalisation as a core strategy to achieve renewable energy growth, Energy Policy, vol. 120 (2018) 650.
248. Articles 45 and 47 of Electricity Act of 2017.
249. Anton Ming-Zhi Gao, Chien-Te Fan, Chao-NingLiao, Application of German energy transition in Taiwan: A critical review of unique electricity liberalisation as a core strategy to achieve renewable energy growth, Energy Policy, vol. 120 (2018).
250. Article 6 of Electricity Act of 2017.
251. Article 49 of Electricity Act of 2017.
252. Article 27 of Electricity Act of 2017: "To ensure the stability and safety of the power supply, the Electricity Generating and Retailing Enterprises in selling the electric energy to users shall prepare

electricity supply situation and all gray/stable electricity obliged to be sold to Tai-Power, there is very little volume in the market. Therefore, the future of the implementation of the green market remains unclear. Apart from this, a lot of unique designs in the Electricity Act of 2017 are important. First, only account[253] and "limited" legal unbundling exists in Taiwan. The reason for this is the combination of the regulatory (transmission/distribution) and potential competitive functions (retailing) in one company under Article 6(1) ("In such circumstance, the Electricity Transmission and Distribution Enterprise may run the Electricity Retailing Utility Enterprise concurrently"). This is different from the standard form of legal unbundling, that is, the transmission/distribution companies should become legal subsidiaries.

174. "Electricity Carbon Emission Factor" (Article 28) in this Electricity Act could create competition with the GHG Reduction Act in terms of emission reduction competence and make the energy authority the climate change authority. Under the 2015 GHG Reduction Act, Tai-Power is not responsible for the carbon emissions produced to meet the needs of users.[254] This is a very unique regime in the world, as since 2013 all electricity producers under the EU ETS should buy 100% emission allowances.[255] Two years after the promulgation of the GHG Act, the government decided to load the emission obligation back on Tai-Power, especially on its "non-emission" retailing function, instead of on its generation function. This approach raised several questions, such as why an electricity retailing utility should be responsible for this, how an electricity retailing utility can intervene in this context, and whether such a retailing utility could decline buying fossil fuel electricity to meet the factor requirement.

175. Finally, the legalization of the community support fund is also problematic. Article 65 of the EA aims to set up a standard formula to establish a community support fund and to facilitate the construction of generation/transmission/distribution facilities.[256] The rationale for this scheme is related to the effects of "not in my back yard" (NYMBY) as a result of these electricity projects. However, these

---

the appropriate level of electricity reserve capacity based on its electricity sales, and duly report to the electricity industry regulatory authority. However, the restriction does not apply to Renewable-Energy-Based Electricity Generating Enterprise below a certain capacity. To meet the required capacity, an Electricity Generating Enterprise may either use its resources to generate power or purchase from other Electricity Generating Enterprise, Self-Use Power Generation Equipment or Demand Response providers."

253. Article 6(3) of the Electricity Act of 2019.

254. Article 20(4) of the GHG Reduction Act of 2015:" The central competent authority shall allocate emissions allowances to public utilities, excluding GHG emissions related to energy generation provided to emission sources for consumption as the indirect GHG emissions in CO2e."

255. EC, Transitional free allocation to electricity generators, available at: https://ec.europa.eu/clima/policies/ets/allowances/electricity_en.

256. Article 65 of the Electricity Act of 2017: "To facilitate the development and operation of the electric power, to develop the areas in the proximity of the Electricity Generation, Transformation and Distribution Facilities, and to bring welfare to the residents thereof, the Electricity Generating Enterprise and Electricity Transmission and distribution Enterprise shall allocate assistance fund to facilitate the development of electric power to assist the competent authority at the level of the municipal government or county (city) government in promoting development of electricity and

rules have also applied to large-scale PV and wind power.[257] Whereas applying it to onshore wind power is understandable, it is less reasonable to apply it to PV and offshore wind power, because of its low NYMBY effects.

§4. Electricity Supply Security

176. Many measures are required to ensure electricity supply security. First, under the old Electricity Business Act, an electricity business is required to maintain "appropriate" reserve capacity to ensure a continual supply.[258] As Taiwan is an isolated island system, Tai-Power has made efforts at increasing reserve capacity. Under this scheme, Tai-Power's electricity power system had a 22% capacity reserve in 2010. Yet, if the nuclear power plants from Nuclear No. 1 to No. 3 of the Tai-Power were all removed from the power system, the capacity reserve would be reduced significantly. Therefore, a lot of fossil fuel power plants and renewables have been planned in recent years.

177. Other measures regarding electricity supply security are stipulated in the Energy Management Act. First, the coal-fired power plants of an electricity supply business with installed capacity over 500 MW are required to stock fuel for thirty days of operation.[259] In addition, as noted above, the CPC is required to store oil for sixty days. This measure may also be an "indirect" one to ensure the oil supply to oil-fired power plants. Recently, there has been discussion on whether to require gas-fired power plants to maintain similar inventories, in the light of the increasing use of gas as a power fuel.

178. Second, in order to deal with the energy shortage and avoid worsening the energy security problem, an Ordinance was passed under the Energy Management Act.[260] This Ordinance does not deal with all energy security issues, but applies only to electricity insecurity.[261] The term "electricity shortage" is defined to be the inability to supply sufficient electricity due to the lack of electricity fuel or capacity, safety maintenance of installations, breakdown of installations, accident, natural disaster, or other "act of God" factors.[262] After making efforts to reduce electricity consumption under the existing contract arrangement (such as the Interruptible Rate), the

harmony with the communities. The given assistance fund is on the basis of a certain percentage of the kilowatts of electricity generated or transmitted."

257. Article 65(3) of the Electricity Act of 2017. This article does not apply to Renewable-Energy-Based Electricity Generating Enterprise except for producers of electricity by wind power and with solar power-generating infrastructure of certain capacity.
258. Article 39 of the old Electricity Business Act.
259. Article 7 of the Energy Management Act; Ordinance on Energy User Using Large Amount of Energy.
260. Article 19 of the Energy Management Act: "During periods of insufficient energy supply, the central competent authority may formulate measures for energy control, restriction, and rationing, which shall become effective upon approval by the Executive Yuan."
261. Ordinance on Limiting Electricity Consumption at the Time of Electricity Supply Shortage.
262. Article 2 of Ordinance on Limiting Electricity Consumption at the Time of Electricity Supply Shortage.

security situation may remain unsecured. There is a sequence for reducing electricity use until the electricity supply is sufficient.[263] The order of reduction starts with large industrial users first that consume the largest proportion.

(1) Large industrial users with contract capacity over 5,000 kW: 5%
(2) Industrial users with contract capacity between 1,000 and 5,000 kW: 5%
(3) Industrial users with contract capacity over 1,000 kW: extra 5%.
(4) Large industrial users with contract capacity over 5,000 kW: extra 5%.
(5) Industrial users with contract capacity between 1,000 and 5,000 kW: additional 5%
(6) Industrial users with contract capacity less than 1,000 kW and regular electricity users: regional electricity outages lasting for 50 minutes each time.

179. Except in cases of emergency electricity outages, other actions to limit electricity supply require advance notification. For example, large industrial users with a contract capacity of over 1,000 kW should be given notification one day before 4 p.m. Smaller industrial users and regular users must be given one day's notice about the region of the power outage and the time, by means of news media.[264] Finally, those users and customers facing limited electricity supply may enjoy certain discounts on their electricity bills.[265]

263. Article 5 of Ordinance on Limiting Electricity Consumption at the Time of Electricity Supply Shortage.
264. Article 8 of Ordinance on Limiting Electricity Consumption at the Time of Electricity Supply Shortage.
265. Article 10 of Ordinance on Limiting Electricity Consumption at the Time of Electricity Supply Shortage.

Part III. Regulatory Framework Concerning Petroleum and Liquefied Petroleum Gas

Chapter 1. General Introduction

180. In Taiwan, LPG is a very important by-product of the refining process of petroleum. Thus, it comes under the same regulatory regime as petroleum. Hence, though LPG may be considered a type of “gas fuel” like natural gas or LNG, it will be discussed in this Part.

181. Unlike the oil law in other countries, which regulates oil and petroleum from upstream (exploration, exploitation, production, transportation, wholesale, import and export, refinery) to downstream retailing, the oil law in Taiwan—the Petroleum Management Act—scarcely regulates the exploration, exploitation, and production. The main Act with regard to these activities is the Mining Act. Since the Mining Act regime treats oil exploration and exploitation in similar fashion to other mining activities, this author will not repeat what has been mentioned above and will focus instead on other processes.

§1. Demand and Supply Situation

182. Originally, coal was the main source of energy in Taiwan. Yet, since 1970, oil consumption has exceeded that of coal and has become the main source of energy. This dominance of oil consumption lasted for around twenty years and was replaced by electricity in 1991–1992. In 2019, petroleum products represented 46.91% of the energy consumed, followed by coal and coal products (29%).[266] No doubt, both petroleum and electricity will continue to play major roles in the future. Petroleum products are used for non-energy purposes (28%), transportation (15.78%), and in the industrial sector.[267]

266. MOEABOE, Energy Supply (by Energy Form)&Total Domestic Consumption (by Sector) available at: https://www.moeaboe.gov.tw/ECW/main/content/wHandMenuFile.ashx?file_id=1395.
267. MOEABOE, Energy Supply and Consumption Flowchart (2019), available at: https://www.moeaboe.gov.tw/ECW/main/content/wHandMenuFile.ashx?file_id=5382http://www.moeaboe.gov.tw/About/webpage/book_en3/page7.htm.

183. Taiwan's oil consumption is heavily dependent on imports. As much as 97.9% percent of the domestic energy consumption depends on imports,[268] of which petroleum accounted for more than 99.99% in 2018. This situation makes Taiwan's energy system vulnerable to the global supply and demand. Since the two oil crises, the Taiwan government has made it a priority to move from relying on oil to using other energy. Yet, so far, the results of such initiatives have not been quite satisfactory.

184. Due to the development of the petrochemical industry and the underdeveloped public transportation system, Taiwan remains highly addicted to oil. In this regard, the policy should focus on a more practical aspect, i.e., how to diversify the source of petroleum supply in order to reduce the risk of relying too heavily on one country or a few. In 2018, Saudi Arabia (30.9%) was the main supplier of crude oil to Taiwan, followed by Kuwait (20.7%), and the United States (13.6%).[269] Even though this may at first appear to be a satisfyingly diverse spread of countries, Taiwan still relies too much on distant and the Middle East suppliers. There seems to be a need to find much closer supply sources (such as Indonesia, which was only 2.3% in 2018, etc.) in order to avoid the risks associated with political or transportation difficulties.

§2. Petroleum and LPG in Energy Policy

185. Since the two oil crises, the Energy Management Act was promulgated in 1980. In this Act, the idea of "alternative energy" was promoted as an alternative to fossil fuel energy, i.e., coal, gas, and oil, especially oil. Then the wording of "new" and/or "renewable energy" became a focus to shift energy use from oil to other forms of energy, such as the measures in the 1996 Taiwan Energy Policy and Measures. From the viewpoint of climate change, oil was also described as a "high-carbon" energy source that should be replaced by other sources of energy, such as natural gas. Due to these efforts, oil's role was replaced by in relative terms, though the actual consumption of oil is increasing in real terms. Hence, the reduction of oil use is a dream!

186. Finding itself unable to curb the desire for oil and petroleum products, the government's priority became that of maintaining oil security, so that it has adopted a more practical approach. On the one hand, domestic oil companies are encouraged to increase overseas exploration and exploitation to increase oil output and to diversify the countries of origin from which oil is imported as noted above. On the other hand, domestically, the stockpiling of enough oil in case of emergency ("emergency oil stockpile") is also high on the regulatory agenda. This stockpile policy of

268. Energy Supply and Total Domestic Consumption & Energy Supply (Indigenous & Imported), available at: https://www.moeaboe.gov.tw/ECW/english/content/ContentLink.aspx?menu_id=1540.
269. MOEA, Energy Statistics Handbook 2018, October 2019, available at: https://www.moeaboe.gov.tw/ECW_WEBPAGE/FlipBook/2018EnergyStaHandBook/2018EnergyStaHandBook.pdf.

"Management of oil security stockpile" is also highlighted and emphasized by the MOEABOE as one of the two key oil policies. With high oil-import dependency, it is necessary for Taiwan to maximize its energy security through oil stockpiling. According to Article 24 of the Petroleum Administration Act, oil refinery operators and importers should maintain an oil security stockpile of no less than sixty days of supply while the government must also maintain an oil security stockpile of no less than thirty days. The stability of domestic oil supply is secured through aperiodic government inspections in combination with monthly reports from refinery operators and importers.[270]

187. Even though the overall policy direction is to reduce the use of oil, this does not mean that "all" petroleum products are discouraged. The status of LPG is somewhat equivocal as regards this policy direction. In the household sectors, LPG is predominantly used for cooking and heating water for showering and other domestic use purposes, as the basic infrastructure for a natural gas pipeline is underdeveloped in rural areas. In this regard, it is suggested that LPG be replaced by solar water heaters or natural gas water heaters. Yet, in the transportation sector, LPG has become the preferred energy. LPG vehicles enjoy the advantage of investment subsidies and LPG is sold to taxi drivers at preferential prices during high oil price times, such as in 2009. Yet facing low gasoline prices in recent years, the reduction of the number of LPG filling stations, and the promotion of electricity vehicles, the LPG promotion policy faces challenges.

188. Apart from the general policy on supply and demand, the liberalization and privatization of the oil industry in order to improve its efficiency is highlighted in almost every energy policy document, such as the 1996 Taiwan Energy Policy and Measures. The petroleum market was legally liberalized in 2001 after the passing of the Petroleum Management Act. Yet, the incumbent oil giant—the CPC—remains state-owned so far. Owing to the concerns of quality in the competitive liberalized oil market, the "Administration of Petroleum Product Quality" became one of the two key petroleum policies.[271] According to Article 29 of the "Petroleum Administration Act": (1) Only petroleum products that meet the national standards can be imported or sold in the domestic market, and (2) The central competent authority may send personnel or entrust a professional institution to examine the quality of the petroleum products sold, and the business may not obstruct, refuse, or evade such examination. There are currently over 2,500 gasoline stations in Taiwan. To ensure the qualities of gasoline and diesel oils in the stations for the protection of people's rights and interests, the authority entrusts the responsibility of conducting inspections of petroleum products every year to professional testing institutions.

270. MOEABOE, Management of oil security stockpile, Dec. 24, 2019, available at: https://www.moeaboe.gov.tw/ECW/English/content/Content.aspx?menu_id=8675.
271. MOEABOE, Administration of Petroleum Product Quality, Dec. 24, 2019, available at: https://www.moeaboe.gov.tw/ECW/English/content/Content.aspx?menu_id=8676.

§3. Authorities and Regulators in the Petroleum and LPG Sector

189. Unlike the separation of energy authorities from energy regulators in many European countries and the US, in Taiwan, the main authority responsible for formulating oil policy and regulating the oil industry is the MOEABOE. However, since the CPC remains a state-owned enterprise, the State-Owned Enterprise Commission of the MOEA also supervises the operation of the CPC. Before liberalization, the price of oil was regulated and set by the government under the guidance of the Advisory Commission on Oil and Electricity Prices, established in July 1991. Yet, after oil liberalization, this commission was renamed "The Advisory Commission on Electricity and Gas Prices." Taiwan formally adopted a floating fuel price mechanism from January 1, 2007, with the state-run CPC Corp. (formerly Chinese Petroleum Corporation) and adjusted its prices every week in line with international crude oil price movements.[272] The BOM of the MOEA is also in charge of the EHS of oil fields. The LPG industry is also under the supervision of the MOEA. In general, as petroleum and LPG are closely tied to the country's economic affairs, these industries are regulated by the MOEA.

190. In spite of the lack of a specific energy regulator, the petroleum business and oil business are also subject to the oversight of the FTC. Recently, there were several investigations into the anti-competitive behaviors of LPG businesses. So far, the accumulated fines imposed on LPG businesses is the highest among all industries. Besides, the Consumer Protection Commission is also involved since it regulates the "standardization contract"[273] for Household LPG supply and the contracts between Tai-Power and electricity users. Finally, the EPA may also regulate the pollution from LPG and petroleum businesses.

§4. Main Players in the Petroleum and LPG Market

191. The Taiwan petroleum and LPG markets were originally dominated by the CPC (though the downstream LPG retailing business already had many players). Yet, from 1987 until 2001, the government took a step-by-step approach to liberalizing the market. It started with the liberalization of downstream petroleum marketing, when, in 1987, the private sector was allowed to run gas stations. Then, in 1993, the establishment of a Naphtha crack plant was permitted on the condition that it sell its gasoline and diesel to the CPC. In 1996, the petroleum refinery industry was liberalized. A private company, FPCC, entered this business in September

272. F&L, Taiwan to formally adopt floating fuel price, Dec. 29, 2006, available at: https://www.fuelsandlubes.com/knowledge-base/taiwan-to-formally-adopt-floating-fuel-price/.
273. Executive Yuan, Standard form contract of Liquefied Petroleum Gas, Sep. 21, 2018, available at: https://www.ey.gov.tw/Page/AABD2F12D8A6D561/72347b72-8744-48ad-88b5-1e9ce0aae9e6.

2000. Since January 1999, the import ban on certain petroleum products (LPG, aviation fuel oil, and fuel oil) was abolished. Finally, the importation of petroleum products was freely allowed after the promulgation and implementation of the "Petroleum Management Act" on October 11, 2001.[274]

192. At upstream level, the major players in the oil and LPG sector are the two petroleum refining companies in Taiwan, the CPC Corporation, Taiwan (CPC), and the FPCC. The former refines more crude oil per day than the latter, whereas the latter even has excess gasoline and diesel that can be exported to overseas markets. In addition, since the opening up of fuel imports, including aviation fuel oil and LPG in January 1999, Lee Chang Yung Chemical Industry Corporation (LCYCIC), Chien Huei Industrial, and China Global Petroleum have also secured import licenses for importing LPG, gasoline, and diesel. Apart from these major players, there are more than 189 companies running gasoline and diesel wholesale businesses, over 2487 gas stations (the top 2 players are CPC (606) and FPCC (115)),[275] 49 LPG refilling stations in 2011 (run by several companies including the CPC), reduced to less than 30 recently more than 2800 household LPG retailers, and several LPG suppliers, distributors, and packing companies.

---

274. MOEABOE, About, available at: http://www.moeaboe.gov.tw/About/webpage/book_en2/page1.htm.

275. Petroleum Price Information Management and Analysis System, available at: https://www2.moeaboe.gov.tw/oil102/oil2017/A04/A0409/report.asp.

Chapter 2. Statutory Structure and Legal Regime

§1. MANAGEMENT OF PETROLEUM AND LPG "BUSINESS"

I. Act on the Management of State-Owned Enterprises

193. Taiwan's oil and LPG sector was dominated by the national enterprise, the CPC, before opening up in 1987. The operation of the CPC was regulated and supervised by the MOEA under the provisions of the Act on the Management of State-Owned Enterprises.[276] Besides, the CPC is also subject to the budgetary and related control of Parliament.

II. Regulatory Regime under Energy Management Act

194. Before the promulgation of the Petroleum Management Act, the main law governing the regulation of the petroleum business by the energy authority was the Energy Management Act. This Act provides demand-side and supply-side regulations. From the supply side, the main clause governing the oil business is Article 7 of the Energy Management Act, which mandates the 1. Submission of operation data; 2. Establishment of energy storage facilities; and 3. Storage of security stockpiles. Additional rules on the submission of operation data are defined in Annex Table 2 of the Ordinance on the Submission of Operation Data by the Energy Supply Business.[277] Oil refineries, importers, exporters, and recycled oil businesses are all obliged to submit monthly data by the 20th of each month.[278] For the latter two, the further legal regime is provided in Petroleum Management Act.

195. Finally, as certain petroleum chemical companies may be considered "Energy users producing large amounts of steam and heat" under Article 10 of the Energy Management Act, they are subject to a technology mandate to set up CHP facilities. Once a CHP installation is set up, it is required to follow a format similar to that noted above, which will be elaborated on in the latter Part of "Interaction between Energy Law and Environmental Law."

III. Regulatory Regime under Petroleum Management Act

196. In order to create a comprehensive legal framework to regulate the petroleum and LPG sectors, and to liberalize their market, the Petroleum Management Act was adopted in 2001. The definition of "petroleum and its related products" is

---

276. Act on the Management of State-Owned Enterprises, Jan. 20, 1949; last revised on Feb. 1, 2008.

277. Ordinance on the Submission of Operation Data by Energy Supply Business, 2018-03-09, available at: https://www.moeaboe.gov.tw/ECW/populace/Law/Content.aspx?menu_id=6872.

278. Ordinance on Energy User Using Large Amount of Energy., 1993-10-22, Amended on 2018-03-09, available at: https://www.moeaboe.gov.tw/ECW/populace/Law/Content.aspx?menu_id=615.

defined very broadly to cover the associated use of petroleum. It widely covers crude oil, diesel, coal oil, light oil, LPG, fuel oil, flight oil, etc.[279] Different chapters in this Act provide further detailed regulations for different petroleum supply chains, including a refinery business under Chapter 2, an export and import business under Chapter 3, a retailer and wholesaler of gasoline, diesel, and LPG under Chapter 4. For example, a licensing scheme was developed for refiners and exporters under Article 6 and Article 10, respectively. Then, Chapter 5 provides cross-sector regulations. This includes ensuring petroleum products meet national standards before importing or marketing, once there is a national standard in place.[280] Furthermore, there is a licensing scheme for petroleum businesses setting up oil storage facilities.[281] For those petroleum businesses infringing this Act, Chapter 7 provides a penalty.

197. Yet, it should be noted that LPG business regulation is limited to the Petroleum Management Act of 2001. The issue of LPG is dealt with solely under the business regulations for upstream refining, imports and exports, and downstream LPG filling stations. The other important supply chain, that of "household LPG," was unresolved under this legal framework. In this regard, legislative reform of the Petroleum Management Act began in 2008 to complete the unfinished job of household cylinder LPG regulation.[282] Business management stipulations for middle and downstream household LPG, including LPG suppliers, distributors, can packers, and retailers are given in the Act that was passed and published on January 26, 2011.

198. The other purpose of the Petroleum Management Act is to liberalize the oil sector. As Taiwan mainly relies on oil imports, the best means of liberalization is the abolishment of the "import ban" on all oil-related products. As noted above, parts of the import and the downstream market were already liberalized before the Petroleum Management Act. The Petroleum Management Act completed the whole liberalization process and introduced a free market for all petroleum products on December 26, 2001, including crude oil, bitumen mineral oil, gasoline, diesel, kerosene, light oil, LPG, aviation fuel, and fuel oil.[283]

199. Six years after the petroleum sector liberalization, on January 16, 2008, a large-scale amendment was proposed, adopted, and published to deepen liberalization. Further, the security reserve threshold for petroleum import businesses was lowered to avoid unnecessary barriers to entering the import market. The security reserve requirement of petroleum import businesses was reduced from 50,000 kiloliters (kl) to 10,000 kl, while the reserves of the petroleum refinery was maintained

279. Article 2 of the Petroleum Management Act.
280. Article 29 of the Petroleum Management Act.
281. Article 33 of the Petroleum Management Act.
282. Executive Yuan, Public Attachment, available at: www.ey.gov.tw/public/Attachment/85141354437 1.doc.
283. Article 11 of the Petroleum Management Act, and Ordinance on the Abolishment of Import Ban on Crude oil, Bitumen mineral oil, Gasoline, Diesel, Kerosene, Light oil, LPG, Aviation fuel and Fuel oil: https://www.moeaboe.gov.tw/ECW/populace/Law/Content.aspx?menu_id=621.

at 50,000 kl.[284] Finally, partial import tariffs (customs duties) on petroleum products were relaxed. The Ministry of Finance has already accepted the suggestion of diminishing the tax difference between petroleum products and crude oil, i.e., the tariff on gasoline, kerosene, jet fuel oil, and diesel should be reduced to 0% as a supplementary measure.

200. In 2011, the most recent major revision was made. Two provisions were added. First, to respond to an unexpected accident in the domestic oil market that results in the imbalance between oil supply and demand or any doubt of it, the BOE can levy fees to raise the Petroleum Fund on oil exporters for their export of oil.[285] The second provision pertained to the duties of submitting data and labeling on part of LPG businesses: LPG distributors and packing companies must periodically report to their authoritative units their supply and sale of LPG. LPG retailers must display information on source of gas and the retail price in the business place. LPG packing companies must fill high-pressure gas containers with LPG according to the labeled weight.[286]

§2. Siting and Management of LPG and Petroleum Infrastructure

201. Apart from "business" regulation under the Petroleum Management Act, further detailed rules have been developed to regulate the siting and management of petroleum-related "infrastructure." A series of Siting and Management Ordinances are provided for gas stations,[287] LPG filling stations,[288] fishing boat filling stations,[289] self-service oil and gas filling facilities,[290] gas and oil filling facilities at airports, commercial harbors, and industrial harbors,[291] and "oil storage facilities of petroleum businesses,"[292] etc. In spite of different detailed regulations, the relevant issues in these Ordinances are quite similar. They include the planning law in

284. MOEABOE, About, available at: www.moeaboe.gov.tw/About/webpage/book_en2/page1.htm.
285. Article 15-1 of the Petroleum Management Act of 2011.
286. Article 19(1) and (2) of the Petroleum Management Act of 2011.
287. MOJ, Siting and Management Ordinances on Gas Stations, 2017-09-13, available at: https://law.moj.gov.tw/LawClass/LawAll.aspx?PCode=J0120032.
288. MOJ, Siting and Management Ordinances on LPG Filling Stations, 2017-11-22, available at: https://law.moj.gov.tw/LawClass/LawAll.aspx?pcode=J0120052.
289. MOJ, Siting and Management Ordinances on Fishing Boat Filling Stations, 2015-10-15, available at: https://law.moj.gov.tw/LawClass/LawAll.aspx?pcode=J0120034.
290. MOJ, Siting and Management Ordinances on Self-use Oil and Gas Filling Facilities, 2004-09-08, available at: https://law.moj.gov.tw/LawClass/LawAll.aspx?pcode=J0020041.
291. MOJ, Siting and Management Ordinances on Gas and Oil Filling Facilities in Airports, Commercial Harbors, and Industrial Harbors, 2011-12-26, available at: https://law.moj.gov.tw/LawClass/LawAll.aspx?pcode=J0020038.
292. Siting and Management Ordinances on Oil Storage Facilities of Petroleum Businesses, 2004-12-15, available at: https://law.moj.gov.tw/LawClass/LawAll.aspx?pcode=J0020039.

respect to the use of land and sites,[293] the regulation on installations and facilities,[294] the application procedure and documents,[295] regulation on operation and management,[296] and particularly the "safety" regulation on these hazardous facilities.[297] In addition, other regulations are also available for oil storage facilities,[298] for diesel for fishing boat use,[299] and for the tanks of petroleum businesses;[300] there are also land regulations concerning LPG.[301]

202. Yet, it should be noted that the development of a siting and management legal regime for LPG filling stations (2002) and other related facilities came later than for other petroleum activities, such as gas stations (1993) or fishing boat gas stations (1993). A lot of siting and management Ordinances were available for other petroleum activities before the adoption of the Petroleum Management Act of 2001, whereas all Ordinances concerning LPG filling stations were all developed after 2001. However, the main Siting and Management regulation pertaining to LPG remains that on "transportation for LPG filling stations," rather than household matters. Yet, after the revision in 2011, the legal basis to regulate LPG distributors and packing companies was finally introduced and another ordinance was promulgated.[302]

§3. Oil Security

203. As Taiwan relies considerably on oil imports via oil tankers, instead of pipelines, energy security concerns arising from oil are important. In order to improve oil security, three measures were developed under the current legal regime.

---

293. For example, Chapter 2 of Siting and Management Ordinances on Gas Stations; Chapter 2 of Siting and Management Ordinances on LPG Filling Stations.
294. Article 5 of Siting and Management Ordinances on Fishing Boat Filling Stations; Art. 5 of Siting and Management Ordinances on Self-service Oil and Gas Filling Facilities.
295. Article 6 of Siting and Management Ordinances on Gas and Oil Filling Facilities at Airports, Commercial Harbors, and Industrial Harbors; Chapter 4 of Siting and Management Ordinances on Oil Storage Facilities of Petroleum Businesses.
296. For example, Chapter 7 of Siting and Management Ordinances on Gas Stations.
297. For example, Art. 10 of Siting and Management Ordinances on Gas and Oil Filling Facilities at Airports, Commercial Harbors, and Industrial Harbors.
298. Ordinance on Inspecting Oil Storage, 2013-07-25, available at: https://law.moj.gov.tw/LawClass/LawAll.aspx?pcode=J0020040.
299. Ordinance on Black Dye for Fishing Boat Diesel, 2003-08-19, available at: https://www.moeaboe.gov.tw/ECW/populace/Law/Content.aspx?menu_id=626.
300. Ordinance on Applying for Extension of Inspection Period, 2006-03-01, available at: https://www.moeaboe.gov.tw/opengovinfo/Laws/oil/LOilMain.aspx?PageId=l_oil_16.
301. Ordinance on the Change of Non-urban Land to be used for LPG Canning Site, 2018-06-28, available at: https://www.moeaboe.gov.tw/opengovinfo/Laws/gas/LGasMain.aspx?PageId=l_gas_07.
302. Ordinance on the Management of LPG distributors and packing companies, 2018-02-06, available at: https://law.moj.gov.tw/LawClass/LawAll.aspx?pcode=J0130062.

I. Oil Stockpile Duty for Petroleum Business and Government

A. Petroleum Business: Refiners and Importers

204. According to the Petroleum Management Act, oil refinery operators and importers are required to maintain an oil security stockpile of no less than sixty days of supply and an LPG security stockpile of no less than twenty-five days of supply.[303] The total storage quantity of an oil refinery must be no less than 50,000 kl, and that of oil importers must be no less than 10,000 kl.[304]

205. In spite of the Act mentioning the basic calculation rules,[305] how to calculate the oil stockpile requirement is further elaborated on in an Ordinance.[306] In addition, in order to ensure compliance with this legal duty, a special Ordinance provides rules for inspecting the compliance of oil refiners and oil importers.[307]

B. Government

206. An additional oil security obligation is placed on the government. This is a unique mechanism, since most extant energy laws mainly deal with the relationship between the government and the one that is regulated. This special regime also reflects either the priority of oil security or the weaknesses of Taiwan's oil supply situation.

207. Under the Petroleum Management Act, the government is obliged to maintain an oil security stockpile of no less than thirty days' supply.[308] This duty is only half that of the oil refiners and importers, but still very strict. The resources to fund this stockpile duty come from a Petroleum Fund. Certain oil importers, exploiters, and manufacturers of petrochemical feedstock may be subject to this levy requirement.[309] Notification of the levies for different types of petroleum products (crude oil, fuel oil, kerosene, kerosene type jet fuel, LPG, gasoline, and diesel oil) is published by the government.[310]

---

303. Article 24(1) of Petroleum Management Act.
304. Article 24(2) of the Petroleum Management Act.
305. Article 24(1) of Petroleum Management Act: "The supply amount will be based on the average domestic sales and private consumption of the past twelve months."
306. Ordinance on the Standard for Calculating Oil Security Stockpile for Oil Refiner and Importer, 2008-07-29, available at: https://law.moj.gov.tw/LawClass/LawAll.aspx?pcode=J0130030.
307. Ordinance on the Inspection of Oil Security Stockpile, 2006-04-24, available at: https://www.moeaboe.gov.tw/opengovinfo/Laws/oil/LOilMain.aspx?PageId=l_oil_03.
308. Article 24(3) of the Petroleum Management Act.
309. Article 34 of Petroleum Management Act.
310. MOEABOE, Notification of Payment for Petroleum Fund, 2013-12-31, available at: https://www.moeaboe.gov.tw/ECW/populace/Law/Content.aspx?menu_id=623.

208. In order to further implement this duty, a special Ordinance on the Management of the Governmental Oil Stockpile was provided.[311] As it is impossible for government to store the oil in its own facilities, this Ordinance mainly deals with the process to entrust this duty to outside qualified companies and their eligibility. The basic principle is to store oil domestically. Overseas stockpiles are allowed only under certain conditions: 1. the lack of domestic oil storage facilities; 2. the cost of domestic stockpiling is too high; 3. the need for compliance with international treaties. Most importantly, this Ordinance provides four ways for government to stockpile oil:

- Bailment stockpile: The MOEA entrusts eligible companies to store "specific" oil in "specific" storage facilities. Eligible companies are not allowed to take and use the oil without the prior consent of the MOEA.
- Conditional stockpile: The MOEA entrusts eligible companies to store "specific" oil of defined "quality" in "specific" storage facilities. The MOEA would consent and allow these companies to change oil storage facilities or keep the flow of oil (withdraw or inject), on the basis of the pre-conditions that this would not affect the oil quantity and quality.
- Accounting stockpile: The MOEA entrusts eligible companies to store oil. The MOEA signs a contract with eligible companies. The MOEA would inspect the stockpile to verify the oil stockpile account amount. Eligible companies are allowed to use their own or rented oil storage facilities to store oil and keep the flow of oil (withdraw or inject).
- Overseas stockpile: The MOEA and its agent may contract with foreign qualified institutes and store oil abroad.

C. The Result

209. According to the 2007 statistics, the amount of government security reserves reached 2,830,000 kl by the end of 2007, equivalent to more than thirty days' demand or consumption of domestic petroleum. The amount of private security reserves is about 6,740,000 kl and the number of days' reserves are all more than eighty-five days, higher than the stipulated sixty-day security reserves. This amount exceeds the requirement under the Petroleum Management Act. The oil stockpile is still increasing. In February 2011, the stockpile of oil was 454 million kl, while that of petroleum products was 516 million kl. This amount is equivalent to around 126–128 days of security reserves. Private security reserves account for ninety days, while government's accounts for around thirty-eight days.

311. Ordinance on Management of Governmental Oil Stockpile., 2005-05-06, available at: https://www.moeaboe.gov.tw/opengovinfo/Laws/oil/LOilMain.aspx?PageId=l_oil_08.

210. In November 2019, the stockpile was increased further to the equivalent of around 134 days of security reserves with 44 and 90 days of government and company stockpiles respectively.[312]

II. Oil Security at the Time of Emergency Phase

211. An emergency phase is defined as an oil supply shortage, or oil price-hike, which would affect the national security or the continual supply of oil.[313] As the defining of this moment would affect the right and duty of existing private oil companies a great deal, a further parameter to define this moment is provided in a special Ordinance.[314]

212. In order to handle this situation, a cross-ministerial commission would be created[315] to deliberate on potential solutions. Overall, the MOEA is also authorized to take certain oil control measures, such as imposing restrictions or prohibitions on oil exports, demanding that oil refineries should adjust refined oil types and quantity, demanding that oil importers should adjust imported oil types and quantity, and prohibiting oil businesses from stocking up oil.[316] Specifically, the MOEA

312. MOEABOE, National Safety Energy Stock of November 2019, available at: https://www.moeaboe.gov.tw/ecw/populace/content/wHandStatistics_File.ashx?statistics_id=2763&serial_no=2.

313. Article 2(1) of the Ordinance on Oil Emergency Phase: "'Emergency' prescribed in the measure refers to the period where deficient oil resources and the acutely fluctuating oil price have an influence on domestic oil supply or national security, as determined by the central competent authority; and enforcement of oil controls, quotas, price limits and adjustment, appropriation and operational measures of oil stockpiling are announced by the central competent authority."

314. MOEABOE, Ordinance on Defining Shortage of Supply or Price-hike, Limitation, and Measures, 2002-11-15, available at: https://www.moeaboe.gov.tw/ECW/populace/Law/Content.aspx?menu_id=1014.

315. Article 4 of the Ordinance on Oil Emergency Phase: "Before enforcing the Measure Governing Oil in Emergency Management, the central competent authority shall establish the Council Governing Oil in Emergency Management where the chief of the central competent authority (i.e., the Minister of the MOEA) assumes the directorship concurrently. The following persons may be invited (or designated) to hold concurrent posts as members of the council (composed of 14–16 members):

1. Vice-Minister of the Ministry of the Interior
2. Vice-Minister of the Ministry of National Defense
3. Vice-Minister of the Ministry of Finance
4. Vice-Minister of the Ministry of Justice
5. Vice-Minister of the Ministry of Economic Affairs
6. Vice-Minister of the Ministry of Transportation and Communications
7. Vice-Minister of the Council for Economic Planning and Development, Executive Yuan
8. Vice-Minister of the Council of Agriculture, Executive Yuan
9. Vice Chairperson of the Fair Trade Commission, Executive Yuan
10. Secretary-General of the Consumer Protection Commission, Executive Yuan
11. Two or three oil refinery representatives
12. Two or three scholars, professionals."

316. Article 7 of the Ordinance on Oil Emergency Phase.

may set a price cap for oil,[317] and release the governmental oil stockpile to the market.[318] In general, Article 21 of the Petroleum Management Act confers a wide range of powers for the MOEA to rely on in order to intervene in the situation:[319] "In the event of an oil shortage or a great fluctuation in oil prices that may impact the steady supply of oil or national security, the central competent authority may institute measures on oil control, such as quotas, price controls, and security stockpile adjustments and utilization." The Ordinance on the Oil Emergency Phase also provides detailed regulations.[320]

§4. PETROLEUM FUND

213. At the time of liberalization, a Petroleum Fund was created to serve as the public benefit fund to provide financial support for universal service, facilitation of exploration and exploitation, R&D activities, etc.; the detailed issues respecting the Fund, such as the levy amount,[321] keeping and spending,[322] and refund,[323] are dealt with by individual Ordinances.

214. Several expense purposes are elaborated in the Petroleum Management Act.[324] Apart from the above-mentioned governmental oil stockpile expense, three

---

317. Article 11 the Ordinance on Oil Emergency Phase: "In an emergency, the central competent authority may specify the upper limit of the oil price for the following oil businesses.

    1. The oil wholesale price and the retail price of the oil refinery and importer.
    2. The oil retail price of the gasoline station, the LPG station, and the gasoline station for fishing boats.
    3. The LPG wholesale price and the retail price of the LPG dealer and the distributor."

318. Article 13 of the Ordinance on Oil Emergency Phase: "In an emergency, the central competent authority may release the governmental oil stockpile."
319. Article 21 of the Petroleum Management Act.
320. MOJ, Measure Governing Oil in Emergency Management, Amended Date: 2009-11-02, available at: https://law.moj.gov.tw/ENG/LawClass/LawAll.aspx?pcode=J0020024.
321. Ordinance on Levy Amount of Petroleum Fund, 2001-12-26, Amended Date: 2016-02-26, available at: https://www.moeaboe.gov.tw/ECW/populace/Law/Content.aspx?menu_id=623.
322. MOJ, Ordinance on Keeping and Spending of Petroleum Fund, Amended Date: 2005-10-26, available at: https://law.moj.gov.tw/LawClass/LawAll.aspx?pcode=J0020020.
323. Special Refund Ordinance for Petroleum Refiners and Importers; Special Refund Ordinance for Petroleum Refiners When Importing Oil for Certain Purposes, 2009-02-23, available at: https://www.moeaboe.gov.tw/ECW/populace/Law/Content.aspx?menu_id=628.
324. Article 36 of the Petroleum Management Act: "1. To maintain the governmental petroleum security stockpile.

    2. To subsidize the establishment of petroleum facilities in mountain and offshore areas as well as transportation outlays, and offer price subsidies.
    3. To encourage the exploration for and development of oil and natural gas reserves.
    4. To implement research and development on energy policy, oil development technology, and alternative energies.
    5. To ensure the security and reasonably effective use of oil and gas (including LPG), as well as to develop and promote oil-saving technology and methods.

expenses are relatively more important. First of all, as Taiwan depends heavily on oil imports, the discovery and securing of potential resources is always the government's main concern. In this regard, the Petroleum Fund developed further rules concerning the subsidy for "exploration," "exploitation," and "development" of oil and natural gas.[325] The main subsidized items include essential geological, geophysical, and geochemical surveys and studies, drilling, and other related expenses. Second, there is another expense item related to the R&D subsidy for oil development technology.[326] Finally, a subsidy for the use of oil products in the rural mountainous and island areas was also introduced.[327] This is to subsidize mainly high transportation, shipping, maintenance, and personnel costs resulting from "rural" factors.

§5. Quality Control of Petroleum-Related Products and Legitimate Operation of Petroleum Businesses

I. Quality Control

215. In the age of liberalization, the for-profit factor may lead to a drop in the quality of petroleum products. In order to protect consumer interests and ensure fair trade, the government placed the quality control of petroleum-related products high on its agenda after oil liberalization. The policy's targets are ensuring the quality of petroleum products sold by gas stations, protecting consumers' rights in petroleum consumption, and deterring illegal profiteering, with the aim of ensuring legal enterprise and upholding consumers' rights.

---

6. To offer a subsidy rewarding the use of renewable energy to replace petroleum energy.
7. To provide an operation subsidy of a municipality, a county, or a city competent authority to implement the oil management and the ban, inspection or auditing as stated in the first paragraph of Art. 54 in this Law.
8. To implement other necessary measures deemed necessary by the central competent authority to stabilize the oil supply and maintain the oil market's order."

325. Ordinance on Application for Exploration and Exploitation Subsidy, 2002-02-26, Amended Date: 2020-06-01, available at: https://www.moeaboe.gov.tw/ECW/populace/Law/Content.aspx?menu_id=633; Ordinance on Application Guide for Exploration and Exploitation Subsidy, 2009-02, Amended Date: 2020-07-31, available at: https://www.moeaboe.gov.tw/ECW/populace/Law/Content.aspx?menu_id=632.

326. Ordinance on Application for Subsidy of R&D for Oil Development Technology, 2002-02-26, Amended Date: 2018-03-09, available at: https://www.moeaboe.gov.tw/ECW/populace/Law/Content.aspx?menu_id=629; Ordinance on Application Guide for Subsidy of R&D for Oil Development Technology, 2018-04-19, available at: https://www.moeaboe.gov.tw/ECW/populace/Law/Content.aspx?menu_id=630.

327. MOJ, Ordinance on Subsidy for the Higher Oil Cost in Rural Mountainous and Island Areas, Amended Date: 2018-02-06, available at: https://law.moj.gov.tw/LawClass/LawAll.aspx?pcode=J0020060.

216. The quality of related petroleum products was prescribed under the Ordinance on Quality of Petroleum Products.[328] The energy content and composition of liquefied petroleum gas, gasoline, naphtha, aviation fuel, kerosene, diesel, and fuel oil are all defined and the CNS national standards for petroleum products are provided. The MOEABOE promulgates auditing rules[329] and engages a professional auditing institute to check related products on the spot market. Business owners selling petroleum products that violate the national standard shall be fined according to the Petroleum Management Act. Of all the auditing targets, the gas station is the government's first priority. Random inspections increased from 400 gas stations in 2002 to 3,000 gas stations in 2007. A qualified rate in terms of petroleum products during inspection is up to 99.8%. In 2016, the qualified rates for gasoline and diesel were 99.98% and 99.94%, respectively.[330]

II. Legitimate Operation of Petroleum Business

217. Before the liberalization, certain illegal oil businesses, so-called underground oil shops, operated oil businesses without governmental permission. In order to unearth and penalize these illegal behaviors, a special cross-ministerial commission hosted by the MOEA was created to advise, coordinate, and review work.[331] In order to encourage the exposure of those underground and illegitimate petroleum business operations, a "reward" incentive was established in 2001.[332] It encourages citizens and governmental investigation officers to actively uncover both the underground oil business and the aforementioned sales of low-quality oil products. As these two measures were very important following oil liberalization, these measures have been maintained and revised several times to meet the latest needs of the MOEABOE.

III. Management of and Regulation on Solvent Oil and Lubricating Oil

218. Solvent oil and lubricating oil may be used illegally to mix with gasoline and diesel and for other illegal or illegitimate purposes. The Petroleum Management Act provides a regulatory regime consisting of two provisions. First, the

328. Ordinance on Quality of Petroleum Products, 2003-05-07, Amended Date: 2019-01-17, available at: https://www.moeaboe.gov.tw/ECW/populace/Law/Content.aspx?menu_id=622.
329. Ordinance on Auditing the Quality of Petroleum Products, Amended Date: 2019-03-14, available at: https://www.moeaboe.gov.tw/ECW/populace/Law/Content.aspx?menu_id=1011.
330. Energy Magazine, The quality test for gas stations, Aug. 5, 2015, available at: https://energymagazine.itri.org.tw/Cont.aspx?CatID=&ContID=2560.
331. Ordinance on Special Commission on Revealing illegitimate Operation of Petroleum Businesses, 2010-05-03, available at: http://www.rootlaw.com.tw/LawContent.aspx?LawID=A040100051000200-0990503.
332. MOJ, Ordinance on Reward of Citizens or Investigation Officers for Uncovering Illegitimate Oil Business and Low-Quality Oil Products, Amended Date: 2011-08-02, available at: https://law.moj.gov.tw/LawClass/LawAll.aspx?pcode=J0020023.

importer should be subject to a reporting duty under Article 12(5).[333] The reporting format is further developed in the Ordinance.[334] Second, the government is also given the authority to trace the flow of solvent oil and lubricating oil after importation. An administrative inspection power is conferred on government,[335] allowing the authority to access data and inspect companies to trace the flow of these two oils.[336]

§6. Other Ancillary Measures

I. Incentives for LPG Filling Stations

219. To facilitate fuel diversity in the transportation sector, the promotion of LPG has been placed on the policy agenda. Yet, there are cost barriers to setting up LPG filling stations. With a view to encouraging the establishment of LPG filling stations; dual filling stations of gasoline and LPG; as well as dual use LPG distribution stations and filling stations, an Ordinance was promulgated to provide an investment subsidy.[337] Even though the title of the subsidy looks as if the main subsidized item is the station itself, the main subsidized item is rather the underground or ground-level LPG storage infrastructure. This scheme differentiated the investment subsidy according to two parameters: 1. whether it is underground or ground level; 2. the size of the storage. However, in order to promote the rapid establishment of LPG filling stations, an extra incentive in the form of an increased subsidy of 40% for early bird stations set up between October 17, 2008, and the end of 2012 was also provided.

220. However, as noted above, with the low oil prices and the emerging role of electricity vehicles, the use of LPG vessels is decreasing. The government decided to abolish the subsidy scheme in June 2016.[338]

333. Article 12(5) of the Petroleum Management Act: "An oil or non-oil business that imports petroleum grade solvent oil or lubricant must file a report with the central competent authority within ten days of any importation. The report must state the name and location of the principal business, the name and domicile or residence of the person responsible, and the types, quantity, and usage of the product imported. Imports by petrochemical enterprises sanctioned by the industrial authority are exempt from this provision."
334. Ordinance on Reporting Format of Solvent Oil and Lubricating Oil, Amended Date: 2017-06-15, available at: https://www.moeaboe.gov.tw/ECW/populace/Law/Content.aspx?menu_id=639.
335. Article 28(2) of the Petroleum Management Act: "The central competent authority may ask the manufacturers of petrochemical feedstock to report on their use of imported petroleum products. Or, the central competent authority may ask oil or non-oil businesses to name who bought the solvent oil and/or lubricant products the businesses imported or sold. Likewise, the central competent authority may send personnel or entrust a professional institution to conduct an inspection on the same issues. A business may not obstruct, refuse, or evade such inspection."
336. Ordinance on Tracing and Inspecting the flow of Solvent Oil and Lubricating Oil, 2006-10-25, available at: https://www.moeaboe.gov.tw/ECW/populace/Law/Content.aspx?menu_id=638.
337. Ordinance on Investment Subsidy for LPG Filling Stations, 2013-05-24, Abrogated on: 2016-06-29, available at: https://law.moea.gov.tw/LawContent.aspx?id=FL070353.
338. Ordinance on Investment Subsidy for LPG Filling Stations, 2013-05-24, Abrogated on: 2016-06-29, available at: https://law.moea.gov.tw/LawContent.aspx?id=FL070353.

II. Tax Incentive

221. In addition to the provision of a project-based exploration and exploitation subsidy under the Ordinance on Application for Exploration and Exploitation Subsidy, "the machine, installations, and materials" used for exploring and exploiting offshore oil and gas mines may be exempted from the import customs duties under the Mining Act.[339]

III. Mandatory Insurance

222. Petroleum-related products are toxic, flammable, and dangerous during all phases of the supply chain. Article 22 of the Petroleum Management Act provides for mandatory public liability insurance and accidental pollution insurance. The obligated entities include oil refiners, importers, exporters, wholesalers of gasoline and diesel, gas stations, LPG filling stations, gas stations for fishing boats, storage facilities at airports, commercial harbors, industrial harbors, "self-use storage and filling stations above a certain scale," etc. Details of the amount insured for different entities are further defined in an Ordinance.[340] A minimum insured amount is provided for "injury and death per person," "injury, death, and property damage per accident," and "total amount during the insurance period." For instance, the amount insured by oil importers for the above three issues is 4 million, 20 million, and 40 million NTD, respectively. In general, in real terms, the insured amount for a refiner is higher than that for an oil importer and gasoline and diesel wholesaler. Oil exporters have the next highest. The last group includes LPG filling stations, gas stations for fishing boats, storage facilities at airports, commercial harbors, industrial harbors, "self-service storage and filling stations above 1.8 kl (LPG) or 5 kl (oil)."

IV. Regulation for Oil Fields and Transportation

223. The detailed regulations concerning storage facilities and other downstream facilities, such as gas stations, have already been mentioned above. Certain regulations are also available for other oil supply chains, which are dispersed in different pieces of legislation.

339. Article 67 of the Mining Act: "All machines, equipment and materials specially used for the exploration or exploitation of sea oil and natural gas mines are exempt from import duties. The categories of machines, equipment and materials mentioned in the preceding paragraph shall be determined by the competent authority in conjunction with the Ministry of Finance."

340. Ordinance on Public Liability and Accidental Pollution Insurance for Petroleum Business, Amended Date: 2011-08-16, available at: https://www.moeaboe.gov.tw/ECW/populace/Law/Content.aspx?menu_id=624.

A. Installation of Oil and Gas Field

224. Apart from the regulation for exploration and exploitation licensing regimes under the Mining Act, there are other requirements when conducting activities covered by the Mining Act, such as the establishment of an offshore "safe zone" to prevent collision with ships.[341]

225. In addition, under the Marine Pollution Act, the operators of exploration and exploitation installations are required to submit a Marine Pollution Prevention Plan for the approval of the competent authority, and establish a continual monitoring recorder to prevent the leakage of oil and gas.[342] They are also principally prohibited from dumping oil and gas during the exploitation period.[343]

226. The sovereignty rights to the oil and gas resources under the Exclusive Economic Zone (EEZ) and continental shelf are owned by the Taiwan government under the Act on the EEZ and Continental Shelf of ROC.[344] In this regard, the establishing of any exploitation and exploration installations are subject to the control of the ROC.[345] The authorization of the construction and the use of offshore exploitation and exploration platforms is further governed by an Ordinance.[346]

341. Article 68 of the Mining Act: "The mineral right holder of offshore petroleum or natural gas shall establish a safety zone for the equipment and installation necessary for exploring and drilling in the drilling area.
The necessary equipment, installation, and safety zone referred to under the previous paragraph shall not obstruct international navigation.
The established equipment, installation, and safety zone under Paragraph 1 shall be properly announced with a warning sign installed to indicate its existence."
342. Article 17 of the Marine Pollution Act.
343. Article 18 of the Marine Pollution Act.
344. Article 5 of Act on EEZ and Continental Shelf of ROC: "The Republic of China shall, in its exclusive economic zone or on its continental shelf, enjoy and exercise the following rights:

1. Sovereign rights for the purpose of exploring, exploiting, conserving, and managing the resources, living or non-living, of the waters superjacent to the seabed and of the seabed and its subsoil."

345. Article 8 of Act on EEZ and Continental Shelf of ROC: "For the undertaking of construction, use, modification, or dismantlement of artificial islands, installations or structures in the exclusive economic zone or on the continental shelf of the Republic of China, permission from the Government of the Republic of China shall be required. The related permission regulations shall be decided by the Executive Yuan.
Laws and regulations of the Republic of China shall apply to artificial islands, installations, or structures prescribed in the preceding paragraph.
A safety zone shall be established around artificial islands, installations, or structures prescribed in paragraph 1 where appropriate measures shall be taken to ensure the safety both of navigation and of the artificial islands, installations, or structures.
The width of the safety zones prescribed in the preceding paragraph shall be in accordance with general international standards or as recommended by the related international organizations."
346. Ordinance on Authorization Payment Standard for Man-made Installations in EEZ and Continental Shelf, 2009-05-06, available at: https://law.moj.gov.tw/LawClass/LawAll.aspx?pcode=D0070179; Ordinance on Authorization for Man-made Installations in EEZ and Continental Shelf, 2000-10-04, available at: https://law.moj.gov.tw/LawClass/LawAll.aspx?pcode=A0030122.

B. Pipeline Transportation

227. The Petroleum Management Act makes two provisions to govern the development of an oil pipeline. One is related to the laying, site principle, and land use principle;[347] the other is associated with the operation of the pipeline.[348] For instance, the laying of a pipeline may not adversely affect the safety or landscape or the original use of the premises on which the pipeline is laid. The materials of the pipeline must conform to national standards or other comparable standards.

228. A special regime for offshore pipelines is also provided in the Marine Pollution Act. The above-mentioned regime for oil and gas field installations is also applicable to offshore oil pipelines.[349] In addition, the pipeline operator is required to have "financial guarantee or liability insurance in case of an accident," and have an Emergency Response Plan in place.[350]

---

347. Article 31 of the Petroleum Management Act: "Where necessary, oil refinery operators or importers may lay pipelines using rivers, irrigation canals and ditches, coastal areas, bridges, dikes, ports and harbors, roads, forest land, green land, parks, and other public lands.

Laying the pipeline may not adversely affect the safety or landscape or the original use of the premises on which the pipeline is laid. Before laying the pipeline, those who will do so, must get the approval of the central competent authority and the agency in charge of the land. The operator or importer must compensate for any damages incurred to the premises on which the pipeline is laid.

Oil refinery operators or importers who have oil pipelines may accept the request of other businesses to transmit oil through those pipelines."

348. Article 32 of the Petroleum Management Act: "Oil refinery operators or importers must observe the following requirements in laying oil pipelines:

1. The materials of the pipeline must conform to national standards or other comparable standards.
2. The business must immediately replace corroded pipelines that pose a safety concern.
3. The business must conduct periodic inspections of its oil pipelines each year and save the inspection results for the competent authorities to review.
4. The competent authorities may send personnel or entrust a professional institution to conduct inspections of the pipelines. The business may not refuse such inspection.
5. The business must draw up a pipeline maintenance, inspection, replacement, anti-burglary, leak-proofing, and contingency plans for the following year before the end of October of each year. Before the end of January of each year, it must also produce a report on the inspection and replacement status of the pipeline for the previous year. This report must then be filed with the competent authorities.
6. The business must submit its oil pipeline layout diagrams, final acceptance drawings, and other relevant data to the competent authorities for the setup of a pipeline management information system.

If an inspection of the pipeline shows that the corrosion of pipes poses a safety concern, the competent authorities may demand that the business take remedial actions within a prescribed time period."

349. Articles 17 and 18 of the Marine Pollution Act.

350. Article 13 of the Marine Pollution Act.

229. According to the Act on the EEZ and Continental Shelf of ROC,[351] the ROC has sovereignty over offshore pipelines. The laying of pipelines should be subject to the approval of the ROC.[352] When decisions on such matters are to be made, environmental pollution and biodiversity will be the two principal concerns.[353] The authorization for the laying, maintenance, and change of oil and gas pipelines is further regulated by a special Ordinance.[354]

C. Ship Transportation

230. Marine pollution from ships is highly regulated under the Marine Pollution Act. The above regulations concerning the transportation of oil, including shipping permit, emergency response plan, monitoring obligation, and liability insurance,[355] are also applicable. Also, a mandatory liability clause is provided for ships.[356]

---

351. Article 5(3) of Act on the EEZ and Continental Shelf of ROC: "The Republic of China shall enjoy and exercise jurisdiction over laying, maintaining, or modifying submarine cables or pipelines."
352. Article 15(1) of the Act on the EEZ and Continental Shelf of ROC: "For delineating the course for the laying, maintaining, or modifying of any submarine cables or pipelines on the continental shelf of the Republic of China, permission of the Government of the Republic of China is required. The permission regulations shall be decided by the Executive Yuan."
353. Article 15(2) of the Act on the EEZ and Continental Shelf of ROC: "The Government of the Republic of China may withhold such permission as prescribed in the preceding paragraph on the grounds of exploring, exploiting, managing, conserving the non-living or sedimentary resources over its continental shelf, or preventing, reducing, and controlling the pollution from such pipelines."
354. Ordinance on the Authorization for Laying, Maintaining, Changing Seabed Cable and Pipeline, Amended Date: 2017-11-09, available at: https://law.moj.gov.tw/ENG/LawClass/LawAll.aspx?pcode=K0060041.
355. Article 13 of the Marine Pollution Act.
356. Article 33 of the Marine Pollution Act: "The ship owner shall bear liability for compensation for the damage caused by the pollution of the sea by a ship.

    The ship owner of a ship with a gross tonnage in excess of 400 tons or of an oil tanker or chemical tanker with a gross tonnage in excess of 150 tons shall purchase liability insurance or provide a guarantee based on the gross tonnage of the ship and may neither suspend nor terminate the insurance or guarantee.

    The central competent authority in consultation with the Ministry of Finance shall determine the amount of the liability insurance coverage or guarantee in the foregoing paragraph.

    The ship owner designated in the foregoing article and Paragraph 1 of this article includes the owner, lessee, agent, and operator of a ship."

231. In addition, there is a whole Chapter in the Marine Pollution Act dealing with ships' pollution.[357] The provision relating to oil shipment includes the regulation on the discharge of oil into the ocean from ships,[358] the special discharge prevention measures for oil-carrying ships,[359] and the prevention of oil discharges at the time of ship construction, fixing, dismantling, or cleaning.[360]

V. The Selling of Oil after Distress Warrant

232. Once a petroleum business violates the requirement under the Petroleum Management Act, it may face an administrative fine, criminal punishment, and "forfeiture."[361] Where the oil seized is not suitable or cannot be held, the competent authority may ex officio sell the articles to an oil refinery operator and keep custody of the proceeds. The oil refinery operator designated by the competent authority may not refuse such a purchase request.[362] The price for such sales is defined by a

357. Chapter 6 of the Marine Pollution Act.
358. Article 29(1) of the Marine Pollution Act: "The wastewater or sewage, oil, waste and other polluting substances of a ship shall remain on board or be emitted into on-shore reception facilities with the exception of those circumstances in which it may in accordance with the law be emitted into the sea."
359. Article 30 of the Marine Pollution Act: "Ships loading, unloading, or transporting oil, chemical goods or other cargo that might cause pollution of the sea shall adopt appropriate emissions prevention measures."
360. Article 31 of the Marine Pollution Act: "For those circumstances in which the construction, repair, demolition, salvage, or tank or cargo hold cleaning of a ship causes marine pollution or a concern about pollution, the following measures shall be adopted and polluting substances cleaned up.

Establish appropriate equipment for the containment or removal of floating oil on the surface of the waters surrounding work areas.

Provide appropriate reception facilities in work areas for waste oils, wastewater or sewage, waste, and other hazardous substances.

Prevent the emission into the sea of oils, waste oils, wastewater or sewage, waste, residue, and hazardous substances.

Adopt other measures designated by the central competent authority."
361. For example, Art. 39 of the Petroleum Management Act: "A business in any of the following situations will be fined a minimum of NTD 2,000,000 and a maximum of NTD 10,000,000:

1. In violation of the provisions specified in the first paragraph of Art. 6 herein (i.e., failing to obtain an oil refinery operation license while conducting oil distillation, refining, or blending other than for the purpose of a trial run).
2. In violation of provisions specified in Art. 10 herein (i.e., failing to obtain an oil import operation license) and in violation of Arts. 12 or 13 herein (i.e., failing to acquire a special permit for oil imports) while conducting oil imports.

Oil distilled, refined, blended, or imported as described in the preceding paragraph will be confiscated.

If any of the violations described in the first paragraph results in public endangerment, the offender will be sentenced to a maximum of three years imprisonment or detention and/or be fined a minimum of NTD 1,000,000 and a maximum of NTD 5,000,000.

If the offender of the preceding paragraph is a corporate person, its acting responsible person will be punished and the corporate person itself will also be subjected to the fine prescribed in the preceding paragraph.
362. Article 52(1) of the Petroleum Management Act.

further Ordinance.[363] For oil, the price is set at 60% of the wholesale price of fuel oil, after deducting fuel oil-related taxes; while for LPG, it is 70% of the wholesale price of the oil refinery operator.[364]

VI. The Role of Local Government in Management of the Petroleum Business

233. In general, Taiwanese constitutional law adopts the idea of a separation of powers between the central and local governments. This means the local government is supposed to enforce the related law and regulations. Specifically, the Petroleum Management Act also reflects this spirit in Article 3.[365] However, in reality, due to the local government's lack of financial resources and the heavy administrative and regulatory expense involved in conducting professional and technical petroleum management, there is a special subsidy regime for local government when conducting "oil installation siting management" and when "clamping down on illegal petroleum business."[366] For example, the additional personnel fee resulting from managing an oil installation can be subsidized. Moreover, the cost for laboratory tests of oil is also subsidized to the sum of 40,000 NTD per case. These measures can thus be seen as a "capacity building" mechanism to facilitate the "substantial" implementation of the Petroleum Management Act, using a "bottom-up" approach. Otherwise, insufficient financial resources may lead to the local government being unable to oversee and regulate the petroleum business.

VII. Regulatory Fee and License Fee

234. According to Article 58 of the Petroleum Management Act, the petroleum business has to pay for its regulatory (review) and license fee. A different tariff scheme is further developed for oil refiners,[367] oil importers,[368] "the producer, importer, mixer, seller of bioethanol, biodiesel and renewable petroleum,"[369] the petrochemical industry,[370] oil exporters, "wholesalers of biodiesel and gasoline,"[371]

---

363. Ordinance on the Selling of seized Oil, 2011-06-13, available at: https://law.moj.gov.tw/LawClass/LawAll.aspx?pcode=J0020021.
364. Article 4 of the Ordinance on the Selling of seized Oil, 2011-06-13, available at: https://law.moj.gov.tw/LawClass/LawAll.aspx?pcode=J0020021.
365. Article 3 of the Petroleum Management Act: "The competent authorities referred to in the Act are the Ministry of Economic Affairs on the central level, the municipal governments on the special municipality level (Taipei and Kaohsuing), the county, or city governments on the county or city levels."
366. Ordinance on Subsidy to Local Government for "oil installation siting management" and "clamping down on illegal petroleum business," 2011-07-18, available at: https://www.moeaboe.gov.tw/ECW/populace/Law/Content.aspx?menu_id=634.
367. Article 3(1) of the Ordinance on Regulatory and License Fees for Petroleum Business, Amended Date: 2008-06-18, available at: https://law.moj.gov.tw/LawClass/LawAll.aspx?pcode=J0120037.
368. Article 4 of the Ordinance on Regulatory and License Fees for Petroleum Business.
369. Article 5 of the Ordinance on Regulatory and License Fees for Petroleum Business.
370. Article 6 of the Ordinance on Regulatory and License Fees for Petroleum Business.

operators of gas stations, LPG filling stations, fishing boat gas stations,[372] "the installers of storage in airports, commercial harbors, and industrial harbors," oil storage installers, and installers of self-service gas and LPG filling and storage facilities.[373] In general, the license fee is a fixed rate for all licenses—2,000 NTD. Yet, there is a different review fee or regulatory fee for different petroleum businesses. That for refiners is the highest at NTD 5,000,000. The lowest is NTD 10,000 for oil exporters.

371. Article 7 of the Ordinance on Regulatory and License Fees for Petroleum Business.
372. Article 9 of the Ordinance on Regulatory and License Fees for Petroleum Business.
373. Article 10 of the Ordinance on Regulatory and License Fees for Petroleum Business.

Part IV. Regulatory Framework Pertaining to Gas and LNG

235. Before elaborating on the regulatory framework pertaining to gas, there is a need to discuss Taiwan's unique legal framework for gas. Unlike the gas law in other countries, which regulates the gas industry from upstream (exploration, exploitation, production, transportation, wholesale, import and export) to downstream retailing, the gas law in Taiwan—the Natural Gas Business Act—scarcely regulates the exploration, exploitation, and production procedure.[374] This situation is similar to the Petroleum Management Act as noted above. The main legislation pertaining to this matter is the Mining Act. Since the Mining Act regime treats gas exploration and exploitation in a manner quite similar to other mining activities, this author will not repeat what has been mentioned above and will focus on other processes in this Part.

§1. Gas Demand and Supply

236. Unlike the importation or use of LNG and pipeline gas for fuel purposes in Europe and the US, Taiwan's importation of LNG is done mainly via LNG tankers. In the early stages, Taiwan had a small amount of indigenous natural gas that represented only a limited part of domestic gas consumption, e.g., 3.8% in 1982. With the exhaustion of its gas field, Taiwan began to import LNG from 1990, which represents 0.6% of energy consumption.[375] The quantity of imported gas increased almost four-fold by 2009 and represents 1.2 percent of energy consumption (compared to 1% of indigenous gas). Yet, as 80% of the LNG is used to generate electricity, LNG should be much more than 1.2%. According to the recent statistics on the island's primary energy mix, LNG accounted for 15.06%, while indigenous gas accounted for only 0.12% in 2018.[376] The indigenous natural gas is mainly used in the electricity and industrial sectors. Recently, with the development of distribution gas pipelines in urban areas, natural gas began to compete with cylinder LPG and

374. Of all 72 provisions of the Natural Gas Business Act, only two provisions mention the "gas production business." One is provided in the legislative definition of a gas production business. The other is provided in Art. 5, which regulates the application document to set up a natural gas production business. Yet, this Act does not provide for the exploitation or exploration permit.
375. MOEAEC, Energy Policy White Paper of 1998 80 (1998).
376. MOEA, Energy Statistics Handbook 2018, Oct. 2019, available at: https://www.moeaboe.gov.tw/ECW_WEBPAGE/FlipBook/2018EnergyStaHandBook/2018EnergyStaHandBook.pdf.

has become an important energy source for households where it is used for cooking or water heating. However, it should be noted that as there is little heating demand during the winter, the main heaters in Taiwan are electricity heaters, rather than gas heaters.

§2. Energy Policy on Gas

237. In 2018, imports of LNG reached a total of 22,431 million cubic meters. In 1998, it was 5,108 million cubic meters. LNG imports depicted an average annual increase of 7.68%. In 2018, the consumption of LNG was 20,834 million cubic meters, while in 1998 it was only 4,283 million cubic meters, depicting an average annual increase of 8.23%. Of the total in 2018, power generation accounted for 85.13%, industrial use accounted for 13.92%, services use accounted for 0.63%, residential use accounted for 0.29%, and agricultural use accounted for 0.02%.[377]

238. Of all fossil fuel types, gas enjoys a unique status in the energy policy. Unlike the coal and petroleum consumption reduction measures in the 1996 Energy Policy and Measures and all other policy documents, the policy direction in relation to gas is to promote its use. For example, in the 1986 Energy Policy and Measures, it explicitly states that there is a need to reduce the reliance on oil and increase the imports of LNG.

239. In addition, there are two other concerns with regard to gas, i.e., supply security and gas liberalization, which will be elaborated on below.

I. Supply Security of Gas

240. Even though gas and petroleum are treated differently under the above-mentioned policy, their similar status as imports and as fossil fuels makes them subject to a similar principle: that is the diversification of country sources for of oil, gas, coal, and nuclear fuel imports as directed in the 1996 Taiwan Policy and Measures. The strategy does not seem to work very well. The top two country sources accounted for almost 80% of the LNG imports in 2007 (40.7% of imported LNG was from Indonesia, 36.2% from Malaysia). The other countries accounted for just over 20% (8.8% from Egypt, 5.2% from Qatar, 2.3% from Oman, 2.9% from Australia, 1.5% from Algeria). In this regard, the CPC aggressively negotiated with Australia, the Middle East, and South America for long-term contracts. This situation improved significantly as seen in the 2018 statistics. The sources of imports have diversified. The four main countries are Qatar (28.8%), Malaysia (16.7%), Australia (15.2%), and Papua New Guinea (6.9%).[378]

377. MOEA, Energy Statistics Handbook 2018, Oct. 2019, available at: https://www.moeaboe.gov.tw/ECW_WEBPAGE/FlipBook/2018EnergyStaHandBook/2018EnergyStaHandBook.pdf.
378. MOEA, Energy Statistics Handbook 2018, Oct. 2019, available at: https://www.moeaboe.gov.tw/ECW_WEBPAGE/FlipBook/2018EnergyStaHandBook/2018EnergyStaHandBook.pdf.

241. The Stable Supply of Natural Gas was recently listed as one of the two priority gas policies.[379] In response to occasional interruptions of LNG importing countries or temporal delays caused by weather conditions, the government has required natural gas import enterprises to reserve a security stockpile of natural gas since 2018. The security stockpile required was at least seven days in 2019 and will be at least fourteen days in 2027; the storage capacity required was at least fifteen days in 2019 and will be at least twenty-four days in 2027.[380]

II. Promoting Use of Natural Gas

242. In order to realize the policy goals, there is a special policy initiative focusing on promoting the use of natural gas. The MOEABOE announced a "Program of Expansion of the Use of Natural Gas in Taiwan" in 2006. Gas is considered a low-carbon energy that can be helpful in achieving emission reduction targets. The MOEABOE planned to expand the deployment of natural gas up to 10.5 million tons in 2010, 16 million tons in 2020, and 20 million tons in 2025.[381] The following are the main objectives to expand the use of natural gas, such as the expansion of LNG terminals.[382]

(1) Grasping the complexities of the international LNG market and aggressively looking for new purchasing sources.
(2) Obtaining a commitment from Tai-Power to purchase natural gas in the future.
(3) Increasing the capacity of the LNG receiving terminal.
(4) Amending the pricing structure of natural gas.
(5) Implementing the pricing guideline for users to install gas pipelines.
(6) Proposing a project for the rationalization of electricity prices.
(7) Increasing the capacity factors of gas-fired generation units and installing more of them, as part of long-term power development.
(8) Having the CPC and gas companies implement promotion plans to boost the rate of those being served in the industrial, residential, and commercial sectors.
(9) Improving public education on natural gas.

243. What activity consumes the majority of LNG? Currently, electricity generation does. In future, in the light of the global trend of emission reduction, it

379. MOEABOE, Stable Supply of Natural Gas, Dec. 24, 2019, available at: https://www.moeaboe.gov.tw/ECW/english/content/Content.aspx?menu_id=8677.
380. MOEABOE, Stable Supply of Natural Gas, Dec. 24, 2019, available at: https://www.moeaboe.gov.tw/ECW/english/content/Content.aspx?menu_id=8677.
381. Yun-Hsun Huang, Jung-Hua Wu, Energy Policy in Taiwan: Historical Developments, Current Status and Potential Improvements, energies, 2009, 2, 623–625, available at: https://www.mdpi.com/1996-1073/2/3/623/pdf.
382. Yun-Hsun Huang, Jung-Hua Wu, Energy Policy in Taiwan: Historical Developments, Current Status and Potential Improvements, energies, 2009, 2, 623–625, available at: https://www.mdpi.com/1996-1073/2/3/623/pdf.

would be difficult to construct new coal-fired power plants. Hence, in order to reduce emissions in the electricity generation sector, the rational approach would be to replace the existing coal-fired plants with gas-fired ones and build new gas-fired power plants.[383] The role of gas-fired power was scheduled to account for more than 25% of power generation in 2025 under the Sustainable Energy Development Framework.[384] A similar policy direction is also mentioned in the 2010 Master Plan on Energy Conservation and Emission Reduction.

244. As noted above, the role of gas-fired power plants will increase in the Taiwan 2025 electricity mixture. The aim is to reach 50% of the power generation in 2025.[385] However, because of the delay in the construction of LNG terminals, it remains uncertain whether such a goal can be reached on time.[386]

III. The Promotion of a Digital Gas Meter

245. To secure consumers' household safety, the MOEA under Article 36 of the Natural Gas Business Act, should formulate a natural gas utility enterprise to promote projects on computerized gas metering systems and to implement projects each year. The computerized gas metering system should include functions of auto shutdown when earthquakes occur or below set supply pressure, linking capability, remote reading, and so on. To conduct detailed planning for the promotion of the microcomputer gas meter, the official Promotion Plan on the Microcomputer Gas Meter was adopted on March 20, 2017.[387] This plan can hopefully facilitate the deployment of such meters among all users ahead of the originally set target year of 2026.

IV. Gas Liberalization

246. Taiwan was affected by the global energy liberalization trend and began to promote this position. However, in the early stages, the liberalization trend had an impact only on the electricity and petroleum sectors, not on the gas sector. In the 1986 Taiwan Energy Policy and Measures, in spite of mentioning an overall energy privatization and liberalization policy, only the electricity and oil sectors were

383. "Expand the use of low carbon (natural gas) fuel: Increase the capacity factor of natural gas generators, and establish new natural gas power plants. The total consumption of natural gas is expected to reach 10.5 million tons in 2010, 16~20 million tons in 2020, and 20~22 million tons in 2025."
384. "Increase the utilization of low carbon natural gas, so that it could account for more than 25% of power generated in 2025."
385. The News Lens, Taiwan's 2025 Energy Goals Demand an "Energy 'Czar'," Jun. 19, 2018, available at: https://international.thenewslens.com/article/98126.
386. Taiwan Business Topics, Energy in Taiwan: Uncertainty in Liquefied Natural Gas, Nov. 9, 2017, available at: https://topics.amcham.com.tw/2017/11/uncertain-path-forward-liquefied-natural-gas/.
387. Official Promotion Plan on the Microcomputer Gas Meter, 2017-03-20, available at: https://www.moeaboe.gov.tw/ECW/populace/content/wHandMenuFile.ashx?file_id=7066.

explicitly mentioned for liberalization.[388] In the Energy White Paper of 1998,[389] only electricity and oil liberalization bills were proposed. The gas bill in this white paper is only an industrial regulatory bill for gas utilities—the Gas Utility Bill.

247. In the second phase since the early 2000s, the idea of gas liberalization began to take hold in the policy stage. For example, the policy direction is explicitly mentioned in 2007: "Speeding up the amendment of the 'Electricity Act' and the legislation of the 'Natural Gas Business Act' to facilitate liberalization of the energy market." Yet, unlike the detailed proposed design for electricity liberalization or restructuring, the actual and detailed plan for the proposed gas industry never appeared in any policy document. Even in the aforementioned 2007 policy, the idea of gas liberalization appeared only in the Implementation Measures for Overall Energy Policy. Even though the gas bill has a liberalization element, this was not mentioned when introducing the gas bill in this policy document. Only the management aspect of the gas industry is highlighted in this gas bill. Yet, in fact, the TPA clause for gas transportation pipelines is integrated in the Natural Gas Business Bill of 2003 and 2006, in spite of the removal of this clause in the adopted version of the Natural Gas Business Act of 2011. From this evidence, clearly, natural gas liberalization is not a governmental policy priority.

§3. Authorities and Regulators in the Gas Sector

248. The regulator and authorities of the gas sector are very similar to those of the petroleum sector, because of the similarity between these two energy sources. The MOEA and its MOEABOE, the SEC, the Advisory Commission on Electricity and Gas Prices (previously Advisory Commission on Oil and Electricity Prices), the BOM, etc., are involved in the regulation of the gas sector. Even inside the MOEABOE, oil and gas affairs are regulated under the same Division—the Division of Oil and Gas, MOEABOE.

249. Since the gas market remains unliberalized in Taiwan, the gas price is set by the MOEA. Yet, this does not mean the anti-competition authority and Consumer Protection Authority have no role in regulating or influencing gas-related tariffs or the gas market. For example, the FTC intervened in the issue of the Basic Gas Rate, which was considered an inappropriate measure that would encourage the waste of energy. Furthermore, the Consumer Protection Authority may have a say in the gas business, such as in matters concerning the investigation of extraordinarily high gas connection fees (between 30 and 100,000 NTD) for installing new gas pipelines.

388. 1996 Taiwan Energy Policy and Measures, available at: http://www.moeaboe.gov.tw/Policy/PoMain.aspx?PageId=executepolicy; http://163.28.10.78/content/junior/life_tech/tc_jr/life_tech03/304/304source09.htm.
389. MOEAEC, Energy White Paper of 1998 169–180 (1998).

§4. Main Players in the Gas Market

250. Beginning with the first gas imports from southern East Asia in 1980,[390] the most dominant player in the gas market is the CPC, which dominates upstream gas production, importation, overseas exploitation, transportation pipelines, underground gas storage and LNG facilities, and LNG storage businesses, besides running a small downstream gas supply business. The gas is reprocessed from LNG and then sold to 25 city gas companies for reselling to final customers, to Tai-Power for gas-fired power plants, and to large industrial users. At the retail and regional level, the city gas companies owned by private chaebol run gas distribution and retailing businesses and also own ball-shaped storage facilities. They are franchised providers of natural gas in their area. Yet, they may face competition from cylinder LPG retailers, when the householder is unwilling to pay to be connected to the pipeline or when the distribution pipeline is not developed.

390. MOEABOE, The Introduction to the Document on the Energy Situation in Taiwan in 2007, Aug. 23, 2009.

Chapter 1. Statutory Structure and Legal Regime

251. Before the promulgation of the Natural Gas Business Act of 2011, there was no specific law regulating the gas industry. At the upstream level, the CPC is regulated under the general legal regime (i.e., State-Owned Enterprise Management Act) that applies to all state-owned enterprises. (This is unlike the situation in South Korea, where a specific law governs national gas enterprises, namely the KOGAS Act).[391] At the downstream level, the city gas companies running gas distribution pipelines, ball-shaped storage, and retailing businesses are regulated under the Act for Regulating Privately Run Utilities.[392] which was revoked recently in November 2019. The Ordinance on Managing Coal Gas Businesses, which was revoked in October 2011,[393] and the Ordinance on Accounting Rules for Utilities, which was revoked in November 2011[394] were promulgated under the authorization of this Act and regulated city gas companies in the early stages. In sum, the downstream city gas companies are subject to more regulations than the CPC.

252. In order to create legislation for regulating the entire gas industry and to develop *sector-specific* laws for each industry, the Bill on Gas Fuel Utilities was proposed and reviewed in the Parliament in the early 1990s. However, this law was not passed by the Parliament. Then, affected by the trend of gas liberalization in the US and Europe, a Natural Gas Business Bill was proposed in the 2000s. Yet, the wheeling clause (TPA) in support of liberalization attracted the attention and objection of state-owned enterprises. In the final version, the liberalization clause was removed. The Natural Gas Business Bill merely served the function of legalizing the regulation of gas, as was the case with the Bill on Gas Fuel Utilities.

§1. Management of Gas Business

I. Before Adoption of the Natural Gas Business Act of 2011

A. Legal Regime Applying to Downstream Gas Distribution and Supply Business

253. It was generally believed that the state-owned enterprise—the CPC—was created to serve the needs of the public and thus could be easily regulated by the related authorities. An industry-specific law appeared unnecessary. Yet, there are

391. "KOGAS was established under the KOGAS Act in 1983." *See* ADBG, Gas domestication in South Korea: Lessons for African countries, available at: https://www.afdb.org/fileadmin/uploads/afdb/Documents/Publications/anrc/Gas_domestication_in_South_Korea_Lessons_for_African_countries_AfDB.pdf.
392. Act for Regulating Privately Run Utility, published in 1929, Amended Date: Apr. 26, 2000. abolished date: Nov. 20, 2019, available at: https://law.moj.gov.tw/LawClass/LawAll.aspx?pcode=J0030008.
393. Ordinance on Managing Coal Gas Business, Apr. 23, 1968; Amended Date: 2005-11-17, available at: https://law.moj.gov.tw/LawClass/LawAll.aspx?pcode=J0030009.
394. Ordinance on Accounting Rule for Utilities, 2003-07-25, Abrogated on: 2011-11-07, available at: https://law.moj.gov.tw/LawClass/LawHistory.aspx?pcode=J0130016.

many pieces of legislation related to the downstream gas business, which is mainly dominated by private companies. This fact suggests that privately owned energy companies should be regulated in order to ensure the service quality and public benefit.

254. The Act for Regulating Privately Run Utilities establishes a general framework for all privately run utilities, such as lighting, electricity, cable car, water, coal gas, bus, ship transportation, and air transportation.[395] The application should be submitted to the local authority first, then be approved by the competent authority of the central government.[396] Other important regulations include the submission of a related annual report to the government,[397] the submission of a tariff schedule and other company codes for the approval of the competent authority of the central government,[398] and one on accounting.[399] Finally, there is also a "nationalization clause" embedded in this Act. The privately run utility may be expropriated by the government, where the expropriation amount is determined by a commission comprising government, company staff, several experts, etc.[400]

255. The Ordinance on Managing Coal Gas Businesses was created to govern the development of private local distribution companies (so-called city gas companies) in Taiwan. This Ordinance is authorized under the Act for Regulating Privately Run Utilities. Several important regulatory issues are dealt with under this Ordinance. First of all, a licensing regime is provided for establishing city gas companies.[401] The gas installations of the company in question should meet certain standards.[402] For instance, the company is required to have safety facilities in place and have a professional coal gas safety technician.[403]

256. Two main concerns are the tariff and the quality regulations. The gas sold by the company should also meet certain quality standards.[404] For example, the heat value of gas per cubic meter should not be less than 4,500 calories.[405] Chapter 5

395. Article 2 of Act for Regulating Privately Run Utilities.
396. Article 4 of Act for Regulating Privately Run Utilities.
397. Article 8 of Act for Regulating Privately Run Utilities.
398. Article 7 of Act for Regulating Privately Run Utilities.
399. Article 10 of Act for Regulating Privately Run Utilities.
400. Article 20 of Act for Regulating Privately Run Utilities.
401. MOJ, Chapter 2 of the Ordinance on Managing Coal Gas Businesses, Abrogated on 2011-10-25, available at: https://law.moj.gov.tw/LawClass/LawAll.aspx?pcode=J0030009.
402. Chapter 3 Facility Standard Ordinance on Managing Coal Gas Businesses, Apr. 23, 1968; last revised on Nov. 17, 2005.
403. Articles 13 and 13-1 of Ordinance on Managing Coal Gas Businesses, Apr. 23, 1968; last revised on Nov. 17, 2005.
404. Chapter 4 Quality Standard Ordinance on Managing Coal Gas Businesses, Apr. 23, 1968; last revised on Nov. 17, 2005.
405. Article 15 of the Ordinance on Managing Coal Gas Businesses, Apr. 23, 1968; last revised on Nov. 17, 2005.

provides the regulation on the calculation and formula of sale prices. In order to review the sale price of city gas companies, a special Ordinance on Reviewing Gas Tariffs has been provided.[406]

257. The operation of the gas utility is regulated under Chapter 6 of the Ordinance on Managing Coal Gas Businesses. The authority is empowered to conduct administrative inspections to investigate the installation and operational situation of the city gas companies.[407] The pipeline between city gas companies and users should be subject to a qualification procedure before supplying gas.[408]

258. Finally, in spite of the comprehensive nature of this Ordinance on Managing Coal Gas Businesses, related accounting rules were stipulated quite late and in other Ordinances. The Ordinance on Managing Coal Gas Businesses was promulgated in 1968, but the Ordinance on Utility Accounting Rules was published in 2003.[409] The key point in this Ordinance is the establishment of a "separation of accounts" in a non-liberalization age. Although this account separation regime is not the same as account unbundling, it remains very helpful in avoiding cross-subsidies between the gas division and other divisions of city gas companies. In this regard, the revenue of the city gas company cannot be used to subsidize non-gas business.

B. Pipeline Contractor

259. As Taiwan is located in an earthquake zone, concerns over pipeline safety are emphasized more. Pipeline safety is partly affected by the material of which the pipeline is made, and partly by the skills of the workers. An Ordinance has been provided to ensure public safety and regulate pipeline contractors.[410] The pipeline contractor business includes not only gas pipelines but also works on gas supply installations.[411] Two types of pipeline contractor businesses are further classified, involving the more skillful A level, which has the ability to install all high-pressure pipelines, etc., and a less skilled B level, which can only install user pipelines.[412] Different qualifications are required for A Level and B Level pipeline contractor

406. Ordinance on Reviewing Gas Tariffs, Abrogated on: 2011-01-25, available at: http://www.rootlaw.com.tw/LawContent.aspx?LawID=A040100051003100-1000125.
407. Article 20 of Ordinance on Managing Coal Gas Businesses, 1968-04-23; Amended Date: 2005-11-17, 2011-10-25, available at: https://law.moj.gov.tw/LawClass/LawAll.aspx?pcode=J0030009.
408. Article 23 of Ordinance on Managing Coal Gas Businesses, 1968-04-23; Amended Date: 2005-11-17, 2011-10-25, available at: https://law.moj.gov.tw/LawClass/LawAll.aspx?pcode=J0030009.
409. The Ordinance on Utility Accounting Rules, 2003-06-25, Abrogated on 2011=11-07, available at: https://law.moj.gov.tw/LawClass/LawAll.aspx?pcode=J0130016.
410. Article 1 of the Ordinance on Management of Gas Pipeline Contractor Businesses. *See* MOJ, Ordinance on Management of Gas Pipeline Contractor Businesses, Abrogated on: 2011-11-30, available at: https://law.moj.gov.tw/LawClass/LawAll.aspx?pcode=J0130025.
411. Article 2 of the Ordinance on Management of Gas Pipeline Contractor Businesses.
412. Article 5 of the Ordinance on Management of Gas Pipeline Contractor Businesses.

businesses.[413] Procedural rules concerning applying, registering, changing, reissuing, and canceling licenses are further provided. Finally, the MOEA holds the exam for certifying technicians of pipeline contractor businesses.[414]

C. *Other Regulations for Gas Business*

Safety Distance of Gas Storage

260. A gas storage site is not permitted within 200 m of factories producing explosive products.[415] A similar provision is made for the location of "explosive magazines."[416] Storage facilities of flammable gas with a capacity of no less than 300 m3 and 3000 kg should keep a safe distance under the Ordinance on Labor Safety with High-Pressure Gas.[417] The manufacturing site of hazardous products[418] should establish a safety zone of 20 m.[419]

EHS Gas Storage Concerns

---

413. Article 6 of the Ordinance on Management of Gas Pipeline Contractor Businesses.
414. Article 23 of the Ordinance on Management of Gas Pipeline Contractor Businesses.
415. MOJ, Ordinance on Site Standard for Factory of Explosive Products, 2006-06-30, available at: https://law.moj.gov.tw/LawClass/LawAll.aspx?pcode=J0020048; Art. 2 of the Ordinance on Site Standard for Factory of Explosive Products.
416. MOJ, Ordinance on Site Standard for Explosive Magazine, 2016-03-31, available at: https://law.moj.gov.tw/LawClass/LawAll.aspx?pcode=J0020044; Art. 7 of the Ordinance on Site Standard for Explosive Magazine.
417. Article 35 of the Ordinance on Labor Safety with High-Pressure Gas. MOJ, Ordinance on Labor Safety with High-Pressure Gas, 2014-06-27, available at: https://law.moj.gov.tw/LawClass/LawAll.aspx?pcode=N0060030.
418. Article 2 of the Ordinance on Site, Safety, and Management of Hazardous Products: "1. Class 1: oxidizing solids; 2. Class 2: flammable solids; 3. Class 3: pyrophoric liquids, pyrophoric solids, and hydrophobic materials; 4. Class 4: flammable liquids; 5. Class 5: self-reactive substances, mixtures, and organic peroxides; 6. Class 6: oxidizing liquids. MOJ," Ordinance on Labor Safety with High-Pressure Gas, 2014-06-27, available at: https://law.moj.gov.tw/LawClass/LawAll.aspx?pcode=N0060030; MOJ, Establishment Standard and Safety Control Regulation for Manufacturing, Storing, Processing Public Hazardous Substances and Flammable Pressurized Gases Places, Amended Date: 2019-06-11, available at: https://law.moj.gov.tw/ENG/LawClass/LawAll.aspx?pcode=D0120025.
419. Article 13 of the Ordinance on Site, Safety, and Management of Hazardous Products: "The safety distance between the exterior wall or the outer side equivalent to an exterior wall of any facility with the Six Materials and any abutting property outside the said facility shall be as follows:

> 3.Not less than 20m from any place used for the manufacturing, storage, or processing of hazardous materials and flammable pressurized gases, gas stations, LPG stations, natural gas storage tanks, flammable high-pressure storage tanks, and places for manufacturing, storage, and retail of firecrackers, and other similar hazardous places."

261. Certain safety installations are required for gas storage, such as leakage prevention installations,[420] safety guards or water spray devices,[421] and fire extinguishers.[422]

262. In addition, the storage is subject to regulatory inspection.[423] For special LNG storage facilities, an additional risk assessment is also required and mandatory.[424]

263. Gas storage tanks, valves, coolers, and filters should be subject to regular cleaning.[425] Gas storage tanks and the exhaust valves should not be too far away from the control room to facilitate the neutralizing of pressure and making of safety checks.[426] The operation of gas storage tanks should follow the safety rules of boilers and pressure vessels.[427]

---

420. MOJ, Art. 37 of Ordinance on Labor Safety with High-Pressure Gas, Amended Date: 2013-06-27, available at: https://law.moj.gov.tw/LawClass/LawAll.aspx?pcode=N0060030.
421. Article 208 of Ordinance on Fire Fighting Installations, Amended Date: 2018-10-17, available at: https://law.moj.gov.tw/ENG/LawClass/LawAll.aspx?pcode=D0120029.
422. Article 228 of Ordinance on Fire Fighting Installations, Amended Date: 2018-10-17, available at: https://law.moj.gov.tw/ENG/LawClass/LawAll.aspx?pcode=D0120029.
423. Article 6(1) of the Ordinance on Safety Inspection for Dangerous Machines and Installations: "The inspection of domestic (home-made) hazardous machines/equipment shall be subject to this regulation and the relevant provisions stipulated in the Labor Safety and Health Act, as well as whole or part of the stipulations contained in the national standards, international standards, or association standards that are endorsed and designated by the central governing authority."
    MOJ, Regulations for Safety Inspection of Hazardous Machines and Equipment, 2016-11-21, available at: https://law.moj.gov.tw/ENG/LawClass/LawAll.aspx?pcode=N0060039.
424. Article 6(4) of the Ordinance on Safety Inspection for Dangerous Machines and Installations: "With respect to application for the inspection of those tanks including underground type storage tanks for liquidized natural gases, double shell-type storage tanks (featured with an outer concrete shell and an inner steel shell) for liquidized natural gases, embedded type storage tanks, etc., which are manufactured by adopting special construction and installation techniques, the owner shall prepare a risk evaluation report in advance according to the following requirements, and submit the same to the central governing authority for review (Unless both the said risk evaluation report and the inspection standards have been respectively approved and designated, the applicant shall not be entitled to apply for the subsequent inspections.):
    1. A narration of the major consideration in the planning/design of the said hazardous machines or equipment as well as the proposed inspection standards, together with a written commitment of the risk obligations shall be provided for the authority's reference and use in review of the above-mentioned risk evaluation report.
    2. The said risk evaluation report and the risk control strategy plan shall be duly signed by the original planning/design personnel or by the manufacturer.
    3. The contents of the risk evaluation report shall consist of a description of the risk circumstances, a quantitative evaluation of the risk, the evaluation results, the risk control strategy plan, and the owner's committed risk control measures."
425. MOJ, Art. 33(3) of Ordinance of the Act on Safety of Mining Sites, 2000-01-26, available at: https://law.moj.gov.tw/LawClass/LawAll.aspx?pcode=J0020018.
426. MOJ, Art. 33(10) of Ordinance of the Act on Safety of Mining Sites, 2000-01-26, available at: https://law.moj.gov.tw/LawClass/LawAll.aspx?pcode=J0020018.
427. MOJ, Art. 33(12) of Ordinance of the Act on Safety of Mining Sites, 2000-01-26, available at: https://law.moj.gov.tw/LawClass/LawAll.aspx?pcode=J0020018.

Site of Pipeline

264. The development of gas pipelines and other networks should follow the regulations under the Act on Common Ducts.[428] The purpose is to reinforce the management of different networks. For example, a common duct policy and strategy should be set up by the central government.[429]

265. In addition, there is an Ordinance governing the use of "road land." The pressure control station of a gas pipeline should be set up outside the "road land."[430] For cross-tunnel gas pipelines, the work should be approved by the competent road authority. The pipeline should be buried underground at a designated place; it is not permitted above ground and overhead.[431] For those pipelines crossing a bridge, the authority must be requested to allocate a space for the pipeline. If there is a need to change the bridge design, the additional cost should be borne by the pipeline developer. The gas pipeline may be attached to the existing bridge after consultation with and approval by the road authority.[432]

D. Bill of Gas Fuel Utility Businesses of 1986

266. Even though the downstream city gas companies are governed by the Act on Regulating Privately Run Utilities and the Ordinance on Managing Coal Gas Businesses, the upstream gas business and the LPG supply chain are not governed by these. The first draft of the Bill on Gas Fuel Utility Businesses was proposed to the Parliament in 1986. Yet, the deliberation process was not very satisfactory and it was not approved by the Parliament until 1995. In order to update the regulation to meet the latest regulatory needs, the Executive Yuan submitted an update on January 17, 2007. Yet, this version failed again.

267. The regulations target household LPG and city gas businesses, and also suppliers of cylinder LPG and pipeline installation businesses. LPG also has a special status in oil and gas law. LPG is treated as a gas energy, even though its supply is highly related to the petroleum business. But as this bill (Bill on Gas Fuel Utility Businesses) did not succeed, LPG is considered an oil product, and is currently regulated under the oil law.

268. As Taiwan is not a centralized governmental regime, the division of the regulatory function is of some importance. The advantage of central government is

428. MOJ, Common Ducts Act, 2000-06-14, available at: https://law.moj.gov.tw/ENG/LawClass/LawAll.aspx?pcode=D0070046
429. Article 4 of the Act on Common Ducts: "The competent authority at the central level takes charge of the following affairs: Stipulates the Common Duct development policy and strategy."
430. Article 16(2) of Ordinance Governing the Use of "Road Land."
431. Article 23 of Ordinance Governing the Use of "Road Land."
432. Article 24 of Ordinance Governing the Use of "Road Land."

that it is well endowed with financial and planning functions. Thus, it is the authority's responsibility to establish common rules and monitor common affairs. However, as central government is located far from local gas businesses, the function of the day-to-day affairs, monitoring, and law enforcement are conducted by local government.

269. A licensing regime for gas fuel utilities has been established. The license duration is thirty years. Detailed operation rules are also provided. This regime is quite similar to that of the current Ordinance on Managing Coal Gas Businesses. In this regard, these provisions can be seen as the "juridification" process.

270. Of course, the main function or the essence of this bill is the provision to protect consumer interests. In order to ensure the appropriate supply, quality, and price of supply, a "law" can do more than an "Ordinance" can. In achieving this goal, many detailed regimes, particularly the penalty regime, are very helpful.

271. Finally, this bill is also concerned with the safety of gas storage, pipelines, composition, gasification, and loading facilities. Safety inspections and the hiring of safety personnel during the work and operational period are both important.

272. Yet, with the adoption of the Petroleum Management Act in 2001 the government started to push a new Natural Gas Business Bill, which dropped the LPG element.

II. Natural Gas Business Bill of 2003

273. Due to the above-mentioned general regulations for public utilities being legislated since 1929, they may not be able to meet the needs of an increasingly changing environment. Moreover, in view of the trend of privatization, the CPC will eventually be privatized, and other companies will probably join the import market in years to come. To ensure sound management of natural gas utilities and to regulate natural gas production and importation, the draft of the "Natural Gas Business Act" was completed and submitted to the Legislative Yuan for deliberation in 2003.[433]

274. The contents of this draft Act lay out the aims of its legislation and define the subjects to be regulated and the competent authorities, as well as give concrete

433. MOEABOE, The Introduction to the Document on the Energy Situation in Taiwan in 2007, Aug. 23, 2009, available at: http://www.moeaboe.gov.tw/About/webpage/book_en2/page5.htm.

provisions for relevant matters such as guiding principles for the operation of relevant businesses, the safety of related facilities, the prevention of disasters, the reasonable assurance of customers' rights, and the establishment of a safety inspection system. Additionally, appropriate penalties are clearly defined for any violation of the regulation.[434]

III. After Natural Gas Business Act of 2011

275. After a long wait, the Natural Gas Business Act was published in 2011 and a formal law to regulate the gas business was finally established. This Act was revised in 2016 and 2020. However, no major changes were seen.[435]

276. A licensing regime has been established for running natural gas production, import, utility (pipeline), and pipeline contractor businesses.[436] The supply (sale) license is also necessary for local utility gas businesses.[437] A gas business can obtain qualification documents attesting to inspection by authorities of the municipal or the county (city) governments after consulting with relevant authorities[438] or civil inspection institutions as approved by such authorities.[439] During the application process of a gas utility, other companies wishing to operate in the same franchise area are required to submit a financial guarantee.[440] The amount is further defined in an Ordinance.[441]

277. Chapter 3 of this Act deals with the standard of installations and safety issues. For instance, Article 13 requires the transportation and storage installations to meet national standards or "standards recognized by other progressive countries approved by central competent authorities."[442] Article 17 outlines the emergency reporting requirement at the time of an accident. Article 19 specifies the odorant for mixing into natural gas. A further regulation concerning the odorant is provided in

434. MOEABOE, The Introduction to the Document on the Energy Situation in Taiwan in 2007, Aug. 23, 2009, available at: http://www.moeaboe.gov.tw/About/webpage/book_en2/page5.htm.
435. MOJ, Natural Gas Business Act, Amended Date: 2020-05-27, available at: https://law.moj.gov.tw/LawClass/LawHistory.aspx?pcode=j0130045.
436. Articles 5-6 of the Natural Gas Business Act.
437. Article 10 of the Natural Gas Business Act.
438. Article 10(2) of the Natural Gas Business Act.
439. Article 10(2) of the Natural Gas Business Act. MOJ, Natural Gas Enterprise Act, Amended Date: 2020-05-27, available at: https://law.moj.gov.tw/LawClass/LawHistory.aspx?pcode=j0130045; Ordinance on the Certification of civil inspection institutions, 2011-08-01, available at: https://law.moj.gov.tw/LawClass/LawAll.aspx?pcode=J0130052.
440. Article 7 of the Natural Gas Business Act.
441. MOJ, Ordinance on Financial Guarantee for Application for Utility Business, 2011-07-06, available at: https://law.moj.gov.tw/LawClass/LawAll.aspx?pcode=J0130047.
442. Ordinance of standards recognized by other progressive countries approved for Material, testing, installation, and other safety regulations-regarding affairs of natural gas enterprise's transmission and storage equipment, 2011-08-02, available at: https://law.moj.gov.tw/LawClass/LawAll.aspx?pcode=J0130059.

an Ordinance.[443] The safety concerns pertaining to the gas pipeline have resulted in a license regime for natural gas utility pipeline installation enterprises.[444]

278. Chapter 4 concerns the land use for a natural gas business. It is mainly related to the land for pipelines and storage infrastructure. For instance, the laying of pipelines or establishing of storage facilities on public land should be subject to the approval of the government.[445]

279. Chapter 5 deals with the management of the business. Articles of Association,[446] the universal service duty,[447] the tariff schedule for such service,[448] the tariff for installing pipelines,[449] and the separate accounting rules[450] are covered; in order to ensure the financial stability of the gas utility, the "paid-in capital" of the gas utility must be maintained at a certain level.[451] The gas utility is allowed to change the paid-in capital, yet should submit its Plan of Changing Paid-in Capital for the approval of the central government.[452] The format of this plan is further outlined in an Ordinance.[453]

280. The tariff scheme is one of the key issues in Chapter 5. Article 34 defines the tariff for sales prices,[454] while Article 35 defines the fees payable by the users when they install natural gas pipeline equipment for families, commercial businesses, and the service sector.[455] Finally, like the petroleum business, the gas business is also subject to a mandatory insurance regime to cover public accident liability.[456] The insured amounts required for "producers and/or importers" and "gas utilities" differ. For the former, the amount is 4 million NTD for personal death and

---

443. Ordinance on adding Odorant, 2011-06-30, Amended Date: 2015-06-23, available at: https://www.moeaboe.gov.tw/ECW/populace/Law/Content.aspx?menu_id=1022.
444. MOJ, Art. 20 of the Natural Gas Business Act. Natural Gas Enterprise Act, Amended Date: 2020-05-27, available at: https://law.moj.gov.tw/LawClass/LawHistory.aspx?pcode=j0130045;The Ordinance on the License of natural gas utility pipeline-installation enterprises, 2015-10-12, available at: https://law.moj.gov.tw/LawClass/LawAll.aspx?pcode=J0130058.
445. Article 22 of the Natural Gas Business Act.
446. Article 29 of the Natural Gas Business Act. The Standard Form for Articles of Association of Natural Gas Utility, 2011-08-02, Amended Date: 2015-08-19, available at: https://www.moeaboe.gov.tw/ECW/populace/Law/Content.aspx?menu_id=1028.
447. Article 30 of the Natural Gas Business Act.
448. Article 33 of the Natural Gas Business Act.
449. Article 35 of the Natural Gas Business Act.
450. Article 43 of the Natural Gas Business Act. Natural Gas Enterprise Act, Amended Date: 2020-05-27, available at: https://law.moj.gov.tw/LawClass/LawHistory.aspx?pcode=j0130045. Ordinance on Accounting Rules of Natural Gas Utility, Amended Date: 2015-09-15, available at: https://law.moj.gov.tw/LawClass/LawAll.aspx?pcode=J0130049.
451. Article 41(1) of the Natural Gas Business Act.
452. Article 41(2) of the Natural Gas Business Act.
453. Ordinance on the Format and Items of Plan of Changing Paid-in Capital, 2011-06-30, available at: https://www.moeaboe.gov.tw/ECW/populace/Law/Content.aspx?menu_id=1027.
454. Ordinance on the Calculation of Basis Sales Price of Gas Utility, Amended Date: 2017-05-31, available at: https://law.moj.gov.tw/LawClass/LawAll.aspx?pcode=J0130055.
455. Ordinance on charging pipeline equipment of gas utility, Amended Date: 2014-01-20, available at: https://law.moj.gov.tw/LawClass/LawAll.aspx?pcode=J0130051.
456. Article 44 of the Natural Gas Business Act.

injury per person, 100 million NTD for death, injury, and financial loss per accident, and 200 million for total insured amount for the insured period. For the latter, the amount is also 4 million per person, but per accident it is only 40 million, and for the insured period it is 80 million.[457]

281. Chapter 6, which deals with Monitoring, provides further regulation of the gas business. For instance, Article 46 requires a gas utility business to submit a "Gas Supply Plan" each year, which should include forecasts of new users, scheduled pipeline length, gas amount, and other related information.[458] The authority can randomly check if the gas business is complying with the plan or not. In addition, Article 47 requires a gas business to set up a "geological information management system for its pipeline and storage" and update the information regularly. The detailed data in this system is further defined by an Ordinance.[459] In addition, a gas business is required to report its "operational data," including gas supply amount and revenue and expense, to the MOEABOE. The format and detailed procedure is further defined in an Ordinance.[460] In addition, there are other regulations, such as the requirement of regular inspection of the customer-side's pipeline[461] and its own pipeline,[462] and the replacement of old or corroded pipelines if necessary.[463]

282. Chapter 7 prescribes administrative fines and criminal prosecution for non-compliance with the regulation in this Act.

283. Chapter 8 lists out the transitional clauses, as the gas law regime was not governed by the Natural Gas Business Act before 2011. For instance, any operation of business by a natural gas utility enterprise holding a coal gas business license according to other regulations before this Act comes into effect should apply to a temporary gas supply business license within a year after the date on which this Act comes into effect.[464] Moreover, the qualifications of the related technical staff can guarantee the safety of the operations of the gas company. Therefore, safety technicians hired by natural gas utility enterprises or full-time technicians hired by natural gas utility pipeline installation enterprises before this Act comes into effect may

457. Ordinance on the Insured Amount of Public Liability Insurance of A Gas Business, 2011-07-06, available at: https://www.moeaboe.gov.tw/ECW/populace/Law/Content.aspx?menu_id=1023.
458. The format and details are further provided in the Ordinance on "Gas Supply Plan," Amended Date: 2015-08-24, available at: https://www.moeaboe.gov.tw/ECW/populace/Law/Content.aspx?menu_id=1024.
459. MOJ, Ordinance on the Establishment of "Geological Information Management System for Pipeline and Storage." 2019-03-28, available at: https://law.moj.gov.tw/LawClass/LawAll.aspx?pcode=J0130046.
460. MOJ, Ordinance on "Operational Data." 2011-07-07, available at: https://law.moj.gov.tw/LawClass/LawAll.aspx?pcode=J0130048.
461. Article 48 of the Natural Gas Business Act.
462. Article 50 of the Natural Gas Business Act.
463. Article 51 of the Natural Gas Business Act.
464. Article 68 of the Natural Gas Business Act, Natural Gas Enterprise Act, Amended Date: 2020-05-27, available at: https://law.moj.gov.tw/LawClass/LawHistory.aspx?pcode=j0130045; The Ordinance on the Permission of applying for gas supply from public gas utility, 2011-08-01, available at: https://law.moj.gov.tw/LawClass/LawAll.aspx?pcode=J0130050.

obtain the qualifications of natural gas pipeline installation professionals by passing a special technician skills certification test conducted by the central skill certification authorities.[465]

284. In order to ensure the gas quality, the government uses the administrative internal rules to govern the gas quality inspection works.[466] Also, with a view to setting up gas price, a special review commission for gas price calculation was set up by Organizational Ordinance.[467]

285. The Charges and Fees Act provides a legal basis for the government to charge a license or reviewing fee.[468] Additional details on charging are provided in a separate Ordinance on the Fees for Gas Utility.[469] For instance, when an application to be registered as a gas production utility is made under Article 5 of the Natural Gas Business Act, the registration fee is NTD 150,000 per case. Finally, as mentioned above, the official Promotion Plan on Microcomputer Gas Meters in promoting digital gas meters, natural gas utility enterprises are obliged to promote computerized gas metering systems.[470] A monitoring ordinance has been adopted to regulate, monitor, and award progress.[471] The MOEA also encourages the participation of local governments and awards innovations on part of the local government.[472]

IV. Energy Management Act

286. Apart from the legal regime mentioned above, according to Article 7 of the Energy Management Act, an energy supply business whose capacity is above a certain amount of energy as defined by the central authority must submit operational data on a monthly basis, set up energy storage installations, and ensure safety stock.

---

465. Article 69 of the Natural Gas Business Act, Natural Gas Enterprise Act, Amended Date: 2020-05-27, available at: https://law.moj.gov.tw/LawClass/LawHistory.aspx?pcode=j0130045; Ordinance on the Management of Professional staffs of natural gas pipeline, Amended Date: 2013-05-16, available at: https://law.moj.gov.tw/LawClass/LawAll.aspx?pcode=J0130057; Ordinance on the Test of Professional staffs of natural gas pipeline, 2011-08-08, available at: https://law.moj.gov.tw/LawClass/LawAll.aspx?pcode=J0130061.
466. Internal Ordinance on Gas Quality Inspection, 2017-07-06, available at: https://www.moeaboe.gov.tw/ECW/populace/Law/Content.aspx?menu_id=8490.
467. Organizational Ordinance for commission to review gas price calculation, 2016-09-22, available at: https://www.moeaboe.gov.tw/ECW/populace/Law/Content.aspx?menu_id=3328.
468. MOJ, Charges and Fees Act, Amended Date: 2017-06-14, available at: https://law.moj.gov.tw/ENG/LawClass/LawAll.aspx?pcode=G0340107.
469. MOJ, Ordinance on Fee for Gas Utility, Amended Date: 2018-01-30, available at: https://law.moj.gov.tw/LawClass/LawAll.aspx?pcode=J0130067.
470. Article 36 of the Natural Gas Business Act.
471. Monitoring Ordinance on progress of gas utility in promote computerized gas metering systems, 2018-04-24, available at: https://law.moea.gov.tw/LawContentSource.aspx?id=GL000556.
472. Ordinance on the Award to the promotion plan of computerized gas metering systems provided by the local governments, 2018-04-24, available at: https://www.moeaboe.gov.tw/ECW/populace/Law/Content.aspx?menu_id=6988.

Under the Ordinance, gas import/production and utility (selling gas to final customers through its own distribution pipeline) companies are subject to different requirements. Both kinds of companies should submit monthly data to the BOE on the 20th of each month.[473] The format is provided by another Ordinance.[474]

287. The demand-side regulation of the Energy Management Act applies to the user consuming natural gas to the tune of over 10,000,000 m^3. First, it should establish its own energy audit system and set objectives for energy conservation and execution and should report the energy consumption data to the competent central authority.[475] Second, it should employ and mandate a certain number of technicians or qualified energy administrators.[476] Finally, users who have massive investment and production plans that establish or expand the energy consumption facilities wherein energy consumption has a significant influence on the total national energy supply and demand as well as structure or regional energy balance, before such establishment or expansion, should submit an energy utilization manual for approval by MOEA.[477]

§2. Gas Liberalization

288. As noted above, since the 2000s, the policy has been to liberalize the natural gas business. In this section, the focus will be on the potential liberalization clause in the Natural Gas Business Bill and Act.

289. Article 32 of the Natural Gas Business Bill of 2003 and 2006 provides for TPA to all gas infrastructure owned by the CPC, including natural gas pipelines, LNG terminals, LNG storage, underground storage, etc. In this regard, the gas producer and importer can request the wheeling service from the CPC. The authority can also order the CPC to provide open access service, if doing so would be in the "public interest."[478] The rate and capacity of the wheeling service is determined by negotiation between the CPC and the requester. Yet, if negotiations fail, the requester can request the authority to make a decision.[479] In order to improve the authority's decision-making capacity, the infrastructure operator (i.e., the CPC) is required to submit the data on "maximum used capacity," "actual used capacity," "predicated used capacity," and other annual data to the authority.[480] The foregoing indicates that Taiwan was to adopt a mixed system of TPA. That is, a mixture of

473. Ordinance on Energy User Using Large Amount of Energy. Amended Date: 2018-03-09, available at: https://www.moeaboe.gov.tw/ECW/populace/Law/Content.aspx?menu_id=615.
474. Annex Table 3: Gas Business Reporting Form, available at: https://www.moeaboe.gov.tw/ECW/main/Law/wHandEditorFile.ashx?file_id=5028.
475. Articles 9, 12 of the Energy Management Act.
476. Article 11 of the Energy Management Act.
477. Article 16 of the Energy Management Act.
478. Article 32(1) of the Natural Gas Business Bill of 2003 and 2006.
479. Article 32(2) of the Natural Gas Business Bill of 2003 and 2006.
480. Article 32(3) of the Natural Gas Business Bill of 2003 and 2006.

negotiated third party access (NTPA) and "conditional (public interest) RTPA."[481] Yet, this TPA clause was deleted in the final adopted version of the Natural Gas Business Act of 2011.

290. However, there are other potential "liberalization" clauses in the current Natural Gas Business Act of 2011. First, an account unbundling scheme is stipulated.[482] Therefore, a gas company is required to create separate accounts for its gas business and other businesses. However, as there is no service unbundling requirement, a gas business is not required to provide its service separately. Since consumers are unable to arrange separately different gas services, such as a pipeline and a supply, it is impossible to encourage competition between gas companies.

291. Another potential liberalization clause is the licensing regime for gas producers and importers. It seems every company can apply for an import or production license[483] and the upstream wholesale market seems open to competition. Yet, in reality, it is impossible to facilitate open competition in Taiwan's current market situation. As Taiwan imports gas in the form of LNG, how can a company become an importer without access to LNG facilities and storage? In addition, as Taiwan is running out of domestic gas, this area of production is not attractive for new entrants.

292. From that perspective, Taiwan's natural gas liberalization bill looks very peculiar. First, there were few liberalization clauses in the Natural Gas Business Bill of 2003 and 2006. Only the wheeling clause can be seen as a liberalization clause. Second, this sole liberalization clause is unclear from a legal standpoint and so is difficult to implement. Fortunately, this clause was not passed. Third, the Natural Gas Business Bill was supposed to be a liberalization bill. Yet, interestingly, the removal of only one wheeling clause can turn it into the regulations for a monopoly gas industry as well. All of these unique features reflect one simple idea: that the Taiwanese government had no intention of injecting liberalization into the gas bill from the very beginning. Gas liberalization is very difficult to achieve in Taiwan, due to the aggressive lobbying of the state-owned CPC.

§3. Gas Supply Security

293. The easiest way to ensure the security of the gas supply is to imitate the oil stockpile regime and develop a gas "stockpile" regime. However, it is more difficult to store gas than oil. In addition, there is also a lack of suitable underground geological storage in Taiwan.

---

481. For a further discussion, *see* Anton Ming-Zhi Gao, Regulating Gas Liberalization. A Comparative Study on Unbundling and Open Access Regimes in the US, Europe, Japan, South Korea and Taiwan (2010).
482. Articles 32, 33, 40 of the Natural Gas Business Act of 2011.
483. Article 5 of the Natural Gas Business Act of 2011.

294. Yet, there has been discussion about introducing a thirty-day stockpile requirement for gas, with a view to improving gas security and responding to the gas supply shortage of the CPC that led to an electricity outage in early 2002. Besides, there was also discussion on whether the operators of gas-fired power plants should adhere to the coal stockpile requirement of coal-fired power plants and stock gas for a certain period. Yet, these discussions were not enacted into law. Even though these discussions were not subsequently incorporated into legislation, the CPC remains very active in expanding its gas stockpile. Based on different scenarios, Taiwan's gas stockpile is around 5–15 days. For example, if the gas is used for base-load power plants, then the gas stockpile would drop dramatically from 15 to 7 days' supply.

295. The Natural Gas Business Act of 2011 authorizes the central authority to determine the gas stockpile requirements for "gas producer" and "gas importers."[484] Recently, with a view to reflect the 50% gas-fired power plants by 2025, the stockpile Ordinance was revised and published on August 27, 2018. The detailed Ordinance requires a gas production company to prepare a half-day storage capacity and to store the half-day volume, and more stringent rules are applied to gas importers.[485] To alleviate the burden on them, there is a gradual timeline to increase the stockpile:

- August 27, 2018 to the end of 2021: Preparing capacity for 15 days/stockpile volume for 7 days.
- January 1, 2021 to the end of 2024: Preparing capacity for 16 days/stockpile volume for 8 days.
- January 1, 2025 to the end of 2026: Preparing capacity for 20 days/stockpile volume for 11 days.
- Starting from January 1, 2026: Preparing capacity for 24 days/stockpile volume for 14 days.

296. The gas rationing scheme is relevant to gas security as well. In the event of a natural gas shortage or great fluctuation in prices that may affect the steady supply of domestic natural gas or national security, the MOEA may carry out regulatory measures that are mandatory, with respect to natural gas supply and sale prices.[486] For instance, the reduction of the supply ratio is defined under Article 5 of the Ordinance[487] at the time of the gas shortage. The sequence and reduction ratio is provided as follows:

---

484. Article 31 of the Natural Gas Business Act.
485. Stockpile Ordinance, Amended Date: 2018-08-27, available at: https://www.moeaboe.gov.tw/ECW/populace/Law/Content.aspx?menu_id=1029.
486. Article 45 of the Natural Gas Business Act.
487. MOJ, The Ordinance on mandatory measures regarding natural gas supply and sell price, 2013-09-17, available at: https://law.moj.gov.tw/LawClass/LawAll.aspx?pcode=J0130054.

297. The gas supply disruption can be caused by disasters. When transmission and storage equipment may involve the risk of causing disasters, natural gas enterprises should immediately take necessary precautions or improvement measures.[488] When disasters, accidents, or urgent circumstances occur, natural gas enterprises should report to the relevant authorities.[489] The reporting detailed rules are provided in the Ordinance.[490] Finally, to prepare well to deal with these disasters, natural gas enterprises should institute disaster prevention measures, including devices on their transmission and storage equipment.[491] These equipment are subject to the maintenance requirement in the Ordinance.[492]

298. There are preventive measures to reinforce transportation facilities. When natural gas enterprises find that their gas transmission pipelines are eroded or are showing signs that pose safety concerns, they should replace them at once.[493] As for planning toward replacement, natural gas enterprises should draft their inspection and replacement projects for the gas transmission pipelines for the next year before October 31 of each year, and report these plans to the MOEA.[494] Each natural gas utility enterprise should set aside a reserve fund for gas transmission pipeline replacement and deposit the amount in a special account created in a financial institution.[495] Additional details are provided by the Ordinance.[496]

(1) Electricity utility: reduction of 10% average daily gas supply
(2) CHP: reduction of 5% average daily gas supply
(3) Industrial users: reduction of 5% average daily gas supply
(4) Electricity utility: further reduction of 10% average daily gas supply
(5) CHP: further reduction of 5% average daily gas supply
(6) Industrial users: further reduction of 5% average daily gas supply
(7) Transportation users: reduction of 10% average daily gas supply
(8) Gas utility: reduction of 10% average daily gas supply.

§4. Private Participation in Developing Gas Infrastructure

299. In order to encourage private participation in public infrastructure projects, an incentive law was adopted in 2001.[497] Gas transportation and storage related

488. Article 16 of the Natural Gas Business Act.
489. Article 17 of the Natural Gas Business Act.
490. The Ordinance on the reporting at the time of gas disaster or urgent accident, 2019-05-30, available at: https://law.moj.gov.tw/LawClass/LawAll.aspx?pcode=J0130060.
491. Article 13(2) of the Natural Gas Business Act.
492. Ordinance on the Maintenance of disaster prevention measures of transmission and storage equipment, 2018-10-24, available at: https://law.moj.gov.tw/LawClass/LawAll.aspx?pcode=J0130056.
493. Article 51(1) of the Natural Gas Business Act.
494. Article 51(3) of the Natural Gas Business Act.
495. Article 54 of the Natural Gas Business Act.
496. Ordinance on the reserve fund for gas transmission pipeline replacement of gas utilities, 2017-11-16, available at: https://law.moj.gov.tw/LawClass/LawAll.aspx?pcode=J0130053.
497. Act on Promotion of Private Participation in Infrastructure Projects, Amended Date: 2016-11-21, available at: https://law.moj.gov.tw/LawClass/LawAll.aspx?pcode=D0070062.

infrastructure are all regarded as "public infrastructure" under this Act.[498] There are six main ways for the private sector to participate in public infrastructure:[499]

(1) The private institution invests in the construction and operation of new infrastructure, and upon the expiration of the operation period, it transfers the ownership of the infrastructure to the government.
(2) The private institution invests in the construction of infrastructure and upon completion, relinquishes the ownership to the government without compensation. The government then lets the private institution operate the infrastructure. Upon expiration of the operation period, the right to operate reverts to the government.
(3) The private institution invests in the construction of infrastructure. Upon completion, the government acquires ownership by paying the construction expenses in a lump sum or in installments. The government then lets the private institution operate the infrastructure. Upon expiration of the operation period, the right to operate reverts to the government.

---

498. Article 3 of Act on Promotion of Private Participation in Infrastructure Projects: "The term 'infrastructure project' as referred to herein shall mean a project for constructing any of following facilities for public use and for promotion of public interest:

1. Transportation facilities and common conduits;
2. Environmental pollution prevention facilities;
3. Sewerage, water supply and water conservancy facilities;
4. Sanitation and medical facilities;
5. Social and labor welfare facilities;
6. Cultural and educational facilities;
7. Tourist attractions and lodgings;
8. Power facilities and public gas and fuel supply facilities;
9. Sports facilities;
10. Parks and green spaces;
11. Industrial, commercial and hi-tech facilities;
12. Development of new towns;
13. Agricultural facilities; and
14. Government office buildings."

Art. 13 of Implementation Ordinance of Act on Promotion of Private Participation in Infrastructure Projects: "The public gas and fuel supply facilities specified in Subparagraph 8, Paragraph 1, Art. 3 of the Act shall mean any of the following facilities designated by the competent central authorities of the relevant industries for public gaseous fuel supply enterprises to pipe, store, and regulate gaseous fuel:

1. Tanks, pipes, sites, and affiliated facilities for gaseous fuel storage;
2. Pipelines, pressure regulating stations, and related distribution facilities laid from the source;
3. Facilities for blending air or other flammable gas to adjust the calorific value of gaseous fuel;
4. Facilities for gasifying and liquefying gaseous fuel; and
5. Facilities for loading and unloading liquefied gaseous fuel."

499. Article 8 of Act on Promotion of Private Participation in Infrastructure Projects.

(4) The private institution invests in the extension, reconstruction, and/or repair of existing infrastructure and operates it. Upon expiration of the operation period, the right to operate reverts to the government.
(5) The private institution operates infrastructure built with investment from the government. Upon expiration of the operation period, the right to operate reverts to the government.
(6) To support government policy, the private institution invests in the construction of infrastructure on private land provided by the private institution itself, has ownership thereof upon completion of the construction, and then either operates the infrastructure by itself or commissions a third party to operate it.

Part V. Regulatory Framework for Nuclear Energy

§1. Nuclear Power in Energy Policy

300. After World War II, the idea of peaceful use of nuclear power as promoted by the US was put high on the agenda. Apart from this international factor, due to the lack of domestic energy resources, the semi-indigenous nature of nuclear power made it an important electricity resource in Taiwan. Unlike the slow development of Taiwan's energy law, the development of nuclear law or atomic energy law and a competent regulating authority was quite rapid. The legal framework was established before the deployment of the technology and the complete construction of nuclear power plants. The Atomic Energy Act was adopted on May 9, 1968,[500] and a very high level authority to regulate the development of atomic energy was created under the Act on the Atomic Energy Council of the Executive Yuan (December 3, 1970).[501] Even the compensation scheme for nuclear disasters was developed in 1971.[502] Under this regime, the first nuclear power plant was approved in 1970 and its construction began in 1971.

301. Due to the effects of the 1973 and 1979 oil crises, the Taiwan government realized the importance of energy security and decided to follow the route taken by Japan and other OECD countries to develop nuclear power plants. Even as Taiwan recognized its reliance on imported energy, the development of nuclear power contributed to energy security. The 1979 Taiwan Energy Policy listed the expansion of nuclear power plants as a priority. The No. 1 nuclear power plant was considered as one of the Top 10 Infrastructures of National Importance and was commissioned and completed in 1977–1979.[503] The No. 2 and No, 3 nuclear power plants were listed among the further Top 12 Infrastructures of National Importance and quickly completed in 1981 and 1984, respectively. This period can be seen as a golden age for nuclear power plants.

---

500. Atomic Energy Act, Amended Date: 1971-12-24, available at: https://law.moj.gov.tw/ENG/LawClass/LawAll.aspx?pcode=J0160001.
501. Act on the Atomic Energy Council of the Executive Yuan, 2000-11-23, available at: https://law.moj.gov.tw/LawClass/LawAll.aspx?pcode=J0000040.
502. MOJ, Nuclear Damage Compensation Law, 1971-07-20, Amended Date: 1997-05-14, available at: https://law.moj.gov.tw/ENG/LawClass/LawHistory.aspx?pcode=J0160003.
503. Taiwan Panorama, 1976 Building the Future: Ten Major Construction Projects, December 2015, available at: https://www.taiwan-panorama.com/en/Articles/Details?Guid=55e423d1-c5c2-4222-b8aa-bdbd01081c08&CatId=9.

302. After the inception of the UNFCCC, the 1996 Taiwan Energy Policy and Measures declared nuclear power to be very important in order to provide energy security, environmental safety, and emission reductions.[504] Yet, the Chernobyl nuclear disaster in 1986 seemed to affect adversely the promotion of the fourth Nuclear Power and drew strong objections from citizens. This controversial project began construction in 1999 but is still not completed as yet (2020).

303. Then from 2000 up to the present, there was a policy and legislative change toward nuclear power. In the early 2000s, the political climate started to turn against nuclear power, as the ruling party in power for more than fifty years lost the 2000 presidential election. In 2000, the pro-green DPP won the presidential election. Then, following Germany's nuclear phase-out in 1998,[505] it proposed a nuclear phase-out and nuclear-free homeland, which would terminate the construction of a fourth nuclear power plant and phase out the operation of the three existing nuclear power plants at the 40th year.[506] In particular, this policy proposal mandated the Taiwan Power Company (Tai-Power), the state-owned electricity provider, not to enforce the budget to construct the fourth power plant, which led to a boycott in parliament by the majority of the opposition Nationalist Party (KMT). These tensions created governmental dysfunctions, and to deal with the impasse, the DPP sought a decision from the Constitutional Court. The Constitutional Court overturned the budget mandate in Interpretation 520.[507] A consensus to promote a nuclear free homeland was reached between the Executive Yuan and the Parliament in 2001. Consequently, the DPP was compelled to resume construction, and it shifted its anti-nuclear position to the softer approach of seeking a nuclear-free homeland. In February 2001, the administrative and legislative branch of the government adopted a nuclear-free homeland agreement.[508] The first version of the nuclear phase-out bill was proposed in 2001. A Nuclear-Free Homeland Commission in the Executive Yuan was established in 2002.[509] The Committee was organized into eight subcommittees, each led by Cabinet members, to manage the various aspects of the plan including education, public outreach, supervising the Lungmen project, creating regulations, managing radioactive waste, decommissioning nuclear power plants, developing clean energy, and adjusting the energy structure.[510] The idea of a

---

504. MOEABOE, Taiwan Energy Policy and Measures (1997).
505. *See, e.g.*, Kerstine Appunn, The history behind Germany's nuclear phase-out, Jan. 2, 2018, available at: https://www.cleanenergywire.org/factsheets/history-behind-germanys-nuclear-phase-out.
506. *See, e.g.*, Wang To-far, Germany's nuclear policy a model, available at: http://www.taipeitimes.com/News/editorials/archives/2003/04/07/0000201189.
507. Toward a nuclear-free homeland, Wednesday, Sep. 26, 2012, available at: http://en-test.taiwantt.org.tw/index.php?option=com_content&view=article&id=3114:toward-a-nuclear-free-homeland&catid=15:taipei-times&Itemid=3.
508. Henry Philippens, A Nuclear-Free Taiwan by 2025? An Unlikely Target, available at: https://www.globalasia.org/v6no4/feature/a-nuclear-free-taiwan-by-2025-an-unlikely-target_henry-philippens.
509. Nuclear Free Homeland Commission, Taiwan's Choice: Nuclear-Free Homeland, 2003, available at: http://www.taiwangreenenergy.org.tw/files/Policy/20071029141155.pdf
510. The 2002 AIT-TECRO JSCCNC Annual Meeting Joint Plenary Session 9 am, Monday, Dec. 9, 2002, General Remarks by Dr. Min-shen Ouyang, Chairman, AEC, available at: https://www.aec.gov.tw/english/historical/files/minister/new_2002.pdf.

nuclear-free homeland was integrated into the Environmental Basic Act at the end of 2002.[511] A National Nuclear-Free Homeland Conference was held and the Nuclear-Free Homeland Bill (the second generation nuclear phase-out law) was proposed; the Nuclear-Free Homeland Action Plan was adopted in 2003. This series of actions turned the tide against the development of nuclear power. However, since 2005, the promotion of a nuclear-free homeland seemed to lose momentum in the second term of this new presidency. The going into effect of the Kyoto Protocol also affected the government's ambition with regard to promoting a nuclear phase out. Hence, the Energy White Paper of 2005 made only passing reference to the concept of a nuclear-free homeland. This was a reflection of the conflict between nuclear phase-out and emission reduction goals. Including the idea of a nuclear-free homeland did not change the nuclear situation. The three nuclear power plants operated as before, and the planned fourth nuclear power plant obtained funding from the DPP government, which enabled its continued construction.

304. In 2008, the climate changed again with a change in government. The idea of a nuclear-free homeland lost momentum in 2008 when the KMT won the presidential election. During the KMT's presidency, the idea of extending the lives of the nuclear power plants from forty to fifty or even sixty years was brought up. Within less than one month of swearing in the new president (May 20, 2008), the new "Sustainable Energy Policy Framework" was adopted, on June 5, 2008, which identified nuclear power as a "no-carbon energy option" in achieving clean energy, low emission energy, and energy diversity targets. After the Copenhagen COP 15 meeting in 2009 and the Taiwanese NAMAs,[512] the new climate and energy package (Master Plan on Energy Conservation and Emission Reduction 2010) seemed to enhance the role of nuclear power to historically high levels. On the one hand, nuclear power's role in tackling climate change was again heavily stressed. Even though it was urged that nuclear power be developed in harmony with the "Nuclear Power Rational Utilization Assessment," the possibility of extending the life of the existing nuclear power plants presented itself. On the other hand, under the energy technology initiative, nuclear power technology is promoted under the National Energy R&D Program, which seems to imply an enhancing of the role of nuclear power to that of an export-oriented industry. This policy direction would be a great help for the development of nuclear power.

305. In February 2011, the draft of the Strategic Environmental Assessment (SEA) Report of the Energy Development Framework (the 2020 energy vision) was announced. Two scenarios, nuclear life expansion and normal decommission, were

511. Article 23 of the Environmental Basic Act: "The government shall establish plans to gradually achieve the goal of becoming a nuclear-free country. The government shall also strengthen nuclear safety management and control, protections against radiation, and the management of radioactive materials and monitoring of environmental radiation to safeguard the public from the dangers of radiation exposure."

512. Taiwan's Bid for Meaningful Participation in the UNFCCC, Oct. 2014, available at: http://www.mofa.gov.tw/Upload/RelFile/1390/145337/103%E5%B9%B4UNFCCC%E8%AA%AA%E5%B8%96(%E8%8B%B1%E6%96%87%E7%89%88).doc.

evaluated and the life expansion scenario was favored by the government. The government's position was severely criticized by the environmental NGOs. After the Fukushima accident in Japan, the government promised to re-evaluate the role of nuclear power. In April 2014, after large-scale demonstrations against nuclear power plants, the pro-nuclear government decided to halt construction. The first reactor was sealed after the completion of safety checks, and construction of the second reactor was stopped. After 2016, the anti-nuclear party won the election. The government asked Tai-Power to return the fuel rods to the United States. Tai-Power had already sent back several fuel rods since mid-2018.[513]

306. This author will discuss the nuclear promotion legislations, nuclear regulatory legislations, and nuclear homeland legislations against this policy background over the years.

§2. Pro-Nuclear Power Legislative Scheme

307. The Atomic Energy Act of 1968 and 1971 were considered to be the first generation of nuclear energy legislations. Under these legislations, nuclear R&D was certainly promoted in Chapter III Research and Development on Nuclear Science and Technology. For example, the establishment of a nuclear science and technology institution is encouraged by Article 10 of the Atomic Energy Act of 1971.[514] Similarly, nuclear energy's peaceful use is encouraged in the fields of agriculture and medicine.[515] Finally, nuclear power plants were also facilitated by the "nuclear power clause" under Article 17 of the Atomic Energy Act.[516] Under this scheme, the Nuclear Power Plants Nos. 1–4 were promoted. However, it is unclear why during the nuclear-free homeland phase, this clause was not revised.

308. In order to respond to the need to regulate Taiwan's energy mix, the idea of an Energy Development Framework was discussed at the 2005 National Energy Conference, which proposed an amendment to the Energy Management Act in 2007; the amendment was adopted by the Parliament and became effective on July 8, 2009. It provides that "in order to maintain nation-wide energy security, while taking into account economic growth and environmental impacts, the competent

513. George Liao, 1st batch of fuel rods for the 4th Nuclear Power Plant has likely been transported out of Taiwan, 2018/07/04, Taiwan News, available at: *https://www.taiwannews.com.tw/en/news/3474254*; Taipower readies 2nd batch of nuclear fuel rods for US return, 2018/09/05, available at: http://focustaiwan.tw/news/asoc/201809050007.aspx.

514. Article 10 of Atomic Energy Act: "The Atomic Energy Council may request the approval of the Executive Yuan to establish departments of research and development for nuclear science and technology at relevant science research institutions."

515. Article 19 of Atomic Energy Act: "As for the application of atomic energy in agriculture, industry, and medicine, the Atomic Energy Council shall supervise and guide related organizations to proceed cooperatively."

516. Article 17 of Atomic Energy Act: "For the purpose of nuclear research and the production of radioactive material for peaceful uses, besides improving the existing research reactor, the Atomic Energy Council may, according to the practical needs, request the Executive Yuan to allocate special funds to set up additional nuclear reactors and other facilities."

authority should enact the Energy Development Framework, and submit it for the approval of the Executive Yuan. If approved by the Executive Yuan, the competent authority should implement it accordingly."[517]

309. Against the policy background to encourage the development of nuclear power plants as a way of dealing with climate change, the Sustainable Energy Policy Framework[518] and related documents[519] promoted the role of nuclear power in the energy mix.

310. The original legislative purpose of this Energy Development Framework was to determine an overall prospective energy mix for a certain period. Thus, it seemed "neutral" with regard to nuclear power, neither promoting nor hindering its development. Yet, as nuclear power would unavoidably be one of the most important items in this energy mix, the future of nuclear power would be either devalued or appreciated under this framework. As noted above, the first draft Energy Development Framework favored the use of nuclear power plants. Hence, this scheme could also be used to promote nuclear power. However, the doubled-edged effects of this scheme were also possible. Thus, the nuclear-free homeland policy by 2025 was now back in the 2017 Energy Development Framework.[520]

311. As three major nuclear disasters have occurred globally and Taiwan is facing the issue of nuclear waste disposal, the government has re-examined the position of nuclear power generation and recognized the necessity of achieving a nuclear-free homeland as soon as possible. The "Basic Environment Act" promulgated in 2002 showed that the government is bound to set a plan to reach the target of a nuclear-free homeland. Therefore, the resources devoted should be increased, and energy transition including energy saving, energy exploration, energy storage, and smart system integration must be comprehensively accelerated to reduce the share of nuclear power generation and achieve the target of a nuclear-free homeland by 2025.

§3. NUCLEAR POWER REGULATORY LEGAL SCHEME

I. Phase I: 1970–2000

312. The development of Taiwan's nuclear power regulatory regime can be divided into phases in accordance with the parallel development of a nuclear policy.

---

517. Article 1(2) of Energy Management Act.
518. "(3) Increase energy supply diversity. Reconsider nuclear power as a no-carbon energy option." *See* MOEA, Framework of Taiwan's Sustainable Energy Policy, 2008.06.05, available at: www.epa.gov.tw/FileLink/FileHandler.ashx?file=11942.
519. "(1) Secure energy supply and promote energy diversity. Carry out the 2.7 million-kilowatt operation of the 4th nuclear power plant project as scheduled, and continue the 5.14 million-kilowatt operations of the 1st, 2nd, and 3rd nuclear power plants."
520. Guidelines on Energy Development (2017 Energy Development Framework), April 2017, available at: https://www.moeaboe.gov.tw/ECW/main/content/wHandMenuFile.ashx?file_id=559.

In the early stages, minor laws were in place, while the regulatory regime focused on the legitimacy of the authority and administrative Ordinances. On the one hand, in order to ensure the legitimacy of the authority and other related nuclear institutions, intense legislation was enacted regarding the nuclear administrative organizations. The Organizational Acts relating to the AEC,[521] the Radioactive Material Management Agency[522] (under the AEC), the Radiation Detection Center (under the AEC),[523] and the Nuclear Research Institution (under the AEC)[524] were promulgated in 1970, 1980, 1980, and 1990, respectively.

313. However, the Atomic Energy Act plays the main role in regulation since there is a dearth of laws regarding regulatory actions. For instance, in the important regulatory fields such as nuclear reactor regulation,[525] radiation protection,[526] and radioactive waste management,[527] there were only administrative regulatory Ordinances available. The only Act at that time was the Compensation Act for Nuclear Damage of 1971.[528] There were no Acts and Ordinances relating to nuclear reactor waste disposal, siting, etc.

314. With regard to the regulation of the nuclear power reactors, the main Act and provision governing the regulation of nuclear power plants is Article 23 of the Atomic Energy Act[529] and the Organization Act on AEC. Under the latter Act, a professional commission was created under an Organizational Ordinance to advise on

---

521. Organizational Acts relating to the Atomic Energy Council.
522. Organizational Acts relating to Radioactive Material Management Agency.
523. Organizational Acts relating to Radiation Detection Center.
524. Organizational Acts relating to Nuclear Research Institution (under the AEC).
525. *See, e.g.*, Monitoring Ordinance on Operation of Nuclear Power Plants, the Ordinance on the Renewal of Licenses for Nuclear Power Plants, etc.
526. *See, e.g.*, Ordinance on the Regulation of Applying for the Sales of Products Containing Radioactive Substances, etc.
527. *See, e.g.*, the Ordinance on Management of Radioactive Waste.
528. Compensation Act for Nuclear Damage of 1971; last revised in May 1997.
529. CHAPTER V Control of Nuclear Source Material, Nuclear Fuel, and Reactors, Art. 23, Atomic Energy Act: "Control of nuclear reactors shall be governed by the following regulations:

(1) Any applicant for the construction of a nuclear reactor shall present a filled-out application to the Atomic Energy Council for approval and the issuance of a construction permit.
(2) Upon the completion of the construction of a nuclear reactor, a request shall be submitted to the Atomic Energy Council for inspection.
(3) Prior to operation of any nuclear reactor, a safety analysis report of the reactor shall be submitted to the Atomic Energy Council for review, approval, and the issuance of an operating license.
(4) Operation of nuclear reactors shall be in compliance with the regulations of the Atomic Energy Council which shall send inspectors for inspection.
(5) Any design change to be made during the construction phase of any nuclear reactor or any change of equipment due to updating of the design after operation of the reactor shall be reported in advance to the Atomic Energy Council for approval.
(6) Without the approval of the Atomic Energy Council, a licensee shall not transfer the license or the privilege granted by the license to any other person.
(7) The transfer or removal of any nuclear reactor, unless approved by the Atomic Energy Council, is not allowed.

nuclear reactor safety.[530] In accordance with the former Acts, there are also very detailed regulations on nuclear plants' components[531] as well as on inspection and monitoring issues during the operation period.[532]

315. The aforementioned AEC and its regulations provide the *ex post* regulations and *ex ante* licensing regime for the development of nuclear power plants. Generally, the AEC, rather than the EPA, is responsible for the EHS concerns resulting from nuclear and atomic energy activities. However, due to these environmental concerns, the EPA seeks to regulate the residue from nuclear power activity. In this regard, the general EIA regime is relevant. The EIA Guideline for Radioactive Waste Storage Sites of 1995, EIA Guideline for Nuclear Power Plants of 1995, and the subsequent EIA Operation Ordinance for Development Projects of 1997[533] all provided regulations for nuclear power plants and related installations. However, because the Nuclear Power Plants No. 1 to No. 3 were developed before 1995, the main facility subject to this requirement is Nuclear Power No. 4.

II. Second Phase: After 2000

316. The aforementioned regulatory environment faced a dramatic challenge after the change in government in 2000. The promotion of the nuclear-free idea led to changes in policy regarding nuclear power plants and also to the evaluation of the current, insufficient regulatory and legal framework that was subject to the whims of the administration in power. A large-scale juridification was launched whose objective was to bring nuclear power plants under legal control.

317. In the most important field of **reactor regulation**, a new Act, the Act on Regulating Nuclear Reactors of 2003, was promulgated.[534] Then the existing eight administrative ordinances were abolished[535] and twenty-eight administrative measures were created under the regulatory regime of this Act.[536] Several important regulatory issues were further developed under this legal regime, including the

---

(8) For the operation of nuclear reactors, the utilization of nuclear fuel, and the production of radioactive materials, complete records shall be kept and submitted periodically to the Atomic Energy Council, and for auditing purposes the Atomic Energy Council may dispatch personnel to carry out inspection from time to time."

530. Organization Ordinance on Advisory Commission on Nuclear Installation Safety.
531. Technical Ordinance on Nuclear Components.
532. Inspection and Monitoring Ordinance on Nuclear Power Plants during Operational Period.
533. Enacted on Dec. 31, 1997; last revised on Feb. 26, 2010. For English version, *see* Standards for Determining Specific Items and Scope of Environmental Impact Assessments for Development Activities, available at: http://law.epa.gov.tw/en/laws/571925793.html.
534. MOJ, Nuclear Reactor Facilities Regulation Act, 2003-01-15, available at: https://law.moj.gov.tw/ENG/LawClass/LawAll.aspx?pcode=J0160019.
535. For example, the abolishment of Organization Ordinance on Advisory Commission on Nuclear Installation Safety, available at: http://erss.aec.gov.tw/law/LawContent.aspx?id=FL010783.
536. The complete list of related regulations, available at: https://erss.aec.gov.tw/law/LawCategoryMain.aspx?CategoryID=003.

health of operational personnel of the nuclear power reactors, and the Ordinance on Applying for Nuclear Reactor Construction Licenses. Furthermore, in the field of **ionizing radiation protection,** the Ionizing Radiation Protection Act of 2002 was enacted, whereas six existing administrative ordinances were abolished[537] and replaced by forty-eight administrative measures.[538] There was a similar development in the field of "radioactive materials management"[539] for nuclear source materials, nuclear fuel, radioactive waste,[540] radioactive waste disposal sites,[541] nuclear accident emergency response,[542] etc. Further, the transparency of and public participation in nuclear affairs are becoming more noticeable. The Ordinance on Governmental Information Disclosure of the AEC[543] and Ordinance for Citizens to Participate in the AEC-related Activities[544] formed part of a spider-web-like regulatory regime from top to bottom that was developed between 2000 and 2008. After this reform trend, the regulatory regime for nuclear activities was transformed from a regime that relied on institutions to a regime that was governed by laws and their sub-legislations. The overall legal framework for nuclear activities is illustrated in Figure 3.

537. AEC, Laws and Regulations Retrieving System, available at: http://erss.aec.gov.tw/law/LawCategoryContentList.aspx?id=004&CategoryList=004 (visited on Oct. 10, 2020).
538. AEC, Laws and Regulations Retrieving System, available at: https://erss.aec.gov.tw/law/LawCategoryMain.aspx?CategoryID=004 (visited on Oct. 10, 2020).
539. Radioactive Material Management Act of 2002, Dec. 25, 2002.
540. Radioactive Materials Management Act of 2002. The Ordinance on Radioactive Waste Management was abolished then.
541. Act on Siting of Final Disposal Site for Low Radioactive Waste of 2006, May 2006.
542. Act on Emergency Response for Nuclear Accidents, Dec. 24, 2003.
543. The Ordinance on Governmental Information Disclosure of the AEC, 2002-05-18, Amended Date: 2019-10-22, available at: https://erss.aec.gov.tw/law/LawContent.aspx?id=GL000021.
544. Ordinance for Citizens to Participate in ACE-related activities, 2002-02-05, available at: https://erss.aec.gov.tw/law/LawContent.aspx?id=GL000018.

Figure 3 Regulatory Legal Framework of Atomic Energy in Taiwan

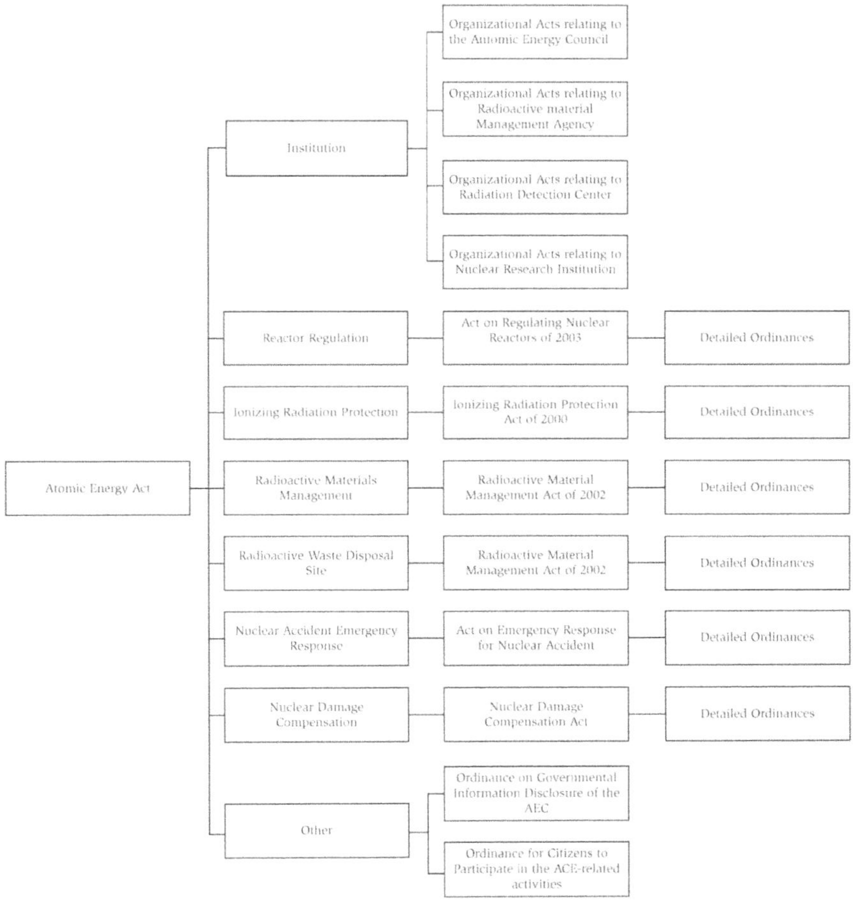

Source: Compiled by the author.

§4. NUCLEAR PHASE-OUT LEGISLATIVE SCHEME: NUCLEAR-FREE HOMELAND BILL

318. After the change in government in 2000, the opposition and the green party took power and started to follow Germany's approach in promoting the idea of "Nuclear Phase out." The Executive Yuan announced the suspension of the construction of Nuclear Power No. 4 at the end of 2000, which suspension led to an issue of political and constitutional law. Even though the issue was dealt with by the Grand Justice of Taiwan, the ambiguous judgment could not resolve this political chaos. There seemed no clear judgment as to whether the suspension decision of the Executive was right or wrong. This issue also led to tension between the Executive Yuan and the Parliament. The functioning of the national machine came to a standstill. In order to resolve this impasse, there were intensive discussions between the ruling party and the opposition party in the Parliament. Finally, a consensus was reached in February 2001 to continue the construction of the Nuclear Power No. 4 plant while pursuing the idea of a "nuclear-free homeland" ("Nuclear-Free Consensus"). It resulted in serious nuclear-free homeland activities in the coming years. However, as there was no concrete context and definition for this new term—Nuclear-Free Homeland—a lot of effort was put into developing this idea.

I. Proposal of Nuclear Phase-Out Bill in 2001

319. In order to pursue the goal of a nuclear-free homeland, in February 2001, the Executive Yuan adopted a bottom-up approach to develop this objective. It ordered the MOEA to consult with the AEC and propose energy-related bills to implement the idea of a nuclear-free homeland, which would be submitted to Parliament for its deliberation. Furthermore, the MOEA was also to consider stopping the operation of the existing three nuclear power plants on the condition that it would not affect the electricity supply security of Taiwan.[545]

320. In view of this call, the MOEAEC started to interpret the idea of a nuclear-free homeland, and proposed the Nuclear Phase-Out Bill to the MOEA. The MOEA then approved it immediately in July 2001 and delivered it to the Executive Yuan for its deliberation.

321. In this bill, the idea of a nuclear-free homeland was only mentioned in the Explanatory Note (the foreword) of the bill. The MOEAEC interpreted the concept of this term as "nuclear phase out." The bill specified the condition for the phasing out of the existing four nuclear power plants in Article 5. The follow is the essence of this bill, notwithstanding its very unclear and ambiguous conditions:

(1) From the date of phase out, the annual electricity reserve capacity is able to be maintained at an excess of 15% for the next seven years.
(2) From the date of phase out, the electricity price does not exceed 15% within seven years.
(3) The compensation to Tai-Power as a result of the phase-out decision would not cause a "significant" financial burden to the government.
(4) The phase out would not cause any infringement of international treaties signed by the government.

545. The Decision of the Executive Yuan on Feb. 14, 2001, available at: http://www.ey.gov.tw/ct.asp?xItem=21449&ctNode=232&mp=21.

322. This bill is unique in Taiwanese energy law from the following two aspects. First, bearing in mind the usual sequence in which policy comes first, then the law, this was the first time in history that the legal instrument came before the policy, as at that time, the energy policy document promoting nuclear power in Taiwan was still in effect. Second, in terms of nuclear development laws, this was also the first time that Taiwan sought to develop a legal regime that "discouraged" the development of nuclear power. However, in the prevailing political climate, the Executive Yuan seemed to consider this bill, particularly the conditions, too weak, too ambiguous, and too difficult to achieve the objective of nuclear phase out. The bill was insufficiently discussed; further, the minister without portfolio at the level of the Executive Yuan began to notice the "German" phase-out approach and decided to adopt a top-down approach, promoting the "Nuclear-free Homeland Bill" idea.

II. Integration into Environmental Basic Act in 2002

323. The bill related to the nuclear-free homeland idea took some time. Yet, the administrative sector was quite eager in promoting the idea of a nuclear-free homeland. As the concerns related to nuclear energy development were also relevant to the environment-related legislations, the concept of the "nuclear-free homeland" was integrated into the final version of Article 23 of the Environmental Basic Act and approved by the Parliament on November 19, 2002. Even though the nuclear-free homeland is an empty and open concept in Article 23, it was helpful in encouraging serious action on the proposal of a Nuclear-free Homeland Bill, the holding of a National Nuclear-free Homeland Conference, and the adoption of a Nuclear-free Homeland Action Plan, etc.

324. The emptiness of this wording is reflected in the following aspect. In comparison with the Nuclear-Free Consensus, Article 23 does not deal with the issue of whether construction of the Nuclear Power No. 4 plant should continue. Second, unlike the phase-out bill dealing with the fate of Nuclear Power Nos. 1–3, this aspect is unclear in the Environmental Basic Act.

325. A closer look at the development of this concept in the Basic Act reveals its stealthy nature during the legislative process. If the Nuclear-Free Consensus were the influence or the inspiration for Article 23, according to the past legislative practice it should have been mentioned in either the Explanatory Note of the overall bill or in giving the legislative reason for it. Yet, none of that happened in this Act. My guess is that as Article 23 is the only provision that deals with nuclear issues, the "nuclear-free homeland" wording was surreptitiously introduced into this Act. The mentioning of this concept thus led to the further development of this idea.

III. Proposal of Nuclear-Free Homeland Bill of 2003

326. The Nuclear-Free Homeland Bill of 2003 can be seen as a "shadow" of the German phase-out mechanism. Following an official visit to Germany in February

2003 led by the Minister without portfolio, steps were taken to integrate the German element into an Explanatory Note, and provide legislative explanation of the Nuclear-Free Homeland Bill, such as the commercial operation of thirty-two years as an index to electricity production. This draft bill was then approved by the Executive Yuan on May 7, 2003, and submitted to Parliament for its deliberation on May 11, 2003. The bill underwent several discussions in the Parliament but was not approved. Even though the bill was formally noted as a "priority bill" of the Executive Yuan, it was ignored in that parliamentary term.

327. The bill has 20 provisions. The issues of future energy mix adjustment, nuclear plant phase outs, clean energy, public participation in nuclear power policy, safety monitoring of nuclear power plants, energy education, etc., are all mentioned in this bill. Yet, it should be noted that the scheme to phase out nuclear power plants remains the core of this bill, while the other elements are merely "decorative." In this regard, three provisions regulate the fate of future nuclear power development. Generally, Article 4 urges the government to adjust the Taiwanese energy mix and gradually reduce nuclear electricity with a view to eliminating gradually the use of nuclear power. Then, more especially, from the implementation date of this Act, there would be no construction license issued (Article 5). In this regard, the development of Nuclear Power No. 5 or the expansion of nuclear power plants at the existing sites of Nuclear Power Nos. 1–4 is no longer possible. Finally, the German phase-out concept of "scheduling a fixed total electricity amount" and "transferring the remaining electricity among different nuclear power facilities" is stipulated in Article 6. The nuclear power reactors should stop operation permanently, once they reach the "scheduled fixed total electricity amount." According to Article 6(2), plant operators are allowed to transfer the unused electricity to other plants after the approval of the Executive Yuan. This mechanism was considered for the less safe and older type reactors of Nuclear Power No. 1 and No. 2, and allows the safer reactors to run longer. Finally, this mechanism would prevent any compensation claim from the nuclear plant operators, which was also a very important element of the German-style phase out.

328. The Explanatory Note of this bill defines the nature of this bill as Basic Law. Yet, a closer investigation reveals that the development of nuclear power plants would be subject to many limitations, similar to a regular legal regime. For the existing reactors (Nos. 1–3 plants), it seems unlikely they would operate until the normal decommission date (i.e., in forty years); not to mention, their life extension for another twenty years. For those reactors under construction (No. 4), their construction would be allowed to continue, but their operation would be limited by this bill as well. The expansion of nuclear generators at the existing sites was clearly prohibited as well. In sum, this bill sets up an inescapable dragnet to avoid potential loopholes. Compared with the previous generation nuclear phase-out bill of 2001, this bill's phase-out conditions are more concrete and workable. Yet, these workable and concrete measures also made the bill difficult to pass in the Parliament, where the opposition party is in the majority.

Table 5 Transition of the Concept of a Nuclear-Free Homeland in Major Policies and Legislation

Contents	*Nuclear-Free Homeland Consensus (2001.2.13)*	*Nuclear Phase-Out Bill 2001*	*Nuclear-Free Homeland Policy (2002)*	*Environmental Basic Act of 2002*	*Nuclear-Free Homeland Bill (2003)*	*Nuclear-Free Homeland Action Plan (2003.9)*	*Energy Policy White Paper 2005*
Continuing the construction of Nuclear No 4	O	O	O	O	O	O	X
Overall energy supply and demand	O	O	O	O	O	O	X
Renewable energy development	X	X	O	O	O	O	O
Dealing with the phase-out issue of existing Nuclear Power Nos 1–3	X	V	O	X	O	O	X

Contents	*Nuclear-Free Homeland Consensus (2001.2.13)*	*Nuclear Phase-Out Bill 2001*	*Nuclear-Free Homeland Policy (2002)*	*Environmental Basic Act of 2002*	*Nuclear-Free Homeland Bill (2003)*	*Nuclear-Free Homeland Action Plan (2003.9)*	*Energy Policy White Paper 2005*
Nuclear safety	X	X	O	O	O	O	X
Radioactive protection	X	X	O	O	O	O	X
Any nuclear weapon	X	X	O	X	O	X	X
Nuclear waste management	X	X	O	X	O	O	X
New nuclear power installations (construction of Nuclear No 5 or expansion at existing sites)	X	X	?	X	O	?	X

Contents	*Nuclear-Free Homeland Consensus (2001.2.13)*	*Nuclear Phase-Out Bill 2001*	*Nuclear-Free Homeland Policy (2002)*	*Environmental Basic Act of 2002*	*Nuclear-Free Homeland Bill (2003)*	*Nuclear-Free Homeland Action Plan (2003.9)*	*Energy Policy White Paper 2005*
Extending the life of the existing Nos 1–3 power plants	X	?	?	X	O	?	X

Source: Compiled by the author.

Note:

O: The issue is clearly dealt with.

X: The issue is not dealt with.

?: It is unclear whether this issue is dealt with or not.

IV. Proposal of the Nuclear-Free Homeland Bill since 2012

329. After the Fukushima accident, the leader of the opposition party (i.e., the party in power at the time the nuclear-free homeland was being promoted) again proposed the Vision of A Nuclear-free Homeland of 2025.[546] Despite losing the presidential election in 2012, the anti-nuclear party proposed the Nuclear-Free Homeland Bill in 2012.[547] In response, the ruling party proposed the Energy Security and Nuclear-Free Homeland Bill in March 2013.[548] Apart from these two main versions, there were also the other three versions proposed by the non-ruling parties, namely the Nuclear-Free Homeland Bill by Taiwan Solidarity Union,[549] Nuclear-Free Homeland Implementation Bill by 21 DPP MPs,[550] and No-Nuclear Power Homeland Promotion Bill by the People First Party.[551] Of the five versions, the government version set criteria before phasing out all nuclear power plants. Furthermore, it provided no fixed timeline for the nuclear phase out, and reserved the possibilities of extending the life of the Nos. 1–3 nuclear power plants and issuing a license to the No 4 nuclear power plant.

546. Taipei Times, Tsai talks "nuclear-free homeland," Jul. 9, 2011, available at: https://www.taipeitimes.com/News/taiwan/archives/2011/06/09/2003505340.
547. Legislative Yuan, Nuclear-free Homeland Bill, available at: https://misq.ly.gov.tw/MISQ/IQuery/misq5000QueryBillDetail.action?billNo=1010303070201300.
548. Executive Yuan, Energy Security and Nuclear-free Homeland Bill, Mar. 7, 2013, available at: https://www.ey.gov.tw/Page/9277F759E41CCD91/9ccacfb2-be1e-421b-a8e8-25192d4e482f.
549. Legislative Yuan, Nuclear Freehomeland Bill by Taiwan Solidarity Union, available at: https://misq.ly.gov.tw/MISQ/IQuery/misq5000QueryBillDetail.action?billNo=1020509070200600.
550. Legislative Yuan, Nuclear Freehomeland Bill by Chen, available at: https://misq.ly.gov.tw/MISQ/IQuery/misq5000QueryBillDetail.action?billNo=1020503070200300.
551. Legislative Yuan, Nuclear Freehomeland Bill by People First Party, available at: https://misq.ly.gov.tw/MISQ/IQuery/misq5000QueryBillDetail.action?billNo=1020425070200800.

Table 6 Comparison of Different Versions of the Nuclear-Free Homeland Bills in the Post-Fukushima Era

<table>
<tr><th></th><th>The Government</th><th>DPP</th><th>Taiwan Solidarity Union</th><th>21 DPP MPs</th><th>People First Party</th></tr>
<tr><td>Pre-conditions for nuclear phase out</td><td>Yes</td><td colspan="4">No</td></tr>
<tr><td>Timeline of a nuclear-free homeland</td><td>No</td><td colspan="3">2025</td><td>No</td></tr>
<tr><td>Prohibition of life extensions or issuing a new license</td><td>No</td><td colspan="3">Yes</td><td>Yes (but excluding the fourth nuclear power plant)</td></tr>
</table>

Source: Compiled by the author.

V. After 2016: The Concept of a Nuclear-Free Homeland in the Taiwan Electricity Act Amendment: Toward a Liberalized and Green Energy Market (January 23, 2017)

Zero Nuclear Power Generation by 2025

330. The legislation for a nuclear-free homeland disappears after 2016. After the MOEA's New Energy Policy was implemented in 2016, Taiwan began tackling the soon to be four nuclear power plants. In contrast to the deliberations on whole legislative bills that focused on a nuclear-free homeland during the previous few years,[552] the DPP took a unique approach. First, the idea of a nuclear-free homeland was integrated into the Amendment (2017) as Article 95. Second, instead of explicitly stating "nuclear-free homeland," Article 95 only provided the operational deadline as follows: "The nuclear energy-based power-generating facilities shall wholly stop operating by 2025." Third, instead of using the word "decommission" (which was in the previous draft about a nuclear-free homeland), it stated, "wholly stop

552. The early draft Act to promote a nuclear-free homeland was proposed in 2003. *See* MOEABOE, Draft Act to promote a nuclear-free homeland, Jun. 11, 2003, available at: https://www.lawbank.com.tw/news/NewsContent.aspx?nid=15938.00 (in Chinese). The bill was again proposed by DPP in March 2013 after the Fukushima accident in 2011. *See* Lawmakers clash over nuclear-free act, Taipei Times, Mar. 28, 2013, available at: www.taipeitimes.com/News/taiwan/archives/2013/03/28/2003558196.

operating." These conceptual changes led to a legal concern about the Amendment's relationship to the legal regime of current atomic energy. The draft Amendment to promote a nuclear-free homeland referred to further revisions of the Nuclear Reactor Facilities Regulation Act;[553] thus, to avoid conflicts, Article 95 would relate to application issues such as whether the three nuclear power plants could meet the "stop operations" requirement while applying for life extension.[554]

331. Previously, under the "Nuclear-free Homeland Draft Act," a comprehensive approach would handle all aspects of decommissioning the nuclear power plants. For example, in one version of the Energy Security and Nuclear-Free Homeland Bill in 2013,[555] an evaluation mechanism would be created to determine whether the phase-out would influence the overall electricity supply. However, a thorough and thoughtful approach is missing from the current Article 95 (Electricity Act) because many unresolved issues remain.

Fate of the Three Nuclear Power Plants

332. Under Article 95 of the Amendment, the entire electricity system gradually moves to a nuclear-free system. However, in mid-2017, the central government approved the operation of two new nuclear reactors: the first reactor of the second nuclear power plant and the second reactor of the third nuclear power plant. Then, on August 15, 2017, due to operational negligence of a gas valve, a chain reaction led to system failure and Taiwan experienced an unprecedented electricity blackout that affected 6.68 million households.[556] About one year later in mid-2018 (just months ago), the government approved a restart of the controversial second reactor at the second nuclear power plant.[557] Apparently, the beginning of Taiwan's journey toward a nuclear-free homeland was not very smooth. Instead, it began with a dramatic increase in nuclear power in Taiwan's electricity mix.

Fate of the Fourth Nuclear Power Plant

333. The fate of the nearly complete fourth nuclear power plant was less positive. Despite the lack of clarity about it in Article 95, the government took deliberate action against it, circumventing the law. Because of the lack of legal measures to deal with sunk assets, the government asked Tai-Power to return the fuel rods to

553. Nuclear Reactor Facilities Regulation Act, 2003.01.15, available at: https://law.moj.gov.tw/Eng/LawClass/LawAll.aspx?PCode=J0160019.
554. The major part of this section was adapted from: OGEL A.M. Gao; "Taiwan's Perhaps Irresponsible Policy and Laws on a Nuclear-free Homeland by 2025: The Missing Piece of Nuclear Assets and Legacy" OGEL 2 (2019), www.ogel.org URL: www.ogel.org/article.asp?key=3819.
555. Energy Security and Nuclear-free Homeland Bill of 2013, available at: https://www.ey.gov.tw/Page/9277F759E41CCD91/9ccacfb2-be1e-421b-a8e8-25192d4e482f.
556. ROUNDUP: Power outage affects 6.68 million households; supply restored, 2017/08/15, available at: http://focustaiwan.tw/news/aeco/201708150034.aspx.
557. Tai-Power seeks to restart No 2 nuclear power plant reactor, 2018/02/05, available at: http://focustaiwan.tw/news/aeco/201802050010.aspx; No 2 reactor at second nuclear plant resumes operations, 2018/07/07, available at: http://focustaiwan.tw/news/aeco/201807070020.aspx.

the United States. Tai-Power had already sent back several fuel rods in mid-2018.[558] Some readers might wonder why Tai-Power was so compliant, but this state-owned company could not challenge the government's implicit order.

334. Dealing with the fourth nuclear power plant has been problematic. The plant is comprised of two advanced boiling water reactors (each 1,350 MWe net). General Electric is the reactor supplier, and the turbines and generators are supplied by Mitsubishi Heavy Industries. The nuclear power plant cost about USD 9.4 billion. As discussed above, the DPP government stopped budgetary funding as a political tactic to halt its construction in 2000 while continuing construction and injecting funding after consensus was reached on a nuclear-free homeland. After the Japanese Fukushima nuclear power plant accident in 2011, the DPP, then the opposition party, again raised the issue. In 2014, the DPP launched a major protest against continuing with the construction, which pressured the KMT government to halt construction of the fourth power plant. Construction of the plant was deferred.[559]

335. As noted, in mid-2018, the government began to return the fuel rods, although many people opposed that action because it could be perceived as a symbol to abandon investment in nuclear power plants.

336. To avoid a dramatic increase in electricity tariffs caused by the sunk costs of this nuclear power plant, the government tried to have Tai-Power not reflect these costs in their accounts. Perhaps it is understandable that in 2014, the construction works differed although the regular maintenance of the power plants remains. Likely, construction will be completed and the plant will go online. However, the recent step of returning the fuel rods seems to signal the end. It is very difficult to imagine that Taiwan, a country under the rule of law, has no legal remedy for dealing with the USD 9.4 billion in sunk costs. A major debate in parliament on this issue is not necessary for such an important decision, which only relies on Tai-Power's decision to return the fuel rods and sink the assets. Further, it seems unnecessary for the government to persuade the public to accept higher electricity prices after abandoning this power plant project.

2018: Referendum to Revoke Article 95

337. In December 2017, the Referendum Act was largely revised.[560] The major change concerned easing the burden of the threshold for the number of proposers

558. Taiwan News, Nuke plant's fuel rods to be shipped to U.S. 2018/03/16, https://www.taiwannews.com.tw/en/news/3383849.
559. Taiwan halts fourth power plant, 16/05/2014, available at: https://www.wiseinternational.org/nuclear-monitor/786/taiwan-halts-fourth-power-plant.
560. Referendum Act, Amended Date: 2018.01.03, available at: https://law.moj.gov.tw/Eng/LawClass/LawContent.aspx?PCODE=D0020050.

by reducing it from about 1 million to around 280,000 people.[561] In March 2018, pro-nuclear groups used this as an opportunity to propose "go green with nuclear power," because municipal elections were set for November 2018 that could include a referendum vote.[562] Thus, in mid-2018, they launched a referendum to remove the nuclear-free homeland clause from Article 95. This referendum was launched by the alumni and a professor of National Tsing Hua University, Taiwan.[563]

338. The proposer documents had to be submitted by mid-September for the referendum to be included on the November 24, 2018 ballot. However, after accepting 315,000 signatures by September 6, the government refused to accept a second attempted delivery of 24,000 signatures on September 13.[564] Shih-Hsiu Huang, cofounder of Nuclear Myth-Busters and the chief organizer of the referendum, staged a hunger strike outside the office of the Central Election Commission (CEC) for several days. The hunger strike ended, but the CEC still refused to accept the signatures. As expected, on October 16, 2018, the referendum failed to pass the CEC review because the number of qualified public endorsements for the proposal did not meet the legally required threshold, falling short by 2,326 signatures.[565]

339. In mid-September, the organizer of the referendum brought the CEC's refusal to accept the signatures before the High Court to request a provisional injunction to order the CEC to accept them. On October 17, the Administrative Court ordered the CEC to accept supplemental signatures for a pro-nuclear power referendum proposal.[566] Finally, the CEC approved the referendum on October 24, 2018.[567]

340. After the vote on November 24, 2018, close to 6 million citizens voted for the revoke of Article 95 of the nuclear-free homeland clause. The clause was officially revoked on May 22, 2019. Even so, the nuclear-free homeland policy continues as there is no life extension of the existing three power plants. The first (No. 1) nuclear power plant was issued a decommission license in July 2019. The two

---

561. Referendum Act, Art. 12: "For the matters prescribed in Paragraph Two of Article 2, the number of proposers shall be not less than 1.5% of the total electors in the most recent election of the President and Vice President."
562. Nicolas Freschi, Taiwan's Nuclear Dilemma: Nuclear energy has long been a contentious issue for Taiwan, but there are few good alternatives. Mar. 14, 2018, available at: https://thediplomat.com/2018/03/taiwans-nuclear-dilemma/.
563. The official website of the referendum, available at: https://www.green-nuclear.vote/.
564. Michael Shellenberger, Sep. 17, 2018, Taiwanese government sparks hunger strike after rejecting signatures for pro-nuclear referendum, available at: https://www.forbes.com/sites/michaelshellenberger/2018/09/17/taiwanese-government-sparks-hunger-strike-after-rejecting-signatures-for-pro-nuclear-referendum/#2dceb91c6af9.
565. CEC approves two more referendum proposals, making nine in total, 2018/10/16, available at: http://focustaiwan.tw/news/aipl/201810160023.aspx.
566. CEC ordered to accept more signatures for nuclear power referendum, Oct. 17, 2018, Focus Taiwan News Channel, available at: http://focustaiwan.tw/news/aipl/201810170022.aspx.
567. Michael Shellenberger, Momentum builds for nuclear power with referendum approved in Taiwan and "Pride Fest" in Germany, Oct. 24, 2018, Forbes, available at: https://www.forbes.com/sites/michaelshellenberger/2018/10/24/momentum-builds-for-nuclear-power-with-referendum-approved-in-taiwan-and-pride-fest-in-germany/.

reactors of the second nuclear power plant are scheduled to cease operations in 2021 and 2023, while the third is scheduled to cease operations in 2025. As the fuel rods of the fourth nuclear power plant have been sent back to the United States, test operations remain unlikely. However, on December 13, 2019, the CEC approved a proposal to hold a referendum on the revival of the contested fourth nuclear plant.[568] August 28, 2021, has been named as the earliest possible date the vote might be held. Thus, the government's response to the coming referendum in 2021 remains to be seen.

568. Taiwan News, Taiwan approves plans for a referendum to revive contested 4th nuclear plant, Dec. 13, 2019, available at: https://www.taiwannews.com.tw/en/news/3836618.

Table 7 Results of the Nuclear Referendum in 2018

Referendum Results									
Question	*For*		*Against*		*Invalid/Blank*	*Total*	*Registered voters*	*Turnout*	*Outcome*
	Votes	*%*	*Votes*	*%*					
Repealing the planned end of nuclear power stations	5,895,560	59.49	4,014,215	40.51	922,960	10,832,735		54.83	Adopted

Source: https://web.archive.org/web/20181124220825/http://referendum.2018.nat.gov.tw/pc/en/00/m00000000000000000.html.

§5. NUCLEAR WASTE MANAGEMENT POLICY AND LAW IN TAIWAN

I. Nuclear Waste Management Policy

Overall Policy/Plan/Program for Nuclear Waste Management

Guideline for Radioactive Waste Management

341. Taiwan's overall nuclear waste management policy is governed by the "Guideline for Radioactive Waste Management," which was established in September 1988 and updated and revised on September 2, 1997.[569] There are thirteen general principles including three chapters: Chapter 1: Target, Chapter 2: Strategy, and Chapter 3: Measures. The guideline provides the following:

Chapter 1. Goals	1. Aiming at strengthening the management of radwaste produced by electric power generation, medicine, agriculture, industry, education, research, and other activities, and therefore assuring public safety, maintaining the quality of environmental ecology, and preventing current and future generations from suffering the adverse effects of radwaste, the Radwaste Management Policy is set hereunder.
Chapter 2. Strategy	2. In performing the treatment, transport, storage, and final disposal of radwaste and the decommissioning of storage facilities, current and practicable technologies shall be adopted as the foundation. Active research and development shall be conducted to meet the actual national needs in securing safety.
	3. Radwaste producers shall endeavor to minimize the amounts and volumes of radwaste production.
	4. The treatment, transport, storage, and final disposal of radwaste shall be performed by respective producers or entrusted organizations as approved by the government. Producers of radwaste shall bear the related necessary costs.
	5. In the management of radwaste, public safety and environmental protection shall be considered and relevant international conventions shall be direly observed.
	6. Research and development, education, and public communication shall be enhanced to lay a solid foundation for the management of radwaste.

569. Guideline for Radioactive Waste Management, Amended Date: 1997-09-02, available at: http://erss.aec.gov.tw/law/LawContent.aspx?id=FL015688.

7. Comprehensive systems of codes and regulations, management structures, and information management shall be established to enhance the effectiveness of radwaste management.

8. Both the domestic and extraterritorial disposal options for radwaste shall be equally evaluated and actively pursued. Regardless of the feasibility of the extraterritorial disposal option, a domestic disposal site shall be engaged for possible use.

Chapter 3. Measures

9. Strengthening a comprehensive regulation and management structure: (1) Review and revise relevant codes and regulations. Enhance the management of radwaste produced by electric power generation, medicine, agriculture, industry, education, research, and other activities. (2) Strengthen a viable entrustment structure for the treatment, transport, storage, and final disposal of radwaste. (3) Establish an appropriate funding system to levy upon radwaste producers the costs for radwaste management. (4) Establish a safe management structure for the radwaste produced of naturally occurring radioactive materials to avoid adverse effects on the environment.

10. Protecting natural, social, and cultural resources: (1) Storage sites or disposal sites for radwaste shall be located in low-population zones to as realistic an extent as possible. (2) Storage sites or disposal sites for radwaste shall be located so as not to interfere with the sustained utilization and preservation of regional resources. (3) When transporting a large amount of radwaste, marine transport shall be adopted to as realistic an extent as possible, and accordingly, land transport minimized. (4) When decommissioning a radwaste treatment or storage facility, dismantling shall be the principle approach, such that the site can be reused for development.

11. Reinforcing tasks relating to safety analysis and environmental impact assessments: (1) Before installing a radwaste management facility, a safety analysis report for facility operation shall be submitted. An environmental impact assessment shall be performed if such an assessment is mandatory according to the environmental impact assessment regulations. (2) An environmental radiation monitoring system shall be established at each radwaste management facility. (3) Establish a comprehensive audit system and enhanced inspection program to ensure the safety of the treatment, transport, storage, and final disposal of radwaste.

12. Furthering the planning on the implementation programs for the storage and final disposal of radwaste: (1) Enhance safety for the storage of low-level radwaste, and study the feasibility of various options for long-term safe storage. (2) Strengthen development programs for the domestic disposal of low-level radwaste, accelerate implementation for the corresponding environmental impact assessment, and conduct safety analysis studies. (3) Continue developing programs for the extraterritorial disposal of low-level radwaste, and emphasize conformance to international regulations to ensure the safety of transport and disposal operations. (4) Strengthen the implementation for spent fuel on-site interim storage. (5) In accordance with the international nuclear safeguards agreement, study the feasibility of the extraterritorial reprocessing options for spent fuel. (6) Continue planning for final disposal programs for spent fuel and high-level radwaste, and accelerate the development of a preliminary feasibility study program and an implementation program.

13. Strengthening research and development, education, and public communication on radwaste management: (1) Develop medium-level and senior-level human resources for radwaste management, and recruit senior-level personnel from overseas to participate in the research and development on radwaste management. (2) Consolidate the research resources of academic and research organizations with organizations producing radwaste to strengthen research activities on radwaste management. (3) Establish a nation-wide radwaste management information system, and promote social education and public communication on radwaste management. (4) Actively participate in international cooperation programs and attend international conferences on radwaste management to grasp relevant technologies and experiences. (5) Promote private sector participation in the operation, research, and technology development on radwaste management. (6) Expand sources of funding to support research and development on radwaste operation and management technologies.

Source: http://www.aec.gov.tw/english/radwaste/file/national_report_20110414.pdf.

342. According to the EIA Ordinance, this type of policy should be mandatorily subject to a SEA. Thus, the SEA report was completed in 1999[570] and subject to public hearings in October 2000.[571]

343. Furthermore, individual waste management plans for final disposal and site selection have been further developed under these guidelines.

II. Policy/Plan/Program for Final Disposal and Site Selection

A. Overall: For High and Low Radioactive Waste

344. In general, no overall plan for *both* low and high radioactive waste (LRW, HRW) existed. However, as noted in the "Guideline for Radioactive Waste Management," certain guidelines such as 10, 11, and 12 could be related to the overall planning for final disposal and site selection.

345. From the planning, we see the trend of development of two different and divergent routes for HRW and LRW, respectively, as identical principles are included in guideline 12. The tendency is that "LRW is first and HRW second." Furthermore, it seems that much of the burden of planning is borne by Tai-Power, the operators of the nuclear power plants.

570. AEC, Final Report of the Strategic Environmental Assessment on Radioactive Waste Management Policy, August 2002, available at: https://www.aec.gov.tw/webpage/UploadFiles/headline_file/2010255142002.pdf.

571. AEC, Public Hearing of the SEA Report on Radioactive Waste Management Policy, available at: *www.aec.gov.tw/webpage/UploadFiles/headline_file/2010286143652.pdf.*

B. LRW

1. Final Disposal Plan for LRW

346. According to Article 29 of the Nuclear Materials and Radioactive Waste Management Act, it is the responsibility of nuclear operators to plan for final disposal.[572] Tai-Power proposed the first version of the final disposal plan for LRW in 2004.[573] The plan has been subject to revision several times: in 2007, 2014, and 2015.[574]

347. However, based on opposition from the local county during the site selection process, Tai-Power was ordered in December 2016 to propose an alternative program for final disposal of LRW. A centralized LRW storage site is planned,[575] which will be used to store the LRW before the final disposal site is available.

348. To continue evaluating technical aspects of the final disposal of LRW, Tai-Power also conducted related research. The research report[576] can be viewed as a soft approach to proceeding with the site selection process.

2. Site Selection Plan

349. According to Article 7 of the Act on Sites for the Establishment of a Final Disposal Facility for Low-Level Radioactive Waste," the site selection group shall within six months after organizing draft a disposal facility site selection plan. In August 2006, the site selection group was established, which proposed the selection

572. Article 29 of the Nuclear Materials and Radioactive Waste Management Act: "The treatment, carriage, storage and(/or) final disposal of radioactive waste shall be done by the producer of radioactive waste itself solely or be entrusted to an entrepreneur who or which has the technical capability to finally dispose of the domestic or foreign radioactive waste, or holds the facilities thereof. The producer shall be responsible for minimizing the generation amount and the cubic measure of radioactive waste. The plan for final disposal shall be proceeded in accordance with the planned schedule. The fee scale of the entrepreneur entrusted to implement the treatment, carriage, storage, and(/or) final disposal referred to in the preceding Paragraph shall be reported and determined (approved) by the competent authorities."
573. Final disposal plan for LRW (2004), available at: http://www.aec.gov.tw/webpage/control/waste/files/index_07_a-93.pdf.
574. For example, the final disposal plan for LRW 2007, 2012, 2014, 2015, etc. 2007, available at: https://www.aec.gov.tw/webpage/control/waste/files/index_07_a-96.pdf; 2012, available at: https://www.aec.gov.tw/webpage/control/waste/files/index_07_a-101-1.pdf; https://www.aec.gov.tw/webpage/control/waste/files/index_07_a-101-2.pdf; 2014, available at: https://www.aec.gov.tw/webpage/control/waste/files/index_07_a-103-1.pdf; 2015, available at: https://www.aec.gov.tw/webpage/control/waste/files/index_07_a-104-1.pdf.
575. *See* Tai-Power, A Study on LRW Final Disposal, available at: http://www.aec.gov.tw/webpage/control/waste/files/index_07_d-1.pdf.
576. AEC, Technology Assessment Report on LRW Final Disposal (2017), available at: http://www.aec.gov.tw/webpage/control/waste/files/index_07_e-1.pdf.

plan.[577] In August 2008, three potential sites were selected, including Taitung County Daren Township, Pingtung County Peony Township, and Penghu County Wangan Township.[578]

C. High Radioactive Waste

350. Taiwan's strategies for HRW are threefold: short-term—on-site spent fuel pool storage, mid-term—dry storage, and long-term—promoting final disposal.[579]

1. Research Plan

351. Since December 1983, the AEC, Tai-Power, INER, Central Geological Survey (CGS), and Energy and Resources Laboratories (ERL) of the ITRI have organized a task force to draft the "*Research Plan* on Disposal of Spent Fuel" and carried out four stages of HRW final disposal R&D. Progress in this regard has been made).[580]

2. Plan for Spent Fuel

352. For HRW, in compliance with the "Nuclear Materials and Radioactive Waste Management Act of 2002," Tai-Power submitted the "Spent Fuel Final Disposal Plan" (2004) to the AEC for review and approval. It was approved by the AEC in 2006. At this stage, "Potential Host Rock Characterization and Evaluation" is being carried out. The first version of the plan was approved in 2006.[581] This plan was subject to a Technical Feasibility study in 2009 and 2010.[582] In 2009, Tai-Power proposed the "Preliminary Technical Feasibility Evaluation Report on Taiwan's Spent Fuel Final Disposal Program," which reported the research results of Taiwan's spent fuel disposal programs over the past twenty years and deliberated on matters related to final disposal in nuclear-advanced countries. The AEC approved this report in July 2010. The preliminary technical feasibility evaluation

577. MOEABOE, Current Status and Policy of Radioactive Waste Management in Taiwan, available at: *web3.moeaboe.gov.tw/ECW/main/content/wHandEditorFile.ashx?file_id=794.*
578. Gillan Chi-Lun Huang • Tim Gray • Derek Bell, Environmental justice of nuclear waste policy in Taiwan: Taipower, government, and local community, available at: http://140.116.249.155/pluginfile.php/455273/mod_resource/content/0/Environmental_justice_of_nuclear_waste_policy_in_Taiwan.pdf.
579. Id. Summary of Radioactive Waste Management Policies, 88-89, available at: www.aec.gov.tw/english/radwaste/file/national_report_20070802.pdf.
580. Atomic Energy Council, National Report, 2016, pp. 95–96, available at: http://www.aec.gov.tw/english/radwaste/file/national_report_2016.pdf.
581. AEC, LRW Final Disposal Plan (2006), available at: http://www.aec.gov.tw/webpage/control/waste/files/index_06_a1.pdf.
582. Preliminary Technical Feasibility Study for Final Disposal of Spent Nuclear Fuel - 2009 Progress Report (Summary) June 2010, available at: http://www.aec.gov.tw/webpage/control/waste/files/index_06_a8.pdf.

report was completed, which confirmed that in Taiwan, potential host rocks need further research and exploration.[583] According to Article 37 of the "Enforcement Rules for the Nuclear Materials and Radioactive Waste Management Act," the final disposal plan for HRW shall be reviewed and amended every four years. Tai-Power submitted the "Spent Fuel Final Disposal Program 2010 Revision" to AEC for review on May 27, 2010. AEC approved the program on January 24, 2011. After the review, a new version of the Spent Fuel Final Disposal Plan was proposed at the end of 2010.[584]

353. Later, in 2014, a revised version was made public.[585] To monitor the progress of the final disposal of HRW, annual working programs[586] and annual working result reports[587] are available.

354. The plan includes the following five stages: potential host rock characterization and evaluation, candidate site selection and confirmation, detailed site investigation and testing, repository design and license application, and repository construction. The repository is scheduled to start operation in 2055. Taiwan's plan for the final disposal of HRW is currently in stage one, namely potential host rock characterization and evaluation.[588] Given that the international promotion of spent fuel disposal programs are subject to hindrance and delayed schedules, we proposed an alternative contingency plan. According to the plan, in 2028, after the completion of stage two—candidate site selection and confirmation—if we are still unable to propose a candidate site, we shall in 2029 start an alternative measure, namely a centralized spent fuel storage facility. This site shall be confirmed and its EIA completed by 2038. The centralized spent fuel storage facility shall be completely constructed and start operation by 2044.[589]

---

583. Tai-power, Preliminary Technical Feasibility Study for Final Disposal of Spent Nuclear Fuel - 2009 Progress Report, https://www.aec.gov.tw/webpage/control/waste/files/index_06_a8.pdf.
584. AEC, Spent Fuel Final Disposal Plan (2010), available at: http://www.aec.gov.tw/webpage/control /waste/files/index_06_a10.pdf.
585. AEC, LRW Final Disposal Report (2014); Spent Fuel Final Disposal Plan of 2014, available at: http://www.aec.gov.tw/webpage/control/waste/files/index_06_a16.pdf.
586. For example, Annual Working Programme of 2017, available at: http://www.aec.gov.tw/webpage/control/waste/files/index_06_c-106.pdf; Annual Working Programme of 2016, available at: http://www.aec.gov.tw/webpage/control/waste/files/index_06_c-105.pdf; Annual Working Programme of 2015, available at: http://www.aec.gov.tw/webpage/control/waste/files/index_06_c-104.pdf.
587. For example, Annual working result reports of LRW Final Disposal projects of 2016, available at: http://www.aec.gov.tw/webpage/control/waste/files/index_06_b-105.pdf; 2015, available at: http://www.aec.gov.tw/webpage/control/waste/files/index_06_b-104.pdf ; 2014, available at: http://www.aec.gov.tw/webpage/control/waste/files/index_06_b-103.pdf; 2013, available at: http://www.aec.gov.tw/webpage/control/waste/files/index_06_b-102.pdf.
588. AEC, Tai-Power, Plan on Spent Fuel Final Disposal (2010), available at: www.aec.gov.tw/english /radwaste/file/national_report_2016.pdf.
589. Tai-power, Preliminary Technical Feasibility Study for Final Disposal of Spent Nuclear Fuel - 2009 Progress Report, https://www.aec.gov.tw/webpage/control/waste/files/index_06_a8.pdf.

3. Site Selection Plan

355. While the draft HRW Site Selection Bill of 2016 is similar to the LRW Site Selection Act, the site selection plan and ideas of the site selection group are not included in the current bill. Thus, the development of site selection remains part of the aforementioned plan or program.

III. Institutional Design

A. General Radioactive Waste Management

1. Public Authorities

356. The Executive Yuan is the highest administrative organization in Taiwan. The MOEA, EPA, and AEC are at the ministerial level. The MOEA is responsible for supervising the operation of nuclear power generation. The EPA is responsible for regulatory measures regarding the EIA and protection measures related to spent fuel and radioactive waste facilities. The AEC is responsible for supervising and regulating the safety management of spent fuel and radioactive waste. The Fuel Cycle and Materials Administration (FCMA), which is an affiliated agency under the AEC, is responsible for safety regulations regarding spent fuel and radioactive waste in Taiwan, including small producers such as medical, agricultural, industrial, and research applications of radioactive materials.[590]

Figure 4 Institutional Design for Radioactive Waste Management in Taiwan

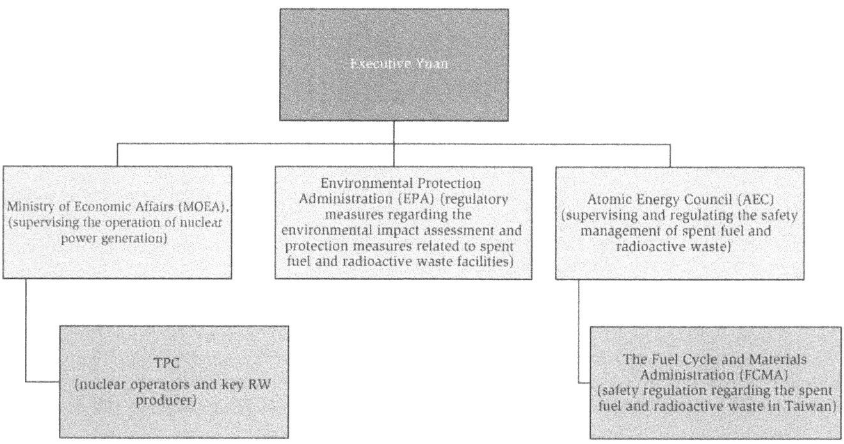

Modified from the AEC: http://www.aec.gov.tw/.

---

590. AEC, Summary of Radioactive Waste Management Policies, *id.* at 66., available at: *www.aec.gov.tw/english/radwaste/file/national_report_20070802.pdf.*

A. The Nuclear Regulator (Such as the NRC in the United States): The Authority for Nuclear Reactor Operators

357. The AEC was founded in 1955 at the ministerial level under the Executive Yuan. Its original mission was to foster peaceful applications of atomic energy and to coordinate international cooperation on nuclear energy.[591]

358. The primary mission of the AEC is to protect public health and safety, and the environment from the effects of radiation from nuclear materials and facilities. To carry out its mission, the AEC sets strategies and formulates policies as directed by the Minister, develops regulations[592] and guidance documents related to atomic energy, and conducts licensing and enforcement for reactor safety[593] of nuclear power plants and for protection against ionizing radiation.[594] International cooperation also plays an important role in this and other regulatory activities.[595,596]

B. Special Commission or Agency in Charge of Nuclear Waste Management

359. The Radwaste Administration (RWA) was established in January 1981 as an affiliated agency under the AEC to meet the growing need for radioactive waste management. Its original responsibility included planning, overseeing, and regulating the treatment, storage, and transport of radioactive waste, and operating the Lan-Yu Radioactive Waste Storage Facility.

360. In September 1988, the government of Taiwan decided that radioactive waste producers should be responsible for and bear the cost of the treatment, storage, transport, and disposal of radioactive waste. In July 1990, the operation of Lan-Yu Storage Facility was therefore turned over to Tai-Power, the largest radioactive waste producer, leaving RWA as a purely regulatory agency. With the rapid growth in civilian use of nuclear energy since RWA was set up, and the corresponding growth in demand for radioactive waste management, RWA's structure and status were no longer aligned with its operational needs. In early 1996, the legislative process to restructure RWA was completed. New regulatory standards related to nuclear materials, nuclear fuel, and spent fuel were added, and RWA was renamed as the Fuel Cycle and Materials Administration (FCMA to reflect the regulatory standards changes. FCMA is comprised of three technical divisions: a secretariat as well as the personnel and accounting functions.[597]

591. AEC, Our History, http://www.aec.gov.tw/english/intro/article1.php.
592. AEC, Laws & Regulations, http://www.aec.gov.tw/english/laws/index02.php.
593. AEC, Nuclear Power Plants of Taiwan, http://www.aec.gov.tw/english/nuclear/index01.php.
594. AEC, Radiation Protection, http://www.aec.gov.tw/english/protection/index.php.
595. AEC, International Cooperation, http://www.aec.gov.tw/english/international/index01.php.
596. AEC, About AEC, http://www.aec.gov.tw/english/intro/article4.php.
597. *Id.* at 64. Summary of Radioactive Waste Management Policies, available at: *www.aec.gov.tw/english/radwaste/file/national_report_20070802.pdf.*

2. Utilities

a. Nuclear Power Reactor Operators

361. In general, Tai-Power is responsible for the construction, operation, and decommissioning of spent fuel and radioactive waste facilities. As noted, the final disposal plan is the main scheme to promote these matters. Moreover, Tai-Power is designated as the site selection operator under Article 6(1) of the LRW Site Selection Act.[598] The site selection operator shall provide the site selection group with data on selection of the site of the disposal facility; carry out the site survey, safety analysis, public communication and land acquisition; and publicize quarterly the progress of the site survey on the website.[599]

b. A Different Company/Organization for Nuclear Waste Management Created by Electricity Utilities

362. Tai-Power has already tried very hard to implement a final disposal plan and site selection process. However, because of its position as a state-owned monopolistic electricity company, difficulties are delaying the progress of both LRW and HRW. To improve this situation, Tai-Power has conducted many studies on the regimes of various countries including Finland, Sweden, and Japan. The results seem to suggest that an institution outside Tai-Power would be a better situation. As noted, the bill on Administrative Institutions for Radioactive Waste Management was already proposed during the deliberation process in Parliament. According to Article 3 of the draft bill, the Institution is responsible for the following actions:

- Site selection, design, construction, operation, maintenance, closure, and monitoring of the final disposal facilities of RW
- Site selection, design, construction, operation, maintenance, and decommission of the storage facilities of this administration
- Foreign final disposal of RW
- Foreign reprocessing of spent fuel
- R&D and international collaboration

598. The implementing authority shall consult with the competent authority to select or designate a major domestic LRW-producing institution as the operator selecting the site of disposal facility (hereafter, "site selection operator").

599. Article 6(2) of the Act on Sites for the Establishment of a Final Disposal Facility for Low Level Radioactive Waste: http://law.moj.gov.tw/Eng/LawClass/LawContent.aspx?PCODE=J0160079.

3. Related Associations

A. A Nuclear Waste Management Association and Think Tanks/Research Institutes

363. Based on a mandate from the AEC, the INER is responsible for collecting, treating, and storing radioactive waste from small producers.

364. INER is responsible for the collection, treatment, and on-site storage of all radioactive waste arising from medical, agricultural, industrial, and research activities. LRW is classified as Class A, Class B, Class C, and Greater than Class C (GTCC).

365. In addition, CGS and ITRI are relevant in the handling of nuclear waste. Since December 1983, the AEC, Tai-Power, INER, Central Geological Survey (CGS), and Energy and Resources Laboratories (the ERL) of the ITRI (ITRI have organized a task force to draft the "*Research Plan* on the Disposal of Spent Fuel" and conducted four stages of R&D on the final disposal of HRW. Progress in this regard has been made.

B. Site Selection Process

1. LRW

366. Several interesting institutional designs are included under the authority clause of the LRW Site Selection Act.

367. Apart from the **competent authority** of AEC in the LRW Site Selection Act, the MOEA is designated as the "**implementing authority**" under Article 2.[600] Moreover, a **special work group, namely the siting committee or site selection group,** was created to facilitate the site selection process.[601] Figure 5 shows the flow, which is elaborated in the next session.

---

600. Article 2 of the Act on Sites for the Establishment of a Final Waste Disposal Facility for Low-Level Radioactive: "The competent authority of this Act is the Atomic Energy Council (AEC), Executive Yuan, and the implementing authority is the Ministry of Economic Affairs (MOEA)."

601. Article 5, Act on Sites for the Establishment of a Final Disposal Facility for Low-Level Radioactive Waste: "The implementing authority shall organize a work group on the selection of the site of disposal facility (hereafter, 'site selection group') within three months after this Act takes effect to carry out the work of disposal facility site selection in accordance with the provisions of this Act."

Figure 5 Siting Flowchart for the Final Disposal Facility for Low-Level Radioactive Waste[602]

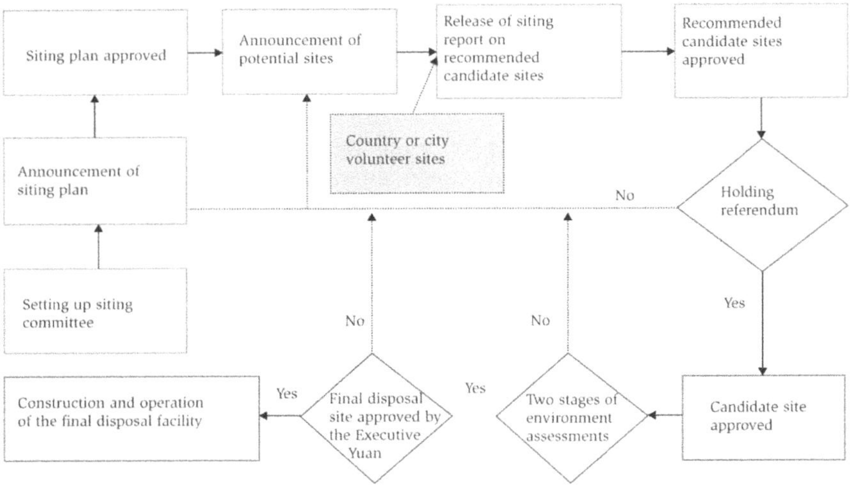

2. Competent Authority for HRW

368. According to Article 2 of the draft HRW Site Selection Bill, the competent authority for HRW is scheduled to be the MOEA. Interestingly, unlike the LRW Site Selection Act, the current draft bill does not include an implementing authority or "work group on the selection of the site of the disposal facility."

IV. Legal Regime

A. *Overview of the General Waste Management Regime*

369. Before the promulgation of The Nuclear Materials and Radioactive Waste Management Act on December 25, 2002, Taiwan's nuclear waste management has long been governed by the general regime under the Atomic Energy Act and aforementioned guideline. Since 2002, The Nuclear Materials and Radioactive Waste Management Act provides a legal basis for the regulation of both nuclear materials and radioactive waste. The Act is outlined below.

– Chapter I General Principles §1
– Chapter II Administration of Nuclear Source Material and Nuclear Fuel §8

602. AEC, Summary of Radioactive Waste Management Policies, p. 105, available at: *www.aec.gov.tw/english/radwaste/file/national_report_20070802.pdf.*

- Chapter III Administration of Radioactive Waste §17
- Chapter IV Penal Provisions §32
- Chapter V Supplemental Provisions §46

370. Chapter III (Articles 17–31) of this Act deals with the issue of radioactive waste management. Important clauses include the licensing requirement for the construction or operation of the treatment, storage, and/or final disposal facilities and installations.[603] Furthermore, it renders the submission of regular monitoring reports mandatory.[604] Unless approved by the competent authorities, radioactive waste shall not be imported, exported, transited, transhipped en route, carried, discarded, or assigned.[605]

371. According to the "Nuclear Materials and Radioactive Waste Management Act," the AEC of the Executive Yuan published the "Regulations on the Final Disposal of Low-Level Radioactive Waste and Safety Management of Facilities," which is enacted pursuant to Article 21 of the Nuclear Materials and Radioactive Waste Management Act to regulate the requirements on final disposal of low-level waste and ensure the safety of the disposal facility. Articles 28 and 29 further elaborate general management issues. According to Article 28, Tai-Power is obliged to bear the financial responsibility.[606] The treatment, carriage, storage, and(/or) final disposal of radioactive waste shall be done by the producer of radioactive waste itself solely or be entrusted to an entrepreneur who or which has the technical capability to finally dispose of the domestic or foreign radioactive waste, or holds the facilities to do so.[607]

B. Site Selection Regime

372. Despite the existence of the Nuclear Materials and Radioactive Waste Management Act, a separate legal regime deals with issues pertaining to site selection in Taiwan. Furthermore, two separate regimes are scheduled for HRW and LRW as

603. Articles 17 and 18 of Nuclear Materials and Radioactive Waste Management Act: "For the construction of treatment, storage, and(/or) final disposal facilities of radioactive waste, an application for a construction license shall be filed with the competent authorities, and the construction shall not commence until the application has been reviewed and approved (by the competent authorities) to satisfy the following prescription and the competent authorities have issued a construction license therefor." Article 18: "Even after the completion of the construction of treatment, storage, and(/or) final disposal facilities of radioactive waste, the facilities shall not be formally operated until the competent authorities have approved and issued an operation license thereof."
604. Article 20 of the Nuclear Materials and Radioactive Waste Management Act: "The operator of treatment, storage, and(/or) final disposal facilities of radioactive waste shall submit regularly to the competent authorities reports related to the operation, radiation protection, environmental radiation monitoring, irregularity, and(/or) emergency events, and(/or) any other reports designated by the competent authorities. The competent authorities shall publicize the relevant reports."
605. Article 25 of Nuclear Materials and Radioactive Waste Management Act.
606. Article 28 of the Nuclear Materials and Radioactive Waste Management Act: "The producer of radioactive waste shall bear the necessary expenses for the treatment, carriage, storage, and(/or) final disposal of waste, and(/or) the decommission of facilities."
607. Article 29 of Nuclear Materials and Radioactive Waste Management Act.

well. Even so, the current draft bill for HRW is almost identical to the LRW Site Selection Act. Thus, this article first elaborates on the design of the LRW Site Selection Act, and then on that for HRW.

1. LRW

373. The "Act on Sites for the Establishment of a Final Disposal Facility for Low-Level Radioactive Waste" was formulated to govern this activity and ensure conformance to the requirements for safety and environmental protection.

374. In the previous section, several key contents of the Act were elaborated, including the institutional design of the site selection work group (Article 5) and site selection operator (Article 6), and site selection plan (Article 7). This article introduces the rest of the regime.

A. Principles of LRW

375. As noted, the guideline provides the following principles concerning the site selection of LRW:

10. (1) *Enhance safety* for the storage of low-level radwaste, and study the feasibility of various options for long-term safe storage.
    (2) Strengthen development *programs* for the domestic disposal of low-level radwaste, accelerate implementation of the corresponding *environmental impact assessment and safety analysis studies.*
    (3) Continue developing *programs* for the *extraterritorial disposal of low-level radwaste*, and emphasize conformance to international regulations to ensure the safety of transport and disposal operations.
12. Furthering the planning of implementation programs for the storage and final disposal of radwaste: (1) Enhance safety for the storage of low-level radwaste, and study the feasibility of various options for long-term safe storage. (2) Strengthen development *programs* for the *domestic disposal* of low-level radwaste, and accelerate implementation of the corresponding environmental impact assessment and safety analysis studies. (3) Continue developing programs for the *extraterritorial disposal* of low-level radwaste, and emphasize conformance to international regulations to ensure the safety of transport and disposal operations.

376. Article 4 of the Act further elaborates the controversial issue of zones prohibited from the final disposal site as follows:

1. Area where active faulting or geological conditions could endanger the safety of the disposal facility;

2. Area where geochemical conditions are unfavorable for effectively suppressing the diffusion of radioactive nuclides and are likely to endanger the safety of the disposal facility;
3. Area where the hydrologic conditions of surface water or groundwater are likely to endanger the safety of the disposal facility;
4. Area with a high population density; and
5. Areas that cannot be developed according to the law.

377. These prohibited zones are similar to those in Article 7 of the Ordinance on the Safety Management of the Final Disposal of LRW of July 9, 2012.[608] The Ordinance includes additional safety and management rules.

378. In addition, several principles are found in all provisions, particularly regarding public participation and access to information. For instance, in the procedure in the site selection plan,[609] in the identification of potential[610] and recommended sites,[611] the public is empowered to *participate* in the procedure and the authorities have the duty to respond to their concerns. Furthermore, *public participation* is also seen in the local referendum to determine the final disposal site.[612] Finally, Article 12 includes a *compensation principle*, which can be considered another aspect of public participation.

1. Phase I: Potential Sites

379. The purpose of the first phase of the site selection process is to identify "potential sites."

380. As noted, Article 7 stipulates that the site selection group shall within six months after organizing, draft a disposal facility site selection plan and submit it to the implementing authority, namely the MOEA. After consulting with the general public[613] and related authorities,[614] the plan will be approved. The potential sites selected during this process will be announced.[615]

---

608. AEC, Ordinance on the Safety Management of LRW, Amended Date: 2012-07-09, available at: http://erss.aec.gov.tw/law/LawContentDetails.aspx?id=FL026397&KeyWordHL=%E4%BD%8E%E6%94%BE%E5%B0%84%E6%80%A7%E5%BB%A2%E6%A3%84%E7%89%A9&StyleType=1.
609. Article 7(2) of Act on Sites for Establishment of Low Level Radioactive Waste Final Disposal Facility.
610. Article 7(2), Act on Sites for Establishment of Low Level Radioactive Waste Final Disposal Facility.
611. Article 9(2)(3), Act on Sites for Establishment of Low Level Radioactive Waste Final Disposal Facility.
612. Article 11, Act on Sites for Establishment of Low Level Radioactive Waste Final Disposal Facility.
613. Article 7(2), Act on Sites for the Establishment of a Final Disposal Facility for Low-Level Radioactive Waste: "The implementing authority shall, within 15 days after receiving the site selection plan referred to in the preceding paragraph, publish the plan in the Executive Yuan Gazette and publicize it on the website for 30 days. In this period of public announcement, any government agency,

381. In August 2008, three potential sites were selected for further survey. The MOEA named two recommended candidate sites in March 2009, but later, the local government recommended the "Basal Reservation Area" as another candidate site. Because the Act specifies that at least two recommended candidate sites are needed to hold a local referendum, siting operation was restarted immediately. On September 10, 2010, the MOEA declared Daren Township of Taitung County and Wuchiou Township of Kinmen County as potential sites.

2. Phase II: Recommended and Voluntary Sites

382. After identifying potential sites, the next phase involves identifying recommended sites. Article 9(1) stipulates that the site selection group shall within six months after the list of potential sites is publicized, submit a report on the selection of recommended candidate sites to the implementing authority and include *at least two recommended candidate sites*. These sites will be further subject to a similar process of consulting the public[616] and related authorities[617] before the final decision is made.

383. Following this process, on March 29, 2011, the "Report on the Selection of Recommended Candidate Sites" of Nantien Village Daren Township and Shaochiou Village Wuchiou Township was released for public comments. In total, seventy-six comments were collected and handled. The MOEA announced Nantien and Shaochiou Villages as the two recommended candidate sites on July 3, 2012.[618]

individual, juridical person, or civil association may submit to the implementing authority comments in a written document stating the name or appellation and the address thereof."

614. Article 7 (3), Act on Sites for the Establishment of a Final Disposal Facility for Low-Level Radioactive Waste: "The implementing authority shall consult with the competent authority and other relevant government agencies and consider the opinions brought by the government agencies, individuals, juridical persons, and civil associations to approve the site selection plan referred to in the first paragraph within two months after the end of the period of public announcement referred to in the preceding paragraph."

615. Article 8, Act on Sites for the Establishment of a Final Disposal Facility for Low-Level Radioactive Waste: "The site selection group shall submit a list of potential sites to the implementing authority and have it publicized within six months after the site selection plan is approved by the implementing authority."

616. Article 9(2), Act on Sites for the Establishment of a Final Disposal Facility for Low-Level Radioactive Waste: "The implementing authority shall, within 15 days after receiving the report referred to in the preceding paragraph, publicize on the website and exhibit or announce in a proper place in the recommended candidate sites for 30 days. In this period of exhibition, any government agency, individual, juridical person, or civil association may submit to the implementing authority comments in a written document stating the name or appellation and the address thereof."

617. Article 9(3), Act on Sites for the Establishment of a Final Disposal Facility for Low-Level Radioactive Waste: "The implementing authority shall consult with the competent authority and other relevant government agencies to compile the sources and contents of the opinions brought by the government agencies, individuals, juridical persons, and civil associations, and give a reply on the adoption of the opinions one by one."

618. MOEA, The Announcement of the Recommended LRW Final Disposal Sites, Jul. 3, 2012, available at: http://www.llwfd.org.tw/notice_view.aspx?id=422.

384. Local economic development is considered a contributor to the potential host community. Therefore, the MOEA proposed a compensative subsidy program to enhance the local economy and quality of residential life. The host community and municipality are continuously influenced by the implementation of public engagement work to facilitate acceptance of the LRW repository. It is expected that the compensative subsidy program could be an incentive in site selection.

385. Apart from this top-down approach to identifying candidate sites, local government can seek voluntary participation in the "competition" for recommended sites after potential sites are announced. According to Article 10 of the LRW Site Selection Act, a county (city) government that volunteers to establish a disposal facility in the area under its jurisdiction shall after the county (city) council and township (city) council have adopted the decision, publicize the plan of establishment, hold a public hearing, and then submit a written application enclosed with relevant documents to the implementing authority within four months after potential sites are publicly announced. This site could be prior to the top-down recommended sites during the selection decision-making process.[619]

386. The main idea of this alternative bottom-up approach is to use a financial incentive to encourage a local government to participate in the process. According to Article 12, the Executive Yuan approves the total amount of the community support fund (feedback subsidies) for the disposal facility site. The amount must be no more than *NTD 5 billion*. The distribution of the subsidies is as follows:

(1) No less than 40% to the township (city) in which the disposal facility site is located.
(2) No less than 30% to all townships (cities) nearby the disposal facility site. In the absence of a nearby township (city), 15% more will be allocated to each township (city) and county (city) in which the disposal facility site is located.
(3) No less than 20% to the county (city) in which the disposal facility site is located.

387. As local economic development is considered a contribution for the potential host community, the MOEA has proposed a compensative subsidy program to enhance the local economy and quality of residential life. The host community and municipality are continuously influenced by the implementation of public engagement work to facilitate acceptance of the LRW repository. It is expected that the compensative subsidy program could be an incentive in site selection.[620]

---

619. Article 10(2) of the Act on Sites for the Establishment of a Final Disposal Facility for Low-Level Radioactive Waste: "The implementing authority shall turn the application referred to in the preceding paragraph to the site selection group for review. If it is confirmed that the application conforms to the provisions of Article 4, the site may have the priority to be listed as a recommended candidate site, and a public announcement shall be made."

620. AEC, Summary of Radioactive Waste Management Policies, p. 106, available at: www.aec.gov.tw/english/radwaste/file/national_report_20070802.pdf.

388. Based on the draft regulation on the use of feedback subsidies laid down by the MOEA, the first subsidies are expected to be dispatched to the local community only after the Executive Yuan approves the site. To accelerate the site selection process, the MOEA set up a draft encouragement regulation of the site investigation of the LRW final disposal program. After the site investigation application is approved by the local community and the first geological drill performed by Tai-Power, NTD 10 million in subsidies from the Nuclear Back-end Management Fund will be dispensed to the local community. These additional subsidies can be used for public construction, a business renaissance, social welfare, education, culture, and medical aid. Welfare measures such as free lunches for students and job opportunities are reserved for local tribal people.[621]

389. However, despite the incentives, no local governments adopted this approach.

3. Phase III: Candidate Site and Local Referendum

390. As multiple recommended sites exist, a local referendum scheme remains in place to determine the candidate site. A *local referendum* shall be held in the county (city) in which the site is located within thirty days after the end of the period of public announcement. With the consent of the public through a referendum, the site may be listed as a candidate site.[622] Where there are two or more candidate sites, one shall be selected by the implementing authority.[623]

391. On August 17, 2012, the MOEA requested the local governments of Taitung and Kinmen Counties to agree to accept the commission to hold local referendums on the sites of LRW. However, neither of the counties agreed to accept the commission. The MOEA will plan and carry out the referendum on its own. The AEC is watching the development of the event closely and will in due course urge the MOEA and Tai-Power to actively communicate with the public to hold a successful referendum.[624] However, thus far, the local governments have refused to conduct a local referendum for the sites.[625] The MOEA has also not held a referendum. Thus, there is currently no candidate site for the final disposal facility of

621. AEC, Summary of Radioactive Waste Management Policies, at p. 105, available at: www.aec.gov.tw/english/radwaste/file/national_report_20070802.pdf. *See also*, MOJ, Act on Sites for the Establishment of a Final Disposal Facility for Low-Level Radioactive Waste, available at: https://law.moj.gov.tw/ENG/LawClass/LawAll.aspx?pcode=J0160079.
622. Article 11(1), Act on Sites for the Establishment of a Final Disposal Facility for Low-Level Radioactive Waste.
623. Article 11(2), Act on Sites for the Establishment of a Final Disposal Facility for Low-Level Radioactive Waste.
624. Summary of Radioactive Waste Management Policies, p. 104, available at: www.aec.gov.tw/english/radwaste/file/national_report_20070802.pdf.
625. AEC, The AEC's official statement on the refusal of local government to host a referendum, http://www.aec.gov.tw/webpage/service/qna/files/index_05_7-01.pdf.

LRW, and the issue remains pending. This has also delayed the original planned schedule of completion of site selection work by 2016 and operation of the final disposal site by 2021.[626]

4. Relationship with Other Legal Regimes

392. The Site Selection Act also deals with the relationship with the legal regime for the environment and land.

Environmental Impact Assessment

393. According to Article 13 of the LRW Site Selection Act (Act on Sites for the Establishment of a Final Disposal Facility for Low-Level Radioactive Waste), where the establishment of a disposal facility is likely to seriously impact the environment, the site selection operator shall submit an Environmental Impact Statement according to the EIA Act. After the statement is turned to the competent authority in charge of environmental protection for reference through the implementing authority, the *second-stage assessment* of environmental impact shall be conducted in accordance with the provision of Article 8 of the EIA Act.

394. The site selection operator shall submit the relevant documents on the EIA to the Executive Yuan through the implementing authority within one month after the candidate site passes the review of the EIA. After the candidate site is approved by the Executive Yuan as the selected disposal facility site, a public announcement shall be given in the county (city) hall and township (city) office where the disposal facility site is located.[627]

Land Taking and Planning Issues

395. Articles 15 to 18 are related to issues pertaining to land and planning of the LRW site selection.

396. According to Article 15 of the LRW Site Selection Act, where public land is needed for establishing a disposal facility, the site selection operator shall apply to the implementing authority for *land appropriation*. Where private land is needed, the site selection operator shall apply to the implementing authority for *land expropriation*. When conducting the land appropriation or expropriation referred to in the preceding paragraph, the implementing authority may state in the appropriation or expropriation plan that the development, construction, and operation of the disposal facility be carried out through joint development, consigned development, cooperative operation, leasing, the setting right of superficies, trust, or investing by land right or rent without being limited by the provisions of Article 25 of the Land Act, Article 28 of the National Property Act, and local governments' regulations on the

626. AEC, Brief on LRW Management Strategy and Site Selection Works, https://www.aec.gov.tw/webpage/waste/files/index_04_1_2_02.pdf.
627. Article 14 of the LRW Site Selection Act.

management of public properties.[628] Article 17 of the LRW Site Selection Act provides further regulation regarding issues pertaining to taking land.[629]

397. According to Article 16 of the Act on Sites for the Establishment of a Final Disposal Facility for Low-Level Radioactive Waste, where the land for the disposal facility involves an alteration of *urban planning*, the implementing authority shall coordinate the competent authority in charge of urban planning to conduct the alteration quickly in accordance with the provision of Article 27 of the *Urban Planning Act.* Where the alteration of non-urban land utilization is involved, the implementing authority shall coordinate the competent authority in charge of regional planning to conduct the alteration in accordance with the provision of Article 13 of the *Regional Planning Act.*

5. Funding Sources for LRW

398. According to Article 19 of the LRW Site Selection Act, the expenses required for selecting the disposal facility site shall be allocated from the Nuclear Back-end Management Fund, and the properties acquired shall be vested in the Fund. This fund has been in place in accordance with Article 28 of the "Nuclear Materials and Radioactive Waste Management Act." The producer shall bear the necessary expenses for the treatment, storage, transportation, and disposal of spent fuel and radioactive waste, and decommissioning of the facilities. A nuclear back-end fund was established in 1987 to meet the abovementioned requirements. The fund was redefined as a non-operational fund and the administration thereof was switched from Tai-Power to the Nuclear Back-End Fund Management Committee under the MOEA's supervision.[630]

6. Current Status of LRW Storage: Temporary Storage Sites

399. All existing radioactive waste management facilities except the Lan-Yu Storage Facility are located within the originating nuclear power plants or research reactor facilities. The Lan-Yu Storage Facility has been in operation since 1982. Only the LRW disposal facility has recently required siting activity. Therefore, this subsection concentrates on the siting of the LRW disposal facility.[631]

---

628. Article 15(2) of the LRW Site Selection Act.
629. Article 17 of the LRW Site Selection Act: "The land expropriated under this Act shall be used according to the expropriation plan within six years after the completion of the payment of compensation without being limited by the provision of Subparagraph 1, Paragraph 1, Article 219 of the Land Act, and Subparagraph 1, Paragraph 1, Article 9 of the Land Expropriation Act. Where the land is not used within the time limit set forth in the preceding paragraph, the original landowner may apply for its redemption at the expropriated price originally paid him/her. However, if the cause is not attributable to the implementing authority, the original landowner may not apply to redeem his land."
630. Summary of Radioactive Waste Management Policies, p. 10, available at: *www.aec.gov.tw/english/radwaste/file/national_report_20070802.pdf.*
631. Summary of Radioactive Waste Management Policies, p. 102, available at: *www.aec.gov.tw/english/radwaste/file/national_report_20070802.pdf.*

2. HRW

400. Regarding the management of HRW, Taiwan has three strategies: short-term—on-site spent fuel pool storage, mid-term—dry storage, and long-term—promoting final disposal. A team was created in December 1983, which comprises members from the AEC, Tai-Power, INER, CGS of MOEA, and IER of the ITRI, to delineate "Spent Fuel Research Projects" that include four R&D stages for the final disposal of HRW. Tai-Power also submitted the "Spent Fuel Disposal Plan" to the AEC in 2004, which was approved in 2006.

401. The "Spent Nuclear Fuel Final Disposal Plan" will be conducted in five phases: Taiwan's SNFD plan also refers to this approach, which has five stages. It is currently in the "potential host rock characterization and evaluation stage" (2005–2017), and consequently, has not yet entered the siting process. The five stages are as follows:

(1) Potential host rock characterization and evaluation (2005–2017)
(2) Candidate site investigation and confirmation (2018–2028)
(3) Detailed site investigation and testing (2029–2038)
(4) Repository design and license application (2039–2044)
(5) Repository construction (2045–2055).

402. Currently, Tai-Power is conducting a study on the potential host rock characterization and evaluation. Tai-Power also submitted the "Preliminary Feasibility Study Report on Spent Fuel Final Disposal" to the AEC in 2009 for its review and approval. The AEC completed its review in July 2010. According to the report, potential host rocks exist in Taiwan, such as granite, mudstone, and Mesozoic bedrock. The current priority option is granite. Tai-Power submitted the "Technical Feasibility Study for the Final Disposal of Spent Nuclear Fuel" (SNFD2017 report) in 2017 to show the results of characterization and facilitate the determination of the technical feasibility of disposal.[632]

A. Development before the Draft Bill for HRW Site Selection in 2016

403. There is still no legislation for siting the final disposal repository of HRW in Taiwan. According to the development experiences of other countries, the key point of siting is garnering local communities' acceptance of the repository and developing appropriate disposal technology. Tai-Power has promoted the disposal plan with reference to international experience.[633]

404. According to the requirements set forth in the "Nuclear Materials and Radioactive Waste Management Act," approval by the competent authority (AEC)

632. Summary of Radioactive Waste Management Policies, p. 21, available at: *www.aec.gov.tw/english/radwaste/file/national_report_20070802.pdf*.
633. Summary of Radioactive Waste Management Policies, pp. 88-89, available at: *www.aec.gov.tw/english/radwaste/file/national_report_20070802.pdf*.

must be obtained before the construction, operation, decommissioning, or closure of a spent fuel or radioactive waste facility.

405. Article 17 of the Act stipulates that the construction of the treatment, storage, and final disposal facilities of radioactive waste shall not commence until the construction license application has been reviewed and approved by the competent authority. Article 23 of the Act stipulates that the decommissioning plan for a spent fuel storage facility or radioactive waste treatment and storage facility shall be implemented after the decommissioning plan is reviewed and approved by the competent authority. Article 23 of the Act also stipulates that the closure of a final disposal facility shall be implemented after both the closure plan and institutional control plan are reviewed and approved by the competent authority.

406. The longest validity period of the operating license for the production or storage facility of nuclear source materials and nuclear fuel, and for the radioactive waste treatment or storage facility, is forty years. However, this period is extended to sixty years for a radioactive waste final disposal facility. When the operating license expires and the facility needs to operate, the facility manager shall apply to the competent authority to renew the license two years before its expiration. Failing to renew the operating license according to the provisions will result in ceasing the operations of the facility.

407. The competent authority in issuing a license for spent fuel or radioactive waste management facilities must consider the following elements: whether the equipment and facility are capable of protecting public health and safety, whether the environmental and ecological effects comply with the relevant laws and regulations, and whether the technology and management capability and financial base are capable enough to operate the facility. Those elements are set out in Articles 8 and 17 of the "Nuclear Materials and Radioactive Waste Management Act."[634]

408. In January 2012, the AEC promulgated an Ordinance on the Final Disposal and Safety Management of HRW.[635] This Ordinance also provides regulations for site selection. For instance, Article 3 deals with deep geological disposal, and Article 4 with prohibited zones. Article 4 is similar to the provision in Article 4 of the LRW Site Selection Act.[636] Article 5 of the Ordinance stipulates the extra location requirement of a "prohibited zone," which refers to the following areas:

---

634. Atomic Energy Council, 2016, National Report, at p. 57, http://www.aec.gov.tw/english/radwaste/file/national_report_2016.pdf.

635. Ordinance on HRW Final Disposal and Safety Management, Amended Date: 2013-01-18, available at: http://erss.aec.gov.tw/law/LawContentDetails.aspx?id=FL036833&KeyWordHL=%E9%AB%98%E6%94%BE%E5%B0%84%E6%80%A7%E5%BB%A2%E6%A3%84%E7%89%A9&StyleType=1.

636. 1. Area where active faulting or geological conditions could endanger the safety of the disposal facility.

2. Area where the geochemical conditions are unfavorable for effectively suppressing the diffusion of radioactive nuclides, and it is likely to endanger the safety of the disposal facility.

– Very likely to have landslides, land subside, volcanic activities
– Geological structure is very likely to change significantly
– Hydrological conditions are highly likely to change
– The disposal rock is subject to major deterioration
– The earth crust is raising significantly or highly susceptible to erosion

409. The AEC should approve a detailed site investigation plan,[637] and the investigation results should be reported to the AEC regularly.[638]

410. Articles 8–13 provide further provisions concerning the design and safety of HRW disposal facilities. The important provisions are as follows:[639]

– Article 8: "Multiple barrier" design is mandatory.
– Article 9: The disposal site should not have annual radiation above 0.25 mSv for people outside the facilities.
– Article 11: The HRW can be withdrawn safely after being stored for fifty years.

B. MP Chen's Draft HRW Site Selection Bill of 2016

411. The draft HRW Site Selection Bill of 2016 is identical to the LRW Site Selection Act. For instance, Article 16 of the draft bill on the funding source of HRW is similar to that in Article 19 of the LRW Site Selection Act. In addition, the draft bill spends five provisions (Articles 11–15) on the EIA, land taking, and planning issues, similar to the LRW Site Selection Act (Articles 13–17).

412. Despite the similarities, the draft bill is unique.

a. Principles

413. The prohibited area for HRW is expanded and more detailed than that outlined in Article 4 of the LRW Site Selection Act. For instance, the listed items are expanded from five in the LRW Site Selection Act to ten in Article 5 of the draft bill.[640] The new items include the urban planning area announced by the government. Furthermore, quantitative criteria have been added in the HRW draft bill. For instance, the population density of 55 people per km^2 is considered an "area of high population density," while areas that have elevated more than 300 m within the last

3. Area where the hydrologic conditions of surface water or groundwater are likely to endanger the safety of the disposal facility.
4. Area of high population density.
5. Areas that cannot be developed according to the law.

637. Article 6, Ordinance on HRW Final Disposal and Safety Management.
638. Article 7, Ordinance on HRW Final Disposal and Safety Management.
639. Other design criteria are included in Arts. 10, 12, and 13.
640. For example, prohibited areas have a population density of 55 people per km^2 and include urban planning areas.

100,000 years are considered "Areas where active faulting or geological conditions could endanger the safety of the disposal facility."

414. Thus far, after the preliminary study, potential sites for HRW are likely to be located in areas populated by indigenous people. Therefore, two special requirements are included. First, the setting up of a HRW disposal site cannot be *against the will of the indigenous people.*[641] Second, the HRW Selection Bill cannot be contrary to the provisions in The Indigenous Peoples Basic Law.[642] Thus, respecting the rights of indigenous people are new principles in the draft bill. However, there seems to be difficulties regarding understanding the ambiguous wording.

b. Annual Radiation Effects on Humans

415. According to Article 6 of the draft bill, the design of the HRW disposal facility should ensure that within 1 million years of the disposal period, the radiation on humans outside the facility cannot exceed 1 mSv annually.

c. Design of the Site Selection Phase

416. The design of this phase of the HRW differs from that of the LRW.

> First, there is no *potential site* phase in the HRW draft bill.
> Second, there is no recommended site phase in the HRW draft bill, and no bottom-up approach enabling local governments to voluntarily participate.
> Third, only a candidate site phase is in place,[643] although the design of this phase differs from that for LRW. For instance, there is no community support scheme for candidate sites. Furthermore, Articles 8 and 9 include a multi-level veto system. Within an 8-km radius of a candidate site, the village head, township mayor, borough chief, county magistrate, and municipality mayor have the right to veto a site designation.[644] Finally, the local referendum may involve the citizens of more than one local government. Local governments located within a 50-km radius of the candidate site are required to hold the referendum for that site.[645]

§6. Summary

417. A responsible nuclear-free homeland requires not only a regime for setting up a nuclear power decommission schedule, but also one for both LRW and HRW.

---

641. Article 7(1) of the HRW Site Selection Bill.
642. The Indigenous Peoples Basic Law, available at: http://law.moj.gov.tw/Eng/LawClass/LawContent.aspx?PCODE=D0130003.
643. Articles 8, 9, and 10 of the HRW Selection Bill.
644. Articles 8 and 9 of the HRW Selection Bill.
645. Article 10 of the HRW Site Selection Bill.

For instance, in 2011, Germany committed to phasing out nuclear power by 2022. A Site Selection Act for controversial HRW was adopted in 2013,[646] and revised in 2017.[647] However, this responsible attitude is not evident in Taiwan.

418. Even if Tai-Power has already fulfilled its legal duties to submit a plan for LRW and HRW, a deadlock is evident. In terms of LRW, the deadlock is the unresolved passive attitude of holding a local referendum by the local government. For HRW, no definite legislative timeline was set for selecting a site, and the current draft bill is badly drafted. The multi-level veto and broader local referendum could be expected to worsen site selection for HRW more than for LRW. The resolution to both deadlocks requires the determination of parliament, the president, and the cabinet. Otherwise, the only way out seems to be the continued use of existing LRW and HRW sites.

---

646. BGR, Site Selection, available at: https://www.bgr.bund.de/EN/Themen/Endlagerung/Standortauswahl/standortauswahl_node_en.html.

647. Bundesamt für Kustiz, Gesetz zur Suche und Auswahl eines Standortes für ein Endlager für hochradioaktive Abfälle, abrufbar auf: https://www.gesetze-im-internet.de/standag_2017/BJNR107410017.html.

Part VI. Regulatory Framework for Renewable Energy

419. A carrot-and-stick approach can be used to regulate the development of renewable energy. The carrot side usually involves the development of incentives, while the stick side often deals with the environmental aspect of renewables. This Part will discuss only the incentive side, while leaving the environmental side for discussion in the latter Part on Interaction between Energy law and Environmental law.

Chapter 1. General Introduction

§1. Renewable Energy Situation

420. Even though Taiwan is located in a subtropical and tropical area and has abundant renewable energy resources, the development of renewable energy remains in its infancy. According to the energy statistics, Taiwan's energy supply remains heavily reliant on imported fossil fuel and nuclear energy. The total supply of renewable energy in the energy supply mix was relatively low. However, it should be noted that the actual supply volume of renewable energy has been increasing over the past fifteen years, which also reflects the recent policy efforts at encouraging the development of renewable energy that will be elaborated on later. The energy supply is illustrated in Figure 6.

Figure 6 Energy Supply (By Energy Form) in Taiwan

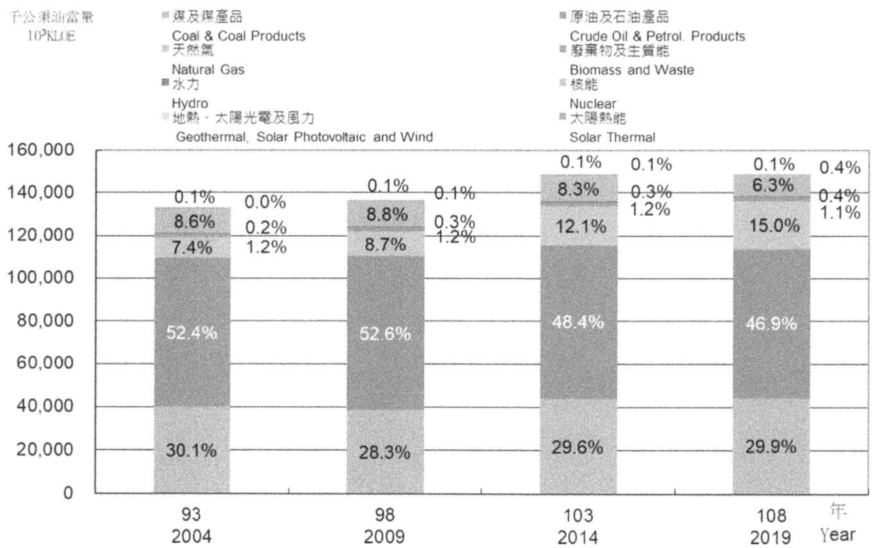

Source: Energy Supply (by Energy Form) and Total Domestic Consumption (by Sector), available at: https://www.moeaboe.gov.tw/ECW/main/content/wHandMenuFile.ashx?file_id=1395.

§2. Role of Renewable Energy in Energy Policy

421. Due to the lack of domestic energy fossil fuel resources, Taiwan is heavily reliant on imported energy. In order to improve its energy sufficiency, the Taiwan government has put considerable effort into developing renewable energy over the years. In the early stages, a qualitative approach was highlighted in the 1996 Energy Policy and Measures approved by the Executive Yuan, whereby renewable energy was seen as an important no-carbon and alternative energy option.[648] After the Kyoto Protocol, the government pondered whether to set a quantitative target for the renewables. For instance, the renewable electricity target was set at 8% in the Sustainable Policy Development Framework[649] and 12% in another policy document.[650] The most detailed step-by step plan to realize this target was scheduled by the New Energy Promotion Commission of the Executive Yuan on August 16, 2010. The top three renewable electricity sources so far are hydroelectricity, waste incinerators, and onshore wind power.

648. 1996 Taiwan Energy Policy and Measures, available at: http://www.moeaboe.gov.tw/Policy/PoMain.aspx?PageId=executepolicy.

649. "Develop carbon-free renewable energy. Effectively explore its power-generating potential, so that the share of renewable energy in the electricity system can reach 8% by 2025." MOEABOE, Taiwan's Sustainable Energy Policy, available at: http://www.moeaboe.gov.tw/Download/English/files/Framework%20of%20Taiwan's%20Sustainable%20Energy%20Policy.pdf.

650. "(1) Secure energy supply and promote energy diversity: Actively develop and promote the use of carbonless renewable energy: The long-term target for the production of renewable energy is 12% of the total electricity capacity." (http://www.moeaboe.gov.tw/About/webpage/book_en3/page3.htm).Bureau of Energy, Ministry of Economic Affairs, Taiwan's Energy Policy and Supply-Demand Situation-Implementation Measures, available at: http://www.moeaboe.gov.tw/About/webpage/book_en3/page3.htm.

Table 8 2030 Renewable Electricity Target of Taiwan (Unit: MW)

Year/Type		*2009*	*2010*		*2011*		*2015*		*2020*		*2025*		*2030*	
		Aggregate	*New*	*Aggregate*	*New*	*Aggregate*	*2012–2015 New*	*Aggregate*	*2016–2020 New*	*Aggregate*	*2021–2025 New*	*Aggregate*	*2026–2030New*	*Aggregate*
Hydro power		1938.7		1,945	61	2,006	46	2,052	60	2,112	390	2,502	0	2,502
Wind power	Onshore	436	70	506	70	576	230	806	150	956	100	1,056	100	1,156
	Offshore	–	–	–	–	–	150	150	750	900	500	1,400	600	2,000
PV		11	64	75	70	145	285	430	820	1,250	750	2,000	500	2,500
biomass	Waste	790	0	790	0	790	58 (18)	848	77	925	444	1,369	0	1,369
	biogas	24.5	0	24.5	0	24.5	4.7	29.2	0	29	2	31	0	31
Marine energy		–	–	–	–	–	1	1	29	30	170	200	400	600
Geothermal		–	–	–	–	–	4	4	62	66	84	150	50	200
Fuel cell		–	0.07	0.07	0.15	0.22	6.7	7	53	60	140	200	300	500
Total		3,200	140.4	3,340	201.2	3,541	785.4	4,327	2,001	6,328	2,580	8,908	1,950	10,858

Source: The Development of Renewable Energy Industry in Taiwan, May 6, 2011, available at: http://homepage.ntu.edu.tw/~ntuperc/pdf_meet/0506_1.pdf.

422. Shortly after President Tsai's inauguration on May 20, 2016, the MOEA announced its New Energy Policy to realize the 2025 Nuclear-Free Homeland Initiative it had promised during the presidential campaign.[651] The policy slides stated that: (1) there would be no life extensions to the existing nuclear power plants and (2) the construction of the fourth nuclear power plant would be stopped. To fill the deficit in the electricity supply, an electricity mix of **50 (natural gas) – 30 (coal) – 20 (renewables) by 2025** (Target 50-30-20-0) was proposed. As shown in Figure 7, this means a dramatic increase in renewable energy sources (from 5% to 20%) and natural gas (from 36% to 50%), and there would be accompanying decreases in coal (from 37% to 30%) and nuclear power (from 13% to 0%).

Figure 7 Distribution of Electricity Sources in 2016

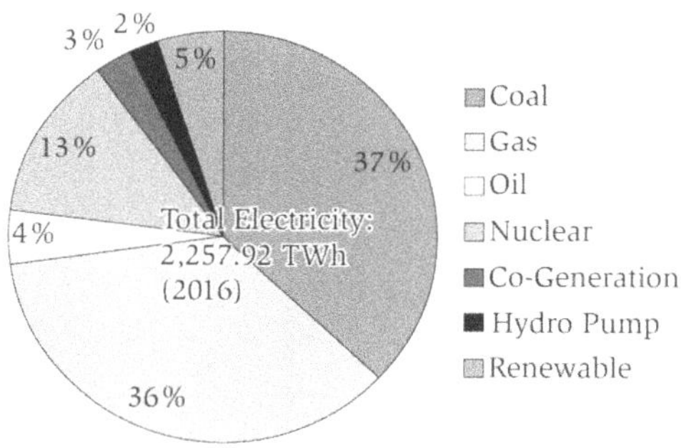

Source: Justin Chou and John A. Mathews, Taiwan's Green Energy Transition Under Way, https://apjjf.org/2017/21/Chou.html.

423. Apart from the "energy security" benefit of renewable energy, there is also the economic motivation. The government seeks to enhance Taiwan's energy R&D capability[652] with a view to promoting the green energy industry as a very important export industry.[653]

424. In the Master Plan on Energy Conservation and Emission Reduction 2010, an effort was made to launch a Renewable New Age Program, with PV cells, biomass electricity, and wind power as the Top 3 priorities, while keeping geothermal,

651. MOEA, New Energy Policy (in Chinese), available at: https://www.moeaboe.gov.tw/ECW/populace/content/wHandMenuFile.ashx?menu_id=3165&file_id=7.
652. "(4) Enhancing R&D and expanding technological capacity. Planning integrated projects in terms of energy technology development, which focus on the improvement of energy efficiency and development of renewable energy to achieve the national goal of developing renewable and clean energy."
Yun-Hsun Huang, Jung-Hua Wu, Energy Policy in Taiwan: Historical Developments, Current Status and Potential Improvements, 2009, Energy Policy, 2(3), 623-645.
653. "d. Promote green energy industry, including energy conserving industries and renewable energy industries, to move toward a clean energy economy." APEC, Peer Review On Energy Efficiency In Chinese Taipei, Nov. 5, 2010, available at: https://apecenergy.tier.org.tw/database/db/ewg40/03/9b_PREE_Chinese_Taipei_final_report.pdf.

hydropower, and marine energy in the short term. Yet, in the long run, marine energy and fuel cells would become more important as indicated in the Table 8.

425. The recent efforts in combining energy security policy and industry policy could be considered from the viewpoint of policies pertaining to the promotion of offshore wind power. The government wished to take the opportunity to develop 5.7 GW of offshore wind power to replace nuclear power by 2025 and to establish a national manufacturing team of M(arine engineering) and W(ind).[654] The technology scheduled to be localized by 2025 is indicated in Table 9.

654. Our Participation and Contribution to Taiwan Offshore Wind Energy Development, 2020: https://mct-eng.com/latest-news.

Table 9 Industrial Development Bureau: Offshore Wind Power Industrial Relevance Implementation Program Plan

Timetable for Grid Connection	*2021*	*2022*	*2023*	*2024*	*2025*
Phase	*Pre-stage*	*Pre-stage*	*Phase 1*	*Phase 2*	*Phase 2*
Industrial develop ment items	– Tower – Foundation – Electrical Components: 1. Transformer 2. Switch-gear 3. Distribution panel(the above refers to onshore electric equipment) – Marine engineering planning, design, construction, supervision, and manufacturing: 1. Construction and supervision of investigation, cable laying, exploration, etc. Planning of ship and machine tool design and safety 2. Shipbuilding: Development of ship industry supply chain for new ships or ship restoration (including ships for investigation, support, seabed preparation, transportation, and cable laying) as per the IDB.		– Wind turbine components: Rotor nacelle assembly, transformer, distribution panel, uninterruptible power supply, spinner, cable, rotor hub, bolts – Submarine high voltage cable – Marine engineering planning, design, construction, supervision, and manufacturing: 1. Construction and supervision of tower, foundation, etc. Planning of ship and machine tool design and safety (BOE) 2. Ship building: Provide the construction ship industry supply chain for new ships or ship restoration (including ships for transportation and construction) as per the IDB.	– Wind turbine components: Gearbox, generator, power converters, rotor blade & epoxy resin, nacelle cover, nacelle bed frame/plate – Marine engineering planning, design, construction, supervision, and manufacturing: Construction and supervision of wind turbines and others. Planning of ship and machine tool design and safety (BOE)	Pre-stage items for 2021 and 2022 Phase 1: items for 2023 Phase 2: items for 2024

Timetable for Grid Connection	*2021*	*2022*	*2023*	*2024*	*2025*
Phase	*Pre-stage*	*Pre-stage*	*Phase 1*	*Phase 2*	*Phase 2*
			– Pre-stage items for 2021 and 2022	– Pre-stage items for 2021 and 2022 – Phase 1 items for 2023	

Source: Huang, TW. Taiwan offshore wind industry promotion policy, Taiwan-Netherlands Offshore Wind Industry Networking Meeting, April, http://www.cieca.org.tw/v_comm/inc/download_file.asp?re_id=2998&fid=35542; 2018 (accessed June 10, 2020).

§3. Authority for Renewable Energy

426. The main authority in charge of the promotion of renewable energy is the MOEABOE (in the past the MOEAEC). It plays an important role in providing RD&D funding for nascent renewable technology, and provides investment subsidies or establishes FITs or net-metering schemes for renewable electricity. Most importantly, it drafted the Renewable Energy Bill in 2002. It also cooperates with the major state-owned electricity (Tai-Power) and petroleum and gas companies (CPC) in facilitating the deployment of renewable energy. For instance, Tai-Power launched a voluntary FIT scheme to purchase renewable electricity in 2003, while it is also mandated to construct its own wind power and PV plants. The CPC launched certain schemes to evaluate the use of biodiesel and ethanol.

427. Another very important authority with regard to the promoting of renewable electricity is the EPA. In order to curb GHG emissions from waste, the EPA has encouraged the production of electricity from biogas since 1999.[655] Yet, due to climate change concerns, the EPA is very keen on pushing the issue higher on the energy agenda and is competing with the MOEABOE in doing so. It remains to be seen whether this competition will have a positive effect on the development of renewable energy, as the EPA is often toothless during the formulating of renewable energy legislations.

§4. Major Players in Renewable Energy Sector

428. Renewable energy can be further divided into three different sectors, including renewable electricity, renewable thermal use, and renewable transportation fuels.

429. With regard to the electricity sector, the main player in the past was Tai-Power, which runs most of the hydropower plants (35.36% of renewable generation), and is still No. 1 as regards renewable electricity in Taiwan. The second most important renewable electricity players are the biomass/waste electricity providers (around 30%). The third player can be viewed as the competition between private onshore wind power and PV developers. Since 2003, there has been an upsurge in the use of wind power. The Germany-based company, Infravest, and Tai-Power are quite keen on harvesting Taiwan's wind resources. However, after 2010, PV energy saw a boom with the coming into effect of the Renewable Energy Act in 2009. Many households, farmers, and private companies are starting to install PV. In 2018, PV accounted for 21.68% (generation) and 43.84% (renewable installation capacity), while wind power accounted for 13.34% (generation) and 11.27% (renewable installation capacity).[656]

---

655. Biogas Feed-in Tariff Ordinance.
656. MOEA, Energy Statistics Handbook 2018, October 2019, available at: https://www.moeaboe.gov.tw/ECW_WEBPAGE/FlipBook/2018EnergyStaHandBook/2018EnergyStaHandBook.pdf.

430. Further, the government repeatedly emphasizes, in policy documents and statements, Taiwan's achievement in the use of solar hot water heaters, since it is among the world's Top 5 for installation intensity per square kilometer. Household users play a major role.

431. Finally, in the renewable transportation fuel sector, the two major oil companies, the CPC and the FPCC, are required to achieve a 2% mix.[657] However, there has been no percentage mandate since May 2014.[658]

432. This author will discuss and elaborate on the incentive scheme to attract these players as follows.

657. MOEABOE, Biodiesel Ordinance, 2010-06-10, available at: https://www.moeaboe.gov.tw/ECW/populace/Law/Content.aspx?menu_id=1078.
658. MOEABOE, Biodiesel Ordinance, 2010-06-10, available at: https://www.moeaboe.gov.tw/ECW/populace/Law/Content.aspx?menu_id=1078.

Chapter 2. Incentives for Renewable Electricity

433. Of all three types of renewable energy, renewable electricity can be seen as the first priority on the governmental agenda, which reflects the fact that most of the provisions in the Renewable Energy Act seek to promote renewable electricity. The development of incentives for renewable electricity can be divided into three stages.

§1. First Stage: Before Drafting Renewable Energy Bill in 2002

434. Before 2002, the main form of renewable electricity in Taiwan's electricity mix, i.e., hydropower, was not developed under any incentive and legislative scheme. Rather, it was ambitiously developed during the Japanese colonization of Taiwan; Tai-Power has continued to follow governmental policy in exploiting hydropower since the KMT's moving to Taiwan after World War II, in the 1940s. Hydropower has been rapidly developing during this stage and large-scale hydropower is heavily exploited, so that room for only small hydropower plants remains in the future. In addition to hydropower, there is also a geothermal electricity site developed voluntarily by the CPC.

435. The development of biomass electricity was influenced by incentives. Renewable electricity from municipal waste was encouraged by the Energy Management Act[659] and CHP Ordinance.[660] Tai-Power is obliged to buy the electricity from municipal waste incinerators at a preferential price. A similar regime is also applied to biogas from the landfill site.[661] As there is a net-metering scheme in place, these forms of renewable electricity are developing rapidly.

436. Compared with the aforementioned early development of renewable electricity, the development of PV and wind power came quite late. Since 2000, they have been promoted by investment and a demonstration subsidy scheme, respectively.[662] However, since there is no FIT scheme in place, they are not promoted very well.

§2. Second Stage: Transition Period Between 2002 and 2009

437. As noted above, a similar scheme was used to promote electricity from biogas[663] and municipal waste incinerators.[664]

---

659. Article 10 of Energy Management Act.
660. CHP Ordinance (first enacted on Jul. 15, 1988).
661. Biogas Feed-in Tariff Ordinance, http://ivy5.epa.gov.tw/epalaw/docfile/049146.doc.
662. Ordinance on Demonstration Investment Subsidy of Wind Power Plants (Mar. 22, 2000); Ordinance on Demonstration Investment Subsidy of PV Plants (May 31, 2000).
663. Biogas Electricity Feed-in Tariff Ordinance (enacted on Jan. 22, 2003; last revised Oct. 13, 2009).
664. Article 10 of Energy Management Act.

438. Regarding the development of a stationary biopower system, currently, a total installed capacity of 772 MW for power generation has been achieved through biomass energy utilization, which is primarily based on MSW incineration generation, biogas power generation, and the utilization of agricultural and industrial wastes. There are currently 25 operational large incineration plants, with a total installed capacity of 622.5 MW. The biogas electricity generation systems with a total installed capacity of 24.5 MW include four landfill sites. As for the utilization of agricultural and industrial wastes—bagasse, paper rejects, waste plastics and rubber, and rice husks—these densified RDF are used for generation with an installed capacity of 125 MW.[665]

439. Even though Taiwan is located in the Pacific Rim, there are limited suitable sites to develop large-scale geothermal electricity. The Tatun volcanic area has the largest geothermal resource in Taiwan. Its development, however, was halted due to severe corrosion resulting from acid fluids and constraints on land accessibility under the National Park Act. Other than the Tatun volcanic area, Ching-Shui of Ilan County is currently considered more appropriate for geothermal development. In August of 2005, the BOE in the MOEA announced the "Ordinance on Exploration Subsidy Program for Geothermal Power Generation and Demonstration."[666] Up to the present, the County Government of Ilan has been awarded a project to implement "The Study of Geothermal Resource and Power Generation Potential in Ching-Shui, Ilan." The MOEABOE will continue to help Ilan County in establishing a demonstrative showcase for the integration of power generation and recreation. In addition, the Geothermal Exploration Subsidy Program granted an application by Taitung County Government in 2007, for help in conducting geothermal exploration and an evaluation of power generation potential in the Jinlun area.[667]

440. The wind power promotion scheme underwent dramatic change during this phase. As the investment subsidy was not sufficient to encourage the deployment of wind power, this scheme was abolished in 2003. A "temporary" FIT scheme was developed by Tai-Power. Tai-Power voluntarily enacted its "FIT Ordinance" in 2003.[668] According to Article 6 of this Ordinance, the buy-back tariff for all renewable electricity is set at 2 NTD/kWh. This scheme was intended to promote many types of renewable electricity (PV, marine energy, wind, geothermal, small hydropower, biomass [excluding municipal waste incinerators]).[669] Yet, due to the fixed 2 NTD/kWh incentive, mainly wind power plants were introduced at this stage. The

---

CHP Ordinance I (first enacted on Jul. 15, 1988); CHP Ordinance II (enacted on Sep. 4, 2002; last revised Dec. 27, 2010).

665. MOEABOE, About, p. 3, available at: http://www.moeaboe.gov.tw/About/webpage/book_en1/page3.htm.
666. Ordinance on Exploration Subsidy for Geothermal Electricity Demonstration System.
667. MOEABOE, About, p. 5, available at: http://www.moeaboe.gov.tw/About/webpage/book_en1/page5.htm.
668. Tai-Power Feed-in Tariff Ordinance (Nov. 11, 2003).
669. Article 2 of Tai-Power Feed-in Tariff Ordinance, 2003-11-11, available at: http://energy.ie.ntnu.edu.tw/policy/download/d48b750a63d455fccb3c8ab06e0dbe41.

aforementioned Infravest private company developed many wind turbines during this period. According to the statistics in 2007, Tai-Power and Infravest were the two major players in building wind turbines. Taiwan has completed 155 sets of wind turbines with a total capacity of 281.6 MW, built by Tai-Power and some private sector organizations. Assuming that 1 kW of the installed capacity produces on average 2,700 kWh per year, wind power can generate 760 million kWh annually, providing enough electricity for 190 thousand households (a family of 4). Moreover, projects under construction, being approved, and being planned will offer a total installed capacity of 467.8 MW (equivalent to 230 sets of wind turbines).[670]

441. Please see Table 10 for the complete list of developers by 2007.

Table 10 Main Onshore Wind Power Developers in Taiwan by 2007

	Wind Farm	*Developer*	*Number of Wind Turbines*	*Capacity (MW)*
1	Penghu JhongtunFirst-phase	TPC	4	2.4
2	Shihmen (1st NPP)	TPC	6	3.96
3	Hengchun (3rd NPP)	TPC	3	4.5
4	Penghu JhongtunSecond-phase	TPC	4	2.4
5	Taoyuan Datan	TPC	3	4.5
6	Taoyuan Dayuan Guanyin	TPC	20	30
7	Taichung Power Plant	TPC	4	8
8	Taichung Harbor	TPC	18	36
9	Changbin Industrial Park	TPC	23	46
10	Hsinchu Siangshan	TPC	6	12
Subtotal			91	149.76
11	Yunlin Mailiao	Formosa HeavyIndustries Corp.	4	2.64
12	Hsinchu Chunfong	Cheng Loong Corp.	2	3.5

670. MOEABOE, About, p. 1, available at: http://www.moeaboe.gov.tw/About/webpage/book_en1/page1.htm.

	Wind Farm	*Developer*	*Number of Wind Turbines*	*Capacity (MW)*
13	Miaoli Jhunan	InfraVest GmbH	4	7.8
14	Miaoli Dapeng	InfraVest GmbH	21	42
15	Changbin Lugan	Luway	33	75.9
Subtotal			64	131.84
Total			155	281.6

442. As there is limited onshore space for wind turbines and the wind is often much stronger offshore around Taiwan, there was a policy initiative to promote offshore wind power parks—The Program for the First Stage of Offshore Wind Development[671]—approved by the Executive Yuan in August 2007, with a view to developing 300 MW offshore wind farms. However, unlike the successful onshore wind farm under the FIT scheme, this program has not gone very well, and so far, no offshore wind power plants have been built. Numerous technical issues are challenging the viability of offshore wind farms, particularly concerns about the effect of typhoons and earthquakes on the wind turbine base.

443. As a 2 NTD/kWh FIT is not very attractive to PV installers, the use of PV was encouraged by a more ambitious "demonstration investment subsidy scheme"[672] and "investment subsidy scheme"[673] before 2009 Renewable Energy Act. According to 2007 statistics, the BOE subsidized the establishment of 243 PV systems sites, with a total installed capacity of 2,066 kWp, which can generate electricity of up to 2,180 kWh, enough to meet the needs of 542 households for one year. Many PV systems have been installed on public buildings for demonstration purposes, such as the Presidential Building, Legislative Yuan, and MOEA offices. Moreover, the system is also widely installed in schools and remote areas on offshore islands for demonstration and disaster reduction purposes.

444. There are also support measures for green procurement, that is, the development of PV units by public sector organizations. In order to deal with the financial crisis, the government sought to launch a large-scale Public Investment Program on PV Demonstration, under a special 2009 Ordinance.[674]

671. The Program of the First Stage of Offshore Wind Power Development, available at: http://www.moeaboe.gov.tw/opengovinfo/Laws/secondaryenergy/LSecondaryMain.aspx?PageId=l_secondary_08.
672. Ordinance on Demonstration Investment Subsidy for PV Plants (enacted Mar. 6, 2002; revised on Apr. 30, 1993 and May 30, 1994).
673. Ordinance on Investment Subsidy of PV Plant (2006).
674. Public Investment Program on PV Demonstration, 2009, available at: http://www.moeaboe.gov.tw/opengovinfo/Laws/secondaryenergy/LSecondaryMain.aspx?PageId=l_secondary_13.

445. In addition, the government is also very keen on establishing a special program to encourage the development of special forms of PV. These programs are summarized in Table 11.

Table 11 PV Programs in Taiwan since 2007

Promotion Projects	*Project Contents*
Solar Community (2007~)	PV systems for residential houses in special communities designated by local governments. 2,000 kWp will be installed by 2009. The total installation capacity will be up to 4,000 kWp.
Solar Top Project for each county (2007~2010)	PV systems integrated with landmark buildings, designed by local governments.
Solar Campus Project (2008~)	PV systems installed in junior high schools and elementary schools for education purposes
Public Building Installation Project (2009~)	Public construction projects with budgets over 50 million NTD must install PV systems with at least 5% expense of the total project budget being for PV installations.

Source: MOEABOE, Sustainable Development of Renewable Energy, available at: http://www.moeaboe.gov.tw/About/webpage/book_en1/page2.htm.

446. Finally, there are also certain measures to encourage the development of a relatively infant technology-fuel cell. In order to encourage the initial application of the fuel cell, a Demonstration Subsidy Ordinance on Fuel Cells[675] was promulgated in January 2009. This Ordinance provides subsidies for not only the installations but also the operational fuel, as fuel cost is also a barrier to the use of fuel cells.

§3. Third Stage: Adoption of Renewable Energy Act in 2009

The Subsidy Scheme in the Renewable Energy Act of 2009

447. After a long discussion in Parliament, the Renewable Energy Act was passed right after the National Energy Conference of 2009. In general, even though this Act is called "renewable energy," the measures mainly focus on the development of a "FIT" scheme for "renewable electricity." It also reflects the fact that of

675. Demonstration Subsidy Ordinance on Fuel Cell, Abrogated on: 2013-03-06, available at: http://www.moeaboe.gov.tw/opengovinfo/Laws/secondaryenergy/LSecondaryMain.aspx?PageId=l_secondary_12.

all the 23 provisions, only 1 provision deals with renewable heating and renewable transportation fuel. With a view to improving the previously insufficient 2 NTD FIT, which was mainly based on the avoidance cost, the new FIT scheme will be mainly based on the real cost of each renewable electricity installation. The major measures in this Act to promote different forms of renewable energy have been illustrated in Table 12.

Table 12 Main Measures to Promote Renewable Energy under the Renewable Energy Act

Types of renewable energy	*Measures*	
Renewable electricity	*Main mechanisms*	Renewable Energy Development Fund for R&D, investment subsidy, demonstration subsidy, and feed-in tariff
		Feed-in tariff
		Investment subsidy for installations and demonstration installations
		Interconnection (grid connection) obligation for utilities
	Others	Renewable electricity target
		Tax incentives for import of renewable installations
		Green procurement
Renewable heating	Investment subsidy for solar water installations	
Renewable transportation fuel (biodiesel and biofuel)	Mandatory Mixture Obligation (2% for biodiesel) Voluntary program for ethanol (3% for ethanol)	

Source: Compiled by the author.

448. In the second stage, the funding for the FIT comes mainly from Tai-Power's budget. In order to provide a solid financial basis for the FIT, a Renewable Energy Development Fund was established under Article 7 of the Renewable Energy Act. The fund's resources come mainly from the non-renewable electricity generators of Tai-Power, IPPs, and (≥300 MW) cogenerators. The government may also use its budget to finance this fund. In this regard, as there are sufficient funds for the FIT, a more preferential FIT scheme will likely be introduced. The preferential tariff for 2020 is illustrated in Tables 13 (renewable energy except for solar PV) and 14 (solar PV).

Table 13 Feed-in Tariff for Renewable Energy (Except Solar PV) in 2020

Renewable Energy Type	*Category*	*Capacity Size*	*Feed-In Tariffs (NTD/kWh)*			*Duration*
Wind	Land	1 kW and above but under 30 kW	7.7998			20 Years
		30 kW and above	Installed LVRT		2.3219	
			Non-installed LVRT		2.2888	
	Offshore	1 kW and above	Fixed 20-Year Tariff (upper limit on the tariff)		5.0946	
			Phased tariffs	1st 10 years	5.8015	
				2nd 10 years	3.8227	
Hydropower	–	1 kW and above	2.8599			
Geothermal	–	1 kW and above	Fixed 20-Year Tariff		5.1956	
			Phased tariffs	1st 10 years	6.1710	
				2nd 10 years	3.5685	
Biomass	Non-anaerobic digestion facilities	1 kW and above	2.6871			
	Anaerobic digestion facilities		5.1176			
Waste	–	1 kW and above	3.9482			

Table 14 2020 Feed-in Tariff for Solar PV

Renewable Energy Type	*Category*	*Capacity Size*		*First Phase 1 (NTD/kWh)*	*Second Phase 1 (NTD/kWh)*	*Add Recycling Costs (NTD/kWh)*	*Add Connected to the EHV2 Grid (NTD/kWh)*	*Duration*
Solar PV	Roof-top system	1 kW and above but under 20 kW		5.7132	5.7132	0.0656	–	20 Years
		20 kW and above but under 100 kW		4.4366	4.3701		–	
		100 kW and above but under 500 kW		4.1372	4.0722		–	
		500 kW and above	Not connected to the EHV2 Grid	4.0571	3.9917		–	
			Connected to the EHV2 Grid				0.4674	
	Ground-mounted system	1 kW and above	Not connected to the EHV2 Grid	3.9383	3.8752		–	
			Connected to the EHV2 Grid				0.4506	
	Floating system	1 kW and above	Not connected to the EHV2 Grid	4.3319	4.2709		–	
			Connected to the EHV2 Grid				0.4358	

Source: https://www.moeaboe.gov.tw/ECW/main/content/wHandMenuFile.ashx?file_id=6803.

449. Even though the original purpose of the Renewable Energy Act was to promote all types of renewable electricity, due to the failure to consider all the costs involved during the drafting of the Act, such as that of marine energy, only PV is given preferential treatment in the early stage. This phenomenon led to a "dash for PV" in 2010. The original scheduled target for 2010 was 75 MW but the accelerated development of PV resulted in 754 MW being reached, which is equivalent to the target for the years between 2015 (430 MW) and 2020 (1250 MW).

450. Even though the FIT was used to replace the investment subsidy and already plays a major role in encouraging the development of renewable electricity, the demonstration investment subsidy is also being used. This subsidy supports investment in nascent technologies such as building-integrated photovoltaic (BIPV) and oceanic energy.[676] As there is no relevant category on the FIT table, it is impossible to encourage these expensive renewable forms of electricity under an FIT-only system. In addition, the aforementioned Subsidy Ordinance for fuel cells is proving effective in providing demonstration subsidies for fuel cells. After the Fukushima accident, offshore wind power is becoming more important under the 2011 Thousand Onshore and Offshore Wind Turbines program. Because of the low FIT for offshore wind power (4.1982 NTD/kWh in 2010; 5.5626 NTD/kWh in 2011), the extra demonstration subsidy is provided by the subsidy ordinance.[677] The name of the Ordinance makes it seem as though the subsidy is a grant. However, according to Article 6 of the Ordinance, the grantee must pay back the funds when starting to receive a FIT subsidy. Markedly, this type of subsidy may be similar to a *zero interest loan.*

451. The government also plays a pioneering role in PV implementation. After the aforementioned 2009 Public Investment Program for PV installations, the second wave Public Investment Program Ordinance of 2010[678] was announced after the enactment of the 2009 Renewable Energy Act. This legislation also showed the government's role in promoting PV installations. Indeed, by this stage, the government was seeking to provide funding for "local governments" to install PV units on their public buildings.

452. From the above, it is evident that the Taiwan government is very keen on promoting PV use after the passing of the Renewable Energy Act. The main reason is quite simple. PV is the only renewable electricity that Taiwan has the ability to

676. Demonstration Subsidy Ordinance on Renewable Electricity Installations, Amended Date: 2012-08-29, available at: http://www.moeaboe.gov.tw/opengovinfo/Laws/secondaryenergy/LSecondaryMain.aspx?PageId=l_secondary_24.
677. Ordinance for Demonstration Subsidy for Wind Power (offshore) of 2012, 2012-07-03, available at: https://law.moj.gov.tw/LawClass/LawOldVer.aspx?pcode=J0130063&lnndate=20120703&lser=001.
678. Public Investment Program Ordinance of 2010, 2002-03-30, available at: http://www.moeaboe.gov.tw/opengovinfo/Laws/secondaryenergy/LSecondaryMain.aspx?PageId=l_secondary_19.

export as a product around the world. In this regard, the creation of a domestic PV market would further strengthen the competitiveness of Taiwanese industry.

Tendering Scheme after PV Proliferation in 2010

453. After the passing of the Renewable Energy Act in 2009, the government promulgated the rate schedule for the FIT of 2010.[679] The PV rate schedule for 1–<10 kW, ≥10–500 kW, and >500 kW installations is 11.1883, 12.9722, and 11.1190 NTD, respectively.[680] As this does not consider the sharp cost reduction of PV in 2010, the rate was considered too preferential.[681]

454. This preferential rate attracted more than ten times the application cases (more than 800 MW) than scheduled (75 MW).[682] The government began to launch FIT reform. On one hand, in the new Ordinance,[683] the government cut the rate dramatically, sparking widespread outcry from the PV industry and installers.[684] The new rate for a rooftop PV of 1–<10 kW, ≥10–100 kW, ≥100–500 kW, and >500 kW is 10.3185, 9.1799, 8.8241, and 7.9701, respectively, equivalent to a rate cut of -29.34%, -29.23%, -31.98%, and -28.32%, respectively. The new rate for all ground-type PV is 7.3297 (-34.08%).

455. On the other hand, Taiwan implemented the combo scheme on March 17, 2011.[685] The installations will be divided into four categories by equipment type, installed capacity, and whether the installation is self-owned or not. The exception is for category 1 (applied capacity between 1–10 kW, rooftop installation owned by the building owner), which will be subject to the unchanged FIT rate noted above. Applications for the remaining three categories[686] will be subject to a tendering scheme. The government will later publish the call for tenders, which will also set the cap for each call. Bidders will then be invited to submit their expected installed capacity and tendering rate, which is usually lower than the FIT rate schedule, to

679. Ordinance of the FIT Rate Schedule of 2010.
680. For >500 kW installations, extra investment subsidy of 50,000 NTD is provided. Taking into account this factor, the FIT is around 14.6030 NTD.
681. This part is mainly adapted from Ming-Zhi Gao, A. (2014). A more sustainable way to promote PV: Transformations from FIT to FIT/FIT tendering schemes in Taiwan and France. Legal issues of renewable energy in the Asia Region: Recent development in a post-Fukushima and post-Kyoto Protocol Era. The Netherlands, Kluwer Law International: 38.
682. Lin, Policy U-turn of PV Promotion Scheme, 2010-12-27, Liberty Times, available at: http://www.libertytimes.com.tw/2010/new/dec/27/today-e8.htm.
683. Ordinance of FIT Rate Schedule of 2011.
684. *See* Yang, The 30% Rate Cut of PV Purchasing Rate; the future is dim for the PV industry, 2011-03-15, The Economy Times, available at: http://www.ezsell.com.tw/mep082/app/eip.asp?dblabel=mep082&apid=message.asp&act=detail&dept_id=370_310&fno=11901&dsn=&sort=a&seo=%A4%D3%B6%A7%A5%FA%B9q%A6%AC%C1%CA%B6O%B2v%B6%5E%A4T%A6%A8+%B7~%AA%CC%A1G%B5o%AEi%A8%FC%AA%FD+1000415.
685. PV Tendering Ordinance of Phase I of 2011.
686. (1) Rooftop with an installed capacity between 1–10 kW and not owned by the building owner; (2) Rooftop installation with an installed capacity superior to 10 kW; (3) ground-type installation with an installed capacity superior to 1 kW that fulfills the "Land Use Regulations." *See* Art. 3 of PV Tendering Ordinance of Phase I of 2011.

win the bid. The winners will be awarded the favor of selling electricity to Tai-Power at the same rate for twenty years. In this regard, Taiwan actually has a *FIT-rate-indexed* tendering scheme in which the rate schedule is a reference to the "rate ceiling." This seems to provide more certainty and investment security than other non-FIT tendering schemes.

456. The tendering scheme is regulated by five administrative ordinances: PV Tendering Ordinance of Phase I of 2011, PV Tendering Ordinance of Phase II of 2011, PV Tendering Ordinance of Phase III of 2011, PV Tendering Ordinance of 2012, and PV Tendering Ordinance of 2013. The evolution of the different ordinances demonstrates a trend of expansion of the effective timeline of a tendering ordinance. In the first year, 2011, the three tendering ordinances were published only slightly before the tender date, and these only applied to one/several tenders within a year for several tenders, which resulted in relative uncertainty for investors. To increase certainty and reflect the government's experience in tendering, the Ordinance of 2012 was published in advance and valid for the whole year. In 2013, the new tendering ordinance became effective for the rest of the year, meaning there is no need to publish a new Ordinance annually.

Tendering Target and Cap

457. Table 15 summarizes the tendering target and cap.

Table 15 Tendering Target and Cap for the Tendering Scheme (2011–2013)

<table>
<tr><th>Related Ordinance</th><th>Tendering Cap</th><th>Other Caps</th></tr>
<tr><td>PV Tendering Ordinance of Phase I of 2011</td><td>15 MW (for this phase)</td><td>Cap for rooftop: 12 MW
Cap for ground-type PV: 3 MW</td></tr>
<tr><td rowspan="2">PV Tendering Ordinance of Phase II of 2011</td><td rowspan="2">17.6 MW (for this phase)</td><td>Caps for each further subphase:
Subphase 1: 5 MW (July 20, 2011); subphase 2:5 MW (August 5, 2011); subphase 3:7.6 MW (August 19, 2011)</td></tr>
<tr><td>Cap for ground-type PV for each subphase:
1 MW</td></tr>
<tr><td rowspan="2">PV Tendering Ordinance of Phase III of 2011</td><td rowspan="2">6.2 MW (for this phase)</td><td>No cap for each subphase:
Subphase 1 (September 30, 2011); subphase 2 (October 14, 2011); subphase 3 (October 21, 2011)</td></tr>
<tr><td>Cap for ground-type PV for each subphase:
1 MW</td></tr>
<tr><td rowspan="3">PV Tendering Ordinance of 2012</td><td rowspan="3">70 MW

(Was expanded to 83 MW on August 1, 2012)</td><td>Cap for each subphase: 10 MW
<table>
<tr><th>Subphase</th><th>Deadline for submission</th></tr>
<tr><td>1</td><td>February 20</td></tr>
<tr><td>2</td><td>March 19</td></tr>
<tr><td>3</td><td>April 16</td></tr>
<tr><td>4</td><td>May 21</td></tr>
<tr><td>5</td><td>June 18</td></tr>
<tr><td>6</td><td>July 16</td></tr>
<tr><td>7</td><td>August 20</td></tr>
<tr><td>8</td><td>September 17</td></tr>
<tr><td>9</td><td>October 15</td></tr>
<tr><td>10</td><td>November 12</td></tr>
</table></td></tr>
<tr><td>Cap for all ground-type PV: 5 MW</td></tr>
<tr><td>Cap for ground-type PV for each subphase:
2 MW</td></tr>
<tr><td rowspan="3">PV Tendering Ordinance of 2013</td><td rowspan="3">90 MW (Was expanded to 135 MW in August 2013.)</td><td>Cap for each sub-phase: 10 MW
(However, if the total submission capacity (X) for each subphase is over 10 MW, the cap for each subphase can be increased to 10 MW + (X-10 MW)/2)
<table>
<tr><th>Subphase</th><th>Deadline for submission</th></tr>
<tr><td>1</td><td>January 14</td></tr>
<tr><td>2</td><td>February 25</td></tr>
<tr><td>3</td><td>April 1</td></tr>
<tr><td>4</td><td>April 29</td></tr>
<tr><td>5</td><td>June 3</td></tr>
<tr><td>6</td><td>July 1</td></tr>
<tr><td>7</td><td>August 5</td></tr>
<tr><td>8</td><td>September 2</td></tr>
<tr><td>9</td><td>October 7</td></tr>
<tr><td>10</td><td>November 4</td></tr>
</table></td></tr>
<tr><td>Cap for all ground-type PV: 5 MW

Cap for ground-type PV for each subphase:
2 MW</td></tr>
<tr><td>Cap for all large rooftop PV: 15 MW

Cap for large rooftop PV for each sub-phase: 5 MW</td></tr>
</table>

Source: Compiled by the author.

458. From this development, several evolutions are evident. First, the phase of each schedule has become more certain and scheduled. Second, the annual cap could be increased to a certain limit to encourage the development of PV. Third, there is a tendency to discourage ground-type PV in favor of rooftop PV. Finally, in terms of rooftop PV, a smaller rooftop is preferred over a larger one.

I. Eligibility

A. *Installation Capacity*

459. In 2011, all ground-type PV were subject to the tendering scheme, and rooftop PV was preferred; specifically, smaller rooftop PV (between 1–10 kW, rooftop installation installed by the owner of the building). In 2012, the PV Tendering Ordinance loosened the regulations for rooftop systems, and the threshold of a tendering exemption was made 30 kW. Other exemptions included: (1) PV installations subsidized in a form of investment or demonstration subsidy by MOEABOE, and (2) PV installations set up by the government or state-owned companies.

460. In 2013, exemptions for the tendering scheme became "all" cases related to installing PVs on government and public school's own or managed buildings (A); and PV (B) on such buildings rented to private parties and approved by the local governments. Furthermore, the aggregative capacity (A+B) must not exceed 5 MW. However, for state-owned company cases, the annual capacity under 5 MW is also exempted from the tendering scheme.

B. *Capacity Requirement for Each Case*

461. Under the three PV Tendering Ordinances in 2011, the capacity range for each case is 1 kW–2 MW, which was applicable to both rooftop and ground-type PV. In 2012, the cap for each application case (5 MW) favored rooftop PV over ground-type PV (1 MW). This capacity requirement of 5 MW and 1 MW was maintained in the 2013 PV Tendering Ordinance.

C. *Other Criteria*

462. Compared with the very complex requirements under France's simple and complex tendering scheme launched in 2011, the extra requirement in Taiwan is relatively simple.

463. First, those tendering are required to pay a security deposit to participate in the scheme.[687] According to Article 6 of the 2013 PV Tendering Ordinance, the amount is 0.1 million, 0.2 million, 0.3 million, 0.4 million, 0.5 million, and 1 million NTD for a capacity range of 1–100 kW, 100–200 kW, 200–300 kW, 300–400 kW, 400–500 kW, and ≥500 kW, respectively.

464. Second, local governments were allowed to participate in the tendering bid under the PV Tendering Ordinance of Phase I of 2011. However, because of different financial and subsidy situations, one local government submitted a very low

687. *See, e.g.*, Art. 6 of PV Tendering Ordinance of 2012.

price (only 75% of the FIT rate) and disrupted the tendering scheme. Thus, since the PV Tendering Ordinance of Phase II of 2011, a PV under other special subsidy schemes including the compulsory 6% of green elements of public buildings and those subsidized by the MOEA or MOEABOE are excluded from the tendering scheme.[688] As mentioned, the exclusions or exemptions were further expanded to other government or state-owned companies,[689] and private parties developing PV on governmental buildings.[690]

465. Finally, for ground-type PV, an extra requirement to comply with land-related regulations was added.

II. Ratio of Rooftop to Ground-Type PV

466. In the PV Tendering Ordinance of Phase I of 2011, the capacity ratio between rooftop and ground-type PV is 4 (12 MW) to 1 (3 MW). Since the PV Tendering Ordinance of Phase II of 2011, only the installation cap for ground-type PV is provided. However, the trend indicates the gradually increasing preference for rooftop PV. For instance, under the "three subphases" of the PV Tendering Ordinance of Phase II of 2011, the ratio is 5 (total cap of rooftop and ground-type PV) to 1 (1 MW for ground-type PV) or 7.6 MW (total cap of rooftop and ground-type PV) to 1 MW (ground-type PV). Under the PV Tendering Ordinance of Phase III of 2011, it is 6.2 MW (total cap of rooftop and ground-type PV) to 1 MW (ground-type PV). In the PV Tendering Ordinance of 2012, it is 70 MW (total cap of rooftop and ground-type PV) to 5 MW (ground-type PV) (14:1) for the cap for the whole year, and 10 MW to 2 MW for each phase.

467. Recently, under the PV Tendering Ordinance of 2013, an even higher ratio is seen: 18:1 [90 MW (total cap of rooftop and ground-type PV) to 5 MW (ground-type PV)] for the annual cap of the original schedule.[691]

III. Administrative Procedure for Tendering

A. *Submission of Related Documents*

468. Applicants are required to provide the relevant documents to participate in the bidding process. Compared with the complex documents required under the

688. Article 3 of PV Tendering Ordinance of Phase II of 2011 and PV Tendering Ordinance of Phase III of 2011.
689. Article 2, PV Tendering Ordinance of 2012.
690. Article 2 of the PV Tendering Ordinance of 2013.
691. The new and additional 45 MW (with 5 MW cap for ground-type PV) was increased to the original cap in August 2013.

simple and complex tendering scheme in France, the mandatory documents in Taiwan are very simple.[692] First, applicants must submit a document preparing for the author's permission for future installation, including[693] an identity document, site explanation, photos of the site, and so on. Second, following the format of Annex 3, proof of the security deposit payment must be provided.[694] Finally, applicants must follow the format of Annex 1 and submit a Tender Document, which indicates the "discount rate" from the FIT rate schedule. This discount rate is an important element during the review process. In addition, for ground-type PV, a document proving compliance with land use regulations by land and related authorities must be obtained.

B. Review Process

469. After receiving the bid (bid deadline), the government first checks the "formal" issues. For cases that do not qualify, applicants will be asked to submit related documents if further information can remedy any shortcomings. Cases that do qualify will then undergo the second round of the review process (day of open bid). On the day, the sealed document indicating the discount rate—the "Tender Document"—is opened. After comparing the bidding price, the results of the bid are finalized and published.

470. The evolution of different regulations concerning the duration between the "bid deadline" and "day of the open bid" is interesting. It seems as though there is a wider gap between these two dates, which delays the tendering process. For instance, the gap is only one day (April 28/April 29, 2011) under the PV Tendering Ordinance of Phase I of 2011. This lengthens to more than ten days under the PV Tendering Ordinance of Phase II of 2011 and PV Tendering Ordinance of Phase III of 2011: July 20/July 29, August 5/August 17, August 19/August 31, September 30/October 13, October 14/October 26, and October 21/November 3. In 2012 (*see* Table 16) and 2013 (*see* Table 17) Ordinances, the gap increases to more than twenty days.

Table 16 PV Tendering Ordinance of 2012

Subphase	*Deadline for Submission*	*Date of Open Bid*
1	February 20	March 14
2	March 19	April 11
3	April 16	May 9
4	May 21	June 13

692. *See*, e.g., Art. 4 of PV Tendering Ordinance of 2012.
693. *See*, e.g., Art. 6 of the Ordinance on Renewable Electricity License and Registration.
694. *See*, e.g., Art. 6 of the PV Tendering Ordinance of 2012.

Subphase	*Deadline for Submission*	*Date of Open Bid*
5	June 18	July 11
6	July 16	August 8
7	August 20	September 12
8	September 17	October 11
9	October 15	November 7
10	November 12	December 5

Table 17 PV Tendering Ordinance of 2013

Subphase	*Deadline for Submission*	*Date of Open Bid*
1	January 14	February 6
2	February 25	March 20
3	April 1	April 24
4	April 29	May 22
5	June 3	June 26
6	July 1	July 24
7	August 5	August 28
8	September 2	September 25
9	October 7	October 30
10	November 4	November 27

471. However, upon closer examination, this is crucial in avoiding unintentionally precluding inexperienced bidders from the latter process. This has also made the tendering scheme more friendly. During the gap period, if the government finds that more documents should be submitted to remedy any procedural flaws in an application, it will ask the applicant to submit this information. Thus, this "mercy" period and measures could improve the capability of small PV installers or household installers during the application process, and reduce the rate of rejection due to filing incomplete documents.

IV. Criteria for Winning the Bid

472. Price determines who wins the tender or bid. In general, the lowest price wins the tender.[695] However, if the discount rate is the same, there are two priorities: (1) the smaller rooftop, and (2) rooftop PV rather than ground-type PV.[696]

695. *See*, *e.g.*, Art. 8 of the PV Tendering Ordinance of 2012.
696. *See*, *e.g.*, Art. 8 of the PV Tendering Ordinance of 2012.

473. The tendering cap would also indirectly determine who wins the tender or bid. Once the tendering cap is reached, a *certain* (not all) extent of surplus capacity is still considered qualified for winning the bid. For instance, under the PV Tendering Ordinance of Phase II of 2011, the cap is 5 MW, but if adding a final rooftop candidate would cause the 5 MW to be exceeded, this case would be accepted. However, for ground-type PV exceeding 1 MW, a maximum exceeding volume of 3%*17.6 MW is set.[697]

V. Procedure after Winning the Bid and Avoiding the Delay Construction Clause

474. For bid winners, the MOEABOE will issue a certificate to confirm that permission to construct has been granted.[698] To avoid a delay in completing construction and starting operation, the candidate must sign a contract with Tai-Power within two months,[699] and must complete construction and obtain an installation registration certificate within the duration specified by the related Ordinance.[700] In general, the duration is within one year after signing the contract with Tai-Power (transmission operators and buyers of electricity), and an extension of six months is likely.

475. As noted, red tape in Taiwan is relatively less bothersome during the bid preparation process. However, for those winning the tender, Taiwan's licensing and registration process is bureaucratic. For instance, PV installers are required to submit numerous documents under the Ordinance on Renewable Electricity License and Registration. For example, for small PV, ten documents are required, including the Registration Format, Completion of Construction Photo and Layout, Receipt of Buying a PV Installation, and the related Certificate of National Standards or ISO.[701]

VI. Results of the Tender: 17 Times of Experience

476. Below, the important findings regarding the tender results are summarized.

477. First, based on **the effectiveness of tendering in reaching the tendering target,** tendering seven times in the first year is not satisfactory. The number of applications is usually lower than the expected cap. As such, it took seven tendering attempts to reach the annual target at the end of 2011. However, after this learning stage, in 2012, applicants began increasing: the number of applications in each subphase was higher than the scheduled cap. This lead to reaching the expected target

697. Article 8 of the PV Tendering Ordinance of Phase II of 2011.
698. *See, e.g.*, Art. 9 of the PV Tendering Ordinance of Phase III of 2011.
699. *See, e.g.*, Art. 10 of the PV Tendering Ordinance of 2012.
700. Article 9, the Ordinance on Renewable Electricity License and Registration.
701. Article 10 of the Ordinance on Renewable Electricity License and Registration.

early in August 2012. (Extra capacity was provided and the case was closed in September.) A similar situation occurred in 2013: it took only three bidding rounds to reach the annual target in 2013.

478. How do we explain this situation? Several reasons can be provided. The applicants became more familiar with the bidding rules and associated red tape. Moreover, the government revised the PV tendering ordinance several times and made the bidding procedure more convenient and predicable, and increased investment security. In addition, the collapse of the export market for Taiwan's PV industry led PV industries to develop the local market. Furthermore, in the sunnier southern part of Taiwan, the local government provided extra incentives such as a loan scheme and building code preference. The Million PV Roof Programme under the New Energy Policy also seemed to have played a role.

479. Second, this article further explores if the tendering scheme achieved its goal of dealing with issues pertaining to the installation of PV through control *developing volume* and *cost*. For the former, it was found that the control volume effect was better in 2011 than in 2012 and 2013. Furthermore, it is more effective in ground-type PV than in rooftop PV.

480. For the latter, cost control is reflected in the factor *average discount rate*. A high discount rate of 25% only appeared once under the PV Tendering Ordinance of Phase I of 2011. The discount rate was only more than 10% twice,[702] and was usually 5%[703] or less than 5%.[704]

Evaluation

481. Taiwan was already following Germany's Renewable Energy Sources Act, (Erneuerbare-Energien-Gesetz, EEG), introduced the FIT scheme before 2016, and promulgated the Renewable Energy Development Act in 2009.[705] The FIT obliges the state-owned electricity company Tai-Power to buy renewable electricity at a very favorable rate for twenty years. Table 18 presents the changes between 1997 and 2016 in the installation capacities of various electricity sources. The FIT scheme contributed to the prosperity of renewable energy, particularly photovoltaic and wind power: photovoltaic power increased to four digits by 2016, and wind power almost doubled over eight years. Thus, the FIT scheme played a key part in facilitating the development of renewable energy.

702. 12.74 (2012-7); 10.59 (2013-3).
703. 6% (102-1); 6.95% (102-2); 5.54% (2011-3-3).
704. 2.62%, 0.31%, 2.95%, 0.31%, 3.12%, 0.31%, 3.37%, 4.40%, 4.35%, 4.72%, 2.06%, 3.20%, 2.53%, 3.09%, 4.37%.
705. Renewable Energy Development Act, 2009.07.08, available at: https://law.moj.gov.tw/Eng/LawClass/LawAll.aspx?PCode=J0130032.

Table 18 Renewable Energy Installation Capacities in Taiwan, 1997–2016 (Unit MW)

Year	*Run of the Rive Hydro Power*	*Wind*	*PV*	*Geothermal Electricity (MW)*	*Biomass Electricity (MW)*	*Waste Electricity (MW)*
1997	1686.00	–	–	–	68.77	75.10
2003	1908.75	8.54	0.45	–	103.05	512.41
2004	1909.73	8.54	0.57	–	103.05	541.81
2005	1909.73	23.94	1.04	–	99.05	573.81
2006	1909.73	101.99	1.41	–	116.77	609.46
2007	1921.23	185.99	2.44	–	116.77	622.46
2008	1937.93	250.39	5.58	–	116.77	622.46
2009	1936.93	374.29	9.51	–	116.77	622.46
2010	1977.43	475.89	22.02	–	116.77	622.46
2011	2040.73	522.69	117.89	–	111.32	624.43
2012	2081.44	570.99	222.51	–	111.32	629.13
2013	2081.44	614.19	392.02	–	111.32	629.13
2014	2081.44	637.19	620.08	–	111.32	629.13
2015	2089.44	646.69	842.04	–	111.32	629.13
2016	2089.44	682.09	1061.38	–	111.32	629.13

Source: MOEABOE, the RE installation capacity (updated January 10, 2016), http://www.moeaboe.gov.tw/ECW/populace/web_book/wHandWebReports_File.ashx?type=pdf&book_code=M_CH&chapter_code=L&rport_code=01.

§4. Stage Four: Electricity Liberalization and the Renewable Energy Act of 2019

Electricity Liberalization Act of 2017

482. Because the FIT scheme was successfully facilitating renewable energy development, it seemed rational to further stimulate this development by amending the Renewable Energy Development Act of 2009. However, the government revised the Taiwan Electricity Act to use the electricity liberalization market as a tool to facilitate renewable energy development.[706]

483. The reason for this reform was that the monopolistic electricity supply structure dominated by Tai-Power was not friendly to renewable energy sources. The government claimed that more harm than good would result for renewable energy developers if they could sell only to Tai-Power under the fixed FIT scheme. Thus, the government and energy experts produced a unique idea, that of the "green electricity priority."

484. Under the green electricity priority, only renewable energy generators were allowed to sell on the open electricity market, and the so-called grey power producers such as coal-fired and gas-fired IPPs and CHP (i.e., cogeneration) systems were only allowed to sell to Tai-Power. To gain acceptance of the approach, a promotional video was posted on YouTube presenting an analogy equating the regulated electricity market then in place to a vegetable market with just one vegetable buyer. If farmers were forced to sell to one buyer, there would be no incentive for them to increase their output because they would not be free to sell to other customers.[707]

485. Electricity consumers would also benefit because they would be free to buy renewable energy directly from the generators or from renewable energy retailers. Furthermore, the MOEA created a promotional video stating that many farmers wanted to buy renewable energy from nearby villages, but the monopolistic electricity supply structure limited their options, giving them no choice except Tai-Power for their electricity.[708]

486. It seems clear that assuming "the FIT regime, a regime forcing renewable energy developers to sell all renewable energy to one or a few grid operators, would discourage renewable energy developers from entering the market" is not economically rational. Despite opposition from Tai-Power, renewable non-governmental organizations (NGOs), renewable energy interest groups, and this author, Parliament dominated by the DPP adopted the green electricity priority in January 2017 as the Taiwan Electricity Act Amendment: Towards a Liberalized and Green Energy Market.[709]

---

706. The introduction of the details of this new Electricity Liberalization Act, *see* Anton Ming-Zhi Gao, Chien-Te Fan, Chao-Ning Liao, Application of German energy transition in Taiwan: A critical review of unique electricity liberalisation as a core strategy to achieve renewable energy growth, Energy Policy 120 (2018) 644–654.
707. Apple Daily, 2016. What blocks the Green Energy Development: the Aged More Than 50 years old Electricity Act should be blamed. Dec. 17, 2016, available at: http://www.appledaily.com.tw/realtimenews/article/new/20161217/1011868/.
708. Electricity Liberalization Bill- RE as Gifts, available at: https://www.youtube.com/watch?v=oOKWnRjjeb4.
709. The Electricity Act, 2017.01.26, available at: https://law.moj.gov.tw/Eng/LawClass/LawAll.aspx?PCode=J0030011. The introduction, *see*, *e.g.*, Major Amendments to the Taiwan Electricity Act (20 17), Jan. 16, 2017, available at: https://www.takassocies.com/single-post/2017/01/16/Major-Amendments-to-the-Taiwan-Electricity-Act-2017.

487. As expected, more than three years since the Amendment passed, there have been little achievements. Except for those PV or offshore wind power projects subject to a relatively low power purchase tariff (such as 2.6 NTD for PV in a tendered project in Chiayi County),[710] the price was TWD 2,548 per MWh (approximately EUR 72.3 per MWh) for offshore wind power in tendered projects.[711] Since there is a very good FIT scheme with high investment security effects in place, most renewable energy developers would rather sell all their renewable energy to Tai-Power than on the free market. In addition, from the demand side, all electricity customers seem to prefer buying less expensive electricity from Tai-Power. The claim that Taiwan would be the first country to adopt a green electricity priority has instead been the biggest failure of electricity liberalization.

The Tendering Scheme and Selection Scheme for Offshore Wind Power in 2018

488. Since 2016, the government has been very active in promoting the development of offshore wind power. From 2016, the FIT was fixed between NTD 5.5160 and 6.0437/kWh for twenty years, and the front-end tariff at NTD 6.2795 to 7.4034/kWh for the first ten years and from NTD 3.4586 to 4.1422/kWh for the subsequent ten years. Taiwan's FIT is not only higher but also applicable to a longer period than in the UK (fifteen years: GBP 74.75 and GBP 57.50/MWh) after tendering in 2017 and 2019, respectively, and the twenty years in Germany. Taiwan's FIT is two to three times higher if the duration and effects of the front-end tariffs are considered.

489. In early 2017, the government recognized the problem caused by the unexpected number of applicants. The applications represented more than 10 GW. If these projects were to be awarded a favorable FIT, it would cause a tremendous burden to electricity consumers. In addition, there were concerns over grid connections and the harbor.[712] Thus, reasonable reduction of the 10 GW was a policy concern. Before mid-2017, the favorable FIT was applied to all renewables projects, as there was no quantity cap according to the REDA.

490. In June 2017, the BOE announced a tendering scheme.[713] The announcement was soon criticized, and the MOEABOE stated that there was no intent to limit development.[714] The BOE disclosed further measures in August and included a draft of the offshore WP selection scheme, which was considered a combination of fixed

---

710. Common Wealth, In 2020, Taiwan's Green Energy Will Power Tech Giants Like Apple and Google, Dec. 24, 2019, available at: https://english.cw.com.tw/article/article.action?id=2627.
711. Offshorewind, World's Largest Renewable Energy Corporate Power Purchase Agreement Signed in Taiwan, Jul. 8, 2020, available at: https://www.offshorewind.biz/2020/07/08/worlds-largest-renewable-energy-corporate-power-purchase-agreement-signed-in-taiwan/.
712. Richard C., Companies set up shop in Taiwan. Wind power monthly, Feb. 1, 2018, available at: https://www.windpowermonthly.com/article/1455351/companies-set-shop-taiwan; 2018 [accessed Jun. 10, 2020]. Liberty Times. Government changes the rules arbitrarily and wind power developers flip out, http://news.ltn.com.tw/news/focus/paper/1108163; 2017 [accessed Jun. 10, 2020].
713. Liberty Times. Government changes the rules arbitrarily and wind power developers flip out, http://news.ltn.com.tw/news/focus/paper/1108163; 2017 [accessed Jun. 10, 2020].
714. China Times. BOE: The establishment of offshore wind power friendly environment, http://www.chinatimes.com/newspapers/20170607000280-260210; 2017 [accessed Jun. 10, 2020].

FITs and tendering in which applicants had to compete to qualify and to be granted the favorable FIT. The development target increased from the previous 3 GW to 3.5 GW. Bidders were required to demonstrate a 70% LCR effort, which was also the first time the LCR was officially announced.[715] This draft also faced serious criticism as two-thirds of the projects were cancelled. The European Chamber of Commerce Taiwan heavily criticized the lack of investment certainty.[716]

491. In October 2017, the second draft version was released. The allocation capacity was increased to 5.5 GW, comprising a mixture of 3 GW selection and 2.5 GW tendering scheme to minimize opposition.[717] The final version was released in December, which increased the selection to 3.5 GW and reduced tendering to 2 GW.[718] In the final version, 0.5 of the 3.5 GW had to be completed by 2020, and the remaining 3 GW by 2025, while the role of the LCR evolved from explicit to implicit. In addition, in January 2018, the MOEA immediately announced internal administrative rules for the allocation of offshore wind power.[719]

492. On April 30, the review process for non-price selection was performed, and 3836 MW of grid connection capacity was awarded to 11 offshore wind farms proposed by 7 developers. These results and controversies were soon debated in Parliament, including the high tariffs and rule of law.

493. The offshore wind power policy experienced an unexpected threat. The tendering results, which were released in July, revealed that the MOEA awarded 1,664 MW capacity to two developers with bids of NTD 2.225 and 2.548/kWh, which was less than half the selection tariff from the previous two months (5.8). Considering the front-end tariff of NTD 7.1, this was less than one-third of the value.

Renewable Energy Act of 2019

494. As electricity liberalization attempts failed to give impetus to renewable development, the revision to the older Renewable Energy Act of 2009 began to attract attention. After the inauguration ceremony of the new president on May 20, 2016, amendments to the Renewable Energy Act were already under discussion.

715. Liberty Times. Government changes the rules arbitrarily and wind power developers flip out, http://news.ltn.com.tw/news/focus/paper/1108163; 2017 [accessed Jun. 10, 2020].
716. UDN News. ECCT: Taiwan's policy is lacking persistence, https://paper.udn.com/udnpaper/PID0008/317034/web/#2L-10552527L; 2017 [accessed Jun. 10, 2020]. ECCT. ECCT releases 2018 position papers, https://www.ecct.com.tw/new-online-courses; 2017 [accessed Jun. 10, 2020].
717. China Times, BOE is promoting offshore wind power, https://www.chinatimes.com/newspapers/20171013000066-260202; 2017 [accessed Jun. 10, 2020].
718. Harris J, Chao M, Wang RHY, Brughmans F, Raleigh J, Li SS et al. Taiwan: Taiwan offshore wind farm projects: Guiding investors through the legal and regulatory framework. Jones Day, http://www.mondaq.com/x/673224/Renewables/Taiwan+Offshore+Wind+Farm+Projects+Guiding+Investors+Through+The+Legal+And+Regulatory+Framework; 2018 [accessed Jun. 10, 2020].
719. Bureau of Energy, Ministry of Economic Affairs (BOE). Directions for allocating installed capacity of offshore wind potential zones, https://www.moeaboe.gov.tw/ECW/populace/Law/wHandLawsList_File.ashx?kind=6&id=3296&file_id=3476; 2018 [accessed Jun. 10, 2020].

However, the Electricity Liberalization Bill in July 2016 slowed down the progress of the amendment of the Renewable Energy Act amendment. Compared with the fast track revision of the Electricity Liberalization Act of 2017 between July 2016 (BOE bill) and January 2017 (adoption in Parliament), the amendment of the Renewable Energy Act of 2009 progressed slowly. It took almost 1.5 years for the Executive Yuan (cabinet) to approve the cabinet version to Parliament (May 2016–January 11, 2018).[720] In addition, it took more than one year to review the amendment, which was finally passed in Parliament in April 2019.[721]

495. In general, the overall subsidy structure of new revised Renewable Energy Act of 2019 is similar.

- The main subsidy scheme remains at twenty years FIT, supplemented by investment or demonstration subsidies[722] for geothermal electricity,[723] offshore wind power,[724] BIPV,[725] ground PV in Chiayi County,[726] and projects in the indigenous people's region.[727] To provide a solid financial basis, the Renewable Energy Development Fund for R&D, investment subsidy, demonstration subsidy, and FIT remains.[728] Only the main funding source has changed from generators to electricity retailers.[729] The rules on the Interconnection (grid connection) obligation for utilities have been further revised to accommodate the needs of the new situation.[730]
- The original renewable electricity target has been largely increased. The promotion objectives for the total amount of electricity generated by renewable energy

720. Executive Yuan, Executive Yuan Amended Renewable Energy Act, Jan. 11, 2018, available at: https://www.ey.gov.tw/Page/9277F759E41CCD91/fef00622-28c2-41aa-9d6d-733cda223d60.
721. Taiwan Times, Legislative Yuan passes energy act amendments, Apr. 13, 2019, available at: https://www.taipeitimes.com/News/taiwan/archives/2019/04/13/2003713323.
722. Article 11 of the Renewable Energy Act of 2019.
723. Ordinance of the Demonstration subsidy to geothermal electricity, Amended Date: 2019-08-06, available at: https://www.moeaboe.gov.tw/ECW/populace/Law/Content.aspx?menu_id=2028.
724. Ordinance of the Demonstration subsidy to offshore wind power projects, 2019-07-08, available at: https://www.moeaboe.gov.tw/ECW/populace/Law/Content.aspx?menu_id=1850.
725. Ordinance of the Demonstration subsidy for BIPV, 2019-07-01, available at: https://www.moeaboe.gov.tw/ECW/populace/Law/Content.aspx?menu_id=1090.
726. Ordinance of the Demonstration subsidy for solar PV in Chiayi County, 2019-11-13, available at: https://www.moeaboe.gov.tw/ECW/populace/Law/Content.aspx?menu_id=6963.
727. Ordinance of the Demonstration subsidy to renewables in the indigenous people's region, 2019-10-30, available at: https://www.moeaboe.gov.tw/ECW/populace/Law/Content.aspx?menu_id=8626.
728. Article 7 of the Renewable Energy Act of 2019.
729. Article 7(1) of the Renewable Energy Act of 2019: "The central competent authority should establish a renewable energy development fund to develop renewable energy. The sources of income of the aforesaid fund are as follows:

    1. An amount of fees calculated at a certain percentage of its retailing amount of electricity generated from non-renewable energy charged from electricity retailing enterprises;
    2. An amount of fees calculated as a certain percentage based on the amount of electricity generated by the self-use power generation facilities paid by those who install self-use power generation facilities of non-renewable energy."

730. Article 8 of the Renewable energy Act of 2019.

power generation facilities by 2025 is set as more than 27,000,000 kW.[731] Tax incentives for the import of renewable installations[732] and Green procurement[733] remain similar to those in the original design.

496. Larger changes include the introduction of the promotion scheme to electricity storage and the obligation on large electricity users. First, electricity storage is defined in Article 3 of the Renewable Energy Act of 2019 as a facility for power storage and power maintenance, including storage units, power conversion facilities, and power management systems. The storage is qualified for the demonstration subsidy for those energy storage facilities with development potential, in the preliminary stage of technical development, and for energy storage facilities installed in indigenous areas established by cooperatives or communities.[734]

497. Moreover, Articles 12(3)–(5) of the new Renewable Energy Act of 2019 provide the legal basis for introducing a renewable and storage duty on large electricity users. Thus, the obliged entity could comply with this requirement by choosing between an RE or storage. There are four routes to meet this requirement:

– Compliance Method I: installation of an RE or storage installation by the obliged entity.
– Compliance Method II: renting the land to others to install an RE or storage installation.
– Compliance with Method III: using a corporate power purchase agreement (PPA) to buy RE and bundled RECs.
– Compliance with Method IV: paying an alternative payment for non-compliance.

498. Further discussion of the detailed RPS design remains in opposition to large electricity users. After several public inquiry meetings at the end of 2019, the draft regulations on the implementation of the RPS scheme were published on the MOEA's official website and in the government gazette for public deliberation on February 26, 2020.[735] The obliged entities are limited to those with a contract capacity of more than 5000 kW (506 entities), with a lenient five-year period to meet the 10% obligation. Despite such relaxed measures, opposition remains, particularly after the serious loss of revenue for large electricity users during the COVID-19 crisis. After a consultation meeting with affected companies on June 11, 2020, the measures were further relaxed, but still subject to further deliberation.[736] For instance,

731. Article 6(1) of the Renewable Energy Act of 2019.
732. Article 16 of the Renewable Energy Act of 2019.
733. Article 12(1)-(2) of the Renewable Energy Act of 2019.
734. Article 11(1)-(2) of the Renewable Energy Act of 2019.
735. MOEABOE, Draft Ordinance on Renewable Energy Obligation of the Large Electricity Users, published Feb. 26, 2020. https://www.moeaboe.gov.tw/ECW/populace/news/Board.aspx?kind=3&menu_id=57&news_id=16585.
736. Economic Daily News, The Controversy over the draft Ordinance on the Renewable Energy Obligation of the Large Electricity Users, Jun. 12, 2020. https://money.udn.com/money/story/7307/4630397 (visited on Jun. 18, 2020).

for those who had already constructed PV, this may be considered as the 10% obligation under certain conditions. In addition, it is possible to have an early bird discount treatment if the obliged entity can meet the five-year 10% obligation earlier; specifically, 8% within three years or 9% within four years.

Chapter 3. Incentives for Renewable Thermal Use

§1. First Stage: Before Drafting Renewable Energy Bill in 2002

499. As Taiwan is located around the volcanic area of the Pacific Rim, there is an abundant resource of geothermal heat. Earlier investigations have shown that, except for the Tatun volcanic area, most geothermal reservoirs in Taiwan are developed in regions of metamorphic rocks, and are primarily liquid-dominated. The production of hot water is by and large fracture-controlled. The amount of hot water produced by such a well is much smaller than that of a production well in foreign geothermal reservoirs of volcanic type, as reported in the literature. The geothermal resources in Taiwan are thus considered less suitable for power generation on a large scale. To increase economic incentives, the development of domestic geothermal power generation may be better served in conjunction with the development of local leisure and recreational opportunities.

500. However, unlike the large-scale use of geothermal electricity in Iceland, and similar to Japan, Taiwan mainly uses these geothermals for leisure hot spring use. Hot springs are developed by private persons, entertainment companies, or hotel groups. The law related to the development of geothermal energy was the Mining Act of 2002.[737] Article 2(2) of the Mining Act of 2002 provided that "geothermal (and steam air) are regarded as Mines in this Act." This means that owners of hot spring restaurants are required to apply to operate in a mining zone and are subject to very rigid red tape and regulations.

501. Solar water heating is the most important form of renewable heating encouraged by the government. A formal legal and incentive scheme to encourage the development of solar water heaters can be traced back to 1986,[738] even before the promotion of CHP in 1988. The scheme provides an investment subsidy mainly for household installation.

§2. Second Stage: Transition Period Between 2002 and 2009

502. In order to further regulate hot spring geothermal use and to regulate this kind of unique "mine" in the Mining Act, the Hot Spring Act was enacted in 2003.[739] In this Act, hot spring business operators are required to apply for a "Hot Spring Water Right" and a "Hot Spring Mining Right." The latter is further defined as the right to explore and exploit hot spring air and geothermal (steam) under the

737. Mining Act of 2002, Jun. 12, 2002.
738. Ordinance on Investment Subsidy for Solar Water Heater (1986), Abrogated on: 2003-01-22, available at: https://law.moj.gov.tw/LawClass/LawAll.aspx?pcode=J0130021.
739. Hot Spring Act, published on Jul. 2, 2003.

Mine Act.[740] Yet, due to the private sector's strong objection to geothermal's inclusion in the Mining Act, the Mining Act was revised in 2003, and geothermal activity was removed from it.[741] An amendment to the Hot Spring Act was also proposed.[742] However, the concept of a Mining Right was not totally excluded in the Hot Spring Act of 2005 and 2010. A proposal to remove the Hot Spring Mining Right was again brought before the Executive Yuan in 2010.[743] Yet, in the current Act, the Mining Right is just an empty concept, as a hot spring operator is required to get either a Hot Spring Water Right or a Hot Spring Mining Right. It is illegal to run a hot spring business without either a water right or a mining right.[744] Yet, due to the latter right already having been removed from the Mining Act, it is impossible to apply for that right. It is unclear why it is so hard to remove this bizarre concept from the Hot Spring Water Act but very easy to remove it from the Mining Act.

503. At this stage, solar water heaters remain a governmental priority in the field of renewable thermal use. The same strategy exists of providing investment subsidies for potential installers to replace the existing gas-fired, LPG-fired, or electricity water heater with solar water heaters. Only a slight change was brought to the Subsidy Ordinance. The original Ordinance on Investment Subsidy for Solar Water Heaters of 1986 was renamed the Ordinance on Investment Subsidy and Implementation Guide for Solar Water Heaters.[745] This mechanism was applicable until the passing of the Renewable Energy Act in 2009. Because of the good weather conditions and solar heating conditions in south Taiwan, the development of solar heating has been quite satisfactory. Up to May 2009, 440 thousand households had already installed solar heaters, making Taiwan No. 3 in the world for installations.[746]

All of the companies in the solar thermal industry are small and medium-sized enterprises, mainly producing metal plate solar collectors and requiring the government's support for technological development in the industry. In the future, the BOE will help the industry to improve its technological level and strengthen its competitiveness in areas such as building integration, continuous sputtering, large-scale systems, etc. It was estimated that by the end of 2010 the annual installation areas would reach 130,000 m^2.

---

740. Article 3(3) of Hot Spring Act of 2003.
741. Mining Act of 2003, December 2003.
742. The proposed revision of Hot Spring Act in 2005, available at: www.ey.gov.tw/public/Attachment/041310284471.doc (visited on Oct. 10, 2020).
743. The Executive Yuan proposed the Amendment to Hot Spring Act (Apr. 4, 2010) available at: https://www.ey.gov.tw/Page/9277F759E41CCD91/ca257b6c-433a-4a19-bc8e-eadb10c8441d.
744. Article 22 of Mining Act of 2010.
745. Ordinance on Investment Subsidy and Implementation Guide for Solar Water Heaters of 2003, Feb. 6, 2003; further revised in December 2004.
746. According to other data, by 2007: "the cumulative installed area achieved was 1,660,000m2 or 410,000 households. The installation density based on the land area ranks as the third in the world. There was an annual saving of about 111,000 KLOE of conventional fossil energy, corresponding to 4,130,000 barrels of 20 kilograms each of domestic LPG."

§3. Third Stage: Adoption of Renewable Energy Act in 2009 and 2019

504. In spite of the passage of the Renewable Energy Act, the government's main endeavor in renewable heating remains focused on solar water heaters, instead of biomass heating, biogas heating, or geothermal heating. According to the Renewable Heating Clause of Article 13 of the Renewable Energy Act, an Ordinance on Investment Subsidy for Renewable Heating Use was promulgated.[747] It is very strange that this Ordinance only partially implements the Renewable Heating Clause. In Article 13(1), it clearly authorized the administrative sector to promulgate an Ordinance to encourage the use not only of solar water heaters but also "biofuel and other potential renewable heating resources [such as biomass, biogas, geothermal, etc.]." Yet, the Final Ordinance only set up an investment subsidy mechanism for solar water heaters. As the potential cost-effective option had already been exploited under the previous Subsidy Ordinances, a more preferential investment subsidy was provided in this new Ordinance.

505. Compared with the additional measures to promote renewable "electricity" in the Renewable Energy Act of 2019, the provision to promote renewable thermal use remains unchanged in the 2019 amendment. Unlike the exact target to promote renewable electricity, no exact promotion target is set for renewable thermal use in the Renewable Energy Act of 2019. The promotion objectives and schedule for heat utilization of renewable energy shall be stipulated by the central competent authority depending on the economic benefits, technological developments, and relevant factors.[748] In addition, Article 13 provides a legal basis to promulgate further subsidy in the Ordinance.[749]

§4. Evaluation

506. During these years, the main renewable energy promoted by governmental policy was the solar water heater. Geothermal hot water was developed for leisure purposes. However, the development of other types of renewable heating resources, such as biomass heating, biogas heating, and biofuel heating, was ignored, even if their role was explicitly or implicitly mentioned in Article 13 of the Renewable

747. Ordinance on Investment Subsidy for Renewable Heating Use, Amended Date: 2015-12-09, available at: https://law.moj.gov.tw/LawClass/LawAll.aspx?pcode=J0130036.
748. Article 6(4) of the Renewable Energy Act of 2019.
749. Article 13 (1) of the Renewable Energy Act of 2019: "The central competent authority may consider reasonable costs and profits for the following heat utilization of renewable energy and shall prescribe regulations on subsidies and rewards for heat utilization according to the effectiveness of their energy contribution:

    1. Heat utilization of solar energy,
    2. Biomass fuel, and
    3. Other renewable energy heat utilization technologies with development potential."

Energy Act. The water from these renewable heaters is mainly used for bathing, showering, or swimming pool purposes. Little is used for industrial heating or air conditioning.

507. One of the reasons could be that the geological location of Taiwan makes it less necessary to have a great deal of hot water, unlike the situation in Europe. Hot air and steam are usually considered as "waste," instead of as useful resources. The electricity heater is more frequently used in Taiwan households, as there are a few days requiring heating during the winter's cold front.

508. In this regard, the development of "totally" renewable heating is not particularly viable in Taiwan. The potential application is to combine renewable heat and renewable electricity use, i.e., biomass CHP. This kind of CHP can replace the existing coal-fired, oil-fired, and gas-fired CHP in the industrial sectors and is much more environmentally friendly for Taiwan. The development of CHP in the US and many European countries, such as Germany, the Netherlands, and Denmark, shows there is also a trend from coal-fired to gas-fired, and finally to biomass CHP. As Taiwan is currently relying too much on coal-fired CHP, which makes CHP ironically a larger emitter, there is a need to promote "clean" CHP, such as gas and biomass CHP. However, in the current Renewable Energy Act, the FIT is only provided for biomass electricity generators. It is uncertain whether biomass CHP could benefit from the FIT scheme. There are also barriers in setting up such biomass electricity generators. For instance, the establishment of burning-type biomass energy power plants should be limited to industrial areas with the exception of electricity generated from biogas.[750]

750. Article 15(6) of the Renewable Energy Act.

Chapter 4. Incentives for Renewable Transportation Fuel

§1. First Stage: Before Drafting Renewable Energy Bill in 2002

509. The promotion of renewable transportation fuel usually takes the form of a "mandatory mixture obligation." Therefore, it would be a burden on the existing oil companies and would require a formal legislation to oblige the oil companies. The Petroleum Management Act, which was passed on October 11, 2001, does not incorporate such an obligation clause. In this regard, it is impossible to obligate the two incumbents, CPC and FPCC, to mix bio-elements into their product.

§2. Second Stage: Transition Period Between 2002 and 2009

510. At this stage, the government started to realize the role of biofuel and proposed a legislation to review the Petroleum Management Act. Before the bill was passed in the Parliament, the MOEABOE launched some incentive programs to encourage the use of biodiesel and bioethanol. The Energy Crop Green Bus Program (November 2006–June 2008) was used to encourage public bus operators to fuel vehicles with biodiesel. The Energy Crop Green Bus Program showed remarkable achievements, with 507 public buses, including 428 in Kaohsiung City and 79 in Chiayi County, adopting the use of biodiesel. Kaohsiung and Chiayi are, respectively, the second and third cities where all public buses use biodiesel; whereas Kyoto, in Japan, is the first in Asia. In addition, there was another Green County Demo Program during July 2007–June 2008. The Green County Demo Program was launched on July 27, 2007, providing B1 biodiesel in the gas stations of Taoyuan County, Chiayi County, and Chiayi City to the public, with an estimated consumption amount of 6,500 kl.

511. In addition, government vehicles in Taipei have been mandated to use E3 (3% bioethanol blended with gasoline), available at eight gas stations in Taipei since September 2007 under the Government Vehicles Demo Program.

512. In order to promote the use of biodiesel, a mandatory mixture obligation for oil refiners and importers to mix a certain percent of biodiesel into the vehicle diesel was promulgated in 2008.[751] A Mixture Ordinance was further promulgated.[752] The 1% mixture obligation, so-called B1, went into effect from July 15, 2008. The MOEABOE has a policy target of 45,000 kl to be reached between July 2008 and December 2009.

---

751. Article 38-1 of Petroleum Management Act of 2008 (Jan. 16, 2008).

752. Mandatory Mixture Ordinance of 2008, Jul. 4, 2008.http://1104.lawtw.com/article.php?template=article_content&area=free_browse&parent_path=,1,2169,1484,&job_id=138894&article_category_id=2100&article_id=71104.

§3. THIRD STAGE: ADOPTION OF RENEWABLE ENERGY ACT IN 2009

513. After the adoption of the Renewable Energy Act in June 2009, the government was also very keen on encouraging further development in the field of biodiesel and bioethanol. With regard to the bioethanol, in spite of there still being no mixture obligation, the original incentive program (Government Vehicles Demo Program) was further expanded to apply to all vehicles, instead of just to governmental vehicles, in the two biggest cities of Taiwan. The Subsidy Ordinance for Ethanol in Taipei and Kaohsiung City was promulgated on July 2, 2009.[753] The subsidy covers the extra cost incurred in the sales of E3 ethanol, including the purchase of ethanol and the mixture, storage, and transportation facilities. Of course, this scheme is not mandatory. Several Demonstration Gas Stations are subsidized under this scheme. In this regard, not all E3 petroleum is available in all gas stations in these two cities. The subsidy scheme for E3 ethanol remains unchanged thus far.

514. With regard to further measures to promote biodiesel, the aforementioned Mandatory Mixture Ordinance was further revised again in 2010 and a more rigid mixture obligation of 2% was introduced, which went into effect on June 15, 2010.[754] However, because 100 car owners complained in October 2013 alone that the B2 biodiesel had hindered their cars' performance, CPC decided to phase out B2 biodiesel in 2014.[755] The Mandatory Mixture Ordinance was revised again on May 5, 2014, to remove the mandatory mixture obligation of biodiesel.[756] This regime change also led to the protest of original upstream oil recycling companies,[757] although the scheme remains unchanged.

515. It should be noted that these two measures are not related to the Renewable Energy Act. For instance, the B2 obligation was introduced under the Petroleum Management Act, while the ethanol subsidy is provided at governmental discretion and subject to the budget. Does that mean biofuel has no role in the Renewable Energy Act of 2009? In fact, there are two aspects related to the promotion of biofuel. On the one hand, Article 13(3) provides that the Petroleum Fund under the Petroleum Management Act can be used to fund the promotion of biofuel. On the other hand, Article 13(4) of the Renewable Energy Act mentions a subsidy scheme for the "upstream" aspect of biofuel, i.e., generating energy crops or biomass for production of biofuel by planting suitable crops on fallow land, and other idle agricultural, forestry, and livestock farming land. The funding will come from the Agricultural Development Fund. However, the realization of Article 13(4) required that

753. The Subsidy Ordinance for Ethanol in Taipei and Kaushiun City (Jul. 2, 2009), 2009-07-02, available at: https://www.moeaboe.gov.tw/ECW/populace/Law/Content.aspx?menu_id=1082.
754. Mandatory Mixture Ordinance of 2010 (Jun. 10, 2010), 2010-05-13, available at: https://gazette.nat.gov.tw/EG_FileManager/eguploadpub/eg016092/ch04/type3/gov31/num9/Eg.htm.
755. Focus Taiwan, CPC to phase out B2 biodiesel in three months, May 5, 2014, available at: https://focustaiwan.tw/business/201405050037.
756. Mandatory Mixture Ordinance of 2014, May 5, 2014, 2014-05-05, available at: https://www.moeaboe.gov.tw/ECW/populace/Law/Content.aspx?menu_id=1078.
757. Taipei Times, FEATURE: Taiwan regressing in biofuel, waste oil policy, Dec. 29, 2014, available at: https://www.taipeitimes.com/News/taiwan/archives/2014/12/29/2003607855.

a further Ordinance be passed by the MOEABOE and Committee of Agriculture of the Executive Yuan. Yet, this Ordinance has not been promulgated thus far (already more than nine years).[758] The reason could be the conflict between the agriculture policy and energy policy before 2013, while the delay after 2013 could be related to the aforementioned change in the biodiesel Mandatory Mixture Policy.

§4. EVALUATION

516. So far, the Taiwanese renewable fuel policy focuses on biodiesel and biofuel. However, there is as yet only a mandatory mixture duty for biodiesel. The use of hydrogen remains at the stage of small-scale demonstrations in Kaushiun city. A demonstration plan of hybrid buses fueled by hydrogen and petroleum was launched in the middle of 2008. However, the recent policy priority focuses on electric busses.

517. Unlike the ambitious biofuel plan and mixture obligation in the US and Europe, Taiwan's plan and mixture obligation schedule are less ambitious, and are closely related to the agricultural policy to promote energy crops in a situation where there are not enough large pieces of land to plant energy crops. In this regard, Taiwan relies heavily on the importation of energy crops from other countries, such as Indonesia, or on biofuel to develop biofuel, which also reduces the emission reduction benefit and "energy security" benefit from developing biofuel. Unfortunately, biofuel, which was seen as a domestic energy resource in the US and Europe, remains a foreign resource in Taiwan.

518. Since reliance on petroleum seems inevitable, the government has directed its main effort to encouraging high efficiency petroleum vehicles, LPG vehicles, and hybrid (electricity and petroleum) vehicles, and electric vehicles (and scooters). Another future policy direction is the development of all-electricity vehicles. This policy direction also indicates the different ways of using renewable energy in the transportation sector. In the US and Europe, the trend seems to be toward using biofuel as a transitional transportation fuel between petroleum and all-electricity or hydrogen vehicles. Yet, due to the above-mentioned biofuel limitation and also, perhaps, its technological advantage in the field of battery research, Taiwan is more willing to invest in electricity-related vehicles, instead of in biofuel. In addition, the popular use of scooters makes the government of Taiwan more willing to provide a subsidy. For instance, the EPA, MOEA, and local government provide three layers of subsidies to encourage the development of electric scooters. This strategy also means the main Renewable Transportation Fuel in Taiwan in the future is likely to be "electricity fuel," which is the main focus of the Renewable Energy Act, rather than biofuel.

758. The Subsidy Ordinance of using fallow land to cultivate energy crops for the production of biofuel, 2011-12-01, available at: https://gazette.nat.gov.tw/EG_FileManager/eguploadpub/eg017232/ch04/type3/gov31/num4/Eg.htm.

Part VII. Interaction Between Energy Law and Tax Law

519. The Energy Policy Provisions of 1996 declared that the energy price should be determined by market mechanisms, and reflect the related social costs of energy use.[759] This statement has two meanings. On the one hand, it supports the idea that energy cost should reflect its "true" cost, which should not be artificially subsidized by the government. On the other hand, energy cost should further internalize its external environmental cost. However, the Taiwanese government has long made reasonable, meaning cheap, energy prices a priority and usually subsidizes energy prices when they spike or soar. Besides, in order to provide cheap utility costs to support the development of the manufacturing sector and facilitate the export-oriented high-technology economy, the energy price is usually kept artificially low by the government. State-owned energy companies, including Tai-Power and the CPC, are not allowed to reflect their full cost when selling energy. The electricity price is often frozen before the elections.[760] Not to mention the development of environment-related taxes. As citizens have gotten used to this low-energy cost situation, the prospect of increased electricity and oil prices always attracts much political opposition. Therefore, this artificially low energy price does not encourage emissions reduction and energy conservation, which became a major energy policy issue after the Kyoto Protocol came into effect.

520. In a 2007 policy statement, the importance of "enhancing market mechanisms and promoting the rationalization of energy prices" was again emphasized. The issue of adjustable electricity and oil prices was also raised.[761]

> The electricity price should be allowed to be adjusted flexibly based on changes in fuel costs. A 49~99% increase from 2005 to 2025 is foreseeable, if adjusting in keeping with the wholesale price index. The cost of electricity will be even higher when considering other factors, such as the change in the power generation structure (including the increase of renewable energy and LNG share) and the internalization of external costs.

---

759. 1996 Taiwan Energy Policy and Measures, available at: http://www.moeaboe.gov.tw/Policy/PoMain.aspx?PageId=executepolicy.

760. Taipei Times, Ministry freezes electricity prices again, Mar. 19, 2019, available at: https://www.taipeitimes.com/News/biz/archives/2019/03/19/2003711736.

761. MOEABOE, The Introduction to the Document on the Energy Situation in Taiwan in 2007, Aug. 23, 2009, available at: http://www.moeaboe.gov.tw/About/webpage/book_en2/page5.htm.

521. Besides, a flexible oil price mechanism was due to be implemented to carry out the resolution of the Conference on Sustaining Taiwan's Economic Development, which reads "Rationalize the energy price structure to reflect the fuel cost in the short run and the external cost in the long run."

522. Later, in order to reflect the cost after oil liberalization, the flexible oil price mechanism was adopted. This mechanism is really helpful in encouraging oil saving behaviors at the time of high world oil prices.

523. Apart from this true cost approach, several energy taxes were also applied to different forms of energy. Even though not all taxes are related to the internalization of external costs, they are really helpful in contributing to the further development of a carbon tax regime (Energy Tax).

524. Chapter 1 will provide an outline of the existing Taiwanese energy and environment-related tariffs and taxes. Apart from the narrow scope of these taxes and tariffs, the special levy scheme cannot be ignored as these levies are usually a very important funding source for energy R&D and partially fund environmentally friendly technologies. Finally, the emerging issue of an energy tax (or carbon tax) scheme has recently been much discussed and an Energy Tax Bill was drafted.

Chapter 1. The Existing Energy and Environmental Related Tax

§1. Energy Tax and Tariff

I. Custom Duties

525. According to the Customs Act, imported oil and gas products will attract duties.[762] The taxed products are further defined in the Ordinance on Customs Import Tariffs.[763] Yet, this does not apply to steam coal, coking coal, and electricity imports. The import tariff rate is divided into three columns. The first column applies to goods imported from WTO members or from countries or areas that have reciprocal treatment with the ROC. The second column applies to specified goods imported from specific underdeveloped or developing countries or areas, or from countries or areas that have signed a Free Trade Agreement with the ROC. When the rates in the first and second columns are not applicable, those in the third column apply. The different import tariffs applying to different oil and gas energy are illustrated in Table 19.

Table 19 Import Tariff for Oil, Gas, Coal and Electricity

Item	*Import Tariff*		
	Column I	*Column II*	*Column III*
Crude Oil	0%	0%	2.5%
Fuel Oil	5%	0%	5%
Kerosene	0%	0%	15%
Kerosene Type Jet Fuel	0%	0%	15%
LPG	0%	0%	7.5%
Gasoline	0%	0%	15%
Diesel Oil	0%	0%	15%
Natural Gas	0%	0%	7.5%
Steam Coal	0%		
Coking Coal			
Electricity	–	–	–

Source: Compiled by the author from https://www.moeaboe.gov.tw/ECW_WEBPAGE/FlipBook/2018EnergyStaHandBook/index.html.

762. MOJ, Customs Act, Amended Date: 2018-05-09, available at: https://law.moj.gov.tw/ENG/LawClass/LawAll.aspx?pcode=G0350001.
763. MOJ, Ordinance on Customs Import Tariff, Amended Date: 2019-07-24, available at: https://law.moj.gov.tw/ENG/LawClass/LawAll.aspx?pcode=G0350051.

II. Trade Promotion Service Fee

526. According to Article 21 of the Foreign Trade Act[764] and Article 17 of the Implementation Ordinance of the Trade Act,[765] oil, gas, and coal are subject to a trade promotion service fee. A 0.04% fee is levied on the import value of Crude Oil, Fuel Oil, Kerosene, Kerosene Type Jet Fuel, LPG, Gasoline, Diesel Oil, Natural Gas, Steam Coal, and Coking Coal. Electricity is exempted from this fee.

III. Excise Tax

527. According to Article 10 of the Act on Excise Tax,[766] certain petroleum products are subject to excise taxes:

1. Gasoline: NT$ 6,830/KL
2. Diesel oil: NT$ 3,990/KL
3. Kerosene: NT$ 4,250/KL
4. Fuel oil for aircraft: NT$ 610/KL
5. Fuel oil: NT$ 110/KL
6. (Deleted)
7. Dissolving oil: NT$ 720/KL
8. Liquefied petroleum gas: NT$ 690/MT

528. Therefore, regarding calculations based on a per liter amount, the tax rate for different fuels are as follows: Fuel Oil (0.11NT$/L), Kerosene (4.25NT$/L), Kerosene Type Jet Fuel (0.61NT$/L), LPG (0.69NT$/KG), Gasoline (6.83NT$/L), and Diesel Oil (3.99NT$/L). Natural Gas, Steam Coal, Coking Coal, Electricity, and Crude Oil are all exempt from this tax.

---

764. Article 21 of Foreign Trade Act: "In order to expand foreign trade, cope with the situations of foreign trade, and support trade activities, the competent authority may establish a trade promotion fund by collecting uniformly, through customs, a trade promotion service fee against the goods exported/imported by exporters/importers at a rate not more than 0.0425% of the price of the goods exported/imported, provided that the collection may be exempt from international treaties, pacts/agreements, practices or any other specific reasons." MOJ, Foreign Trade Act, Amended Date: 2019-12-25, available at: https://law.moj.gov.tw/ENG/LawClass/LawAll.aspx?pcode=J0090004.
765. Article 17: "The trade promotion service fee collectable under paragraph 1, Article 21 of the Act shall be paid by the concerned exporter/importer within 14 days from the date of issuance of a payment request statement.
   In collection of the above said trade promotion service fee, if it is for goods imported, the customs shall include the fee into a duty request statement and collect it together with import duties; if it is for goods exported, the fee shall be collected after the sailing of the shipping vessel."
   MOJ, Enforcement Rules of the Foreign Trade Act, Amended Date: 2019-07-16, available at: https://law.moj.gov.tw/ENG/LawClass/LawAll.aspx?pcode=J0090011.
766. MOJ, Commodity Tax Act, Amended Date: 2019-12-25, available at: https://law.moj.gov.tw/ENG/LawClass/LawAll.aspx?pcode=G0340076.

IV. Value Added Tax

529. According to Article 10 of the Act on Value-Added and Non-Value-Added Tax, a 5–10% tax is levied on the sales of energy products.[767] The 5% tax rate is applied to Crude Oil, Fuel Oil, Kerosene, Kerosene Type Jet Fuel, LPG, Gasoline, Diesel Oil, Natural Gas, Steam Coal, Coking Coal, and Electricity. It should be noted that among all the taxes under this Energy Tax and Tariff regime, only electricity is subject to this tax scheme.

V. Auto Fuel Usage Fee

530. To finance the expenditures required by highway maintenance, construction, and safety management, the Ministry of Transportation may collect automobile fuel charges at rates not exceeding 25% of the fuel import or ex-factory price.[768] Article 3 of the Ordinance on Auto Fuel Usage Fees states that gasoline and diesel are to be levied at a rate of 2.5 and 1.5 NTD/per liter, respectively.[769]

531. A Different auto fuel usage fees are further calculated taking into account the fuel consumption index of Annex II created for different types of autos, their purpose, fuel type, and category. The updated complete fee level is provided in Table 20.

767. Article 10: "Except as otherwise prescribed by this Act, the business tax rate shall be no less than 5% and no more than 10%. The applicable collection rate shall be determined by the Executive Yuan."
MOJ, Value-added and Non-value-added Business Tax Act, Amended Date: 2017-06-14, available at: https://law.moj.gov.tw/ENG/LawClass/LawAll.aspx?pcode=G0340080.
768. MOJ, Art. 27, Highway Act, Amended Date: 2017-01-04, available at: https://law.moj.gov.tw/ENG/LawClass/LawAll.aspx?pcode=K0040001.
769. Article 3 of the Ordinance on Auto Fuel Usage Fees states that gasoline and diesel are to be levied at a rate of 2.5 and 1.5 NTD/per liter, respectively, Amended Date: 2019-10-01, available at: https://law.moj.gov.tw/LawClass/LawAll.aspx?pcode=K0040007.

Table 20 Annual and Seasonal Auto Fuel Usage Fee for All Auto Types

	Large Passenger Vehicles				*Small Passenger Cars*				*Goods Vehicles (Including Trailers and Tricycles)*				*Motor Bikes (Every Two Years)*
	Tourism and Rent (Each Season)		*Self-Use (Each Year)*		*Business Use (Each Season)*		*For Personal or Private Use (Each Year)*		*Business Use (Each Season)*		*For Personal or Private Use (Each Year)*		
	Gasoline	*Diesel*	*Gasoline*	*Diesel*	*Gasoline*	*Diesel*	*Gasoline*	*Diesel*	*Gasoline*	*Diesel*	*Gasoline*	*Diesel*	
>50 cc													300
51~125													450
126~250													600
251~500							2,160	1,296	788	473	2,160	1,296	900
501~600					1,440	864	2,880	1,728	1,050	630	2,880	1,728	1,200
601~1200					2,160	1,296	4,320	2,592	1,575	945	4,320	2,592	1,800
1201~1800					2,400	1,440	4,800	2,880	2,100	1,260	4,800	2,880	2,010
1801~2400					3,083	1,850	6,180	3,708	2,700	1,620	7,710	4,626	
2401~3000	4,725	2,835	8,400	5,040	3,600	2,160	7,200	4,320	3,150	1,890	9,900	5,940	
3001~3600	5,670	3,402	10,080	6,048			8,640	5,184	3,780	2,268	11,880	7,128	
3601~4200	6,443	3,866	11,460	6,876			9,810	5,886	4,298	2,579	13,500	8,100	
4201~4800	7,365	4,419	13,080	7,848			11,220	6,732	4,913	2,948	15,420	9,252	
4801~5400	7,988	4,793	14,190	8,514			12,180	7,308	5,325	3,195	16,740	10,044	
5401~6000	8,588	5,153	15,270	9,162			13,080	7,848	6,683	4,010	18,000	10,800	
6001~6600	10,163	6,098	16,260	9,756			13,950	8,370	7,110	4,266	19,170	11,502	
6601~7200	10,860	6,516	17,370	10,422			14,910	8,946	7,605	4,563	20,490	12,294	

	Large Passenger Vehicles				*Small Passenger Cars*				*Goods Vehicles (Including Trailers and Tricycles)*				*Motor Bikes (Every Two Years)*
	Tourism and Rent (Each Season)		*Self-Use (Each Year)*		*Business Use (Each Season)*		*For Personal or Private Use (Each Year)*		*Business Use (Each Season)*		*For Personal or Private Use (Each Year)*		
	Gasoline	*Diesel*	*Gasoline*	*Diesel*	*Gasoline*	*Diesel*	*Gasoline*	*Diesel*	*Gasoline*	*Diesel*	*Gasoline*	*Diesel*	
7201~8000	11,453	6,872	18,330	10,998			15,720	9,432	9,165	5,499	25,530	15,318	
8001~9000	13,328	7,997	19,380	11,628					10,298	6,179	27,000	16,200	
9001~10000	14,145	8,487	20,580	12,348					11,573	6,944	28,650	17,190	
10001~11000	15,068	9,041	21,900	13,140					12,323	7,394	32,880	19,728	
11001~12000	15,750	9,450	22,920	13,752					14,318	8,591	36,810	22,086	
12001~13000	16,500	9,900	24,000	14,400					15,000	9,000	43,710	26,226	
13001~14000	17,325	10,395	25,200	15,120					18,900	11,340	54,000	32,400	
14001以上	17,325	10,395	25,200	15,120					18,900	11,340	54,000	32,400	

Source: Annex II of the Ordinance on Auto Fuel Usage Fees https://law.moj.gov.tw/LawClass/LawGetFile.ashx?FileId=0000122626&lan=C.

Notes:

Seasonal fee: gasoline car=2.5 NTD × monthly estimated consumption × 3 month diesel car = 1.5 NTD × monthly estimated consumption × 3 month.

Annual fee: gasoline car=2.5 NTD × monthly estimated consumption × 12 month diesel car = 1.5 NTD × monthly estimated consumption × 12 month.

§2. ENVIRONMENTAL POLLUTION TAX AND TARIFF

I. Air Pollution Control Fee

532. According to Article 16(2) of the Air Pollution Act,[770] the Air Pollution Control Fee may be collected on the basis of the sales of oil and fuel type and their contents.

533. The fees collected are used for the following purposes:[771]

(1) Matters concerning the implementation of air pollution control work by competent authorities at all levels
(2) Matters concerning the inspection of air pollution sources and the auditing of the implementation and efficacy of such inspections
(3) Matters concerning subsidies and incentives for the performance of air pollution abatement work by each category of pollution source
(4) Matters concerning the commissioning and subsidizing of analysis laboratories for the performance of motor vehicle emissions testing
(5) Matters concerning the commissioning or subsidizing of professional organizations for the performance of the testing, guidance, and evaluation of stationary pollution sources
(6) Matters concerning air pollution control technology research, and development and strategy formulation
(7) Matters concerning international environmental protection work involving air pollution
(8) Matters concerning air quality monitoring and the auditing of the implementation and efficacy of such monitoring
(9) Matters concerning the expenses related to the collection of air pollution control fees
(10) The hiring of personnel required for work related to air pollution control

---

770. Article 16: "Competent authorities at all levels may collect air pollution control fees from stationary and mobile pollution sources that emit air pollutants. The targets of air pollution control fees are as follows:

1. Stationary pollution sources: Fees shall be collected from the owners of the pollution source based on the types and quantity of air pollutants emitted. Fees shall be collected from the actual user or manager if the owner of the source is not the user or manager. Fees shall be collected from the construction project owner if the pollution source is a construction project. For substances designated and officially announced by the central competent authority, fees may be collected from the vendor or importer based on the sales volume of the substance.
2. Mobile pollution sources: Fees shall be collected from the vendor or user based on the types and quantity of air pollutants emitted, or from the vendor or importer based on the type, composition, and quantity of fuel."

MOJ, Air Pollution Control Act, 2018-08-01, available at: https://law.moj.gov.tw/ENG/LawClass/LawAll.aspx?pcode=O0020001.

771. Article 18(1) of the Air Pollution Act.

(11) Related matters concerning air pollution health risk assessments and management
(12) Matters concerning incentives for promoting the use of clean energy and related R&D
(13) Matters concerning rewards for the reporting of air pollution
(14) Other matters concerning air pollution control work.

534. Gasoline and diesel oil are subject to this requirement. There is no air pollution control fee requirement for crude oil, fuel oil, kerosene, kerosene type jet fuel, LPG, and natural gas. Steam coal, coking coal, and electricity are not subject to the Air Pollution Control Fee Scheme. Originally, the different tariff schemes are based on the sulfur content of the fuel. The higher the sulfur contents are, the lower the fuel quality, and the higher the fee that should be levied. The fee scheme is different for gasoline and diesel.

– Gasoline: 1st Grade 0.03 NTD/L; 2nd Grade 0.075 NTD/L; 3rd Grade 0.19 NTD/L
– Diesel Oil: 1st Grade 0.03 NTD/L; 2nd Grade 0.075 NTD/L; 3rd Grade 0.2 NTD/L

535. However, after the revision in August 2017,[772] the rate is used to reflect the PM2.5 contents of gasoline and diesel oil. Thus, diesel oil is higher (0.4 NTD/L) than gasoline (0.3 NTD/L).

II. Soil and Groundwater Pollution Remediation Fee

536. According to Article 28(1) of the Soil and Groundwater Pollution Remediation Act, the central competent authority may, for the purpose of remediating soil and groundwater pollution, levy soil and groundwater pollution remediation fees on manufacturers and importers in accordance with the amounts of officially announced chemical substances manufactured and imported by such enterprises, and shall establish a Soil and Groundwater Pollution Remediation Fund.[773]

537. According to the Regulations Governing the Collection of Soil and Groundwater Pollution Remediation Fees, the following energy types are required to be levied.[774]

– Fuel Oil: 11 (NTD/ton) 11 (NTD/kiloliter)
– LPG (Butane): 11 (NTD/ton) 11 (NTD/kiloliter)

---

772. The rate schedule for mobile air pollution sources, 2017-08-30, available at: https://oaout.epa.gov.tw/laW/LawContentSearch.aspx?id=GL005188.
773. MOJ, Soil and Groundwater Pollution Remediation Act, 2010-02-03, available at: https://law.moj.gov.tw/ENG/LawClass/LawAll.aspx?pcode=O0110001.
774. Table 1 Types of Substances Subject to Soil and Groundwater Pollution Remediation Fees and Respective Fee Rates.pdf, available at: https://law.moj.gov.tw/ENG/LawClass/LawGetFile.ashx?FileId=0000003448&lan=E.

– Gasoline: 11 (NTD/ton) 11 (NTD/kiloliter)
– Diesel Oil: 13 (NTD/ton) 11 (NTD/kiloliter)

538. The following energy types are not subject to this fee scheme: Crude Oil, Kerosene, Kerosene Type Jet Fuel, Natural Gas, Steam Coal, Coking Coal, and Electricity.

Chapter 2. Existing Special Public Levy in Energy Sector

539. A Special Public Levy, derived from a similar regime in Germany, was introduced in Taiwan to serve specific administrative purposes. In general, the Special Public Levy is different from a tax: whereas the latter is used to meet the general financial needs of the nation and is a levy on all citizens, the former is used to meet special needs and is levied on a special group of citizens who are more related to the realization of those goals.

540. In the energy sector, it has long been used to promote special energy goals. So far, three related levies and funds have been created.

§1. Special Public Levy of the Energy R&D Fund

541. The Special Public Levy of the Energy Research and Development Fund is a very old levy scheme created under the Energy Management Act. According to Article 5-1 of the same Act, this fund relies on the following sources:

- Contribution of vertically integrated utilities, oil refineries, and oil importers as a percentage of their income generated from the energy supply business. The contribution shall amount to up to half of one percent (0.5%) of the income generated by the energy supply businesses of the vertical integrated utilities, oil refineries, and oil importers, as determined by the central competent authority.
- Technical service fees, royalties, remuneration, and other associated income.

542. In this regard, Tai-Power, the CPC, and other oil refineries and oil importers are subject to this levy requirement. However, in order to avoid duplicating the levy burden, the law requires that oil companies be subject to only the Special Public Levy of the Petroleum Fund under the Petroleum Management Act. Hence, only Tai-Power is in fact subject to this levy requirement.

543. This fund is to be used mainly for the following purposes:[775]

(1) R&D of technology relevant to the exploitation of energy resources and alternate energies.
(2) R&D relevant to technology and methodology for the rational and efficient use of energy as well as energy conservation.
(3) Economic analysis and collection of information on energy.
(4) Training of experts in energy planning and the professional personnel.
(5) Other spending as approved by the competent authority.

544. Generally speaking, this levy is imposed mainly on the national energy enterprise. There is little opposition to this levy and challenge to the justification of

775. Article 5(2) of Energy Management Act.

this levy, as these state-owned companies have a "public" mission. Perhaps this scheme is inspired by the public benefit fund scheme in the US.[776] However, this author raises the question of why these energy companies should fund the RD&D, which is also funded by the national budget. Why should these energy companies fund the R&D but not the non-energy companies? If these energy companies were to be privatized in the future, these questions would create potential concerns related to constitutional law.

§2. Special Public Levy of Petroleum Fund

545. After oil liberalization, the Petroleum Fund was created for the purpose of a universal service, and for other public benefit fund purposes.

546. According to Article 34(1), certain oil exploitation, import, and petroleum by-products, produced by petrochemical feedstock manufacturers and sold to oil refinery operators, are subject to the levy requirement. In this regard, certain oil importers, exploiters, and manufacturers of petrochemical feedstock may be subject to this levy requirement.[777] The government publishes notification of the levy for different types of petroleum products.[778] The exploiters and manufacturers of petrochemical feedstock are obliged to pay 130 NTD/kl, while the levy for oil importers is as follows:[779]

- Crude Oil: 130 NTD/kl
- Fuel Oil: 137 NTD/kl
- Kerosene: 159 NTD/kl
- Kerosene Type Jet Fuel: 123 NTD/kl
- LPG: 185 NTD/T

---

776. *See*, *e.g.*, Steven Nadel, Marty Kushler, Public Benefit Funds: A Key Strategy for Advancing Energy Efficiency, The Electricity Journal, Vol. 13, Issue 8, 2000, pp. 74–84, https://doi.org/10.1016/S1040-6190(00)00147-0.
777. Article 34 of Petroleum Management Act: "In order to finance the Petroleum Fund, the central competent authority will set and charge fees at fixed rates for the following activities:

    1. The exploration or import of oil with the exception of oil imported under the provisions stipulated in the first paragraph of Art. 12 and Items 2–4 of Art. 13.
    2. Petroleum by-products produced by petrochemical feedstock manufacturers and sold to oil refinery operators in conjunction with the second paragraph of Art. 12. The preceding provision does not apply to the feedstock for any petrochemical products originally purchased from oil refinery operators or importers.

    The rates mentioned in the preceding paragraphs will be charged by volume and based on the average import price of oil. The central competent authority will announce the amounts collected for the fund."
778. MOEABOE, Notification of Payment for Petroleum Fund, 2016-02-26, available at: https://www.moeaboe.gov.tw/ECW/populace/Law/Content.aspx?menu_id=623; http://www.moeaboe.gov.tw/opengovinfo/Laws/oil/LOilMain.aspx?PageId=l_oil_04_04.
779. MOEABOE, Notification of Payment for Petroleum Fund, 2016-2-26, available at: https://www.moeaboe.gov.tw/ECW/populace/Law/Content.aspx?menu_id=623.

- Gasoline: 130 NTD/kl
- Diesel Oil: 172 NTD/kl
- Naphtha: 133 NTD/kl

547. This fund is used for the following purposes:[780]

(1) To maintain the government petroleum security stockpile.
(2) To subsidize the establishment of petroleum facilities in mountain and off-shore areas as well as transportation outlays, and offer price subsidies.
(3) To encourage the exploration for and development of oil and natural gas reserves.
(4) To implement R&D on energy policy, oil development technology, and alternative energies.
(5) To ensure the security and reasonably effective use of oil and gas (including LPG), as well as to develop and promote oil-saving technology and methods.
(6) To subsidize the use of renewable energy in place of petroleum energy for heating.
(7) To subsidize the operations of a municipality, a county, or a city competent authority in its implementation of the oil management and the ban, as well as in inspecting or auditing as stated in the first paragraph of Article 54 in this law.
(8) To implement other measures deemed necessary by the central competent authority to stabilize the oil supply and maintain oil market order.

§3. Special Public Levy of Renewable Energy Development Fund

548. In order to promote the development of renewable energy electricity, the Renewable Energy Development Fund was created under the Renewable Energy Act to fund the FIT scheme in 2009. According to Article 7 of the Renewable Energy Act, electricity generators using traditional fuels, including oil, gas, coal, and nuclear power, are required to be levied for each unit of electricity (kW/hour) produced in accordance with its *carbon* contents. (Yet, for nuclear power plants, the presumption on which the tariff is based is not quite clear.) The electricity generators include not only Tai-Power and IPPs, but also CHP operators whose capacity is above 30 MW. The tariff scheme for this fund is provided as follows:[781]

- Coal-fired plants: 0.0019 NTD$/kWh
- CHP (regardless fuel type): 0.0017 NTD$/kWh
- Oil-fired plants: 0.0017 NTD$/kWh
- Gas-fired plants: 0.0015 NTD$/kWh
- Nuclear power plants: 0.0010 NTD$/kWh

780. Article 36 of the Petroleum Management Act.
781. Tariff Level for 2010, available at: http://www.moeaboe.gov.tw/Download/Policy/Renewable/meeting/files/law/09903824700.pdf.

549. Apart from funding the FIT, this levy is also used for funding R&D, investment subsidies, and demonstration subsidies.

550. However, during implementation, the controversy arose over why the generators should bear such burdens, especially private IPPs and CHPs. Furthermore, in countries introducing the FIT scheme, like Germany, the FIT financial source is usually based on the user pay principle, which means the fee is collected as an electricity surcharge in the electricity price. In this regard, the MOEA adjusted the scheme in the 2019 Renewable Energy Act. Now, the main funding source is collected by Tai-Power's retailing company, in other words, from the final users. An amount of fees calculated at a certain percentage of the retailing amount of electricity generated from non-renewable energy charged from electricity retailing enterprises.[782] However, certain fees still come from generators. An amount of fees calculated as a certain percentage based on the amount of electricity generated by self-use power generation facilities paid by those who install self-use power generation facilities of non-renewable energy. The use purpose is expanded to include storage ("To subsidize the development of power generation and storage of renewable energy") or administrative purposes. ("To spend the fund on or subsidize the recognition and audit of renewable power generation facilities in relation to this Act.")

551. This scheme's design incorporates the carbon tax idea and the polluter pays principle. However, this funding scheme is totally different from the normal FIT scheme. For instance, the regular funding scheme for FIT is based on the "user pays" principle instead of the polluter pays principle. The "renewable promotion tax" levied on electricity generators is unique internationally. It is unclear why the electricity generators should be obliged to fund the development of renewable energy. There may be some constitutional issue at stake. This author strongly recommends that the best way to internalize the external cost of fossil fuel power plants is through energy taxation, which will be elaborated on below. In other words, the funding scheme for renewable electricity should be a "usage fee" on all electricity users' electricity bills. Despite the revision in the 2019 Renewable Energy Act, concerns remain, as self-generators are still subject to the levy scheme.

782. Article 7(1) of the Renewable Energy Act of 2019.

Chapter 3. Carbon Tax? Energy Taxation Bill

552. As a result of the government's long-term plan to keep electricity, oil, and gas prices artificially low to support the development of manufacture, production, and the OEM sectors, the energy price is very distorted and does not reflect costs outside Taiwan. This contributes to the wasteful behavior of consumers and the lack of incentives to improve energy conservation and energy efficiency. Following the discussion at the 2004 National Energy Conference, the government proposed an energy tax scheme. After the Taiwan Economic Sustainable Development Conference of 2006, the idea of energy tax reform was proposed. The conclusion of this conference was as follows:

- The tax rate should be increased gradually in order to reduce the impact on CPI and the economy. The tax should take into account carbon content, heat value, and environmental and energy conservation effects.
- The energy tax should be imposed by "volume." The final tax rate should take into account international tax standards and the impact on CPI and the macroeconomy of Taiwan. The tax rate may refer to the international situation and be adjusted every two years.
- With the implementation of the energy tax, consideration should be given to canceling certain excise taxes at the same time.
- The increased tax should be used to reduce income tax or company tax, maintain tax neutrality, and reduce the social welfare burden of companies. Other uses should include R&D expense, public works, social welfare, and local development.
- The energy cost should be made to reflect its real production costs before the implementation of an energy tax and the canceling of subsidies and incentives for use of fossil fuels.

553. In this regard, the energy tax is not a new tax. It was introduced to replace the excise tax on oil and gas, and auto fuel usage fees. It remains subject to discussion whether the petroleum fund special levy, the air pollution control fee, and the Soil and Groundwater Pollution Remediation Fee will be integrated into this energy tax scheme. In keeping with the above concepts and ideas, the Ministry of Finance began to draft an energy taxation bill in 2012.[783] However, this led to an outcry from the industrial sector, which impeded the timetable for this regime. Compared with most energy bills, such as the GHG Reduction Bill, on which a consensus is usually reached at ministerial level so that they are then approved by the Executive Yuan and submitted to Parliament for deliberation, this controversial tax bill met with no consensus by the Ministry of Finance. This fact also shows how controversial this issue is in Taiwan.

783. eTax Portal, Ministry of Finance began to draft an energy taxation bill, Sep. 18, 2012, available at: https://www.etax.nat.gov.tw/etwmain/web/ETW118W/CON/444/6505630371943250059?tagCode=.

554. The debates on the energy tax occurred in the 2010s. In an important policy announcement, the Master Plan on Energy Conservation and Emission Reduction 2010, the importance of the energy tax bill in reducing emissions was highlighted. This bill is considered one of the three top governmental priority legislations (the others are the GHG Reduction Bill and Sustainable Energy Basic Bill). The energy tax bill was also considered one of the "Top 4 Laws on Emission Reduction and Energy Conservation," along with the Energy Management Act, GHG Reduction Bill, and Renewable Energy Act.

555. After years of discussion, there are eight main versions of the Energy Taxation Bill. Of these, five were proposed by members of parliament (MPs), and the other three by the Ministry of Finance. Hereafter, this book uses the following abbreviations based on history.

(1) Energy Taxation Bill by Member of Parliament (MP) Chen (2006.05) (Bill A)
(2) Energy Taxation Bill by the Ministry of Finance (2006.10) (Bill B)
(3) Energy Taxation Bill by MP Wang (2006.12) (Bill C)
(4) Energy Taxation Bill by MP Tian (2008.05) (Bill D)
(5) Energy Taxation Bill by the Tax Reform Committee (2009.10) (Bill E)
(6) Energy Taxation Bill by the Ministry of Finance (2011.01) (Bill F)
(7) Energy Taxation Bill by MP Tzen (2011.03) (Bill G)
(8) Energy Taxation Bill by MP Lee (2012.05) (Bill H)

§1. Institutional Design

556. In general, all tax in Taiwan is under the authority of the Ministry of Finance (MOF) and its local offices at the municipality and county level. Thus, drafting Energy Bills is no exception, as reflected in Bills B, E, and F. Therefore, the MOF is the main institution for energy tax.[784] However, it does not mean other authorities have no say in the process. For instance, as the tax rate could influence the national economy, the cabinet office, namely the Executive Yuan, may have a say in reducing the tax rate under discretion.[785] Furthermore, the competent authorities for different businesses (e.g., the MOEA) may also be involved in enacting tax exemption issues.[786]

784. *See*, *e.g.*, Art. 3 of Bill A.
785. *See*, *e.g.*, Art. 7(4) of Bills B and C; Art. 7(7) of Bill D.
786. *See*, *e.g.*, Art. 5(2) of Bill B. However, Art. 5(2) of Bill D gives the tax exemption decision power to the MOF.

§2. TARGET

I. Time Schedule

557. With regard to the transition period to introduce the full tax, four versions of the bill (Bills A, B, E, and G) adopt a ten-year yearly gradual increase period to the full tax rate. However, two versions (Bills C and D) adopt eight-year periods, and two others (Bills F and H) adopt no transitional period, with the tax taken immediately after passing the law.

II. Tax Rate and Object of Taxation or Taxed Items

558. All taxes in the eight versions of the bill are taxed calculated by volume (ad-valorem tax). In this regard, the tax increases as more energy is consumed. The method used to determine the tax rate is different in each version of the bill. In general, there are three factors: heat value, carbon content, and original excise tax. Most versions adopt a mixed approach (Bills C, F, G, and E). Bill H is based mainly on heat value, and Bill A mainly on excise tax. Bill B is based on the mixture of carbon content and excise tax, and Bill D on excise tax and the automobile fuel usage fee. Thus, the determinants differ between the eight versions of the bill.

559. The tax rate is the main battleground for the bills. Table 21 shows the tax rates for the different types of energy in each bill.

Table 21 Tax Rate Schedule of Eight Versions of the Energy Tax Bills

	Unit	*A*	*B*	*C*	*D*	*E*	*F*	*G*	*H*
Gasoline	NTD/L	27.50	16.83	27.50	26.73	26.15	7.74	26.56	2.00–6.00
Diesel	NTD/L	25.00	11.99	23.50	23.49	23.76	5.08	19.09	1.64–4.92
Kerosene	NTD/L	18.25	12.25	20.00	18.25	16.24	5.27	16.50	2.18–6.54
Flight kerosene	NTD/L	16.61	1.61	18.00	18.61	19.00	1.57	5.78	2.05–6.15
Fuel oil	NTD/L	6.40	0.61	6.30	14.11	2.24	1.30	2.24	2.46–7.38
LPG	NTD/kg	18.25	0.84	14.70	18.69	11.49 (per L)	1.96	15.90 (per L)	1.70–5.10 (per L)
Coal	NTD/kg	1.20	0.40	1.20	1.40	1.86	1.01	1.86	1.64–4.92
Natural gas	NTD/m^3	6.40	0.70	6.60	7.00	1.95	0.97	1.95	Exemption
Solvent oil	NTD/L	20.00	–	20.00	18.72	–	1.73	–	–

Nuclear power	NTD/ kWh	–	–	–	–	0.19	–	–	–
Lubrication	NTD /L	–	–	–	–	–	–	–	2.46–7.38
Naphtha	NTD /kg	–	–	–	–	–	–	–	2.00–6.00

Source: Article 4 of Bill A; Annex of Bill B; Article 7(1),(3) of Bill C; Article 7 and Annex of Bill D; Article 8(2) and Annex of Bill G; Article 5(1)(2) of Bill H.

560. To apply the tax rate more flexibly, certain versions of the tax bill include a flexible clause to adjust the tax rate. Bills B, D, and G give the administrative branch the power to reduce or increase the tax rate up to 50%,[787] while Bill A only allows a 30%[788] change and Bill C 20%.[789] Bill H also gives implicit flexibility. Bill H only provides a tax rate range, empowering the administrative branch to determine the exact tax rate (e.g., gasoline 2.00–6.00 NTD/kg).

III. Types of Gases Covered

561. Not all versions of the Energy Tax Bill provide details concerning the tax calculation of carbon content. In terms of tax based on carbon content, Bill E sets the carbon tax at 750 NTD/TCO2, and Bill F at 400 NTD/T. The energy tax of these bills is a mixture of carbon contents and other taxable elements. With the Bill F price, the carbon tax for gasoline is 0.91 NTD/L and 1.09 NTD/L for diesel. The total energy taxes per liter for gasoline and diesel are 0.91 + 6.83 NTD and 1.09 + 3.99 NTD, respectively. In Bill E, the carbon tax elements for gasoline and diesel are relatively higher at 1.70 NTD/L and 2.05 NTD/L, respectively.

IV. Taxable Entities (Upstream or Downstream)

562. In general, energy producers and importers are required to pay the tax.[790] Although there is limited domestic production of energy, the energy tax for energy export is still likely because the tax regime includes energy products (such as gasoline).

563. The energies to be taxed have commonalities and differences across the various versions of the bill (Table 21). Commonly taxed types of energy in Bills A to H include gasoline, diesel, kerosene and flight kerosene, fuel oil, LPG, and coal. Bills A to G tax natural gas, while Bill H provides an exemption. For other types of energy such as solvent oil, nuclear and lubrication, and naphtha, the views are different. More detailed information is provided in the tax rate section.

§3. Reduction of Economic Burden: Border Tax Adjustment

564. To reduce the negative effects on local industries, certain tax reductions, exemptions, or refund clauses are provided in all versions of the bill except for Bill H. The most common scheme is total exemption from tax for certain purposes such

787. Article 7(4) of Bill B; Art. 7(7) of Bill D; Art. 8(4) of Bill G.
788. Article 4(3) of Bill A.
789. Article 7(4) of Bill C.
790. Article 4 of Bills B, C, D, and H; Art. 5 of Bill G.

as energy used as industrial raw material, transport to foreign countries for exhibition purposes without any sale, and the use of energy for national defense purposes.[791] Bills C and D provide relatively narrower tax exemptions.[792] However, Bill D also provides a relatively flexible clause for the MOF to determine further exemptions.[793]

565. The other method of tax reduction is designed as a form of tax refund (pay first and get a refund later). For instance, Bill A refunds the tax partially or totally for energy used for industrial raw materials,[794] while Bill D provides a partial or total tax refund for solvent oil tax.[795] In sum, most of the bills adopt a tax exemption approach, although Bill A adopts a tax refund approach. Bill D adopts a mixed tax exemption and refund approach.

566. Finally, note that the spending of the tax is also partly related to the tax exemption and tax refund regime. Table 22 provides a summary.

Table 22 Tax Integration, Exemption, and Tax Refund

	A	*B*	*C*	*D*	*E*	*F*	*G*	*H*
Integration of oil and gas-related excise taxes	V (8(2))	V (21)	V(24)	V(24)	V	V	V(23)	
Integration of automobile fuel usage fee	V (8(2))		V(24)	V(24)	V	V	V(10)	
Integration of special public levy of the Petroleum Fund					V		V(10)	
Integration of the vehicle air pollution control fee					V			
Cease existing drink and electric appliance excise taxes					V	V	V(10)	
Cease stamp and entertainment taxes					V	V	V(10)	

Source: Compiled by the author.

791. *See* Art. 5 of Bill B and Art. 6 of Bill G.
792. Article 5 of Bill C provides an exemption only for export and energy used as raw material for another taxed energy. *See also* Art. 5 of Bill D.
793. Article 5 of Bill D.
794. Article 4(4) of Bill A.
795. Article 7(6) of Bill D.

Note: "V" indicates the existence of this function in the related Bills.

The numbers below "V" are the related Articles in the Bills.

§4. Revenue Use

567. In the eight versions of the bill, there are two approaches to spending the taxes brought in thereby. The first approach is for the tax to go to the national treasury to be used for general financial and budgetary purposes[796] or for tax replacement or integration purposes. This practice is more associated with the tax law system in Taiwan. When a fee is considered a tax rather than a special levy, that tax is under the charge of the MOF and goes to the national treasury.

568. However, this approach does not meet the expectations of the public in terms of spending the money on CO2 emission reduction and energy conservation, or other related purposes. Thus, the idea of a purpose-oriented tax, which is a mixture of the traditional sense of a tax and a special levy, is embodied in the recent versions of the energy tax bill, such as Bills C, D, E, F, G, and H.

569. This book later elaborates the related spending purposes including the former (tax integration) and latter approaches (purpose-oriented tax).

I. Tax Integration Function: Tax Reform

570. There are three main ways to spend the tax. The first way is similar to existing related taxes. The purpose of the energy tax is to conduct tax reform and integrate the taxes such as the excise or automobile fuel tax. Thus, part of the tax revenue will be spent on these tax purposes. From this point, the role of energy tax is to replace or integrate existing taxes (Table 23).

Table 23 Tax Integration Function of the Energy Tax

	A	*B*	*C*	*D*	*E*	*F*	*G*	*H*
Integration of oil and gas-related excise taxes	V (8(2))	V(21)	V(24)	V(24)	V	V	V(23)	
Integration of the automobile fuel usage fee	V (8(2))		V(24)	V(24)	V	V	V(10)	

796. Article 5 of Bill A; Art. 3 of Bill B.

	A	*B*	*C*	*D*	*E*	*F*	*G*	*H*
Integration of the special public levy of the Petroleum Fund					V		V(10)	
Integration of the vehicle air pollution control fee					V			
Cease existing drink and electric appliance excise taxes					V	V	V(10)	
Cease stamp and entertainment taxes					V	V	V(10)	
Reduce business income tax or personal income tax			V(9)	V(8)	V			
Reduce personal income tax			V	V(8)	V	V		

Source: Compiled by the author.

Note: The mark "V" is used to demonstrate the existence of such function in the related Bills.

The numbers below the mark V is the related Articles in the Bills.

II. Economic Growth and Promotion of Environmental Industries

571. The second function of the energy tax is related to industrial transformation. It is true that the energy tax on energy intensive industries would harm part of the economy. However, if the revenue can be properly used and spent, it also offers good news for low-carbon and environmentally friendly industries, which could lead to another form of economic growth (Table 24).

Table 24 Economic Growth and Environmental Industry Promotion Functions of the Energy Tax

	A	*B*	*C*	*D*	*E*	*F*	*G*	*H*
Reduce business income tax			V(9) (1/3)	V(8)	V			
Subsidize energy-related research and development			V(9) (1/3)	V(8)	V	V	V(10)	

	A	*B*	*C*	*D*	*E*	*F*	*G*	*H*
Spend on emission reduction and energy conservation measures						V		

III. Consumer and Social Welfare

572. The main concern of the public is the increased cost of living resulting from the energy tax. This concern could partly be dealt with through the tax spending method. First, the energy tax can be used to reduce personal income tax. This could counterbalance part of the loss. Moreover, if energy consumption behavior can be changed, then many subsidies (such as a subsidy for public transportation) are available. Finally, the extra money can be used to ease or supplement the existing budgets of other areas such as social welfare, health care, and education (Table 25).

Table 25 Consumer and Social Welfare Functions of the Energy Tax

		A	*B*	*C*	*D*	*E*	*F*	*G*	*H*
Reduce personal income tax				V(9) (1/3)	V(8)	V	V		
Subsidy for transportation and green energy	Subsidy for public transpor tation				V(8)	V	V	V(10)	
	Subsidy for energy and public policy research				V (8)				

		A	*B*	*C*	*D*	*E*	*F*	*G*	*H*
Budget for other ministries	Extra funding for education				V (8)				
	Subsidy for transportation maintenance and management				V (8)				
	Subsidy for low-income households				V (8)			V (10)	
	Funding for universal health care								V (6(1))
	Funding for care of the elderly								V (6(1))
Budget for local government									V (6(2))

Source: Compiled by the author.

Note: "V" indicates the existence of this function in the related Bills.

The numbers below the "V" are the related Articles in the Bills.

§5. SUMMARY

573. Based on the above analysis, it seems Taiwan aggressively promotes the idea of energy tax to tackle the issue of climate change. The idea for and research on energy tax, environmental tax, or carbon tax arose much earlier than 2005. The introduction of an energy tax takes advantage of the status of global warming as a hot topic to reform long-standing problems in the Taiwanese energy market and pursue the tough policy goal of rationalizing the energy price. Reform of the energy market and promotion of energy conservation, efficiency, and emission reduction have faced many challenges because of the artificially low energy price (the price is lower than the cost) and public resistance to increasing it. It is very difficult to reflect the true energy cost, environmental cost, carbon cost, heating value, and so on. Thus, the development of an energy tax is viewed as a remedy to this long-standing problem.[797]

574. Against this backdrop, we see the politically sensitive nature of the energy tax issue. This is also reflected in divergent views on the design of the energy tax regime and how to persuade industry and the public to accept high taxation for energy. Many transitional designs and compromises are found in the different versions of the Energy Taxation Bill. Interestingly, unlike legislative processes in which bills proposed by the cabinet dominate the discussion (such as the Energy Management Act, Renewable Energy Act of 2009, Petroleum Administration Act, Natural Gas Business Act, Electricity Business Act, and GHG Reduction Act), that on the energy tax in Taiwan is dominated by bills proposed by MPs (Bills A, C, D, G, and H). The cabinet bills remain proposals and are not approved by the cabinet (Bills B, E, and F). Several draft bills (particularly E and F) could not be found on the Internet and can only be collected from related research reports. This also shows the sensitive nature of these bills. As such, the energy tax bill may be the most secret bill in Taiwan's legislative history.

575. Despite the divergent views and designs for the energy tax, particularly in terms of the tax rate (e.g., ranging from 27.5 to 2 NTD/L for gasoline tax), it is still possible to identify key similarities. We found common key elements in the bills (e.g., purpose, who and what should be taxed, tax rate, tax principles, the function and spending of the bills, and tax reduction and refund schemes). In addition, the *transition* plan and a progressive nature were found in many detailed designs, such as the progressive tax rate over ten years, flexible power of the cabinet or MOF to intervene in the tax rate, and tax reduction and refund schemes.

797. Jeffrey Shih-Jey Chen & Anton Ming-Zhi Gao, Recent Development of an Emissions Trading Scheme and Energy/Carbon Tax in Taiwan, in: Economic Instruments to Combat Climate Change in Asian Countries, Kluwer, 2015, Vol. 29.

Part VIII. Interaction Between Energy Law and Environmental Law

576. The first wave to trigger the development of energy law in Taiwan was naturally the "energy" issue, that is, the global oil crises of 1973 and 1979. Since then, several measures including measures to improve the demand-side management, enhance energy efficiency, and encourage energy conservation were introduced. The Energy Management Act was promulgated in 1980. Even though this Act was inspired by energy security concerns, it was also seen as playing a very important role in climate change policy.

577. Further, after the upsurge of the environmental movement in the 1970s, environmental protection also became the main concern of government. Indeed, energy projects often have a larger environmental impact than do other projects. One of the important mechanisms to regulate the environmental impact of energy projects is the assessment mechanism, which includes the EIA and SEA. In this article, this author will focus on the environmental aspects of energy projects' pre-development stages, while the environmental issues arising post-development, such as air pollution and water pollution, will not be dealt with here.

578. The most significant event affecting the development of energy law in Taiwan would doubtless be the issue of climate change. The important National Energy Policy Conferences and related policy documents in the past are all related to the climate change "moment." For instance, the National Energy Conferences of 1998, 2005, and 2009 are related to the Kyoto Protocol on timing of adoption, timing of effectiveness, and the important Copenhagen meeting, respectively. The 1996 Taiwan Energy Policy Measures and the 2005 Energy White Paper were influenced by the climate change issues. The convergence between energy and climate change in policy and legal measures seems to be a global trend, which also leads to the proposing of many climate change-related energy laws and policies. Taiwan adopted an approach similar to the climate change and energy package in Europe in 2007, and proposed its climate change and energy package, the 2010 Master Plan on Energy Conservation and Emission Reduction. In this plan, the "Four Laws of Emission Reduction and Energy Conservation," which include the GHG Reduction Bill, Renewable Energy Act, Energy Management Act, and Energy Tax Bill, were created. The GHG Reduction Bill was passed in 2015. This author will focus on the GHG Reduction Act and the overall legal framework when discussing climate change and energy, leaving the discussion of other Acts and Bills for another section.[798]

798. For a discussion of the Renewable Energy Act, please *see* "Regulatory Framework for Renewable Energy" in this book; for a discussion of the Energy Management Act, please see: Chapter 1 of this Part; for a discussion of the Energy Tax Bill, please *see* "Interaction between Energy Law and Tax Law" in this book.

Chapter 1. Energy Rationalization: Energy Efficiency and Energy Conservation

§1. Policy Concerning Energy Rationalization

579. After the second oil crisis, the Energy Management Act was promulgated that reflected the role of energy rationalization. Apart from this legal instrument, many policy measures were also used to improve the energy efficiency and conservation of all sectors. These energy rationalization measures were all considered to be the best way to achieve the 3E energy policy goal simultaneously. This Act has long been the main policy direction of the government and its role can be seen in the aforementioned important energy policy document, the 1996 Taiwan Energy Policy and Measures.

580. As a result, the energy intensity of Taiwan has continuously decreased since 2003. It was 9.54 and 9.24 LOE/Thousand NTD in 2005 and 2007, respectively, with an average annual growth rate of -1.6%. According to the statistics, Taiwan's energy efficiency has significantly improved.

581. The energy rationalization policy has not lost its momentum but has been reinforced under the challenge of climate change. Two recent important policy documents, the Sustainable Energy Development Framework and the Master Plan on Energy Conservation and Emission Reduction, indicate the energy efficiency target to be "Improving energy efficiency: The goal is to improve energy efficiency by more than 2% per annum, so that when compared with the level in 2005, energy intensity decreased 20% by 2015. Supplemented by further technological breakthroughs and proper administrative measures, energy intensity will decrease 50% by 2025."

582. Generally, there are overall and sector-specific strategies for achieving these ambitious goals. These measures can be summarized as follows:

(a) Overall measures:
  - Expanding technology and research, assisting industrial development.
  - Enhancing educational promotion, promoting energy-conservation activities among citizens.
  - Putting reasonable energy prices into effect, inducing energy conservation through the market mechanism.

(b) Sector specific measures:
  - Reducing the ratio of energy consumption in the industrial sector.
  - Restraining the growth of energy consumption by the commercial, residential, and transportation sectors.
  - Improving the performance efficiency of the power industry, restraining the peak loads.

583. In the 2017 Guideline on Energy Development, the role to "Strengthen Energy Saving on the Demand Side" is considered the priority for the first issue (Energy Security) of the four key guiding principles. The seven policy directions are as follows:

(1) Adopt the new economic development model of "Innovation, Employment, and Equitable Distribution" to continue with the optimization and transition of the industrial structure.
(2) Implement the preliminary management of energy use for large-scale investment in production plans, and adopt the best available commercialized technology to enhance energy efficiency.
(3) Expand the implementation of an energy audit, deploy an energy management system, raise energy efficiency standards for vehicles and equipment, and enhance the energy efficiency of industrial, transportation, residential, and commercial sectors via R&D, and demonstrate the application of energy saving technologies while providing proper energy saving incentives.
(4) Strengthen regulations related to energy saving design for new buildings, encourage the improvement of energy saving in existing buildings, raise building energy saving standards, improve the transparency of buildings' energy consumption information and promote its application in the market to reach the target of net-zero energy buildings and communities.
(5) Promote voluntary energy saving measures through the government's lead, industrial response, and public participation; and regulate energy consumption behaviors and activities to avoid waste to fully achieve energy-saving production, consumption, and living modes.
(6) Integrate energy saving, energy management, and energy storage; strengthen the demand response; disseminate load management measures such as Time-of-Use Rates; and introduce innovative business models to increase users' participation to curb the peak-load demand.
(7) Regulate the obligations of promoting energy saving and complementary mechanisms for the power industry.

584. The Energy Management Act plays a very important role in realizing these policy measures. Its role is also highlighted in the Master Plan of 2010 under the concept of the so-called Four Laws concerning Energy Conservation and Emission Reduction. This author will further elaborate on how the Energy Management Act and other related Ordinances facilitate the transformation of the energy system in Taiwan. The Energy Management Act and its related Ordinance adopted mainly a regulatory carrot-and-stick approach.

§2. Regulation under the Energy Management Act

585. The Energy Management Act mainly uses the stick approach to improve the energy efficiency of energy users. However, before elaborating on the Energy Management Act, there is a need to clarify the concepts of "energy industry" and "energy users." As noted above, there are industry-specific legislations for the petroleum, gas, and electricity industries. Since these industries provide energy for the final customers, this seems to imply that they are energy "suppliers." Yet, as they consume much energy, they come under the scrutiny of the Energy Management Act and are also treated as energy "users."

I. Large Energy Users

586. The Energy Management Act intends to use the regulations to catch the big fish first, as these big energy users consume the most energy and have more potential for improving energy efficiency.

587. There are four types of big energy users in the Energy Management Act.

(1) Energy user consuming large amount of energy
(2) Energy user producing large amounts of steam and heat
(3) Energy user having large air conditioning facilities
(4) Energy user as designated by the authority.

588. Yet, it should be noted that the scheme that applies for one category may also be applicable to another category; for instance, a CHP operator may be considered an energy user producing large amounts of steam and heat as well as an energy user consuming large amounts of energy. In this regard, it should be subject to both the legal regimes of Category 1 and 2.

A. *Energy User Using Large Amount of Energy*

589. Energy users consuming large amounts of energy include:[799]

(a) Large energy users (Annex Table 2):
- The coal users whose annual use exceeds 6,000 tons
- Fuel oil users whose annual use exceeds 6,000 kl
- Gas users whose annual use exceeds 10,000,000 m^3
- Electricity users whose contractual capacity is more than 800 Kw.

(b) Large energy users (Annex Table 3)
- Coal users of electricity generators/steel makers/other industries whose annual use is more than 1000 tons.
- Electricity users of railway/mass transportation/pipeline transportation electricity whose contract capacity is more than 800 kW.

799. Ordinance on Energy Users Using a Large Amount of Energy, 2018-03-09, available at: https://www.moeaboe.gov.tw/ECW/populace/Law/Content.aspx?menu_id=615.

590. Energy users consuming large amounts of energy (Annex Table 2) are subject to the following requirements:

(1) The establishment of an energy auditing system, of energy conservation and efficiency goals, and of an implementation plan[800] as well as the submission of energy consumption data to the MOEABOE by the end of January each year.[801]
(2) The recruitment of energy management personnel to do the audit and related works.[802] The qualifying process for energy management personnel is further specified in the related Ordinances.[803]
(3) Requirement to provide an energy utilization manual for the approval of the central competent authority.[804] Further details on the energy utilization manual are specified in the related Ordinances.[805]

591. Unlike the complicated legal burden for large energy users (Annex Table 2 of the Ordinance), only one duty applies to these energy users (Annex Table 3 of the Ordinance). They are obliged to submit energy utilization data to the MOEA-BOE by the 20th day of each month.[806] Coal users and electricity users above certain thresholds or in different sectors may be subject to different requirements under the Energy Management Act.

592. Finally, noteworthy is that based on the abstract legal provision of Article 9 of the Energy Management Act ("An energy user whose energy consumption meets the level stipulated by the central Competent authority, shall … and set

800. Article 9 of Energy Management Act: "The energy user, whose energy consumption is up to the level as stipulated by the central competent authority, should establish its own energy audit system in conjunction with the objectives for energy conservation and the implementing plan, which shall be carried out upon approval by the central competent authority."
801. Article 12 of the Energy Management Act.
802. Article 11 of the Energy Management Act: "The energy user whose energy consumption meets the level stipulated by the central competent authority or the user that has set up a central air conditioning system should be manned by an administrator in charge of energy management; whereas the central competent authority shall define the qualification, responsibility, and quota of the said administrator."
803. Accrediting Ordinance on Energy Management Personnel; Registration Ordinance on Energy, Amended Date: 2019-08-01, available at: https://www.moeaboe.gov.tw/ECW/populace/Law/Content.aspx?menu_id=1067; Management Personnel, 2016-08-11, available at: https://www.moeaboe.gov.tw/ECW/populace/Law/Content.aspx?menu_id=1068; FAQs of Energy Management Personnel, 2016-09-07, available at: https://www.moeaboe.gov.tw/ECW/populace/Law/wHandLawsList_File.ashx?kind=7&id=202&file_id=16.
804. Article 16 of the Energy Management Act.
805. Ordinance on the Review Fee for the Energy Utilization Manual, 2015-11-24, available at: https://www.moeaboe.gov.tw/ECW/populace/Law/Content.aspx?menu_id=2968; Ordinance on the Reviewing Procedure for the Energy Utilization Manual, 2017-04-18, available at: https://www.moeaboe.gov.tw/ECW/populace/Law/Content.aspx?menu_id=4369; Ordinance on the establishment of an Advisory Group for the Energy Utilization Manual, 2017-03-24, available at: https://www.moeaboe.gov.tw/ECW/populace/Law/Content.aspx?menu_id=3322; Ordinance on the Format of the Energy Utilization Manual, 2015-11-24, available at: https://www.moeaboe.gov.tw/ECW/populace/Law/wHandLawsList_File.ashx?kind=1&id=9&file_id=1.
806. Article 12 of the Energy Management Act.

objectives for energy conservation and execution … "), the MOEA interprets it in a way that the objectives could be considered an "energy saving obligation." Therefore, the Ordinance further stipulates that all legal or natural persons with an electricity contract capacity of more than 800 kW (with a few exceptions) are obliged to follow the energy conservation goals.[807] For instance, according to Article 5 of the Ordinance, the annual average electricity saving rate should be 1% between 2015 and 2024. The plan to achieve this energy saving target should be more than 1% each year. Otherwise, the MOEABOE will not approve the plan.[808]

B. Energy Users Producing Large Amounts of Steam and Heat

593. According to Article 10 of the Energy Management Act, those energy users producing a certain amount (100 tons per hour) of steam heat are subject to a CHP mandate.[809] This scheme seems to be a "stick" at first sight; it intends to encourage the reuse of waste heat during the industrial production process and facilitate the development of CHP and cogeneration, and improve energy efficiency. However, such energy users may also constitute those consuming a large amount of energy, as noted above. Thus, the legal duty such as the submission of energy utilization data each month[810] may still be applicable.

594. Yet, a closer look at Article 10(2)(3) indicates that for qualified CHPs,[811] the surplus electricity produced by these cogenerators will be purchased by TaiPower at a very preferential price. This net-metering scheme was provided for in the CHP Ordinance.[812]

C. Energy User Having Large Air Conditioning Facilities

595. Air conditioning is frequently used in office buildings and the industrial sector and is also the main concern of the Energy Management Act. The Energy

807. Ordinance on Large Electricity Users to set energy conservation goals and execution plan, 2019-12-25, available at: https://www.moeaboe.gov.tw/ECW/populace/Law/Content.aspx?menu_id=2340.
808. Article 3 of such Ordinance on Large electricity Users to set energy conservation goals and execution plan.
809. Article 10(1) of the Energy Management Act: "Where the amount of steam generated by an energy user reaches the level established by the central competent authority, the user shall install a cogeneration system." *See also*, Ordinance on Energy Users Using a Large Amount of Energy.
810. For the data submission form for fossil-fired power plants, incinerators, and CHPs, please *see* https://www.moeaboe.gov.tw/ECW/main/Law/wHandEditorFile.ashx?file_id=5373; https://law.moea.gov.tw/Download.ashx?FileID=168828.
811. Ordinance on the accreditation of qualified CHPs, 2016-05-05, available at: https://www.moeaboe.gov.tw/ECW/populace/Law/Content.aspx?menu_id=1033.
812. MOJ, CHP Ordinance, 2019-12-24, available at: https://law.moj.gov.tw/LawClass/LawAll.aspx?pcode=J0130014.

Management Act provides for two types of regulations: one type focuses on the "energy user," the other focuses on the efficiency of the installation. The latter will be elaborated on later.

596. Air conditioning installations, whose use is not for production purposes and whose frozen main machine exceeds 100 horse power, are subject to the regulations under Article 18 of the Energy Management Act. Installations are required to be equipped with independent electric meters and circuits for such systems,[813] In this regard, the central authority is allowed to adopt load management to control these large central air conditioning systems.

D. *Energy Users Designated by the Authority*

597. The above-mentioned energy users are generally large "industrial" or "commercial" energy users in Taiwan. However, there remain other, smaller, but also very important energy users. They can be seen as medium fish in the flow of regulating energy efficiency. According to Article 8 of the Energy Management Act, the Designated Energy Users are required to comply with the efficiency and user guide for lighting, power, electric heating, air conditioning, refrigerating facilities, or other energy consuming facilities. The designated energy users include mainly commercial leisure, wholesale, and retailing businesses:[814] hotels, department stores, chain wholesale malls, chain store supermarkets, chain store convenience stores, chain store cosmetic and pharmaceutical retailers, electrical appliance retailers, banks, security brokers, post offices, mass transit locations, restaurants, chain store clothing stores, hairdresser salons, book and stationery retail stores, optometrists, shoe retail stores, ordinary hotels, car and motorcycle dealers, and so on.

598. These stores or hotels are required to follow the energy conservation regulations. First, they are obliged to install an air door and improve the insulation of windows, etc., with a view to preventing the leakage of cool air to outdoors and the entry of hot air from outdoors. Second, incandescent bulbs are to be phased out in two stages. The first stage involves prohibiting the use of (≥25 kW) incandescent bulbs, but allowing their use in light dimmers. In the second stage, all incandescent bulbs will be prohibited now.[815] Further Ordinances on Inspection Procedures for Compliance Regarding Cool Air Leakage and the incandescent bulbs prohibition are provided.[816]

813. For the detailed requirements, *see* Ordinance on Meter and Circuit of Central Air Conditioning, 2002-07-17, available at: https://www.moeaboe.gov.tw/ECW/populace/Law/Content.aspx?menu_id=1055.
814. Ordinance on Designated Energy Users to comply with energy conservation regulations, 2016-11-21, available at: https://www.moeaboe.gov.tw/ECW/populace/Law/Content.aspx?menu_id=1063.
815. Ordinance on Designated Energy Users to comply with energy conservation regulations.
816. Ordinance on Inspection Procedure for Compliance Regarding Cool Air Leakage, 2017-03-16, available at: https://www.moeaboe.gov.tw/ECW/populace/Law/Content.aspx?menu_id=4353; Ordinance on the Inspection SOP for indoor air conditioning temperature, 2017-03-16, available at: https://www.moeaboe.gov.tw/ECW/populace/Law/Content.aspx?menu_id=4354; Ordinance on

599. Originally, such regulations on designated energy users covered those not included in the aforementioned "big fish" energy efficiency and conservation measures. However, the abstract nature of the legal basis of Article 8—("The utilization and efficiency of the lighting, power, electric heating, air conditioning, refrigerating facilities, or other energy consuming facilities used by existing energy users designated by the central competent authority shall comply with the energy conservation regulations promulgated by the central competent authority.")—means that the regulations can be applied to various industries including petrochemicals,[817] pulp/paper,[818] steel,[819] cement,[820] textile,[821] and electronics.[822]

600. Large-scale energy users using steamers are also subject to the requirement to conduct certain energy conservation behaviors[823] with a few exceptions.[824] Therefore, this energy conservation regulation completes the regulations applying to the aforementioned energy users who produce large amounts of steam and heat or those using a large amount of energy. The ITRI and Taiwan Green Productivity Foundation audit compliance with this steamer conservation requirement.[825] A site inspection SOP Ordinance is also in place.[826]

Inspection Procedure for Compliance Regarding the Prohibition of Incandescent Bulbs, 2017-03-16, available at: https://www.moeaboe.gov.tw/ECW/populace/Law/Content.aspx?menu_id=4355.

817. Ordinance on Energy Conservation and Efficiency Use Regulations for the Petrochemical Industry, 2014-07-29, available at: https://www.moeaboe.gov.tw/ECW/populace/Law/Content.aspx?menu_id=2339.
818. Ordinance on Energy Conservation and Efficiency Use Regulations for the Pulp and Paper Industry, 2013-11-15, available at: https://www.moeaboe.gov.tw/ECW/populace/Law/Content.aspx?menu_id=2181.
819. Ordinance on Energy Conservation and Efficiency Use Regulations for the Steel Industry, 2013-09-13, available at: https://www.moeaboe.gov.tw/ECW/populace/Law/Content.aspx?menu_id=2111.
820. Ordinance on Energy Conservation and Efficiency Use Regulations for the Cement Industry, 2012-09-24, available at: https://www.moeaboe.gov.tw/ECW/populace/Law/Content.aspx?menu_id=1881.
821. Ordinance on Energy Conservation and Efficiency Use Regulations for the Textile Industry, 2015-10-30, available at: https://www.moeaboe.gov.tw/ECW/populace/Law/Content.aspx?menu_id=2959.
822. Ordinance on Energy Conservation and Efficiency Use Regulations for the Electronic Industry, 2015-03-04, available at: https://www.moeaboe.gov.tw/ECW/populace/Law/Content.aspx?menu_id=2735.
823. Ordinance on Energy Conservation Regulations for Designated Energy Users using Steamers, 2012-03-22, available at: https://www.moeaboe.gov.tw/ECW/populace/Law/Content.aspx?menu_id=1108.
824. Ordinance on the Exemption of Ordinance on Energy Conservation Regulations for Designated Energy Users using Steamers, 2017-03-15, available at: https://www.moeaboe.gov.tw/ECW/populace/Law/Content.aspx?menu_id=4356.
825. Public announcement on the implementation works of the Energy Conservation Regulations for Designated Energy Users using Steamers, 2017-03-07, available at: https://www.moeaboe.gov.tw/ECW/populace/Law/Content.aspx?menu_id=4346.
826. Ordinance on the Site Inspection SOP for Energy Conservation Regulations for Designated Energy Users using Steamers, 2017-03-20, available at: https://www.moeaboe.gov.tw/ECW/populace/Law/Content.aspx?menu_id=4357.

601. Finally, the obligated entity is expanded to also cover public agencies. The legal person in charge of the streetlights in the central or local government should follow the energy conservation guide, such as the prohibition to use mercury streetlights since January 1, 2017.[827]

II. Efficiency Standard for Energy Appliances or Vehicles

A. *Energy Appliances*

602. The best way to improve energy efficiency is to regulate the efficiency standard of energy appliances. Standards have been developed for different appliances in different sectors. The ultimate goal is to encourage the use of the "right" appliance in manufacturing (industrial), commercial, and residential sectors.

1. Energy Efficiency Standards

603. In the manufacturing and industrial sectors, the policy focus is on improving energy efficiency by promoting high-efficiency motor programs and boiler efficiency plans; specific energy consumption indicators are established. The Ordinances on Energy Efficiency Standard for Boilers,[828] Low-Voltage Single-Phase Induction Motors,[829] and Three-Phase Low-Voltage Cage Induction Motors[830] were promulgated with a view to implementing this policy direction. As for the boiler standard, different efficiency standards between 87 and 93.5% were established in accordance with the type of boilers (oil-fired straight water tube boiler, gas-fired straight water tube boiler, oil-fired or gas-fired smoke tube boilers) and their capacity (tons per hour). With regard to the Low-Voltage Single-Phase Induction Motors, the minimum requirement for full-load efficiency is defined as between 53 and 71% in accordance with the type of motors (PSC, RSIR, CSIR), the output (kW or HP), number of poles, and the rpm at 60 Hz. A similar regime is also applied to three-phase low-voltage cage induction motors in accordance with their output (kW and Horse Power), number of poles, and the rpm at 60 Hz.

827. Ordinance on the Energy Conservation Regulations for Streetlight Management Entities/Bodies, 2015-08-13, available at: https://www.moeaboe.gov.tw/ECW/populace/Law/Content.aspx?menu_id=2893; Inspection Ordinance on the Energy Conservation Regulations for Streetlight Management Entities/Bodies, 2017-11-08, available at: https://www.moeaboe.gov.tw/ECW/populace/Law/Content.aspx?menu_id=5527.
828. Ordinance on Energy Efficiency Standard for Boilers, 2001-09-12, available at: https://www.moeaboe.gov.tw/ECW/populace/Law/Content.aspx?menu_id=1036.
829. Ordinance on Energy Efficiency Standard for Low-Voltage Single-Phase Induction Motors, 1999-12-31, available at: https://www.moeaboe.gov.tw/ECW/populace/Law/Content.aspx?menu_id=1041.
830. Ordinance on Energy Efficiency Standard for Three-Phase Low-Voltage Cage Induction Motors, 2014-12-22, available at: https://www.moeaboe.gov.tw/ECW/populace/Law/Content.aspx?menu_id=1038.

604. For energy efficiency in the commercial and residential sectors, the policy priority is to enhance the energy efficiency of various types of electrical appliances; expand electrical products' energy efficiency management; and promote the use of high efficiency, low standby power products. This policy direction is similar to that in the industrial sectors. Yet the target appliances are different.

605. Several Ordinances were developed for commercial and household appliances, which can be summarized into four categories. Apparently, air conditioners and lights are two top priorities. Different Ordinances are provided for different types of air conditioning: "Window Type Air Conditioner,"[831] "Packaged Air Conditioner,"[832] and "No-Air-Duct Air Conditioner."[833] Furthermore, the air conditioner's associated products—namely, water coolers for air conditioning system[834] and steam compression ice-water units[835]—are also regulated.

606. Similar intensive regulation is also provided for lighting, which fact indicates the high energy consumption of lighting in businesses and households. In general, the efficiency standard differentiates between the pipe-shaped "tubular fluorescent lamp" and the ball-shaped "light bulb." Further, detailed regulations are provided for the regular tubular fluorescent lamp,[836] ballasts for fluorescent lamps,[837] and compact fluorescent lamps.[838] As for the light bulb, energy efficiency

---

831. Energy Efficiency Ordinance on "Window Type Air Conditioner," 2001-09-12, available at: https://www.moeaboe.gov.tw/ECW/populace/Law/Content.aspx?menu_id=1039.
832. Energy Efficiency Ordinance on Packaged Air Conditioner, 2001-09-12, available at: https://www.moeaboe.gov.tw/ECW/populace/Law/Content.aspx?menu_id=1040.
833. Energy Efficiency Ordinance on "No-Air-Duct Air Conditioner," Amended Date: 2010-12-17, available at: https://www.moeaboe.gov.tw/ecw/populace/Law/Content.aspx?menu_id=1044.
834. Energy Efficiency Ordinance on Water Coolers for Air-Conditioning Systems, 2001-09-12, available at: https://www.moeaboe.gov.tw/ECW/populace/Law/Content.aspx?menu_id=1037.
835. Energy Efficiency Ordinance on Steam Compression Ice-Water Units, 2019-08-20, available at: https://www.moeaboe.gov.tw/ECW/populace/Law/Content.aspx?menu_id=8553.
836. Energy Efficiency Ordinance on Regular Tubular Fluorescent Lamp, 2017-04-21, available at: https://www.moeaboe.gov.tw/ECW/populace/Law/Content.aspx?menu_id=4366.
837. Energy Efficiency Ordinance on Ballasts for Fluorescent Lamps, 2006-01-06, available at: https://www.moeaboe.gov.tw/ECW/populace/Law/Content.aspx?menu_id=1043.
838. Energy Efficiency Ordinance on Compact Fluorescent Lamp, 2007-01-19, available at: https://www.moeaboe.gov.tw/ECW/populace/Law/Content.aspx?menu_id=1046.

standards are provided for incandescent bulbs[839] and self-ballasted fluorescent lamps,[840] as well as the LED lighting of stabilizer built-in LEDs[841] and double-capped LED lamps.[842]

607. Finally, the objective of the policy is to launch a "lighting revolution." The government would also launch a demonstration scheme of the use of LED lighting in 2012.[843] On the other hand, the retirement subsidy for traditional mercury street lighting, namely the sunset program for mercury streetlights—is also provided.[844] Since 2015, a subsidy is provided to the research and demonstration project on smart lighting in university libraries.[845] Recently, a subsidy has been provided for indoor advanced LED lighting in local government buildings.[846] Finally, as noted, the public or local government is obliged to follow the related Ordinance in the operation of streetlights.

608. Finally, as household and commercial refrigerators consume a lot of energy, there are also energy efficiency standards focusing on refrigerators.[847] In addition, as Taiwan has an island-type climate, there is a need for dehumidification. In this

839. Energy Efficiency Ordinance on Incandescent Bulbs, 2009-03-02, available at: https://www.moeaboe.gov.tw/ECW/populace/Law/Content.aspx?menu_id=1049.
840. Energy Efficiency Ordinance on Self-ballasted Fluorescent Lamps, 2007-01-19, available at: https://www.moeaboe.gov.tw/ECW/populace/Law/Content.aspx?menu_id=1047.
841. Energy Efficiency Ordinance on stabilizer built-in light-emitting diode bulbs, 2014-01-24, available at: https://www.moeaboe.gov.tw/ECW/populace/Law/Content.aspx?menu_id=2207; Inspection Guide for Energy Efficiency Ordinance on stabilizer built-in light-emitting diode bulbs, 2019-03-21, available at: https://www.moeaboe.gov.tw/ECW/populace/Law/Content.aspx?menu_id=8429; Energy Efficiency Classification Ordinance on stabilizer built-in light-emitting diode bulbs, 2002-12-06, available at: https://www.moeaboe.gov.tw/ECW/populace/Law/Content.aspx?menu_id=1072.
842. Energy Efficiency Ordinance on Double-capped LED Lamp, 2020-06-23, available at: https://www.moeaboe.gov.tw/ECW/populace/Law/Content.aspx?menu_id=12016.
843. Demonstration Subsidy Ordinance for LED Street Lighting, 2012-10-15, available at: https://www.moeaboe.gov.tw/ECW/populace/Law/Content.aspx?menu_id=1770; Ordinance on the Expansion of the Deployment of LED Street Lighting, 2012-04-02, available at: https://www.moeaboe.gov.tw/ECW/populace/Law/Content.aspx?menu_id=1501.
844. Ordinance on the Sunset Programme of Mercury Street Lighting, 2017-03-15, available at: https://www.moeaboe.gov.tw/ECW/populace/Law/Content.aspx?menu_id=4351.
845. Ordinance on the Subsidy to Research and Demonstration Projects on Smart Lighting in University Libraries, 2015-07-06, available at: https://www.moeaboe.gov.tw/ECW/populace/Law/Content.aspx?menu_id=2874.
846. Subsidy Ordinance on the Promotion of Advanced LED lighting, 2020-01-06, available at: https://www.moeaboe.gov.tw/ECW/populace/Law/Content.aspx?menu_id=3326; The application period of Subsidy Ordinance on the Promotion of Advanced LED lighting in 2020, 2020-02-04, available at: https://www.moeaboe.gov.tw/ECW/populace/Law/Content.aspx?menu_id=5792; Technical Ordinance on Smart and High Efficiency lighting, 2020-02-04, available at: https://www.moeaboe.gov.tw/ECW/populace/Law/Content.aspx?menu_id=5793.
847. ; Benchmark value for Energy Efficiency for Refrigerators, 2006-01-06, available at: https://www.moeaboe.gov.tw/ECW/populace/Law/Content.aspx?menu_id=1045; Energy Efficiency Ordinance on Refrigerators, 2017-05-12, available at: https://www.moeaboe.gov.tw/ECW/populace/Law/Content.aspx?menu_id=1066.

regard, efficiency regulations for dehumidifiers are also in place.[848] A wide range of efficiency standards are applied to warm drinking water dispensers,[849] rice cookers,[850] air ventilation,[851] electric water heaters,[852] gas water heaters,[853] gas ovens,[854] and incandescent light bulbs.[855]

2. Mandatory Labeling and Energy Efficiency Classification

609. In order to ensure transparency for consumers, in addition to the above standards, certain appliances are subject to mandatory labeling and energy efficiency classification requirements. In this regard, the aforementioned standard can be seen as a minimum requirement. Yet for those appliance makers that wish to appeal to the consumer by going far beyond the basic requirements, these mandatory labeling and energy efficiency classifications are necessary. This additional requirement shows that certain appliances are the main target of energy efficiency regulation in Taiwan. Details on mandatory labeling items and inspection methodology are further provided for all types of air conditioners,[856]

848. Energy Efficiency Ordinance on Dehumidifiers, 2017-04-21, available at: https://www.moeaboe.gov.tw/ECW/populace/Law/Content.aspx?menu_id=4365.
849. Energy Efficiency Ordinance on Storage type electric water boiler, 2020-07-06, available at: https://www.moeaboe.gov.tw/ECW/populace/Law/Content.aspx?menu_id=12024; Energy Efficiency Ordinance on Drinking water dispenser for packaging drinking water, 2018-08-17, available at: https://www.moeaboe.gov.tw/ECW/populace/Law/Content.aspx?menu_id=7031; Energy Efficiency Ordinance on Warm drinking water supply machine, 2016-12-22, available at: https://www.moeaboe.gov.tw/ECW/populace/Law/Content.aspx?menu_id=6943; Energy Efficiency Ordinance on Ice warm drinking water supply machine, 2016-12-22, available at: https://www.moeaboe.gov.tw/ECW/populace/Law/Content.aspx?menu_id=3312; Energy Efficiency Ordinance on Warm drinking machine, 2015-09-21, available at: https://www.moeaboe.gov.tw/ECW/populace/Law/Content.aspx?menu_id=2941; Energy Efficiency Ordinance on IceWarm drinking machine, 2015-09-21, available at: https://www.moeaboe.gov.tw/ECW/populace/Law/Content.aspx?menu_id=2942.
850. Energy Efficiency Ordinance on Rice Cookers, 2018-12-24, available at: https://www.moeaboe.gov.tw/ECW/populace/Law/Content.aspx?menu_id=6937.
851. Energy Efficiency Ordinance on Air Compressors, 2019-01-08, available at: https://www.moeaboe.gov.tw/ECW/populace/Law/Content.aspx?menu_id=7165; Energy Efficiency Ordinance on Ductless Air Conditioners, 2016-12-30, available at: https://www.moeaboe.gov.tw/ECW/populace/Law/Content.aspx?menu_id=3319.
852. Energy Efficiency Ordinance for Storage type electric water heater, 2014-04-28, available at: https://www.moeaboe.gov.tw/ECW/populace/Law/Content.aspx?menu_id=2238; Energy Efficiency Ordinance for Electric thermos, 2013-11-22, available at: https://www.moeaboe.gov.tw/ECW/populace/Law/Content.aspx?menu_id=2183.
853. Energy Efficiency Ordinance for Instant gas water heater, 2012-12-06, available at: https://www.moeaboe.gov.tw/ECW/populace/Law/Content.aspx?menu_id=1853.
854. Energy Efficiency Ordinance for Gas stove, 2012-12-06, available at: https://www.moeaboe.gov.tw/ECW/populace/Law/Content.aspx?menu_id=1865.
855. Energy Efficiency Ordinance for Incandescent Light Bulbs, 2012-03-23, available at: https://www.moeaboe.gov.tw/ECW/populace/Law/Content.aspx?menu_id=1109.
856. Mandatory Labeling Ordinance on Air Compressors, 2019-01-08, available at: https://www.moeaboe.gov.tw/ecw/populace/Law/Content.aspx?menu_id=7165; Mandatory Labelling Ordinance on Ductless Air Conditioners, 2016-12-30, available at: https://www.moeaboe.gov.tw/ecw/populace/Law/Content.aspx?menu_id=3319.

refrigerators,[857] dehumidifiers,[858] and self-ballasted fluorescent lamps,[859] rice cookers,[860] different types of drinking water dispensers,[861] electric water boilers,[862] storage-type electric water heaters,[863] instant gas water heaters,[864] and gas ovens.[865] The labeling requirement is subject to random auditing.[866] The mandatory items differ for different energy appliances. For instance, the refrigerator is required to carry a label of its capacity (in liters) and energy efficiency factor (liter/per kW/per month) (Figure 8).

857. Mandatory Labeling Ordinance on Refrigerators, 2017-05-12, available at: https://www.moeaboe.gov.tw/ecw/populace/Law/Content.aspx?menu_id=1066.
858. Mandatory Labeling Ordinance on Dehumidifiers, 2017-04-21, available at: https://www.moeaboe.gov.tw/ecw/populace/Law/Content.aspx?menu_id=4365.
859. Mandatory Labeling Ordinance on Self-ballasted Fluorescent Lamps, 2012-12-06, available at: https://www.moeaboe.gov.tw/ecw/populace/Law/Content.aspx?menu_id=1072.
860. Mandatory Labeling Ordinance on Rice Cookers, 2018-12-24, available at: https://www.moeaboe.gov.tw/ecw/populace/Law/Content.aspx?menu_id=6937.
861. Energy Efficiency Ordinance on Warm drinking water supply machine, 2016-12-22, available at: https://www.moeaboe.gov.tw/ECW/populace/Law/Content.aspx?menu_id=6943; Energy Efficiency Ordinance on Ice warm drinking water supply machine, 2016-12-22, available at: https://www.moeaboe.gov.tw/ECW/populace/Law/Content.aspx?menu_id=3312; Energy Efficiency Ordinance on Warm drinking machine, 2015-09-21, available at: https://www.moeaboe.gov.tw/ECW/populace/Law/Content.aspx?menu_id=2941; Energy Efficiency Ordinance on IceWarm drinking machine, 2015-09-21, available at: https://www.moeaboe.gov.tw/ECW/populace/Law/Content.aspx?menu_id=2942.
862. Mandatory Labeling Ordinance on, 2013-11-22, available at: https://www.moeaboe.gov.tw/ecw/populace/Law/Content.aspx?menu_id=2183.
863. Mandatory Labeling Ordinance on, 2014-04-28, available at: https://www.moeaboe.gov.tw/ecw/populace/Law/Content.aspx?menu_id=2238.
864. Energy Efficiency Ordinance for Instant gas water heater, 2012-12-06, available at: https://www.moeaboe.gov.tw/ECW/populace/Law/Content.aspx?menu_id=1853.
865. Energy Efficiency Ordinance for Gas stove, 2012-12-06, available at: https://www.moeaboe.gov.tw/ECW/populace/Law/Content.aspx?menu_id=1865.
866. Ordinance on the random auditing energy labeling and related energy efficiency requirement, 2011-11-23, available at:https://www.moeaboe.gov.tw/ECW/populace/Law/Content.aspx?menu_id=1073.

Figure 8 Format of the First-Class to Fourth-Class Labeling for Refrigerators

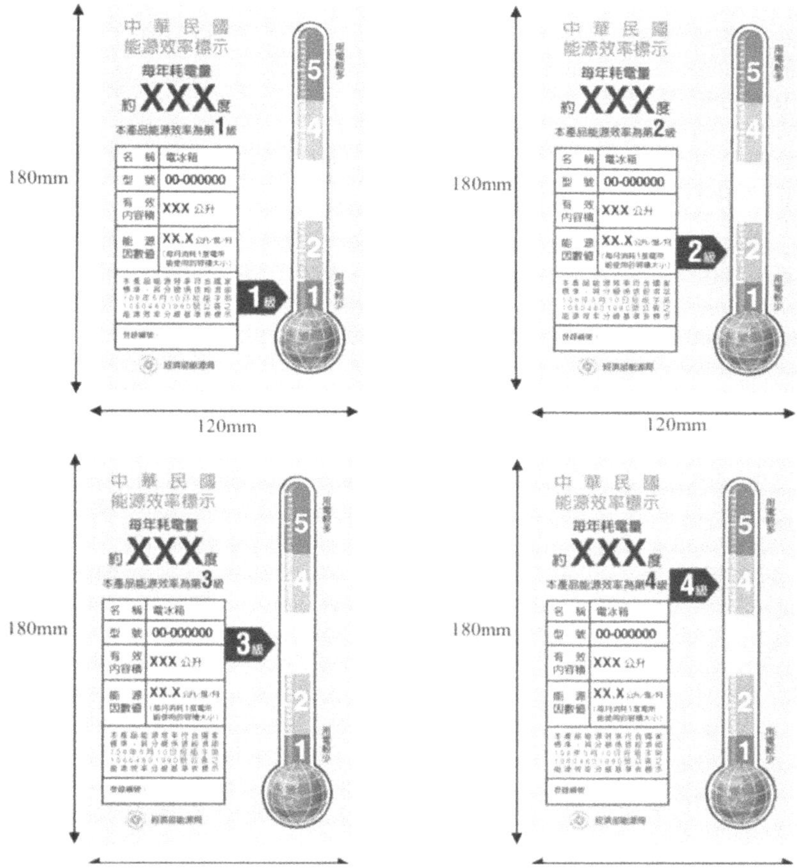

Source: Energy Labeling Ordinance on Refrigerators, available at: https://www.moeaboe.gov.tw/ECW/main/Law/wHandEditorFile.ashx?file_id=3662), 2005-05-06.

3. Incentive

Investment Subsidy (Grant) for Buying Energy Saving Product

610. In addition to encouraging the purchase of these first-class energy efficient products via labeling, the government also promotes an incentive scheme. As these energy efficient products are very expensive, financial barriers on the facilitating and promotion the use is found by the government. In order to reap the potential of energy efficiency measures in achieving the Kyoto target, and, more particularly, to support the endangered Taiwanese electrical appliance industry during the financial crisis in 2008, the government launched a grant scheme to subsidize the purchase of energy-saving products, thus promoting the use of high efficiency, low standby power products. Under the Ordinance on the Grant for Purchasing Energy-Saving Labeled Products,[867] consumers buying air conditioners, refrigerators, and washing machines with an energy saving-mark that was produced in Taiwan between October 1, 2008, and March 31, 2009, were allowed a grant of 3000 NTD. The total subsidy amount is 530 million NTD. This has contributed to electricity saving and emission reduction of 2.6 million tons.

611. However, as this measure focuses on the MIT (made in Taiwan) product, it has also led to concerns about violating WTO or GATT rules on non-discrimination. Those Japanese big brands, such as Panasonic or Hitachi, that have production factories in Taiwan are not much affected by this MIT clause. However, the Korea-based electronics giants, Samsung and LG, launched a complaint to the MOEA over the potential violation of WTO rules. However, they did not file a legal suit in the WTO.

612. In 2017, the MOEABOE launched an equipment subsidy to encourage electricity users with an electricity contract capacity of more than 100 kW to purchase equipment to apply waste heat or cold recycling technology.[868] The subsidized equipment is limited to the following technologies: (1) Organic Rankine Cycle (Organic Rankine Cycle, ORC) waste heat recovery power generation technology, (2) solid state thermoelectric material waste heat recovery power generation technology, (3) industrial heater heat radiation selective absorption technology, (4) regenerative combustion technology, (5) low-temperature waste heat recovery technology of the total heat exchange system, (6) absorption waste heat refrigeration technology, and (7) absorption waste heat refrigeration technology.

613. In 2019, a special subsidy scheme was introduced to encourage public or private legal persons and medical institutions/hospitals to replace old low-efficient

867. Ordinance on the Grant for Purchasing Energy-Saving Labeled Products, 2011, 12, 27, available at: https://www.energylabel.org.tw/index.aspx, http://www.energylabel.org.tw/news/news/upt.asp?uid=&con=&cid=&year=&month=&day=&key=&pageno=&p0=109.

868. Subsidy Ordinance on the Application of Waste Heat and Cold Cycling Technology, 2017-02-16, available at: https://www.moeaboe.gov.tw/ECW/populace/Law/Content.aspx?menu_id=4340; List of Subsidy on the Application of Waste Heat and Cold Cycling Technology 2020, 2020-08-25, available at: https://www.moeaboe.gov.tw/ECW/populace/Law/wHandLawsList_File.ashx?kind=7&id=3398&file_id=3741; List of Subsidy on the Application of Waste Heat and Cold Cycling Technology 2028, 2019-10-29, available at: https://www.moeaboe.gov.tw/ECW/populace/Law/wHandLawsList_File.ashx?kind=7&id=3365&file_id=3621; List of Subsidy on the Application of Waste Heat and Cold Cycling Technology 2017, 2017-02-24, available at: https://www.moeaboe.gov.tw/ECW/populace/Law/wHandLawsList_File.ashx?kind=7&id=236&file_id=137.

air compressors, fans, and pumps with new and higher-efficiency ones.[869] The results for the first year look promising. Therefore, the scheme is being continued in 2020.[870]

Energy Conservation Subsidy for Local Government

614. The local government could play a key role in improving energy conservation. Since 2015, a series of actions have focused on local government participation. In 2015, a one-year smart electricity saving program was launched.[871] Local governments could apply for the funding if they promised energy-saving goals, electricity saving actions in government buildings/residential sector/service sectors, to set up websites to promote energy saving behaviors, etc.

615. However, because of the lack of financial or human resources, local governments are unwilling to participate in planning an electricity saving strategy. To encourage them to formulate a localized electricity saving strategy to improve electricity saving in the service and residential sectors, the MOEABOE provides this capacity building funding.[872] The subsidy ranges between 1–3 million NTD depending on the size of the local county.

616. To attract local governments' participation in promoting electricity saving in the residential and service sectors, office buildings, and the agricultural sector, the central government provided NTD 7.3 billion and 26 million between January 1, 2018 and the end of 2020.[873] The budget will be used to encourage the establishment of energy saving basic works, the smart use of electricity, retiring and replacing old equipment, and tailor-made localization solutions.

Green Procurement

617. In order to comply with the global trend of green production and consumption, EPA proposed the green procurement clause in Article 96 of the Public Procurement Act. Further incentive schemes were developed.

---

869. Special subsidy scheme for Power and utility equipment 2019, 2019-01-03, available at: https://www.moeaboe.gov.tw/ECW/populace/Law/Content.aspx?menu_id=5823. Application on Special subsidy scheme for Power and utility equipment 2019, 2019-03-17 available at: https://www.moeaboe.gov.tw/ECW/populace/Law/Content.aspx?menu_id=5822.
870. Special subsidy scheme for Power and utility equipment 2020, 2020-01-03, available at: https://www.moeaboe.gov.tw/ECW/populace/Law/Content.aspx?menu_id=8910; Application on Special subsidy scheme for Power and utility equipment 2020, 2020-03-17 available at: https://www.moeaboe.gov.tw/ECW/populace/Law/Content.aspx?menu_id=8911.
871. Smart electricity saving program, 2015-05-06, available at: https://www.moeaboe.gov.tw/ECW/populace/Law/Content.aspx?menu_id=2775.
872. Subsidy Ordinance on the Local Government's Participation in Planning an Electricity Saving Strategy, 2016-04-12, available at: https://www.moeaboe.gov.tw/ECW/populace/Law/Content.aspx?menu_id=3077.
873. Subsidy Ordinance on Promoting Local Government's Participation in Electricity Saving in the Residential and Commercial sectors, 2019-08-27, available at: https://www.moeaboe.gov.tw/ECW/populace/Law/Content.aspx?menu_id=5500.

618. In order to encourage the public sector (including government or state-owned enterprises) to buy and use products certified under the energy labeling scheme, the government launched the "Green Procurement Promotion Program" in 2002.[874] Government departments and state enterprises are required to make a certain minimum amount of their total procurement "green content." For instance, the percentage of green contents in 2006 was 88%. Certain energy appliances are also considered green-content products, such as refrigerators, air conditioners, washing machines, microwave ovens, drink water suppliers, lighting facilities, copying machines, fax machines, laptops, etc. In addition to these energy-saving appliances, other products, such as water-saving toilet bowls, furniture using recycled wood, etc., are also considered to be green products.

619. In addition, energy efficient products are considered to be environmentally friendly, and energy-saving labeling is also considered "environmental labeling" as provided for in the Ordinance on Priority Purchasing of Environmentally Friendly Products by the Government.[875] According to Article 2 of the Ordinance, the eco-product involves the "use of a product or its material possesses the function of reducing energy consumption." The Directions for the Performance Appraisal of the Priority Procurement of Government Agencies[876] was developed as a guideline to evaluate the overall performance of the procurement program. A performance appraisal committee was set up to evaluate said performance according to weighted criteria and an appraisal index. The Program clearly defined the category and proportion of the environmentally preferable product the governmental agency shall purchase. The EPA set the green procurement goal as 83% by 2007, which is amended annually according to yearly performance.[877] In 2007, an electronic online reporting system was developed to facilitate monitoring works. The online system can be accessed here: https://greenliving.epa.gov.tw/GreenLife/Anonymous/LoginById.aspx

Soft Loan Scheme

620. For those private or public companies buying energy-saving facilities, the Soft Loan Ordinance on Buying Energy-Saving Installations of 1999[878] and the Soft Loan Ordinance on Buying Energy-Saving Installations (Second Phase) of 2002

---

874. Green Procurement Promotion Program, available at: http://www.purchasing.fcu.edu.tw/wSite/public/Attachment/f1268122364880.pdf.
875. Ordinance on Priority Purchasing Environmentally Friendly Products by the Government MOJ, Regulations for Priority Procurement of Eco-Products, Amended Date: 2001-01-15, available at: https://law.moj.gov.tw/LawClass/LawAll.aspx?pcode=A0030084. The Ordinance is available in English at: https://law.moj.gov.tw/ENG/LawClass/LawAll.aspx?pcode=A0030084.
876. EPA, The Directions for the Performance Appraisal of the Priority Procurement of Government Agencies, 2002-12-17, Amended Date: 2014-12-26, available at: https://oaout.epa.gov.tw/law/LawContent.aspx?id=GL006369.
877. EPA, The Rules and Regulations of Green Procurement in Taiwan, available at: https://greenliving.epa.gov.tw/newPublic/Eng/GreenPurchase.
878. The Soft Loan Ordinance on Buying Energy-Saving Installations of 1999.

provide a soft loan (low-interest rate) scheme.[879] The total amount for the second phase soft loan is 100 billion NTD. The value of the loan cannot exceed 80% of the project cost, or 400 million NTD per project. The main feature of this Ordinance is that it broadly defines what are energy-saving installations. In addition to the traditional energy-saving installations, such as peak-load shifting installations, energy-saving monitoring installations, energy recovery installations, etc., three types of renewable energy sources, namely, electricity installations including wind turbines, geothermal facilities, fuel cells, and PVs; renewable thermal installations; and renewable fuel installations are also incentivized under this scheme. Besides, this loan is also accompanied by a loan guarantee program under the Ordinance on Loan Guarantees of the Credit Guarantee Fund for Small and Medium Enterprises.[880]

621. Later, in 2009, a limited version of the Soft Loan Ordinance for Buying Energy-Saving Installations of 2009 was promulgated.[881] Under this new Ordinance, the definition of energy-saving installations does not include renewable energy facilities. The loan amount is limited to 50 million NTD. The loan guarantee is also included.[882]

622. To emphasize the importance of green finance, in 2015, the National Development Council of the Executive Yuan promulgated the Loan scheme to Update Machine Equipment.[883] The investment in energy conservation equipment could qualify for this loan scheme. Applicants can enjoy a low-interest rate and long loan period (ten years) including a grace period of a maximum of three years. In December 2018, the scheme was renewed and the new Ordinance continues the loans.[884]

623. In sum, Taiwan has followed the route other countries have taken and combined loan guarantees with soft loans to promote energy efficient installations. Finally, it should be noted that the main focus of these loan schemes is not on "small" energy appliances in the household sector, but rather on the big energy appliances, such as motors or boilers, in the industrial and large commercial sectors.[885]

---

879. The Soft Loan Ordinance on Buying Energy-Saving Installations (Second Phase) of 2002, 2002-01-01, available at: http://www.rootlaw.com.tw/LawArticle.aspx?LawID=A040400031000400-0910101; http://www.moeaboe.gov.tw/opengovinfo/Laws/saveenergy/LSaveMain.aspx?PageId=l_save_10.
880. The Ordinance on Loan Guarantees of the Credit Guarantee Fund for Small and Medium Enterprises.
881. Soft Loan Ordinance for Buying Energy-Saving Installations of 2009. http://www.tami.org.tw/sp1/bulletin/government/government_980408.pdf.
882. Ordinance on Loan Guarantees for the Implementation of Soft Loan Ordinance for Buying Energy-Saving Installations of 2009.
883. Ordinance on the Loan Scheme to Update Machine Equipment, 2015-12-30, available at: https://www.moeaboe.gov.tw/ECW/populace/Law/Content.aspx?menu_id=1051.
884. Ordinance on the Loan Scheme to Update Machine Equipment (second phase), 2018-12-24, available at: https://www.bot.com.tw/Business/Loans/PolicyLoan/EnterprisePolicyLoan/Documents/loan17.pdf.
885. "(1) Manufacturing Sector: To establish financial incentives and regulatory mechanisms by: providing preferential loans and investment tax credits, accelerated depreciation, and other financial incentive measures … ."

Tax Incentives

624. Since 1995, companies installing energy saving or new and clean energy facilities qualified for tax incentives under the Ordinance on Investment Tax Credit for Companies Installing Energy Saving or New and Clean Energy Facilities of 1995.[886] This scheme was abolished in 2011, as the Act for Upgrading Industries was abolished. Facilities or technology with a value exceeding 600 thousand NTD is granted income tax deductions. In addition, these facilities are also granted a tax preference of "accelerated depreciation."[887]

625. In the recent revision of the Commodity Tax Act, tax credit is provided for energy efficiency refrigerators, hot/cold air conditioning, and dehumidifiers.[888] Within two years from the effective date of this Article, the commodity tax on new refrigerators, new air conditioners, and new dehumidifiers, which are classified as first- or second-grade of the energy-efficient levels approved by the MOEA and are not for resale, returned, or exchanged, shall be reduced by the maximum amount of NTD 2,000. Thus, household users could receive this tax credit benefit.

B. Transportation Vehicles and Conveyance, and Transportation Lighting

626. The government's policy with regard to the transportation sector focuses on road vehicles and traffic lighting. The legal instrument focuses on the implementation of the road vehicles policy. Fuel economy standards are set for cars and motorbikes.[889] For those vehicles meeting fuel economy standards, a certificate is issued.[890] The government also randomly inspects the fuel economy standards of new vehicles,[891] and recently the energy consumption of electric vehicles.[892] This

886. Article 4 of Ordinance on Investment Tax Credit for Companies Installing Energy Saving or New and Clean Energy Facilities of 1995, Abrogated on: 2011-03-14, available at: https://law.moj.gov.tw/LawClass/LawAll.aspx?pcode=J0040040.
887. Article 5 of the Act for Upgrading Industries, Abrogated on: 2002-05-12, available at: https://law.moj.gov.tw/LawClass/LawAll.aspx?PCode=J0040016.
888. Article 11-1 of Commodity Tax Act, Amended Date: 2019-12-25, available at: https://law.moj.gov.tw/ENG/LawClass/LawAll.aspx?pcode=G0340076.
889. Ordinance on Fuel Economy Standards, Amended Date: 2020-02-05, available at: https://law.moj.gov.tw/LawClass/LawAll.aspx?pcode=J0130009.
890. Ordinance on Issuing Certificates for Fuel Economy Standards, 2002-06-22, available at: https://www.moeaboe.gov.tw/ECW/populace/Law/Content.aspx?menu_id=1056.
891. Ordinance on Sampling and Re-testing of Fuel Economy Standards of New Vehicles, 2004-02-24, available at: https://www.moeaboe.gov.tw/ECW/populace/Law/Content.aspx?menu_id=1057.
892. Ordinance on the Test of Energy Consumption of Electric Vehicles, 2018-12-27, available at: https://www.moeaboe.gov.tw/ECW/populace/Law/Content.aspx?menu_id=3067.

inspection work may also be designated to a competent inspection institute.[893] For rare autos, they can submit energy efficiency improvement plan for the review of the MOEABOE.[894]

627. Transportation vehicles including cars, plug-in hybrid cars, and motorcycles are subject to similar mandatory labeling requirements as are energy appliances.[895] The labels for vehicles and motorbikes are similar though they differ in fuel economy considerations. The fuel economy expected for transportation vehicles is the tested fuel economy on highways and in urban areas, whereas that for motorbikes is the fuel economy at fixed speeds and in urban areas. With the increase in the number of electric vehicles, a voluntary labeling scheme has been provided since 2019.[896] The main information relates to energy efficiency and fuel mile economy (Figure 9).

893. Ordinance on the Designation of Inspection Institutes, 2017/5/18, available at: https://www.moeaboe.gov.tw/ECW/populace/Law/Content.aspx?menu_id=1058.
894. Review Ordinance for the Energy Efficiency Improvement Plan of Rare Autos, Amended Date: 2020-03-25, available at: https://www.moeaboe.gov.tw/ECW/populace/Law/Content.aspx?menu_id=4364.
895. Ordinance on the Format for Fuel Economy of Vehicles (cars, plug-in hybrid cars) and Motorbikes, 2020-03-03, available at: https://www.moeaboe.gov.tw/ECW/populace/Law/Content.aspx?menu_id=1059.
896. Ordinance on the Voluntary Energy Efficiency Labeling of Electric Vehicles, 2019-08-16, available at: https://www.moeaboe.gov.tw/ECW/populace/Law/Content.aspx?menu_id=8555.

Figure 9 The Format for Fuel Economy of Vehicles/Motor Bikes/Electric Vehicles

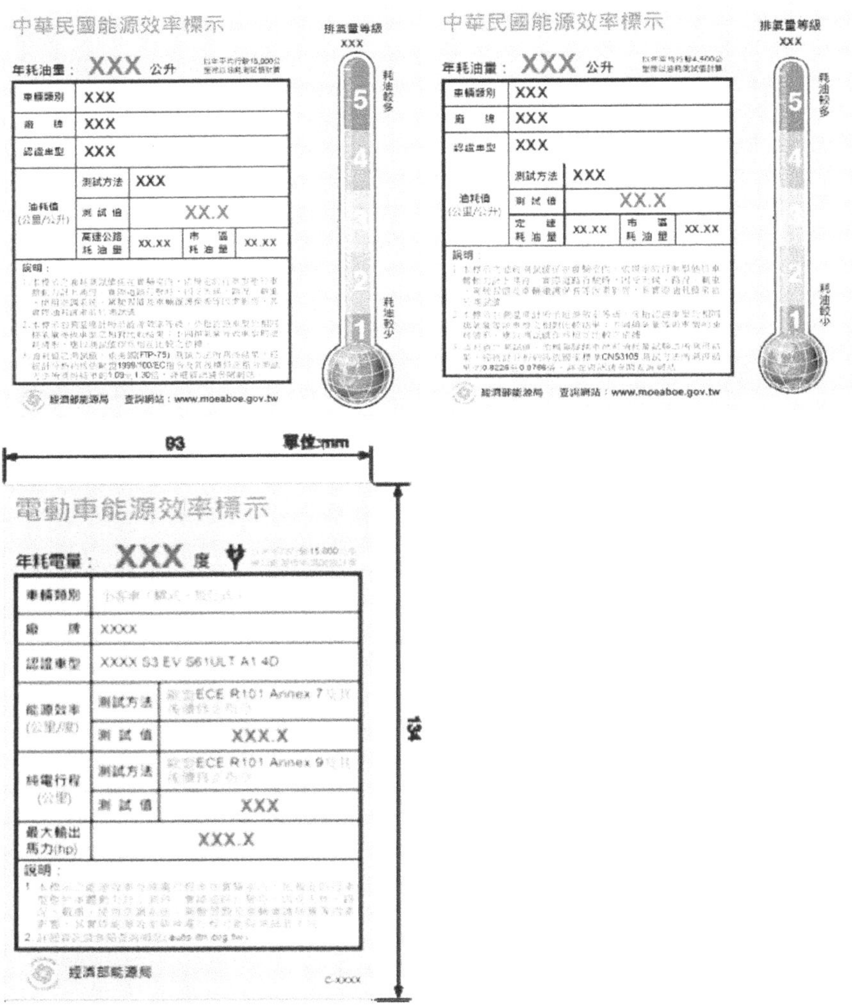

Source: Ordinance on the Format for Fuel Economy of Vehicles and Motor Bikes, and Ordinance on the Voluntary Energy Efficiency Labeling of Electric Vehicles.

628. The measures for LED lighting are used to improve the use of high-performance, energy-saving installations and the energy efficiency in the transportation sector. Several incentive regimes were developed for LED traffic lights[897] and street lights.[898] Since 2012, the scale of the LED traffic lighting scheme has expanded.[899] In keeping with these regimes, local and municipal governments are provided with investment and demonstration subsidies for these installations.

629. Finally, apart from road transportation, a fuel economy standard is also provided for fishing boat engines.[900]

III. Energy Performance Standard for New Buildings

630. In order to improve the energy performance of new buildings, Article 17 of the Energy Management Act stipulates that "Energy conservation standards relevant to the design and construction of new buildings shall be established by the authority in charge of building construction administration in conjunction with the central competent authorities in charge of energy administration." In keeping with this authorization, the Ministry of Interior Affairs proposed a draft Ordinance on Energy Performance of Centralized Air Conditioning for New Building Construction in 2009, and on June 22, 2013, an Ordinance on Energy Performance for New Building Construction.[901] Yet, the main focus is on the standard for the design of "centralized air conditioning," rather than on other aspects of energy performance, such as insulation, lighting, etc. According to Article 3 of the Ordinance, new buildings with a floor area of more than 2,000 m^2 are required to comply with this standard. In addition, the additional energy conservation standards for new buildings would be provided under the Building Act[902] and Ordinance of Building Technical Codes.[903] For example, the technical code for the energy conservation design of buildings provides the technical rules for isolation and ventilation.[904]

---

897. Ordinance on Investment Subsidy for LED Traffic Lighting. http://www.moeaboe.gov.tw/opengovinfo/Laws/saveenergy/LSaveMain.aspx?PageId=l_save_26.
898. Ordinance on Investment and Demonstration Subsidy for High-Efficiency Street Lighting, http://www.moeaboe.gov.tw/opengovinfo/Laws/saveenergy/LSaveMain.aspx?PageId=l_save_37.
899. Ordinance on the Expansion of the Deployment of LED Street Lighting, 2012-04-02, available at: https://www.moeaboe.gov.tw/ECW/populace/Law/Content.aspx?menu_id=1501.
900. Ordinance on Fuel Economy Standards for Fishing Boat Engines, https://law.moj.gov.tw/LawClass/LawAll.aspx?pcode=J0130011.
901. MOJ, Ordinance on Energy Performance for New Building Construction, 2013-06-19, available at: https://law.moj.gov.tw/LawClass/LawAll.aspx?pcode=D0070208.
902. Building Act, Amended Date: 2020-01-15, available at: https://law.moj.gov.tw/ENG/LawClass/LawAll.aspx?pcode=D0070109.
903. MOJ, Ordinance of Building Technical Codes, Amended Date: 2019-11-04, available at: https://law.moj.gov.tw/LawClass/LawAll.aspx?pcode=D0070114.
904. The technical code for the energy conservation design of buildings, 2019-12-31, available at: https://www.cpami.gov.tw/%E6%9C%80%E6%96%B0%E6%B6%88%E6%81%AF/%E6%B3%95%E8%A6%8F%E5%85%AC%E5%91%8A/34535-%E5%BB%BA%E7%AF%89%E7%89%A9%E7%AF%80%E7%B4%84%E8%83%BD%E6%BA%90%E8%A8%AD%E8%A8%88%E6%8A%80%E8%A1%93%E8%A6%8F%E7%AF%84.html.

§3. OTHER ENERGY EFFICIENCY SCHEMES

I. Energy-Saving Mark

631. The energy efficiency standard regulation can be seen as a minimum requirement for energy products entering the market. Yet, meeting this requirement does not mean the product so designated is very energy efficient. In order to differentiate or categorize the energy efficiency of different energy products, the idea of energy labeling was created. The broad meaning of energy labeling includes the above-mentioned mandatory energy labeling and the voluntary energy-saving mark scheme. These two labeling schemes have a quite similar purpose. They are intended to guide the consumers when making their buying decision on certain products. Yet, the former is more complicated and more technical in nature, which is reflected in its use of more technical numbers and details. In this regard, the energy-saving mark is used to simplify the idea of energy efficiency performance. Currently, these two labeling schemes complement each other. For instance, they are both applied to air conditioners, motorbikes, refrigerators, etc. The Energy-Saving Mark of Taiwan label is illustrated in Figure 10.

Figure 10 Energy-Saving Mark of Taiwan

632. In order to apply for the energy-saving mark, the company responsible for the product should pay an application fee[905] and submit its application form for the review of the expert committee established under the Ordinance on the Energy-Saving Mark.[906] Up to now, about 51 types of products, 304 brands, and 8652 products were awarded the energy-saving mark under this scheme.[907] In general, there are seven types of products including home appliances, kitchen equipment, hot

905. Tariff Ordinance on Energy Saving Labeling, Amended Date: 2002-03-16, available at: https://law.moj.gov.tw/LawClass/LawAll.aspx?pcode=J0130029.
906. Ordinance on Energy-Saving Mark, Amended Date: 2018-04-19, available at: https://www.moeaboe.gov.tw/ECW/populace/Law/Content.aspx?menu_id=1060.
907. Products awarded energy-saving mark, available at: https://www.energylabel.org.tw/purchasing/product/index.aspx.

water equipment, drinking equipment, 3C appliances, cars and motorcycles, and ventilation equipment.[908] It is worth mentioning that the 51 types of products include air conditioners, fans, dehumidifiers, refrigerators, TVs, fluorescent tubes, washing machines, dryers, hairdryers, hand dryers, warm & hot-water dispensers, Ice-warm-and-hot-water-type dispensers, cars, motorbikes, ballast built-in fluorescent light bulbs, monitors, gas-fired furnaces, instant gas-fired water heaters, rice cookers, reserve-type electric water heaters, electric hot water pots, exit and evacuation lights, DVD recorders, warm-hot water drinking dispensers, Ice-warm-and-hot-type drinking dispensers, interior lighting appliances, Hi-Fi stereo component systems, compact fluorescent lamps, photocopiers, printers, air cleaners, street lighting, etc.

II. Energy Saving Measures in Governmental and School Sector

633. Apart from the green procurement scheme noted above, a policy measure to promote negative growth in oil and electricity consumption within government agencies and schools, aimed at an accumulated saving of 7% by 2015, was launched in 2007. Subsequently, an Ordinance on Comprehensive Measures of Energy Conservation and Emission Reduction of the Government and Schools was enacted in 2008.[909]

634. To expand the scope of saving beyond energy, in May 2011, a new Program to Encourage the Four Savings of Government and School was adopted. Water and paper savings were added to the savings priority of the government.

635. Such government and school energy conservation initiatives proceed under the current government's energy transition agenda. On December 2, the Executive Yuan approved the "Energy Conservation Action Plan of Government Institutions and Schools."[910] Government Institutions and Schools are obliged to follow the comprehensive measures set out therein to improve their energy conservation for energy consuming appliances such as air conditioning, lighting, computers, and so on. Furthermore, an online progress report platform was established for this purpose: https://egov.ftis.org.tw/. Some local governments proposed their own local

908. Products awarded energy-saving mark, available at: https://www.energylabel.org.tw/purchasing/product/index.aspx.
909. Ordinance on Comprehensive Measures of Energy Conservation and Emission Reduction of the Government and Schools of 2008. Amended Date: 2009-12-16, available at: http://www.rootlaw.com.tw/LawArticle.aspx?LawID=A040100151005000-0970806.
910. Energy Conservation Action Plan of Government Institutions and Schools, 2016-11-28, available at: https://egov.ftis.org.tw/upload/%e3%80%8c%e6%94%bf%e5%ba%9c%e6%a9%9f%e9%97%9c%e5%8f%8a%e5%ad%b8%e6%a0%a1%e7%af%80%e7%b4%84%e8%83%bd%e6%ba%90%e8%a1%8c%e5%8b%95%e8%a8%88%e7%95%ab%e3%80%8d(%e6%a0%b8%e5%ae%9a%e6%9c%ac)-1208.pdf.

plans; for instance, Taipei city proposed its "Energy Conservation Action Plan" for Taipei's public institutions and schools in February 2017.[911]

III. Subsidy Scheme for ESCOs

636. In order to encourage the development of energy service companies (ESCOs) in Taiwan, a subsidy scheme was developed by means of the Subsidy Ordinance on the Energy Performance Guarantee Program.[912] This subsidy scheme provides subsidies for "four" main potential energy savers, including central and local government, public hospitals, public schools, and chain stores, through the arrangement of an energy performance contract with ESCOs to provide energy-saving services. The detailed application rules are also stipulated.[913]

637. As noted above, the MOEABOE is keen to urge the government to play the leading role in energy conservation. ESCO could be very helpful, and its role has been highlighted by the BOE. In 2019, the BOE promulgated the Ordinance of the Demonstration Subsidy to Systematic Energy Conservation Improvement.[914] The qualifying ESCO will receive the reward of 4 NTD/kWh saved electricity. The demonstration site will be in the government or at a medical institution, for example.

IV. Awards and Competition for Energy Conservation

638. To encourage local government and industry participation, and reduce peak hours during the summer, the BOE announced the Electricity Conservation Competition for local governments in the summer[915] and the Energy Conservation Yardstick Award for industries in 2013 and 2016, respectively.

---

911. Energy Conservation Action Plan for Taipei's Public Institutions and Schools, 2017-02-08, available at: http://web2.ycsh.tp.edu.tw/ezfiles/0/1000/attach/95/pta_11588_1508325_17263.pdf.
912. Subsidy Ordinance on Energy Performance Guarantee Progam, 2016-11-04, available at: https://www.moeaboe.gov.tw/ECW/populace/Law/Content.aspx?menu_id=1053.
913. Ordinance on Application for Subsidy of the Energy Performance Guarantee Progam, 2006-01-17, Amended Date: 2009,-02-13, available at: https://law.moea.gov.tw/LawContent.aspx?id=GL000493.
914. Ordinance of the Demonstration Subsidy to Systematic Energy Conservation Improvement, 2019-05-17, available at: https://www.moeaboe.gov.tw/ECW/populace/Law/Content.aspx?menu_id=8481. List of the Demonstration Subsidy to Systematic Energy Conservation Improvement 2020, 2020-06-03, available at: https://www.moeaboe.gov.tw/ECW/populace/Law/wHandLawsList_File.ashx?kind=7&id=3366&file_id=3724.
915. Ordinance on the Electricity Conservation Competition for Local Governments in Summer, 2013-02-23, available at: https://www.moeaboe.gov.tw/ECW/populace/Law/Content.aspx?menu_id=2065.

639. For the former, different awards ranging between 3 to 10 million NTD will be provided for local governments. For the latter, industries will be awarded for their energy conservation, energy management system, electricity saving during the summer, or emission reduction.[916]

V. Voluntary Energy Efficiency Measures in Different Sectors

A. Energy (Electric Power) Sector

640. Some measures were promoted under the authority's supervision and with Tai-Power's cooperation in order to ensure Tai-Power's energy efficiency. For instance, Tai-Power has long been devoted to improving power transmission and distribution facilities, reducing line loss, and raising the efficiency of power generators by replacing old units.[917] Similar measures are also found in the recent Guideline on Energy Development of 2017. Work to enhance efficiency is usually performed by Tai-Power when conducting public procurement of power generators.

- "Introduce clean coal and technologies related to carbon reduction based on a technological progress assessment, and *enhance the efficiency of coal-fired power generation* to reduce carbon emissions from coal consumption.
- *Improve the efficiency of power plants*, regulate new power plants to adopt the commercialized best available technology, and make good use of the potential of a co-generation system in terms of compliance with power dispatching to stabilize the power supply and ensure power quality."

B. Residential and Commercial Sector

641. Due to Taiwan's having kept the price of electricity artificially low for decades, there has been insufficient incentive to reduce electricity consumption. In this regard, since 2007, Tai-Power began to launch an "electricity tariff discount" scheme for the residential and commercial sectors. Residential customers and primary schools, using less than the average daily kWh usage for the same period of the previous year, will be given a discount. This program has been maintained since then. This year, the discount rate is between 5 and 35%. However, there is also a

---

916. Article 4 of the Ordinance on the Energy Conservation Yardstick Award for Industries, 2016-11-17, available at: https://www.moeaboe.gov.tw/ECW/populace/Law/Content.aspx?menu_id=3292; Implementation of the Ordinance on the Energy Conservation Yardstick Award for Industries, 2016-12-26, available at: https://www.moeaboe.gov.tw/ECW/populace/Law/Content.aspx?menu_id=3314.
917. "(1) To improve the proportion of low-carbon and high-efficiency power generation plants by increasing the efficient gas combined-cycle power generation ratio. In 2025, this combination will account for 25% of the power generation system. (2) To introduce the world's best available technology for power generation by speeding up power plant replacement, devising plans to raise the overall efficiency of power plants and calling for the world's best practice power conversion efficiency standards for all new power plants."

weakness to this program. For instance, if the rate of decrease for the previous year is too fast, then the discount rate for coming years might not be substantial, which would leave no incentive for further electricity usage reduction. Thus, it seems that energy taxation remains a better scheme in encouraging reduced electricity consumption. In 2018, Tai-Power proposed a new scheme (2018–the end of 2020) to encourage electricity saving by providing an extra 0.6 NTD/per saved kWh compared with the electricity consumption in the same month of the previous year.[918] This mainly applied to residential electricity users and elementary school (or kindergarten) users. A website was created for participants to register and monitor their usage: https://tpcuip.taipower.com.tw/savepower/.

642. The transformation from an economy based on manufacturing to one based on offering tertiary services is almost the policy priority around the globe. The tertiary sector is usually considered a "chimney free industry." Yet, the energy and electricity consumption in this sector is also of concern to the government. In this regard, certain measures, such as the aforementioned energy efficiency standard for air conditioning, would serve to improve the energy efficiency of the tertiary sector. In order to treat the tertiary sector differently from the manufacturing sector where the stick approach is more prevalent, the government has used voluntary agreements as a tool to encourage the energy-saving goal of 5–10% in this sector.[919] In 2019, the BOE gave the award and praised fifteen companies.[920]

§4. Summary: Energy Saving Hierarchy

643. The best way to reduce energy and electricity consumption is not to buy or use high-energy consumption devices. Yet, with improving life quality and its amenities, this strategy is proving to be impossible.

644. The second best and easier approach is behavior change, such as switching off unused devices. Yet, the laziness of human nature may also make this option impossible. The energy price may incentivize behavior change. However, this is a very politically sensitive issue in Taiwan and an option unlikely to be put into practice. This is also the main reason why Taiwan has had great difficulty in reducing energy consumption.

645. The only strategy left is rationalization measures, including the technology breakthrough of energy saving devices (such as those meeting energy efficiency

918. Tai-power, Electricity Saving Incentive Campaign, available at: https://www.taipower.com.tw/tc/page.aspx?mid=344.
919. TGPF, Achievements in promoting voluntary energy saving in Taiwan, July 2011, available at: https://www.tgpf.org.tw/upload/publish/publish_47/%E6%88%91%E5%9C%8B%E6%8E%A8%E5%8B%95%E9%9B%86%E5%9C%98%E5%BC%8F%E4%BC%81%E6%A5%AD%E8%87%AA%E9%A1%98%E6%80%A7%E7%AF%80%E8%83%BD%E4%B9%8B%E6%88%90%E6%95%88.pdf.
920. MOEABOE, Energy Saving Prize 2019, available at: https://www.moeaboe.gov.tw/ECW/populace/news/News.aspx?kind=1&menu_id=41&news_id=16503.

standards), incentive schemes for applying these technologies, and voluntary schemes (such as the energy-saving mark, or voluntary agreement). These strategies also seem to be related to and may contribute to the prosperity of the domestic electric appliance industries. Whether this strategy will contribute to substantial energy reduction remains to be seen. As there is no price tag on the electricity consumed by these energy appliances, the subsidy for buying another high efficiency device may lead to an increase in the overall energy usage, which would lead to an environmentally perverse subsidy. For instance, the grant for buying energy-saving labeled products may lead to "artificial" demand for air conditioners. The installation of a very energy efficient air conditioner in one household would definitely cause an increase in the overall electricity bill. In this regard, an energy price that reflects both energy's "real" cost and its "external" cost would be a solution to Taiwan's current difficult position.

646. Since 2016, under the government's energy transition agenda, the focus has been on renewable energy development. However, from the introduction of this book, numerous efforts have been made by the government to enhance energy conservation/energy efficiency. However, all these measures are mainly based on policy initiatives/programs or the existing Energy Management Act. Most importantly, unlike the emission reduction goals and renewable energy goals in the GHG Reduction Act and Renewable Energy Act, *no energy efficiency goals* are included in the existing Energy Management Act. Furthermore, the Energy Management Act has not undergone a major revision since 2009.[921] Only one minor revision and a provision were added in November 2016.[922] T*he ignorance of the role of demand side legislations* could be evidenced by the legislation situation that the major revision of the Energy Management Act has been approved by the Cabinet to submit to legislators in March 2018.[923] However, progress is slow and not prioritized by the current government. In addition, the rule of law in the aforementioned energy saving and efficiency measures remains very weak. For instance, the use of an abstract legal basis in regulating the behaviors of "designated" energy users could lead to issues pertaining to constitutional law. Also, the Energy Saving obligation is based on vague legal language in Article 9 of the Energy Management Act: "The energy user …, shall … set objectives for energy conservation and execution..." This seems as if the MOEA interprets voluntary goals as mandatory. Perhaps due to the lack of a clear legal basis, it is impossible to introduce a more flexible "white" certificate trading system like that in Europe.[924]

647. Finally, compared with the EU's legal framework in promoting energy transition, "Energy efficiency first" was highlighted by the Clean Energy Package for

921. Articles 1, 8, 11, 12, 14-1, 16, 21, 23-25 was amended on Jul. 8, 2009, and two provisions added, and two deleted. MOJ, Energy Management Act, available at: https://law.moj.gov.tw/ENG/LawClass/LawAll.aspx?pcode=J0130002.
922. Amended on Nov. 30, 2016 MOJ, Energy Management Act, available at: https://law.moj.gov.tw/ENG/LawClass/LawAll.aspx?pcode=J0130002.
923. Amendment of the Energy Management Act, 2018-03-28, available at: https://www.ey.gov.tw/Page/AE106A22FAE592FD/4d665984-63fb-43e2-8e07-4d6f6e2448c4.
924. EC, Energy Efficiency Obligation Schemes, available at: https://e3p.jrc.ec.europa.eu/node/191.

all Europeans policy[925] and by the real action of updating energy efficiency legislation by amending the Directive on Energy Efficiency ((EU) 2018/844).[926] Taiwan's energy transition approach is unique. Whether such approach could really achieve its energy transition goals remains to be seen in the future.

925. EC, Clean Energy Package for all Europeans, available at: https://ec.europa.eu/energy/topics/energy-strategy/clean-energy-all-europeans_en.
926. The amending Directive on Energy Efficiency ((EU) 2018/844) has been in place since December 2018, available at: https://ec.europa.eu/energy/topics/energy-efficiency/targets-directive-and-rules/energy-efficiency-directive_en.

Chapter 2. EIA and SEA

§1. Introduction

648. Generally, the development of energy activities would lead to EHS concerns. Hence, *sector-specific* legislation and regulations have been created to deal definitely with the EHS concerns arising from developing energy activities. For instance, Article 15 of the Mining Act provides for the establishment of environmental measures during the application for a mining permit. Similar measures can be also found in the Petroleum Management Act and Electricity Act. For instance, Articles 31 and 32 of the Petroleum Management Act provides regulations to maintain the safety of petroleum transportation pipelines.

649. However, the *environmental* concerns resulting from energy activities are mainly dealt with under the environmental legal system, particularly pollution related legislations, such as the Air Pollution Act, the Water Pollution Act, the Marine Pollution Act, the Soil and Underground Water Act, and the Waste Management Act, etc. For instance, those vendors or users of bituminous coal and petroleum coke are subject to a prior permit requirement.[927] In addition, relevant Ordinances deal with the emission standard of air pollutants from electricity power plants[928] and vehicles.[929] Further, gas stations with underground storage are required to install pollution prevention installations and monitoring installations in order to avoid polluting underground water.[930] Gas stations are also required to install petroleum gas recovery systems in order to avoid air pollution.[931]

650. Yet, in order to tackle environmental concerns in a more comprehensive manner, the EIA and SEA play essential roles. Over the past few decades, the EIA has played a more vital role for energy projects. Recently, SEA has begun to be used quite frequently at higher decision-making levels when taking into account environmental effects.

---

927. Article 28(1) of Air Pollution Act: "The fuels and auxiliary fuels that contain bituminous coal or other substances designated and officially announced by the central competent authority and are also used by public or private premises shall meet the standards provided by the central competent authority for fuel types, ratio of fuels in combustion and fuel composition. The use of these fuels may begin only after application for and acquisition of a *use permit* issued by the special municipality, county or city competent authority. Records of the use of these substances shall be maintained and reported to the special municipality, county or city competent authority in accordance with regulations."
928. Ordinance on the Emission Standard of Air Pollutants from Electricity Power Plants, Amended Date: 2014-12-01, available at: https://law.moj.gov.tw/LawClass/LawAll.aspx?pcode=O0020026.
929. MOJ, Air Emission Standards of Mobile Source, Amended Date: 2020-07-27, available at: https://law.moj.gov.tw/ENG/LawClass/LawAll.aspx?pcode=O0020003.
930. Article 33(2) of Water Pollution Act and Management Ordinance on Pollution Prevention Installations and Monitoring Installations, 2002-12-18, Amended Date: 2001-01-14, available at: https://oaout.epa.gov.tw/law/LawContent.aspx?id=FL022348.
931. Article 23(2) of Air Pollution Act, and Management Ordinance on Petroleum Gas Recovery Installations.

§2. EIA and Environmental Permit

651. The EIA Act was enacted in 1994 in order to reflect the need to take into account environmental effects before the development of projects. However, at the first stage, around 1994 to 1997, different rules and guidelines were provided for different development and energy projects. The following Guidelines are related to the energy projects, such as the EIA Guideline for Combustion and Cogeneration Power Plant,[932] the EIA Guideline for Radioactive Waste Storage Sites,[933] the EIA Guideline for Nuclear Power Plants,[934] the EIA Guideline for Municipal Waste Incinerators,[935] the EIA Guideline for Hydropower Plants,[936] the EIA Guideline for General Development Projects,[937] the EIA Guideline for Mining Activities,[938] the EIA Guideline for Industrial Zones,[939] the EIA Guideline for Factories,[940] the EIA Guideline for Education and Medical Facilities,[941] and the EIA Guideline for Road and Railway Transportation.[942]

652. After 1997, this *distributed* approach was revised and a *comprehensive* approach was adopted. A single EIA Operation Ordinance for Development Projects[943] was enacted at the end of 1997 and replaced all aforementioned EIA Guidelines. Electricity, oil, gas, and mining activities are subject to the EIA requirement under certain conditions. The energy projects subject to the EIA requirement are summarized in Table 26.

932. EIA Guideline for Combustion and Cogeneration Power Plants, Abrogated on: 1997-12-31, available at: https://law.moj.gov.tw/LawClass/LawAll.aspx?pcode=O0090025.
933. EIA Guideline for Radioactive Waste Storage Sites, Abrogated on: 1997-12-31, available at: https://law.moj.gov.tw/LawClass/LawAll.aspx?pcode=O0090024.
934. EIA Guideline for Nuclear Power Plants, Abrogated on: 1997-12-31, available at: https://law.moj.gov.tw/LawClass/LawAll.aspx?pcode=O0090023.
935. EIA Guideline for Municipal Waste Incinerators, Abrogated on: 1997-12-31, available at: https://law.moj.gov.tw/LawClass/LawAll.aspx?pcode=O0090017.
936. EIA Guideline for Hydropower Plants, Abrogated on: 1997-12-31, available at: https://law.moj.gov.tw/LawClass/LawAll.aspx?pcode=O0090026.
937. EIA Guideline for General Development Projects, Abrogated on: 1997-12-31, available at: https://law.moj.gov.tw/LawClass/LawAll.aspx?pcode=O0090004.
938. EIA Guideline for Mining Activities, Abrogated on: 1997-12-31, available at: https://law.moj.gov.tw/LawClass/LawAll.aspx?pcode=O0090009.
939. EIA Guideline for Industrial Zones, Abrogated on: 1997-12-31, available at: https://law.moj.gov.tw/LawClass/LawAll.aspx?pcode=O0090005.
940. EIA Guideline for Factories, Abrogated on: 1997-12-31, available at: https://law.moj.gov.tw/LawClass/LawAll.aspx?pcode=O0090022.
941. EIA Guideline for Education and Medical Facilities, Abrogated on: 1997-12-31, available at: https://law.moj.gov.tw/LawClass/LawAll.aspx?pcode=O0090019.
942. EIA Guideline for Road and Railway Transportation, Abrogated on: 1997-12-31, available at: https://law.moj.gov.tw/LawClass/LawAll.aspx?pcode=O0090016.
943. EIA, Standards for Determining Specific Items and Scope of Environmental Impact Assessments for Development Activities, Amended Date: 2020-08-18, available at: https://law.moj.gov.tw/ENG/LawClass/LawAll.aspx?pcode=O0090012. Enacted on Dec. 31, 1997, last revised on Aug. 18, 2020. For English version, *see* Standards for Determining Specific Items and Scope of Environmental Impact Assessments for Development Activities, available at: https://law.moj.gov.tw/ENG/LawClass/LawAll.aspx?pcode=O0090012.

Table 26 Energy Projects Subject to the EIA Requirement in Taiwan

Facilities	*Energy Projects*	*Further Conditions*
Electricity generation	Construction, additional generating units, or decommissioning of the nuclear reactor of a nuclear power plant	No
	Construction or additional generating units of a hydroelectric power plant (excluding any hydroelectric power system that uses existing irrigation channels or other water facilities and whose installed or cumulative installed capacity is below 20 MW)	A. The site is located in a national park. B. The site is located in a wild-life refuge or major wildlife habitat. C. The site is located in an important wetland. D. The site is located in a nature reserve approved and announced under the Taiwan Coastal Area Natural Environ-ment Protection Plan. E. The site is located at an eleva-tion of more than 1,500 meters. F. The site is located in a reser-voir watershed. G. The site is located in a water quality and quantity protection area. H. The site is located in a slope-land where a dam (weir) with a height of at least five meters is installed. I. Installed or cumulative installed capacity is 20 MW or greater.

Facilities	*Energy Projects*	*Further Conditions*
	The construction or expansion of a thermal power plant	However, this restriction shall not apply when black start units are added, or when the generating units are not located in the main island of Taiwan and in the areas specified in items (a) through (e), and the gas-fired installed capacity or cumulative gas-fired installed capacity is less than 100 MW, or installed capacity from oil-fired, coal-fired, or other fuel-generating units or cumulative installed capacity from oil-fired, coal-fired, or other fuel generating units is less than 50 MW. A. The site is located in a national park. B. The site is located in a wildlife refuge or major wildlife habitat. C. The site is located in an important wetland. D. The site is located in a nature preserve approved and announced under the Taiwan Coastal Area Natural Environment Protection Plan. E. The site is located at an elevation of more than 1,500 meters.
	Construction or additional generating units of a power generator for a thermal power plant or of a cogeneration plant	A. The site is located in a national park. B. The site is located in a wildlife refuge or major wildlife habitat. C. The site is located in an important wetland. D. The site is located in a nature reserve approved and announced under the Taiwan Coastal Area Natural Environment Protection Plan. E. The site is located at an elevation of more than 1,500 meters.

Facilities	*Energy Projects*	*Further Conditions*
		F. The site is located on urban land, gas-fired installed capacity or cumulative gas-fired installed capacity is 100 MW or greater, or the installed capacity from oil-fired, coal-fired, or other fuel generating units or cumulative installed capacity from oil-fired, coal-fired, or other fuel generating units is 50 MW or greater. G. The site is located on urban land, gas-fired installed capacity or cumulative gas-fired installed capacity is 200 MW or greater, or the installed capacity from oil-fired, coal-fired, or other fuel generating units or cumulative installed capacity from oil-fired, coal-fired, or other fuel generating units is 100 MW or greater.
	Installation of an offshore wind power generating system	No
	The installation of onshore wind power generation units	A. The site is subject to: A. The site is located in a national park. B. The site is located in a wildlife refuge or major wildlife habitat. C. The site is located in an important wetland. D. The site is located in a nature reserve approved and announced under the Taiwan Coastal Area Natural Environment Protection Plan.

Facilities	*Energy Projects*	*Further Conditions*
		E. The site is located at an elevation of more than 1,500 meters. B. The site is located in a general protected area approved and announced under the Taiwan Coastal Area Natural Environment Protection Plan, the application calls for the installation of five or more generating units, or the sum of the number of generating units in the same protection area called for by the application and the number of generating units already approved by the industry competent authority is 10 or more. C. The site is located in a conservation forest area. D. The straight-line distance between the center of any wind-generating unit and the edge of the nearest building (this refers to a third-party building that received a use license or address number at the time the wind power generation development plan was submitted to the industry competent authority for permit application) is less than 250 meters. An exception shall apply where the building is a water-pumping station or the electrical room of power facilities.
	VII. Installation of a photovoltaic power generation system	The site is located in an important wetland.

Facilities	*Energy Projects*	*Further Conditions*
	Installation of a tidal, tidal current, ocean current, wave, or thermal differential generating unit	However, this restriction shall not apply when the industry competent authority has approved an experimental project.
	IX. Installation of a geothermal generating unit whose installed or cumulative installed capacity is 10 MW or more	
Electricity transmission and distri bution	Installation of power transmission lines, where the transmission lines are more than 161 kV	A. The overhead line passes through one of the areas specified: A. The site is located in a national park. B. The site is located in a wild-life refuge or major wildlife habitat. C. The site is located in an important wetland. D. The site is located in a nature reserve approved and announced under the Taiwan Coastal Area Natural Environ-ment Protection Plan. B. The overhead line passes through the land reserved for indigenous people. C. The straight-line distance between the projected edge of the overhead line, its circuits, or its pylons and the edge of a public elementary school or middle school (including des-ignated land) is less than 50 meters.

Facilities	*Energy Projects*	*Further Conditions*
		D. The straight-line distance between the projected edge of the overhead line, its circuits, or its pylons and the edge of a hospital is less than 50 meters. E. An overhead or underground transmission line with a length of 50 kilometers or more.
	Construction or expansion of a marine substation or land-based substation whose volta ge is more than 161 kV	
Mine	Mining exploration or extraction operation on the ground, underground, or in a marine area, including their expansion or increase of extraction length or application for extension of mining rights for approved mining land	A. The site is located in a national park. B. The site is located in a wildlife refuge or major wildlife habitat. C. The site is located in an important wetland. D. The site is located in a nature reserve approved and announced under the Taiwan Coastal Area Natural Environment Protection Plan. E. The site is located in the land reserved for indigenous people. F. The site is located in a reservoir watershed. G. The site is located at an elevation of more than 1,500 meters. H. The site is located in an agricultural zone or a protection area specified in an urban plan.

Facilities	*Energy Projects*	*Further Conditions*
		I. The site is located in an agricultural land in a special agricultural zone or general agricultural zone. J. The site is located in a marine area. However, this restriction shall not apply when it is not involved in drilling or exploration or is used for natural gas or oil deposits, and the exploration or drilling does not reach the phase of oil gas production. K. The site is located in a slopeland, national scenic area, or a general protected area approved and announced under the Taiwan Coastal Area Natural Environment Protection Plan: the application for development area or cumulative development area (including the area of required road facilities outside the said area) approved for mining use is 1 hectare or more, or the application is involved in a mining length or cumulative mining length of 0.5 kilometers or more along the river approved for mining use.

Facilities	*Energy Projects*	*Further Conditions*
		L. The site is located in a slopeland, national scenic area, or a general protected area approved and announced under the Taiwan Coastal Area Natural Environment Protection Plan, and is also located in a water quality and quantity protection area: the application for development area or cumulative development area (including the area of required road facilities outside the said area) approved for mining use is 0.5 hectares or more, or the application involves an area or cumulative area of land approved for mining use that is in a riverbed extending for 250 meters or more along the river.
		M. The application for development area or cumulative development area (including the area of required road facilities outside the said area) approved for mining use is 5 hectares or more.
		N. When sites under application for mining use are located in a slopeland and one of the following conditions is present, the areas or cumulative areas for which application is made shall be combined for calculation, and the total area reaches the scale specified in Item (k) or (l):

Facilities	*Energy Projects*	*Further Conditions*
		1. The mining sites or cumulative mining sites are located under the same land number. 2. The land of the mining sites or cumulative mining sites is adjacent. 3. The horizontal distance between the boundaries of the mining sites or cumulative mining sites is within 500 meters.
Petroleum	Exploration and exploitation	Similar to mine exploration and exploitationNot applicable to apply for the extension of the mining rights.
	Oil pipeline (excluding those laid only within a park or as a replacement for existing pipelines)	A. The site is located on urban land, with the pipelines extending over a length of at least 5 km. B. The site is located on non-urban land, with the pipelines extending over a length of at least 30 km.
	Construction or expansion of storage tanks for petroleum, petroleum products, or expansion of the storage capacity	A. The site is located in a national park subarea outside of general control areas, or located in a national park general control area, and the total storage capacity of the storage tanks or cumulative storage capacity is more than 300 kiloliters.

Facilities	Energy Projects	Further Conditions
		B. The site is located in a wildlife refuge or major wildlife habitat. C. The site is located in an important wetland. D. The site is located in a nature reserve approved and announced under the Taiwan Coastal Area Natural Environment Protection Plan. E. The site is located in a reservoir watershed. F. The site is located at an elevation of more than 1,500 meters. G. The site is located in a water quality and quantity protection area, and the total storage capacity of the storage tanks or cumulative storage capacity is more than 300 kiloliters. H. The site is located in a slopeland, national scenic area, or a general protected area approved and announced under the Taiwan Coastal Area Natural Environment Protection Plan, and the application for development area or cumulative development area is 1 hectare or more. I. The site is located in an agricultural land in a special agricultural zone, and the application for development area or cumulative development area is 1 hectare or more.

Facilities	*Energy Projects*	*Further Conditions*
		J. The site is located in a port zone, and the total storage capacity of the storage tanks or cumulative storage capacity is more than 30,000 kiloliters. K. The site is located on urban land (excluding the harbor area), and the application for development area or cumulative development area is 5 hectares or more, or the total storage capacity of the storage tanks or cumulative storage capacity is more than 10,000 kiloliters. L. The site is located on non-urban land, and the application for development area or cumulative development area is 10 hectares or more, or the total storage capacity of the storage tanks or cumulative storage capacity is more than 30,000 kiloliters.
Gas	Exploration and exploitation	Similar to mine exploration and exploitationHowever, this is not applicable to apply for an extension of mining rights.
	Gas pipeline	The same as "construction or expansion of storage tanks for petroleum, petroleum products, or expansion of the storage capacity"
	Installation of off-loading facilities (or a port) for liquefied natural gas	No

Facilities	*Energy Projects*	*Further Conditions*
Nuclear activities	Construction or expansion of storage or treatment facilities for radioactive waste or expansion of the capacity or treatment volume of storage facilities	A. The site is located in a national park. B. The site is located in a wildlife refuge or major wildlife habitat. C. The site is located in an important wetland. D. The site is located in a nature reserve approved and announced under the Taiwan Coastal Area Natural Environment Protection Plan. E. The site is located at an elevation of more than 1,500 meters. F. The site is located in a slopeland, national scenic area, or a general protected area approved and announced under the Taiwan Coastal Area Natural Environment Protection Plan, and the application for development area or cumulative development area is 1 hectare or more. G. The site is located in an agricultural land in a special agricultural zone, and the application for development area or cumulative development area is 1 hectare or more. H. The facility provides storage for 1,000 cubic meters or more, or treatment for liquid waste in excess of 100 kiloliters per day or of 2000 kiloliters per month, or treatment by compression equipment in excess of 20 tons per day.

Facilities	*Energy Projects*	*Further Conditions*
	Construction or expansion of the treatment volume of an incinerator for radioactive waste	No
	A facility for the final disposal of radioactive waste	
	A facility for the interim storage of spent nuclear fuels	

Source: Compiled by the author from Standards for Determining Specific Items and Scope of Environmental Impact Assessments for Development Activities, available at: https://law.moj.gov.tw/ENG/LawClass/LawAll.aspx?pcode=O0090012 and https://law.moj.gov.tw/LawClass/LawAll.aspx?pcode=O0090012.

653. From Table 26, it is clear that nuclear and power generation activities are subject to stringent EIA requirements. For instance, there is no EIA threshold for many nuclear activities, such as nuclear waste management and nuclear power generation projects. However, energy R&D projects are generally subject to the exemption from EIA, even for nuclear activities,[944] as these projects are usually developed for improving the environmental quality of existing technology. This exemption can be seen as an incentive as well.

654. However, even though the development of renewable electricity projects is meant to curb the emission from the electricity sector, these projects are also very likely subject to the EIA requirement. These requirements usually impede the deployment of these carbon-friendly, but not environmentally friendly, installations. How to reconcile the potential conflictive nature between carbon targets and, a usually much broader, environmental target, remains a question to be resolved and a future cause for concern. For instance, recently, the large-scale expansion of renewable electricity facilities to meet the 2025 20% renewable target has led to serious

944. Article 30 of the Standards for Determining Specific Items and Scope of Environmental Impact Assessments for Development Activities: "The regulations of the foregoing paragraphs shall not apply to researching radioactive waste disposal or storage facilities or plans that have been approved by the industry competent authority and nuclear competent authority."
EIA, Standards for Determining Specific Items and Scope of Environmental Impact Assessments for Development Activities, Amended Date: 2020-08-18, available at: https://law.moj.gov.tw/ENG/LawClass/LawAll.aspx?pcode=O0090012.

conflict between agricultural land use and PV development.[945] In terms of the development of offshore wind power, concerns have been raised over the influence on white dolphins.[946]

655. Finally, certain important energy technology is not on the EIA list, such as *fuel cell* and *CCS, or recently, electricity storage*. This oversight may cause regulatory uncertainty that requires clarification in the future.

§3. STRATEGIC ENVIRONMENTAL ASSESSMENT

656. In order to deal with environmental effects at a higher level beyond the project level, Taiwan followed the global trend and established the SEA in 2000.[947] According to Article 3 of the Ordinance on Environmental Impact Assessment of Governmental Policy, the several policies that are likely to have significant effects on the environment should be subject to the SEA requirement. Of the nine policies listed, the energy policy is one. However, in terms of the "energy" content, most of the other policies are closely related to energy activities, such as industrial policy, mining development policy, energy policies, transportation policies, and policies of radioactive management.

657. In order to specify the above-mentioned "policies" and exclude unnecessary policies, the Ordinance on the Policy of Compulsory SEA[948] was provided. The policies are further specified in Table 27.

Table 27 Mandatory SEA Policies Concerning Energy under Ordinance on the Policy of Compulsory SEA

Policy Type	*Mandatory SEA Policy*
Industrial policy	The establishment of industrial zone
	Energy intensive industrial policy
Energy policy	Energy Development Framework
Transportation policy	Major rail and road line
Waste disposal policy	Waste disposal policy, such as changing waste incinerators to regional biomass centers

945. PZ Magazine, Restrictions on solar energy on agricultural land may slow PV growth in Taiwan, Jul. 29, 2020, available at: https://www.pv-magazine.com/2020/07/29/restrictions-for-solar-on-agricultural-land-may-slow-pv-growth-in-taiwan/.
946. Taipei Times, Wind farms pose threat to white dolphins, Jun. 25, 2020, available at: https://www.taipeitimes.com/News/editorials/archives/2020/06/25/2003738818.
947. Ordinance on Environmental Impact Assessment of Governmental Policy, enacted on Dec. 20, 2000; last revised on Apr. 7, 2006.
948. The Ordinance on Compulsory SEA Policy, 1998-08-03, Amended Date: 2012-10-17, available at: https://oaout.epa.gov.tw/law/LawContent.aspx?id=GL007321.

Policy Type	*Mandatory SEA Policy*
Radioactive waste policy	Spent fuel reprocessing

Source: Ordinance on Policy of Compulsory SEA

658. Under this requirement, the following energy-related SEA reports have already been conducted and published, such as

- SEA Report of the Policy on the Transportation System between Taipei City and East Taiwan, approved on December 22, 2016.[949]
- SEA report on the Waste Disposal Policy (including changing waste incinerators to regional biomass centers)[950]
- SEA Report of the Policy on Industrial Zone Development[951]
- SEA Report of the steel industry (draft)[952]
- SEA Report the petrochemical industry (draft)[953]
- SEA Report of the draft Energy Development Framework in 2011[954] and 2015[955]
- SEA report on the Radioactive Waste Management Policy (draft)[956]

659. These SEA Reports are mandatory under the Ordinance on the Policy of Compulsory SEA. Because of controversies, several SEA reports did not reach the final approved stage and remained as draft versions. On the other hand, certain energy policies are not mandatory, but still voluntarily develop the SEA reports. For instance, in 2013, the EPA voluntarily developed a draft SEA report and hosted a consultation meeting to gather opinions on the CCS policy.[957] However, opposition from environmental NGOs has led to no final report being approved by the EIA committee. Another voluntary SEA report is the SEA of offshore wind power zonal

949. SEA Report of the Policy on the Transportation System between Taipei City and East Taiwan, 2006-12-22, available at: https://enews.epa.gov.tw/Page/3B3C62C78849F32F/fb778ce4-0acd-4e3c-9618-b9f3d40dab08.
950. SEA report on the Waste Disposal Policy, available at: https://www.epa.gov.tw/Page/DB4B5488A0DC0C71.
951. SEA Report of the Policy on Industrial Zone Development, available at: https://www.epa.gov.tw/Page/83AC0D671BA281A7.
952. The draft SEA report, available at: http://ivy5.epa.gov.tw/EiaWeb/default.aspx; SEA Report of the steel industry (draft), available at: https://www.mirdc.org.tw/FileDownLoad/News/20104915451218.pdf.
953. The draft SEA report on petrochemical industry, available at: http://www.moeaidb.gov.tw/external/ctlr?PRO=indparknews.IndparknewsView&id=1847 (visited on Oct. 10, 2020).
954. MOEA, draft Energy Development Framework, December 2002, available at http://www.tri.org.tw/energy/Web%20information/2/2-1.pdf.
955. SEA, Report of the draft Energy Development Framework in 2015, November 2015, available at: https://www.slideshare.net/ssuser444ec9/2015-176390787.
956. SEA, Report on the Radioactive Waste Management Policy (draft), August 2002, available at: https://www.aec.gov.tw/share/ufile/headline/8laOnaorucuGIMozalWfeg__.pdf.
957. EPA, consultation meeting to gather opinions on the carbon capture and storage policy, Dec. 20, 2013 available at: https://enews.epa.gov.tw/Page/3B3C62C78849F32F/c3f6f986-ac7a-47bf-b8b6-9d3ee8331daf.

development. The policy was submitted to the EPA in December 2015 and approved in July 2016.[958] This SEA report has since then seemed helpful in paving the way for large-scale offshore wind power development. Now, the development of a 5.7 GW installation capacity is under construction and scheduled to be completed by 2025.[959]

958. Chen WH. EPA approves SEA on offshore wind energy development, Taipei Times, http://www.taipeitimes.com/News/taiwan/archives/2016/07/14/2003651002; 2016 [accessed Jun. 10. 2020].
959. Executive Yuan, Offshore wind-power generation, Jun. 13, 2019, available at: https://english.ey.gov.tw/News3/9E5540D592A5FECD/34ff3d6b-412e-458d-afe9-01737d2da52d.

Chapter 3. Climate Change and Energy

§1. Important Policy Dimension

660. The CO2 emissions of Taiwan increased 139.1% from 1990 to 2006, with an average annual growth rate of 5.6%. If we divided this period into two stages with the year of the Kyoto Protocol being the pivotal point, it is found that the CO2 emissions increased 59.6% from 1990 to 1998, with an average annual growth rate of 6.9%, whereas it increased only 46.1% from 1999 to 2006, with an annual growth rate of 4.3%.[960] From 1990 to 2005, Taiwan's GHG emissions increased 110% because of a rise in energy consumption associated with economic growth. However, it only increased by 0.92% between 2005 and 2016.[961] Despite this, Taiwan placed 56th in the Germanwatch Climate Change Performance Index 2019, dropping two places from the previous year's report and ranking among the world's worst performers.[962]

661. As noted above, several policy efforts are related to climate change; the author will focus on the important measures.

I. Development of Nuclear Power?

662. Nuclear power is considered a vital energy source in tackling climate change in Taiwan. Owing to the lack of pipeline gas connections to Taiwan; interconnected electricity networks with other countries; and indigenous energy resources, nuclear power is regarded as the best way to balance energy security and carbon emissions. For instance, the decision to construct the fourth Nuclear Power was made right after the 1997 Kyoto Protocol. The halting of the pursuit of the Nuclear-Free Homeland Policy in 2005 seems related to the effective date of the Kyoto Protocol.

663. However, the nuclear-free homeland clause enacted in Article 23 of the Environmental Basic Act in 2002[963] might potentially limit the development of nuclear power and might increase emissions from the electricity sector. Since the Basic Act is a very special regime in Taiwan, this author is doubtful that the completion of the construction of Nuclear Power No. 4 and the extension of the lives of the existing nuclear power plants will constitute a violation of this clause. In this regard, the nuclear power policy will still contribute to emission reduction in Taiwan, even though this conclusion is not a positive message for many environmental NGOs.

---

960. MOEABOE, About, p. 5, available at: http://www.moeaboe.gov.tw/About/webpage/book_en3/page5.htm.
961. Focus Taiwan, Taiwan lauds progress on greenhouse gas reduction as summit opens, Sep. 23, 2019, available at: https://focustaiwan.tw/society/201909230022.
962. Taipei Times, Tackling Taiwan's carbon footprint, Aug. 28, 2019, available at: https://www.taipeitimes.com/News/feat/archives/2019/08/28/2003721259.
963. "The government shall establish plans to gradually achieve the goal of becoming a nuclear-free country."

664. However, as mentioned in the nuclear power section, the fourth nuclear power plant was put on hold in 2014, and the fuel rods were sent back to the United States in early 2018.[964] Since 2016, the new government has been promoting the policy agenda of a nuclear-free homeland by 2025.[965] This policy direction was highlighted in the 2017 Guidelines on Energy Development:

> III. Development Objectives: Ensure balanced development in energy security, green economy, environmental sustainability, and social equity so that the target of a nuclear-free homeland can be achieved by 2025 and sustainable development in energy can be attained.

665. In spite of the abolishment of the nuclear-free homeland clause in Article 95 of the Electricity Liberalization Act of 2017 after the nationwide referendum in November 2018, the government aims to phase out all nuclear power (the first, second, and third) without life extension by mid-2025.

666. However, the electricity carbon emission factor increased dramatically after the operation of the second reactor of the first and second nuclear power plants was stopped. This factor decreased from 0.555 in 2008 to 0.518 in 2015, but increased for three consecutive years, for example to 0.554 in 2017. After starting operation of the nuclear power plants, the factor decreased again to 0.533 in 2018.[966] Therefore, the expiry of the forty-year license of nuclear power plants would pose tremendous challenges for Taiwan's GHG emission after 2021.

II. Promoting the Use of Natural Gas

667. Following the example of Western countries in viewing natural gas as an important transitional energy to renewable energy, the MOEA has already placed the use of natural gas high on the agenda. After the 2005 National Energy Conference, the MOEA announced a "Plan to expand the domestic use of natural gas" in December 2006. This plan has as its objective the development of more gas infrastructure (pipelines, distribution networks, LNG facilities, and storage) to replace the use of LPG in household cooking and expand the use of natural gas in the electricity sector. The importance of this plan was reconfirmed at the 2009 National Energy Conference, in the 2010 Master Plan, and the aforementioned Energy Development Framework.

---

964. Taiwan News, Nuke plant's fuel rods to be shipped to US, Mar. 16, 2018, available at: https://www.taiwannews.com.tw/en/news/3383849.
965. Executive Yuan, Nuclear-free homeland policy remains unchanged, 2016-06-07, available at: https://english.ey.gov.tw/Page/61BF20C3E89B856/e61c7f0b-9918-4c62-b80b-8a255f1f4aa8.
966. ChinaTimes, Restart Nuclear Power Plant No. 2, available at: https://www.chinatimes.com/newspapers/20190710000638-260110?chdtv.

668. Recently, the expansion of the use of natural gas to achieve a low-carbon society was highlighted in the 2017 Guidelines on Energy Development as a way to "(2) Diversification, Energy Autonomy, and Low Carbon on the Supply Side."

669. Expand the use of natural gas, construct natural gas receiving terminals, transmission and storage facilities, and establish a safety stock mechanism to enhance the supply and security of low-carbon energy.

III. Climate Policy

Nationally Appropriate Mitigation Actions

670. After the Copenhagen COP 15 in 2009, Taiwan submitted NAMAs to the UNFCCC.[967] These NAMAs have triggered several research projects for the capacity building of emission reduction. For instance, a legal instrument to realize NAMAs is also being considered. However, it should be noted that if there is no concrete emission reduction promise in the post-Kyoto period, it is highly likely that Taiwan will remain an outsider in terms of emission reduction.

Master Plan on Energy Conservation and Emission Reduction 2010

671. After COP 15 in Copenhagen, a Master Plan on Energy Conservation and Emission Reduction 2010 was approved by the Executive Yuan to push emission reduction. The target for energy conservation is to improve energy efficiency by 2% annually in the next eight years and reduce energy intensity by 20% and 50% in 2015 and 2050, respectively, as compared to 2005; the target for GHG reduction is to reduce GHG emission in 2020 to the same as that in 2005 and reduce GHG emission in 2025 to the same as that in 2000.[968] Under this master plan, ten more programs have been created, most of which are related to both climate change and energy issues (Figure 11).

---

967. EPA, Nationally Appropriate Mitigation Actions (NAMAs), available at: http://ivy1.epa.gov.tw/unfccc/english/_uploads/20100901/B5-NAMAs_en.pdf.

968. Another Policy Target in Sustainable Energy Development Framework: "(1) Reduce nationwide CO2 emission, so that total emission could return to its 2008 level between 2016 and 2020, and be further reduced to the 2000 level in 2025." *See* MOEABOE, Framework of Taiwan's Sustainable Energy Policy, available at: http://www.moeaboe.gov.tw/Download/English/files/Framework%20of%20Taiwan's%20Sustainable%20Energy%20Policy.pdf.

Figure 11 Ten Programs under the Master Plan on Energy Conservation and Emission Reduction 2010

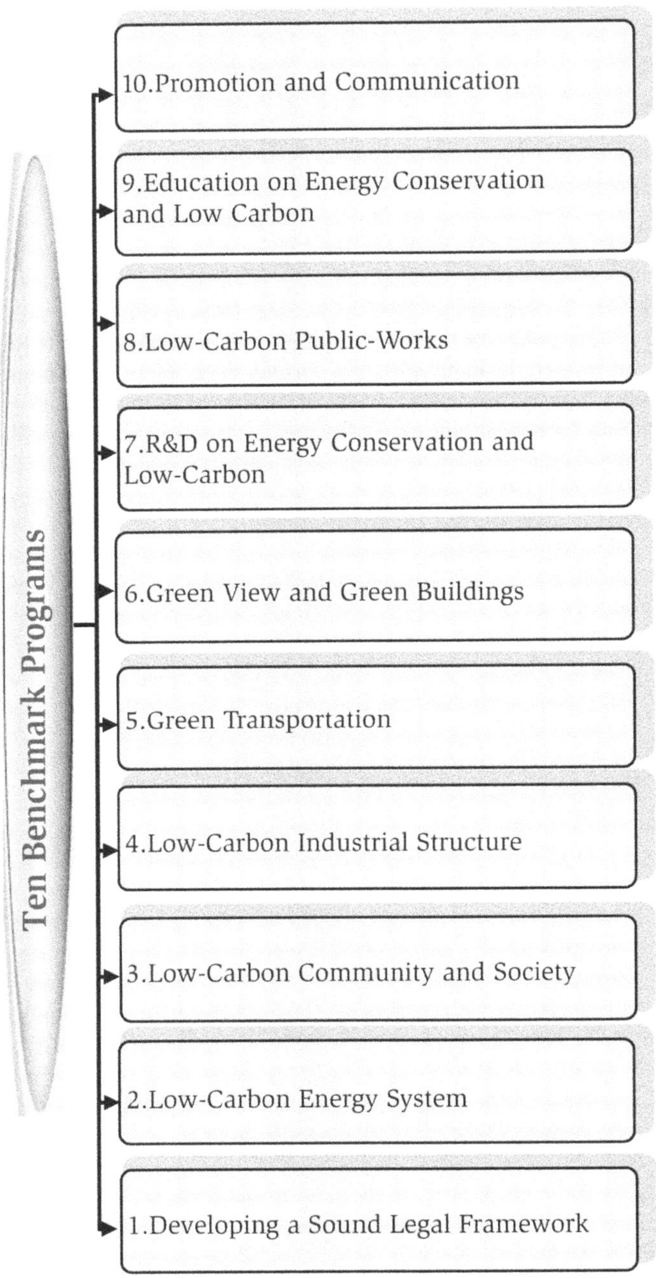

Policy Planning under the GHG Reduction Act of 2015

672. According to Article 9 of the GHG Reduction Act, there are three layers of policy planning for climate change measures. On the top two layers, the EPA plays the key role. To implement the nation's GHG reduction policy, the EPA shall develop a National Climate Change Action Guideline ("Action Guideline") and GHG Reduction Action Plan ("Action Plan") reflecting the nation's economy, energy supplies, environment, current international situation, and assignment of responsibilities. The Action Guideline was published by the EPA in February 2017[969] and the Action Plan in March 2018.[970]

673. As for the third layer, the different ministries charged with the nation's energy, manufacturing, transportation, residential and commercial, and agricultural sectors shall develop "GHG Emission Control Action Programs" for the sectors under its supervision based on the Action Plan. In January 2019, "GHG Emission Control Action Programs" in the energy,[971] manufacturing,[972] transportation,[973] residential and commercial,[974] environmental,[975] and agricultural[976] sectors were all approved by the Executive Yuan and published.

Guidelines on Energy Development of 2017

674. As energy and climate change are closely related, Taiwan's 2017 Guidelines on Energy Development begins by emphasizing the Paris Agreement 2015 and UNFCCC.[977]

675. In "3. Environmental Sustainability," the aspect to "reduce the intensity of greenhouse gas emissions from energy systems" was highlighted. The guidelines focus on reducing GHG and a low-carbon environment as follows:

---

969. EPA, National Climate Change Action Guideline, Feb. 2017, available at: https://adapt.epa.gov.tw/dispPageBox/files/752.pdf.
970. EPA, National Climate Change Action Plan, March 2018, available at: https://www.epa.gov.tw/DisplayFile.aspx?FileID=F8392F55D950E4CD&P=4e6b4fd8-d6a9-445e-9323-a29f51d2a52c.
971. EPA, "GHG Emission Control Action Programs" in the energy sector, available at: https://www.epa.gov.tw/ghgact/68CD0D4FE9D57F49.
972. EPA, "GHG Emission Control Action Programs" in the manufacturing sector, available at: https://www.epa.gov.tw/ghgact/619988F38347E91E.
973. EPA, "GHG Emission Control Action Programs" in the transportation sector, available at: https://www.epa.gov.tw/ghgact/BF698695CF8C04FE.
974. EPA, "GHG Emission Control Action Programs" in the residential and commercial sector, available at: https://www.epa.gov.tw/ghgact/4E3259F94887F9E1.
975. EPA, "GHG Emission Control Action Programs" in the environmental sector, available at: https://www.epa.gov.tw/ghgact/43890392EE8095BC.
976. EPA, "GHG Emission Control Action Programs" in the agricultural sector, available at: https://www.epa.gov.tw/ghgact/2575AED135A13DB2.
977. Considering the shortage of self-produced energy and dependency on imported and fossil fuel energy, which is as high as 98%, in Taiwan, the "Greenhouse Gas Reduction and Management Act" promulgated in 2015 and Paris Agreement reached in UNFCCC COP21, Taiwan is bound to follow the trend of energy transition and seize this opportunity for green growth.

(3) Greenhouse Gas Emissions Reduction	1. Determine the periodic regulatory goal of greenhouse gas emissions for the energy sector in accordance with international convention resolutions related to climate change and situations of international climate negotiations under the principles of maintaining domestic industrial competitiveness and considering the cost benefit to balance economic development and environmental sustainability. 2. Control greenhouse gas emissions by energy industries, assess the potential for emissions reduction, and promote a low-carbon energy structure to gradually reduce greenhouse gas emissions per unit of fuel consumption. 3. Incentivize energy users in reducing emissions, encourage comprehensive and continual actions for emissions reduction by planning for flexible carbon reduction mechanisms such as rewards, offsets, or regulations for different types of energy users by stages.
(5) Establish a Low -Carbon Environment	1. Establish a low-carbon living environment and circular society, promote a low-carbon community renovation plan and national energy saving carbon reduction movement to accelerate the transition to a low-carbon society. 2. Accelerate the construction of a green transportation network, the introduction of a smart transportation system, and promotion of low-carbon energy saving vehicles to establish a human-oriented, safe, and highly efficient green energy low-carbon transportation environment. 3. Integrate local government, utilize local resources to create low carbon cities/villages, construct an energy saving carbon reduction living environment, change the urban texture, and reduce the heat island effect to broaden the horizon of low-carbon governance.

Source: 2017 Guidelines on Energy Development.

§2. Sustainable Energy Basic Bill in the Early 2010s: The Need to Design a Comprehensive Legal Framework

676. In order to handle comprehensively the climate change and energy legal issues, a legal framework has been intensively discussed in Taiwan.

I. Master Plan on Energy Conservation and Emission Reduction 2010

677. According to the Master Plan on Energy Conservation and Emission Reduction 2010, in its First Priority Benchmark Program, developing a sound legal framework was considered the first priority. The legislations relating to this framework involve the Sustainable Energy Basic Bill, Energy Tax Bill, Energy Management Act, Renewable Energy Act, and GHG Reduction Bill. The relationship among these legislations and other related energy legislations is illustrated in Figure 12.

Figure 12 Legal Framework of Energy and Climate Change under the Master Plan on Energy Conservation and Emission Reduction 2010

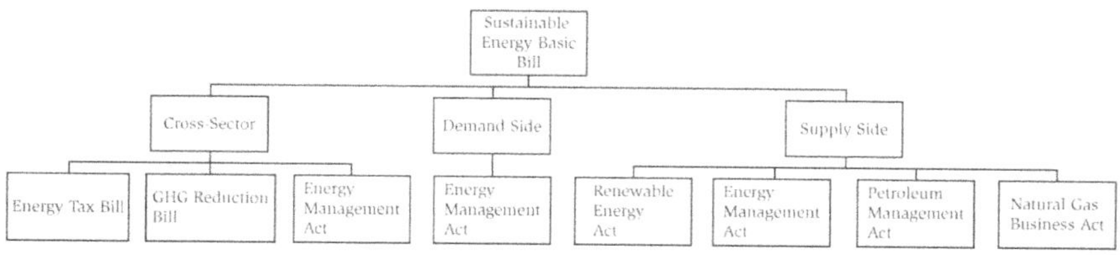

Source: Compiled by the author.

II. The Evaluation of This Legal Framework

678. In fact, the Taiwanese legal framework also reflects the International Energy Agency's (IEA) position. After comparing Taiwan's climate law to the climate change laws in other countries, the weakness of it is quite obvious. That is, there is no appropriate law in place to give effect to the policy. A consideration of the directions and technologies espoused by the IEA[978] and the legal actions of the European Union make it readily evident that Taiwan lacks the laws to realize its policy (Table 28).

Table 28 Legal Regime to Respond to the IEA Climate Change Directions in Europe and Taiwan

IEA Direction	*European Legislations or Regime*	*Taiwan*
Kyoto Mechanisms	European ETS Directive 2009, 2003	GHG Reduction Bill?
Renewable Energy	Renewable Directive 2009, 2001	Act on Renewable Energy 2009

978. IEA, Energy Technology Perspectives 2010, Executive Summary, at p. 3, available at: www.iea.org /techno/etp/etp10/English.pdf.

IEA Direction	*European Legislations or Regime*	*Taiwan*
Energy Efficiency and Conservation	CHP Directive European Directive on Energy Efficiency Buildings, etc ...	Energy Management Act
Nuclear Power	Euratom Treaty	?
Carbon Capture and Storage	CCS Directive 2009	?
Energy and Environmental Tax	Council Directive 2003/96/EC of October 27, 2003: Restructuring the Community Framework for the Taxation of Energy Products and Electricity	Energy Tax Bill?

Source: Compiled by this author.

679. From a comparative legal aspect, without a proper legal framework in place, it is very difficult to implement energy and climate change policy and action plans. This last-lap nature of climate change law also explains why Europe can play a leading role in emissions reduction, while the rest of the world, including the US, Australia, Japan, and Taiwan, are not doing well.

680. Of course, this conclusion is quite harsh. Yet, this is not the end of this type of comparative legal research on climate change law. The next step would be to compare the practical implementation of climate change law in different countries, after the basic climate legal instrument has been adopted in those countries. Currently, this kind of comparison is only possible in Europe. A detailed comparison would show the true value of comparative law. However, whether this desired objective will be realized depends not on the law but on the politics of climate change, and should climate change negotiations fail in the next two years, such an exercise might never become reality.

681. In addition, another weakness of this legal framework is that Taiwan currently focuses mainly on the development of mitigation policy and legal instruments, without paying attention to the "adaptation" aspect of climate law. In fact, this is a result of the lack of an upstream adaptation policy framework. Unlike the early adoption of climate change adaptation policy in other countries,[979] Taiwan's

979. *See*, *e.g.*, Danish strategy for adaptation to a changing climate, 2008, https://www.klimatilpasning.dk/media/5322/klimatilpasningsstrategi_uk_web.pdf.

adaptation policy remains an unfinished draft in 2010.[980] Yet in 2012, the official National Climate Change Adaptation Policy Framework was finally approved by the Executive Yuan .[981] The Action Plan for such Framework for the 2013 and 2017[982] and eight sectoral adaptation plan for disaster, life-saving infrastructure, water resources, land use, coastal area, energy supply and industry, agriculture and biodiversity, health sector was adopted afterward.

§3. GHG Reduction Bill to GHG Reduction Act of 2015

Environmental Basic Act of 2002

682. In order to reduce the GHG emissions, many policy measures have been adopted since 1992. However, the legal instrument to consider GHG is quite slow. The first attempt to consider CO2 in the Taiwanese legal system was Article 22 of the Environmental Basic Act (December 11, 2002), which states that: "Government entities at all levels shall actively adopt measures to control carbon dioxide emissions and establish related plans to mitigate the greenhouse effect." Yet, due to the weak effect of the basic law as well as its policy instruction effect, further detailed and specific laws are required to implement this direction. Besides, it is unclear why this Basic Act only takes CO2 into account, while ignoring five other types of GHG under the Kyoto Protocol.

Evaluation of the GHG Reduction Bill Before 2015

683. One of the most important issues requiring attention by climate change legislation is the establishment of a cap-and-trade emission trading scheme (ETS) under the Kyoto Protocol. In this regard, under the purview of the Environmental Basic Act and the effective date of the Kyoto Protocol in 2005, the government began to prepare and discuss the GHG Reduction Bill. The EPA completed the draft of the GHG Reduction Bill in February 2006 (before the first anniversary of the effective date of the Kyoto Protocol). This bill was then submitted to Parliament after approval by the Executive Yuan. However, during this parliamentary term, only some of the provisions were adopted. After the re-election of the Parliament in 2007, the bill was resubmitted to the Parliament again by the Executive Yuan on February 4, 2008. However, there remains no consensus so far in 2011. This bill was finally adopted in 2015.

---

980. The draft of Taiwan Climate Change Adaptation Framework, available at:http://apf.cier.edu.tw/20100915%E6%B0%A3%E5%80%99%E8%AE%8A%E9%81%B7%E8%AA%BF%E9%81%A9%E6%94%BF%E7%AD%96%E7%B6%B1%E9%A0%98-1-6%E7%AB%A0%EF%BC%88%E8%8D%89%E6%A1%88%EF%BC%89.pdf (visited on Oct. 10, 2020).

981. National Climate Change Adaptation Policy Framework, 2012-06-05, available at: https://www.ndc.gov.tw/cp.aspx?n=5E865E40CA33E974&s=406CB85C0FFDB9E2.

982. NDC, The Action Plan for such Framework for the 2013 and 2017, available at: https://www.ndc.gov.tw/cp.aspx?n=FCB2E59927B8AFFD&s=9513815E1FFFDAD5.

684. This bill was jointly developed by the government and the private sector. It establishes a framework to regulate GHG emissions on the basis of emission efficiencies and new-source emissions, as well as provides penalties for non-compliance. In addition to serving as the legal basis for developing and implementing domestic GHG emission reduction measures, the bill is also expected to demonstrate to the international community Taiwan's willingness to participate in global actions to reduce GHG emissions and to fulfill its responsibilities as a member of the international community.[983] The key elements of the bill (six chapters with twenty-eight articles) are outlined in Figure 13.[984]

Figure 13 Framework of the GHG Reduction Bill

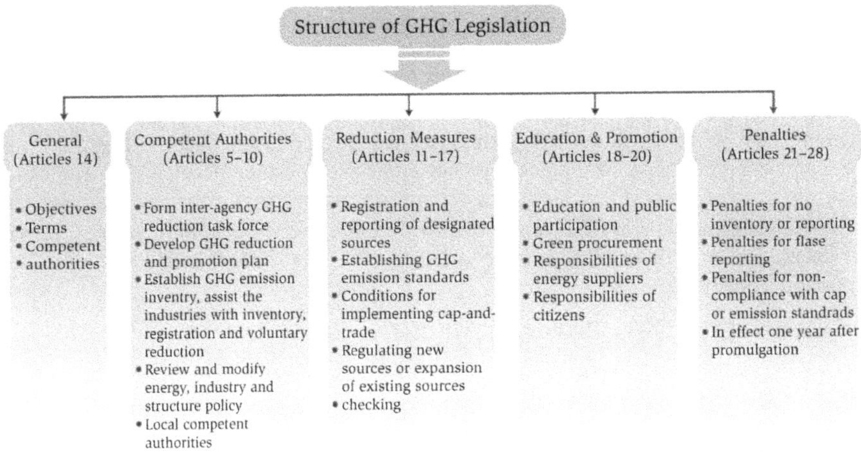

Source: EPA, Mitigating Climate Change-What Taiwan is Doing, at p. 9, available at: http://unfccc.epa.gov.tw/unfccc/english/_uploads/downloads/03_Mitigating_Climate_Change-What_Taiwan_is_Doing.pdf (visited on Oct. 10, 2020).

685. In this bill, a step-by-step approach to establishing a cap-and-trade system will be set up.

686. At the first phase, before the bill takes effect after its passing, voluntary agreements with industries and incentives for early action will be promoted.[985]

983. EPA, Our Effort, available at: http://unfccc.epa.gov.tw/unfccc/english/04_our_efforts/061_policy.html.
984. EPA, Mitigating Climate Change: What Taiwan is doing, p. 9, available at: http://unfccc.epa.gov.tw/unfccc/english/_uploads/downloads/03_Mitigating_Climate_Change-What_Taiwan_is_Doing.pdf.
985. EPA, Our Effort, available at: http://unfccc.epa.gov.tw/unfccc/english/04_our_efforts/061_policy.html.

687. At the second phase, when the bill becomes effective, an emission permit system, inventory verification and reporting, as well as emission performance standards would be enforced. With regard to "GHG Emission Permits," designated emission sources must conduct an annual emission inventory and verification, then register on the EPA platform. Existing, new, or modified emission sources above a certain level must apply for an emission permit from the EPA, and operate, monitor, record, and report emissions in accordance with the permit conditions. Related management regulations will be set by the EPA.[986] In addition, GHG emission performance standards are scheduled. Designated emission sources will be expected to comply with GHG emission standards (the benchmark, e.g., GHG emission per ton of steel production) based on the established emission intensity for new/existing emission sources, installation under various sectors, products, etc. The standards would be set by the EPA in consultation with the central competent authorities, such as the BOE and the IDB.

688. At the third phase, when the national emissions target is established, a cap-and-trade scheme would be enforced. Taiwan will set a national emissions target and implement a domestic cap-and-trade system, as a part of its economic and financial policy instruments to reduce GHG emissions. The timing and stringency of the target setting would depend on the progress of international climate negotiations, as stipulated in the Bill (Figure 14).

Figure 14 Step-by Step Approach to Introducing Cap-and-Trade System under Taiwan GHG Reduction Bill

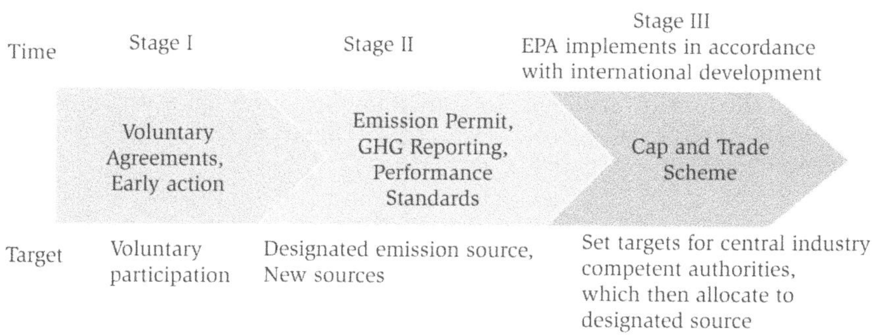

Source: EPA, Mitigating Climate Change-What Taiwan is Doing, at p. 10, available at: http://unfccc.epa.gov.tw/unfccc/english/_uploads/downloads/03_Mitigating_Climate_Change-What_Taiwan_is_Doing.pdf (visited on Oct. 10, 2020).

689. Under this plan, as soon as work begins on a cap-and-trade scheme, a National GHG Reduction Target will be proposed by the EPA after consultation with other related central governmental authorities; the scheme will be set up after the

986. EPA, Mitigating Climate Change: What Taiwan is doing, available at: http://unfccc.epa.gov.tw/unfccc/english/_uploads/downloads/03_Mitigating_Climate_Change-What_Taiwan_is_Doing.pdf.

approval of the Executive Yuan. Except for those emission rights reserved for new entrants, emission targets will be allocated to existing sectors, including energy, industry, transport, residential, commercial, and other sectors. In this regard, the energy sector will be subject to ETS at the third stage.

690. However, due to the outcry and heavy lobbying from the industrial sectors, deliberations on this bill have not been satisfactory before 2015. Before the adoption of this bill, certain measures played a role in regulating GHG.

691. CO2 could be a potential air pollutant; thus it has been regulated in the US under the Clean Air Act, during Barack Obama's Presidency. Similarly, CO2 is listed as a pollutant under the Air Pollution Act of Taiwan after the official designation of six types of GHGs as air pollutants in mid-2012.[987] Under this regime, the EPA began to conduct a GHG registry, which promulgated the Ordinance on GHG Reporting[988] and was involved in the management of GHG inspection and accreditation institutes.[989] Subsequently, work has been done on accumulating emissions information by regulating specific entities contained in the emissions report. In December 2012, the EPA announced the mandatory GHG reporting scheme, and augmented the "Management Regulations of Greenhouse Gas Emission Reporting" and "Stationary Pollution Source in Public or Private Premises that Should Report Greenhouse Gas Emission" pursuant to Article 21 of the Air Pollution Control Act.[990]

692. The early action plan was launched before July 1, 2015. Early Action refers to an offset project proposed by the owner, user, or supervisor of Emission Sources before the Greenhouse Gas Reduction and Management Act was enacted in compliance with the emission intensity designed by the central competent authority. The EPA uses this incentive in five industries, namely in the cement, semiconductor, power generation, steel and iron, and thin-film transistor-liquid crystal display industries. By its termination in July 2015, 69.179 thousand tons of carbon dioxide equivalent (CO_2e) reduction credits were issued.[991]

693. The GHG Offset Project is a mechanism for issuing reward credits to encourage the implementation of voluntary GHG emission reduction by an entity. Emissions reduction is calculated by the difference between the baseline and project scenarios. The implementation of the GHG Offset Project is divided into two stages: registration and the issuance of reward credits, respectively. Regarding the registration procedure, applicants shall propose a suitable approval methodology to

---

987. Ordinance on the Designation of CO2, CH4, N2O, HFCs, PFCs, SF6, as Air Pollutants, 2012-05-09, available at: https://oaout.epa.gov.tw/law/LawContent.aspx?id=GL007322.
988. Ordinance on GHG Reporting, abrogated on Jan. 5, 2016, available at: https://law.moj.gov.tw/LawClass/LawAll.aspx?pcode=O0020093.
989. Ordinance on GHG inspection and accreditation institutes, abrogated on Jan. 7, 2016, available at: https://law.moj.gov.tw/LawClass/LawAll.aspx?pcode=O0020097.
990. EPA, GHG emission reporting, available at: https://ghgregistry.epa.gov.tw/ghgenglish/report.asp.
991. EPA, Early Action Project, available at: https://ghgregistry.epa.gov.tw/ghgenglish/early_project.asp.

describe a project plan document (PDD). All PDD descriptions shall be in accordance with the approved methodology. The PDD shall be validated via Verification Bodies recognized by the EPA, and thereafter, the applicant should provide the validated PDD, validation report, and other related documents to request to register a project with the EPA. In terms of the procedure to issue reward credits, the applicant shall implement and operate the registered PDD in accordance with the description in the registered PDD including all physical features, and then complete the monitoring report. The monitoring report shall be verified via the Verification Bodies recognized by the EPA, and thereafter, the applicant should provide the verified monitoring report, verification report, and other related documents to request the issuance of reward credits by the EPA. When the EPA receives a submission from the applicant, the committee shall assist it by appraising the request for project registration, issuance of reward credits, and the methodology application. The committee shall review and make the final decision for each request.[992]

694. Based on the "Directions for Promoting the GHG Early Action Project and Offset Project," once a reduction project is approved by the EPA, it will issue credits into the accounts of the project proponents. The credits acquired by participants through actual emission reduction approval can be held, transferred, and withdrawn. Each single credit represents 1 ton of CO2e. All approved credits must be held in the registry and will be issued with a unique serial number that includes a project country code, unit type, serial block start, serial block end, applicable period, and project identifier. This is to ensure the ownership and credibility of domestic offsets. From 2000 to 2013, 483 Early Action Projects were approved and the credits were allocated.[993]

992. EPA, Offset Project, available at: https://ghgregistry.epa.gov.tw/ghgenglish/offset_project.asp.
993. EPA, GHG Credits Management, available at: https://ghgregistry.epa.gov.tw/ghgenglish/Credits.asp.

Table 29 Allocated Credits by Early Action Projects (Unit: Metric Tons CO_2e)

Industry Category / Application Year	*Cement*	*Semi-conductor*	*LCD*	*Electricity*	*Steel*	*Total for the Year*
2000	603,861	66,241	–	793,879	119,656	1,583,637
2001	536,577	81,707	–	562,968	711,860	1,893,112
2002	910,874	223,484	–	562,351	1,684,155	3,380,864
2003	886,694	466,213	–	694,568	1,071,551	3,119,028
2004	967,754	467,271	–	614,446	1,202,857	3,252,328
2005	942,609	537,647	2,594,682	385,398	115,965	4,576,301
2006	942,778	813,216	4,199,809	436,474	990,017	7,382,294
2007	863,682	1,348,673	6,244,165	674,252	952,742	10,083,514
2008	782,285	1,570,986	6,009,992	584,744	482,086	9,430,093
2009	792,376	1,404,593	6,007,413	826,736	356,513	9,387,631
2010	792,482	2,957,796	6,228,773	860,628	1,096,230	11,937,909
2011	–	770,631	616,383	258,593	734,950	2,380,557
2012	–	354,378	294,883	25,784	18,125	693,170
2013	–	–	–	35,051	43,311	78,362
Total for industry	**9,023,972**	**11,062,836**	**32,196,100**	**7,315,872**	**9,580,020**	**69,178,800**

Unit : metric tons CO_2e

695. In order to provide incentives for large energy enterprises to measure and verify GHG, a Subsidy Ordinance for GHG Measuring and Verification was promulgated by the MOEA in 2010.[994] The eligible subsidized companies are petroleum refiners, natural gas enterprises, electricity companies, and CHP operators. The qualified projects for subsidy include the following four types of projects:[995]

- GHG Emission Examination and Verification Projects: Up to 300 thousand NTD per project.
- A Confirmation (validation) Project for GHG Voluntary Reduction: Up to 800 thousand NTD per project.
- A Verification Project for GHG Voluntary Reduction: Up to 300 thousand NTD per project.
- A Verification Project whose emission reduction was between 2000 and the passing date of the GHG Reduction Act: Up to 500 thousand NTD per project.

994. Subsidy Ordinance for GHG Measuring and Verification, 2010-03-26; Amended Date: 2011-03-07, abrogated on Jan. 29, 2018, available at: https://www.moeaboe.gov.tw/opengovinfo/Laws/all/LAllMain.aspx?PageId=l_all_07.

995. Point 7 of Subsidy Ordinance for GHG Measuring and Verification.

696. Other important indirect measures that consider GHG emissions are the EIA and SEA. In recent energy policies, projects, plans, and programs, GHG and CO2 emissions were also evaluated by the authorities, even though CO2 was not expressly considered a pollutant under the EIA and SEA schemes.

The GHG Reduction Act of 2015

697. After more than a decade of development, the GHG Reduction Act was finally promulgated on July 1, 2015.[996]

698. Certain aspects of the 2015 GHG Act are unique. Unlike climate laws in other countries,[12] the GHG Act integrates both energy security and energy efficiency; that is, it is not only a climate change law, but also an energy law. The complex nature of the GHG Act led to its accommodation by the energy sector. Another factor leading to acceptance of the act was that even though both mitigation and adaptation are mentioned in its legislative recital, the relatively more forceful regulations focus on mitigation rather than adaptation.[997]

699. Table 30 provides an overview of the GHG Act.

Table 30 Overview of the 2015 GHG Act of Taiwan

Issues	*Relevant Articles*
Institutional design for climate change	Articles 2, 8, 13, 15
General principles regarding climate change and energy	Articles 5, 6
Main measures for addressing climate change	(a) Emission reduction targets (Articles 4, 9, 11, 12) (b) Comprehensive plan for addressing climate change (Articles 9, 15) (c) Six specific measures: – Emission accounting and registration (Article 16) – Emission Performance Standard (Article 17) – Emission Trading Scheme (Article 18, 20, 21, 22) – Climate Change Fund (Article 19) – Incentives and rewards (Article 27) – Education and public awareness (Articles 24, 25, 26)

Source: Compiled by the author.

996. EPA, First Year Implementation of the Greenhouse Gas Reduction and Management Act, Aug. 24, 2017, available at: https://www.epa.gov.tw/eng/F7AB26007B8FE8DF/c36f5c8a-5448-4ae6-a4a8-aa71cb76abae.
997. Anton Ming-Zhi Gao, A Critical Review of the Role of Taiwan's 2015 Emission Reduction Act in the Energy Sector's Mitigation and Adaptation Initiatives, June 2019, The Taiwan Law Review, at 73–105 (2019).

Institutional Design

700. This Act adopts a unique approach to institutional design. Of course, as with all general energy and administrative laws in Taiwan, a "main" competent authority is provided. The EPA is still designated as the competent authority at the central government level, while municipal governments exercise authority at the county or city level.[998] The good news is that the EPA is not alone. Assistance from other central governments and the relative substantive role of local government is also provided.

701. First, at the central government level, different duties are provided for different actors including relevant central government agencies, industry competent authorities, and the Executive Yuan. *Relevant central government* agencies are required to take certain actions to assist the Executive Yuan in discussions on climate change initiatives,[999] and are responsible for climate-related matters.[1000]

---

998. Emission Reduction and Management Act (ERM Act), Art. 2.

999. ERM Act, Art. 8, "The Executive Yuan shall invite *relevant central government agencies*, non-governmental organizations, experts, and scholars to determine and review the division, integration, implementation, and compilation of the work of GHG reduction and climate change adaptation."

1000. ERM Act, Art. 8(2), "Relevant central government agencies shall promote GHG reduction and climate change adaptation through the following actions:

1. Development of renewable energy and energy technology.
2. Improvement of energy efficiency and energy conservation.
3. Reduction in GHG emissions by industrial sectors.
4. Transportation management, development of mass transit systems, and reduction in GHG emissions by other transportation sectors.
5. Implementation of low-carbon energy transportation.
6. Reduction and management of GHG emissions from buildings.
7. Waste recycling and reuse.
8. Forest resource management, biodiversity conservation, and strengthening of forests' carbon sequestration.
9. Reduction and management of GHG emissions from agriculture and guarantee of food security.
10. Green finance and GHG reduction incentive mechanisms.
11. Assessment of the impact of GHG reductions on the economy as a whole and planning of response measures.
12. Establishment of GHG cap-and-trade schemes including the allocation, auction, allowance sale, trade, and facilitation of an international mechanism for cooperation in emission reductions.
13. Research, development, and implementation of GHG reduction technologies.
14. Study of international GHG conventions and laws, and participation in international conferences.
15. Development and implementation of matters connected with climate change adaptation.
16. Education and advocacy of climate change adaptation and GHG reduction.
17. Other climate change adaptation and GHG reduction matters."

702. **The industry competent authorities** play a very important role in governing different types of industries. For instance, the telecommunication industry's industry competent authority is the Ministry of Transportation, while the MOEA is the competent authority for the oil and gas industry. In the ERM Act, industry competent authorities have an extensive role in dealing with climate change matters. During the drafting process of this Act's important climate change plan—the National Climate Change Action Guideline ("Action Guideline") and GHG Reduction Action Plan ("Action Plan")—these industry authorities played an advisory role.[1001] They also have a role under Articles 10,[1002] 11,[1003] 13,[1004] 14,[1005] 15,[1006] 17,[1007] 20,[1008] 21, etc.[1009]

1001. ERM Act, Art. 9, "In order to implement the nation's GHG reduction policy, the central competent authority shall develop a National Climate Change Action Guideline ('Action Guideline') and GHG Reduction Action Plan ('Action Plan') reflecting the nation's economy, energy supplies, environment, current international situation, and the assignment of responsibilities mentioned in Paragraph 1 of the previous Article, and shall implement the Action Guideline and Action Plan in consultation with the central industry competent authorities after requesting approval from the Executive Yuan."
1002. ERM Act, Art. 10, "*The central industry competent authorities* shall regularly review and revise the Action Programs on the basis of changes in the industry and energy supply and demand and deliver an annual report on the implementation of the GHG emissions target and shall propose improvement plans if failing to meet emission targets."
1003. ERM Act, Art. 11, "Regulatory goals will be set in stages on a five-year basis. The central competent authority shall invite scholars, experts, and non-governmental organizations, in conjunction with the *central industry competent authorities*, to form an advisory committee to set the regulations for the goals and regulatory approaches."
1004. ERM Act, Art. 13, "*The central industry competent authorities* shall survey emissions, compile relevant statistics, develop climate change adaptation strategies, and regularly submit survey, statistics, and adaptation results to the central competent authority annually."
1005. ERM Act, Art. 14, "T*he industry competent authorities* shall assist entities in the accounting of emission sources, verification, registration, reduction, and participation in domestic or international offset projects."
1006. ERM Act, Art. 15, "Special municipality, county, and city competent authorities shall develop GHG control implementation plans in accordance with the Action Plan approved by the Executive Yuan and the Action Program determined by t*he central industry competent authorities*; such implementation plans shall be finalized after requesting the approval of the central competent authority in consultation with the central industry competent authorities."
1007. ERM Act, Art. 17, "The central competent authority may establish a GHGEPS to incentivize designated Emission Sources to reduce GHG emissions prior to the cap-and-trade scheme.
 The EPS pursuant to the foregoing paragraph shall be determined and reviewed regularly by the central competent authority in conjunction with the *central industry competent authorities*, considering facilities, products, or other raw materials, output, and consumptions of Emission Sources."
1008. ERM Act, Art. 20, "The central competent authority shall work in conjunction with the *central industry competent authority* to determine regulations regarding the allowance of the entity, the eligibility, approach, and processes of allocation, the approaches of auction or sale, revocation and termination of emissions allowances. Pursuant to Paragraph 4, the reserve of emission allowances, specific scale of new or modified Emission Sources, the designated BAT, the process of ceasing and resuming operation of Emission Sources, and the impact recognition of carbon leakage to the overall national competitiveness and other requirements."
1009. ERM Act, Art. 22, "The regulations regarding the Offset Project, Early Action, EPS, voluntary reduction action of emissions sources not covered under the cap-and-trade scheme and other requirements pursuant to Paragraphs 1 and 2, the central competent authority shall be in consultation with the central industry competent authorities to determine the criteria of reduction actions,

703. Considering the cross-ministerial nature of climate change affairs, the involvement of the Executive Yuan and not just the EPA in making important decisions would give more consideration to the climate change issue. For instance, Article 8 of the ERM Act calls on the Executive Yuan to invite relevant central government agencies, NGOs, experts, and scholars to determine and review the division, integration, implementation, and compilation of the work of GHG reduction and climate change adaptation. The Executive Yuan is also responsible for making important decisions such as on the revision and approval of emission reduction goals and phase goals,[1010] approving the comprehensive climate change plan (action programs),[1011] monitoring progress,[1012] approving the related achievement report,[1013] approving the emission trading system (ETS),[1014] and regulating the spending of the Climate Change Fund.[1015]

704. Finally, a role is provided for local government—i.e., the special municipality, competent county, and city authorities—in drafting local climate change plans[1016] and receiving funding under the climate change fund.[1017]

General Principles

705. The new ERM Act provides many policies and legal principles for the functioning of the new low-carbon future. In general, cross-cutting and climate change-focused principles are provided, respectively. The former category covers the wide issues of "economic policy," "energy policy," and environmental policy, while the latter focuses on climate change aspects.

706. Regarding the former, Article 5 of the ERM Act provides the following seven "general" principles. This article classifies them as shown in Table 31.

---

prerequisites, process of application, review, and approval, as well as the calculated methodology from emission reduction toward emission allowances, requirements of validation and verification, eligibility conditions, and expiry date for reduction credits, and usage limit of reduction credits."

Art. 23 of the ERM Act: "The competent authorities or the industry competent authorities may direct officers, with credentials or proof of authorization presented, to conduct a site visit for the purposes of inspecting an Emission Source's facility operation or requesting relevant information. Emission Source owners, operators, or managers shall not evade this request."

Art. 27 of the ERM Act: "The central competent authority and central industry competent authorities shall reward well-performing facilities, enterprises, schools, organizations, or individuals with grants or subsidies."

Art. 28 of the ERM Act: "The central competent authority shall, in conjunction with the central industry competent authorities, set the aforementioned carbon market price and review regularly taking into consideration domestic and international carbon market trading price."

1010. ERM Act, Art. 4; ERM Act, Art. 11.
1011. ERM Act, Art. 9; ERM Act, Art. 10.
1012. ERM Act, Art. 12.
1013. ERM Act, Art. 13(2).
1014. ERM Act, Art. 18(2).
1015. ERM Act, Art. 19.
1016. ERM Act, Art. 15.
1017. ERM Act, Arts. 19(3)–(4); ERM Act, Art. 5(2).

Table 31 Different Aspects of the General Principles in the ERM Act of 2015

Aspects	*Legal Provisions*
Overall	– The national government shall ensure the sustainable utilization of the nation's resources, maintain balanced energy supply and demand, mitigate and respond to the impacts of climate change, and place balanced emphasis on environmental protection, economic development, and social justice (Article 5(1)). – All levels of government shall encourage technological innovation, and research and development, and enhance financial mechanisms, spur economic momentum, encourage competition, promote low-carbon green growth, create employment opportunities, and boost national competitiveness (5(2)).
Energy	1. To ensure the nation's energy security, the government shall draft mid- to long-term strategies to gradually reduce dependence on fossil fuels with a mid- to long-term aim of renewable energy policies, and the gradual realization of a nuclear-free homeland (5(3)). 3. To respond to the impact of climate change, under the principle of equality and social welfare promotion, the government should implement **tax mechanisms on imported fossil fuels** based on the CO2e. 5. To reduce environmental pollution and GHG emissions, the government should promote resource use efficiency, **energy use efficiency**, and resource recycling.
Climate	2. In line with the "user charge" principle of environmental justice, the free allowances allocation method will be gradually replaced by allowances sold at a fixed price (5(3)). 3. To respond **to the impact of climate change**, under the principles of equality and social welfare promotion, the government should implement tax mechanisms on imported fossil fuels based on the CO2e. 5. To reduce environmental pollution and **GHG emissions**, the government should promote resource use efficiency, energy use efficiency, and resource recycling.
Economy and industry policy aspects	4. The government should actively help traditional industries achieve energy conservation and carbon reduction or transition, develop green technology and a green industry, create new employment opportunities and green economies, and promote a low-carbon green growth plan for the nation's infrastructure.

Aspects	Legal Provisions
Environmental	5. To reduce **environmental pollution** and GHG emissions, the government should promote resource use efficiency, energy use efficiency, and resource recycling.

Source: Compiled by the author.

707. Specifically, Article 6 elaborates on the four climate change principles:

(1) National reduction targets and the schedule shall seek to realize the common but differentiated responsibilities specified in UNFCCC, while also furthering the sustainable development of the nation's environment, economy, and society.
(2) The determination of sector-based periodic regulatory goals shall consider cost effectiveness, and strive to achieve GHG reductions at the lowest possible cost.
(3) The government shall actively adopt preventive measures; seek to forecast, avoid, or reduce the causes of climate change; and mitigate the adverse effects of climate change.
(4) The government shall actively strengthen international cooperation, and strive to maintain the international competitiveness of domestic industries.

708. Apart from these "direct" principles, Article 8(2) also indicates important government initiatives on climate change. These initiatives could be relevant to the policy direction, such as emission reduction in industrial sectors, the promotion of renewable energy, and energy technology development.

Main Measures

Target

709. To achieve emission reductions, the starting point of this ERM Act is to describe the vision or the targets. Three types of targets are described.

710. The first type of target is the long-term vision. Article 4(1) provides *long-term goals* such as "to reduce GHG emissions to no more than 50% of the 2005 GHG emissions by 2050."

711. Such long-term goals are then divided into two types. The *five-year periodical goals* (in this Act, regulatory goals) should be included in the Action Guideline.[1018] Moreover, Article 9(3) requires a *sectoral target* for Sectoral GHG Emission Control Action Programs of energy, manufacturing, transportation, agriculture, and so on. Thus far, these targets are still under deliberation.

1018. ERM Act, Art. 9(2).

712. Of the three types of targets, the regulatory target is subject to very strict rules and monitoring. For instance, there is a very detailed procedural rule, including a public hearing, for the establishment of regulatory goals.[1019] Article 10 requires proposing improvement plans if emission targets under the five-year Action Guideline are not met. Finally, the EPA also has duties to report to the Executive Yuan on its progress in reaching regulatory targets.[1020] Thus, among the three types of targets, the regulatory and periodical target could be considered the most important. This target is also closely related with the emissions trading scheme.[1021]

713. To avoid rigidity in the above targets, they are subject to revision or update. More rules are provided for long-term and/or regulatory targets than for sectoral targets. For the revision of the former two targets, the approval of the Executive Yuan is necessary.[1022] There remains much room for a central industry-competent authority in revising the sectoral target.

Comprehensive Plan

714. To reach the above targets, further comprehensive planning is necessary. A *multi-layer and top-down* approach is adopted. At the top, the EPA prepares the "National Climate Change Action Guideline" ("Action Guideline") and "GHG Reduction Action Plan" ("Action Plan") as required under Article 9(1), while the individual competent industry authorities prepare sectoral GHG Emission Control Action Programs as required under Article 9(3). The local government should then follow the above guideline, plan, and program to develop further "local GHG control implementation plans."[1023]

Six Specific Measures

Emission accounting and registration (16)

715. Understanding the current emission situation could be fundamental for the development of further policies and measures. According to Article 16 of the ERM Act, emission sources designated by the central competent authority shall conduct annual accounting and registration to their holding accounts in the Registry by the deadline. The GHG inventory and relevant information shall be verified by a verification body at least once every three years. The detailed rules are also provided in an ordinance.[1024]

1019. ERM Act, Art. 11.
1020. ERM Act, Art. 12(1).
1021. ERM Act, Art. 20(1), "The central competent authority shall announce the designated Emission Sources, which include: The percentage of the emission allowances on sale shall be determined by regulatory goals in stages and gradually increased to 100%."
1022. ERM Act, Art. 4(2); ERM Act, Art. 12(2).
1023. ERM Act, Art. 15.
1024. Ordinance on Emission Accounting and Registration (Jan. 5, 2016), available at: http://ivy5.epa.gov.tw/epalaw/search/LordiDispFull.aspx?ltype=19&lname=0140.

716. The professional and qualified institute is important to advancing such initiatives. Thus, this provision also provides further rules concerning the qualification of such an institution.[1025]

Emission performance standard (17)

717. Before moving into the ETS scheme, it is worth mentioning a transitional measure in this Act—i.e., the emission performance standard (EPS). According to Article 17, the central competent authority may establish a GHG emission performance standard (GHGEPS) to incentivize designated emission sources to reduce GHG emissions prior to the cap-and-trade scheme.

Emission Trading Scheme (Articles 18, 20, 21, 22)

718. The ETS provisions have very high regulatory intensity. Compared with only one or two provisions of the specific measures, four articles and very lengthy provisions deal with the core of the ERM Act, namely the ETS scheme. Briefly, the features of the ETS are as follows:

- The initiative is nationwide in scope, instead of a local government initiative.
- No specific industry type is listed in the ERM Act; thus, defining the further administrative ordinance is necessary.
- The allocation method is free to tendering and ultimately, a fixed-price.
- Certain emission rights are reserved for new entrants, but they are required to equip themselves with the best available technology (BAT).
- “Carbon leakage″ industries are considered.
- Fixed-price allocation is preferred.
- Special consideration is given once the fossil fuel tax passes.
- Special allocation rules are given for electricity utilities.
- Emissions are non-transferable after closure of the plants or ceasing business operation, and the government has the power to recall all emission rights.[1026]
- As between national and international emission rights, the national and local emission right has priority. To meet a compliance obligation to offset excess emissions, an entity may surrender reduction credits procured from international/foreign GHG trading schemes recognized by the central competent authority by up to 10% of the entity’s total allowances.[1027]

1025. ERM Act, Art. 16(2) “The verification body pursuant to the foregoing paragraph shall be internationally recognized or establish a domestic branch office. Before operating validation and or verification business in accordance with the Act, the verification body must apply and acquire accreditation certificate and permit by the central competent authority or its appointed accreditation body.” The Ordinance on the Management of the Accreditation Body for Greenhouse Gases (Jan. 7, 2016), available at: http://ivy5.epa.gov.tw/epalaw/search/LordiDispFull.aspx?ltype=19&lname=0150.

1026. ERM Act, Arts. 20(5)–20(6).

1027. ERM Act, Arts. 21(3)–21(4).

– Concerning the qualification of the international verification institute, the bodies that provide verification services related to international reduction credits shall be recognized by the associated mechanisms of UNFCCC or the central competent authority.[1028]

Soft tool: Climate Change Fund (Article 19)

719. Climate change mitigation and adaptation initiatives require much funding. In this regard, this Act also creates a fund to facilitate the deployment of climate change initiatives.

720. The main funding sources are scheduled to come from the tendering process of the allocation of emission rights.[1029] The funds collected will be spent on the following purposes:[1030] (1) reducing GHG emissions; (2) inspecting emission sources; (3) providing emission sources with assistance, subsidies, and grants for voluntary efforts to reduce GHG emissions; (4) administrative affairs of holding accounts established in the registry, auctions, sales, and allowance trading; (5) employing staff to carry out administrative services; (6) coordinating, planning, and implementing adaptation to climate change; (7) educating, promoting, and awarding grants; (8) conducting international affairs; and (9) carrying out research and analysis.

721. Certain funding will be provided to the local government.[1031] The function of this fund will be also be monitored by a special committee.[1032]

Incentive and reward (Article 27)

1028. ERM Act, Art. 21(5).

1029. ERM Act, Art. 19(1), "The central competent authority shall establish the GHG Management Fund (Fund) from the following sources:

1. Proceeds from allowances auctioned or sold pursuant to the foregoing Article;
2. Fees collected pursuant to Article 21;
3. Government grant via budget appropriation;
4. Revenues collected under fines and penalties prescribed in the Act;
5. Money received from persons, liable entities, or organizations; and
6. Other incomes."

1030. ERM Act, Art. 19(2).

1031. ERM Act, Art. 20(3)–(4) "Special municipalities, counties, and cities shall be subsidized for activities pursuant to the foregoing paragraph *no less than 30 percent* of the net proceeds collected from allowances auctioned or sold for a fixed price pursuant to Paragraph 1 minus the administrative costs and fees incurred.

The ratios and distribution methods of subsidies pursuant to the foregoing paragraph shall be determined and reviewed regularly by the central competent authority, after consultation with municipalities or county (city) governments considering population, geographical area, and relevant factors."

1032. ERM Act, Art. 20(5), "Pursuant to Paragraph 1, the central competent authority may establish a *committee supervising the operation of the Fund* in accordance with regulations specified by the Executive Yuan regarding revenues, expenditures, safeguard, and utilization."

722. Among all the soft tools (climate change fund, incentive and rewards, and education and public awareness), Article 27 provides a carrot. It provides that the central competent authority and central industry competent authorities shall reward well-performing facilities, enterprises, schools, organizations, or individuals with grants or subsidies. The further subsidy will be specified in an ordinance.

Education and public awareness (Articles 24, 25, 26)

723. Similar to the design of ETS, this Act also uses three provisions to elaborate on the initiatives of education and public awareness. These provisions address climate change, energy education, and public awareness initiatives, respectively.

(1) Climate change: All levels of government are called upon to promote public awareness of the mitigation of climate change and GHG reduction among citizens, schools, and industries, proactively assisting NGOs in the following manner: (1) By developing and promoting education plans on climate change and its impact; (2) providing the public with easy access to relevant information about climate change; (3) engaging industries and the public in relevant measures based on local conditions; (4) training scientific, technological, and managerial personnel; and (5) encouraging research in combination with environmental education on climate change (Article 24(1)).

(2) Energy:
   - All levels of government shall promote public awareness of climate change mitigation and GHG reduction among citizens, schools, and industries, proactively assisting NGOs in the following manner: (6) By promoting energy saving and enhancing energy efficiency; and (7) supporting low-carbon products by establishing a carbon-labeling plan (Article 24(1)).
   - All levels of government, public education institutions, and government-run enterprises shall promote energy saving and use energy-efficient products or services to reduce GHG emission (Article 25).
   - Electricity suppliers and distributors shall encourage energy conservation and energy efficiency amongst customers (Article 25).

Adaptation Measures

724. The idea of adaptation has been integrated into the abovementioned measures. This article provides a summary.

- General principle: Article 5(1) calls on the government to balance the needs of *adaptation* and mitigation.
- The Executive Yuan's initiatives: Article 8(1) calls on the Executive Yuan to invite relevant central government agencies, non-NGOs, experts, and scholars to determine and review the division, integration, implementation, and compilation of the work of GHG reduction and climate change *adaptation*.
- The job of central-related competent authorities: Article 8(2) calls on relevant central government agencies to promote GHG reduction and climate change

adaptation through the following actions: (15) Development and implementation of matters connected with climate change adaptation, (16) education and advocacy on climate change *adaptation* and GHG reduction, and (17) other climate change *adaptation* and GHG reduction matters.

- EPA's reporting duties: Article 13(1) calls on the central industry-competent authorities to survey emissions; compile relevant statistics; develop climate change *adaptation* strategies; and submit surveys, statistics, and adaptation results to the central competent authority annually.
- The funding target of the climate change fund: Article 19 calls on the Fund to serve the following purpose only for GHG emissions reduction and adaptation to climate change: (6) Coordinate, plan, and implement *adaptation* to climate change; … (9) carry out research and analysis relating to mitigation and *adaptation*.
- Reward: Article 27 calls on the central competent authority and central industry-competent authorities to reward well-performing facilities, enterprises, schools, organizations, or individuals with grants or subsidies for their major *adaptation* and mitigation initiatives.

Effects on the Energy Sector

725. The most significant changes are caused by the institutional design and ETS scheme. However, many measures (target, emission accounting and registration, emission performance standard, climate change fund, incentive and rewards, education and public awareness, adaptation measures) have only a very low impact on the energy sector, as this is merely a repeat of the current practice. Finally, this article identifies some uncertainties, namely in the Comprehensive Plan and Emission Trading Scheme. It still relies on the substantive context of the scheme to see if it would heavily influence the energy sector. Therefore, this article emphasizes the uncertainties therein in Table 32.

Table 32 Effect of the ERM Act of 2015 on the Energy Sector

Issues		*Effects on the Energy Sector*	
Institutional Design	2, 8, 13, 15	★★★★★	High
General principles regarding climate change and energy	5, 6	★★★	Mid

Issues			*Effects on the Energy Sector*	
Main Measures	Target (4, 9, 11, 12)		★	Low
	Comprehensive Plan (9, 15)		★or ★★★	Low to mid
	Six specific measures	Emission accounting and registration (16)	★	Low
		Emission performance standard (17)	★	Low
		Emission trading scheme (18, 20, 21, 22)	★★★★★ or★★★	Mid to high
		Climate change fund (19)	★	Low
		Incentive and rewards (27),	★	Low
		education and public awareness (24, 25, 26)	★	Low
Adaptation			★	Low

Source: Anton Ming-Zhi Gao, A Critical Review of the Role of Taiwan's 2015 Emission Reduction Act in the Energy Sector's Mitigation and Adaptation Initiatives, Special Issue on Energy Law, The Taiwan Law Review, 2019/6, 73–105.

726. Finally, even though this author contends that the ETS has had a significant effect on the energy sector, it may not apply to Tai-Power. According to Article 20(4) of the GHG Reduction Act, the EPA shall allocate emissions allowances to public utilities, excluding GHG emissions related to energy generation provided to emission sources for consumption as the indirect GHG emissions in CO2e. This means that the main bodies responsible for emissions from electricity should be loaded on electricity users, namely energy intensive industries, rather than on fossil fuel generators, particularly Tai-Power, under the 2015 GHG Reduction Act.

§4. Electricity Liberalization Act of 2017

727. Even though the 2015 GHG Reduction Act exempts Tai-Power and other fossil fuel generators from responsibility for emission reduction, this responsibility has been added back in the Electricity Liberalization Act of 2017. According to Article 28 of the Electricity Liberalization Act of 2017, when an "Electricity Retailing Utility Enterprise" sells electric power to its users, the sold electric power shall have an Electricity Carbon Emission Factor that meets the electricity carbon emission factor criteria. "Electricity Retailing Utility Enterprise" refers to Tai-Power's retailing division. The carbon emission factor is further defined as 0.492 kg CO2e/kWh by the Ordinance on Electricity Carbon Emission Factor.[1033] Considering the gradual drop of emission in the past few years—0.530 (2016), 0.554 (2017), 0.533 (2018), and 0.509 (2019)[1034]—meeting this year's duty poses a great challenge, even in this COVID-19 year.

728. The integration of emission reduction concerns in the Electricity Liberalization legislation would be unique. It would also turn the energy/economic authority into the climate change authority. Originally, the climate change legislation exempted Tai-Power from its emission reduction burden; however, in less than two years, the burden is back on Tai-Power via the Electricity Liberalization Act of 2017. The violation of this duty would be subject to a fine ranging from NTD 1,500,000 to NTD 15,000,000 imposed by the electricity industry regulatory authority.[1035] This would raise several questions. First, as Tai-Power's "Electricity Retailing Utility Enterprise" has to bear the duty to supply electricity, there is no room for it to refuse to buy high-carbon electricity to meet the factor obligation. Particularly, in the recent time of a low electricity reserve margin and the gradual phase-out of low-carbon nuclear power, and the increase of fossil fuel power plants in the electricity mix, Tai-Power seemed to have no option but to buy high-carbon electricity and get fined. Moreover, as Tai-Power's "Electricity Retailing Utility Enterprise" only has a retail function, it may not be capable of influencing emission directly like the emission performance standards on coal-fired plants in other countries.[1036] Finally, as Tai-Power is an "Electricity Retailing Utility Enterprise," as a utility, it can pass the cost of paying a penalty to electricity users via an electricity tariff calculation formula. This may reduce its incentives to reduce emissions.

1033. Ordinance on Electricity Carbon Emission Factor, 2018-07-16, available at: https://www.moeaboe.gov.tw/ecw/populace/Law/wHandLawsList_File.ashx?kind=5&id=3333.
1034. MOEABOE, Electricity Carbon Emission Factor of 2019, available at: https://www.moeaboe.gov.tw/ecw/populace/content/ContentDesc.aspx?menu_id=12014.
1035. Article 74 of the Electricity Act of 2017.
1036. Chris Simpson Brenda Hausauer Ajith Rao, Emissions Performance Standards In Selected States, August 2010, ResearchBrief, available at: https://www.raponline.org/wp-content/uploads/2016/05/rap-researchbrief-simpson-eps-updated-2010-08-12-2-.pdf.

Selected Bibliography

Anton Ming-Zhi Gao, Chien-Te Fan & Chao-Ning Liao, "Application of German Energy Transition in Taiwan: A Critical Review of Unique Electricity Liberalisation as a Core Strategy to Achieve Renewable Energy Growth," *Energy Policy* vol. 120 (2018), 644–654.

Anton Ming-Zhi Gao, "A Critical Review of the Role of Taiwan's 2015 Emission Reduction Act in the Energy Sector's Mitigation and Adaptation Initiatives," *The Taiwan Law Review*, 73–105 (2019).

MOEABOE, Taiwan Energy Policy and Measures (1997).

MOEA, Energy Statistics Handbook 2018 Revised, October 2019, available at: https://www.moeaboe.gov.tw/ECW_WEBPAGE/FlipBook/2018EnergyStaHandBook/index.html#p=53.

MOEAEC, Energy White Paper of 1998 (1998).

MOEA, Energy Policy White Paper, December 2005.

iReadeBooks, Liberalization of Power Market in Taiwan, 2008, available at: https://www.airitibooks.com/Detail/Detail?PublicationID=P20100203097&DetailSourceType=0.

Yun-Hsun Huang & Jung-Hua Wu, "Energy Policy on Taiwan: Historical Developments, Current Status and Potential Improvements," *Energies*, vol. 2 (2009), 623–645, available at: www.mdpi.com/1996-1073/2/3/623/pdf.

Anton Ming-Zhi Gao, *Regulating Gas Liberalization. A Comparative Study on Unbundling and Open Access Regimes in the US, Europe, Japan, South Korea and Taiwan* (Kluwer 2010).

Anton Ming-Zhi Gao, "Taiwan's Perhaps Irresponsible Policy and Laws on a Nuclear-Free Homeland by 2025: The Missing Piece of Nuclear Assets and Legacy," OGEL 2 (2019), www.ogel.org URL: www.ogel.org/article.asp?key=3819.

Anton Ming-Zhi Gao, *A More Sustainable Way to Promote PV: Transformations from FIT to FIT/FIT Tendering Schemes in Taiwan and France. Legal Issues of Renewable Energy in the Asia Region: Recent Development in a Post-Fukushima and Post-Kyoto Protocol Era* (The Netherlands, Kluwer Law International: 2014).

Jeffrey Shih-Jey Chen & Anton Ming-Zhi Gao, "Recent Development of an Emissions Trading Scheme and Energy/Carbon Tax in Taiwan," in: *Economic Instruments to Combat Climate Change in Asian Countries*, (Kluwer, 2015).

Selected Bibliography

Anton Ming-Zhi Gao & Chien-Te Fan (eds.), *The Development of a Comprehensive Legal Framework for the Promotion of Offshore Wind: The Lessons from Europe and Pacific Asia* (Kluwer, 2017).

Anton Ming-Zhi Gao & Chien-Te Fan (eds.), *Legal Issues of Renewable Electricity in Asia Region: Recent Development at a Post-Fukushima and Post-Kyoto Protocol Era* (Kluwer, 2014).

Ken'ichi Matsumoto & Anton Ming-Zhi Gao (eds.), *Economic Instruments to Combat Climate Change in Asian Countries: Choice Between Emission Trading Scheme and Carbon Tax* (Kluwer, 2015).

Anton Ming-Zhi Gao, "Chapter 9. The Promotion of Renewable Electricity Technology in the Mega-RTA Era: The Preliminary Evaluation of Potential Effects on Regulatory Convergence and Divergence," in: Shin-yi Peng et al. (eds.), *Governing Science and Technology under the International Economic Order: Regulatory Divergence and Convergence in the Age of Megaregionals*, (2018).

Anton Ming-Zhi Gao, "The Legal Regime of Climate Change Adaptation and Disaster Management in Taiwan: Focus on the Major Amendment Following the Devastating Typhoon Morakot of 2009," in: Koh Kheng Lian et al. (eds.), *Adaptation to Climate Change: ASEAN and Comparative Experiences*, World Scientific, pp. 373–408 (2015).

Anton Ming-Zhi Gao, "Chapter 10: Legal Framework to Develop Offshore Wind in Taiwan," in: A.M.Z Gao & C.T. Fan (eds.), *The Development of a Comprehensive Legal Framework for the Promotion of Offshore Wind Power* (Kluwer, .2017), pp. 225–252.

Anton Ming-Zhi Gao, Legal Regime of Taiwan's Offshore Oil and Gas Platforms, Capitulo Especial Sobre Plataformas Costa Afuera (Special Chapter on Costa Afuera Platforms), 1er Congreso Iberoamericano Costa Afuera Hacia Una Regulacion Integral de Las Plataformas Costa Afuera (1st Iberoamerican Congress Costa Afuera Towards a Comprehensive Regulation of the Costa Afuera Platforms), Rama Venezolana Del Instituto Iberoamericano de Derecho Maritimo (Venezuelan Branch of the Iberoamerican Institute of Maritime Law), pp. 50–70 (2016).

Anton Ming-Zhi Gao & Chien-Te Fan, "Transformation of German- and European-Style Feed-in Tariff Schemes in East Asia in the Post-Fukushima Age: Recent Developments in Japan, South Korea, and Taiwan," in: Anton Ming-Zhi Gao & Chien-Te Fan (eds.), *Legal Issues of Renewable Electricity in Asia Region: Recent Development at a Post-Fukushima and Post-Kyoto Protocol Era* (2014), pp. 213–258.

Anton Ming-Zhi Gao, Chien-Te Fan & Jong-Shun Chen, A Critical Review of the World's First Renewable Portfolio Standard (RPS) for Large Electricity Users in Taiwan: The Return of the RPS?," *Energy Strategy Reviews*, vol. 32 (2020), https://doi.org/10.1016/j.esr.2020.100585.

Anton Ming-Zhi Gao, "The Public Acceptance and Legal Issues of Carbon Capture and Storage Technology in Taiwan," *Soongsil Law Review* (法學論叢) vol. 35 (2016), pp. 431–470.

Anton Ming-Zhi Gao et al., "Sustainable Photovoltaic Technology Development: Step-by-Step Guidance for Countries Facing PV Proliferation Turmoil under the Feed-In Tariff Scheme," *Renewable and Sustainable Energy Reviews* vol. 43 (2015), pp. 156–163.

Anton Ming-Zhi Gao, "Europe's Policy Framework for Promoting Offshore Wind Energy: Lessons for Taiwan and Other Countries," *Renewable Energy Policy and Law*, vol. 2015/1 (2015), pp. 3–16.

Anton Ming-Zhi Gao, "The Special Reconstruction Regime after Extreme Weather from the 2009 Morakot Typhoon in Taiwan," *Carbon and Climate Law Review*, vol. 2015/1 (2015), pp. 5–18.

Anton Ming-Zhi Gao, "Evaluation of Electricity Liberalization Legal Framework in Taiwan: What Can We Learn from European Three Waves of Electricity Regulatory Reforms," *International Energy Law Review*, vol. 32 no. 2 (2013), pp. 111–127

Anton Ming-Zhi Gao, "Development of a Legal Framework for Climate Change at the Post-Fukushima Age in Taiwan: Lessons from the Policy and Legal Framework of Europe and Germany," *Carbon and Climate Law Review* (1/2013), pp. 54–70.

Anton Ming-Zhi Gao, "Taiwan's Recent Efforts to Promote Renewable Energy Development: Policy Measures, Legal Measures, Challenges, and Solutions in the Post-Fukushima Era," *Renewable Energy Law and Policy*, vol. 3 no. 4 (2012), pp. 263–279.

Yen-Lin Agnes Chiu & Anton Ming-Zhi Gao, "National Report: Climate Law in the Republic of China (Taiwan)," *Ympäristöjuridiikka* 3/2011 (*Finnish Environmental Law Review*, 3/2011), pp. 107–124.

Anton Ming-Zhi Gao, *An Alternative Way to Deal with Climate Change: A Comparative Study and Critical Review of Basic Acts and Bills on Climate Change and Energy in Japan, South Korea, and Taiwan*, OGEL Special Issue on "Comparative Energy Law," March 2011, OGEL Journal (ISSN 1875-418X)

Michael G. Faure & Anton Ming-Zhi Gao, "Editorial Special Issue: The Rule of Law and Climate Adaptation in the Asian Region," *Carbon and Climate Law Review*, vol. 2015/1 (2015), pp. 1–4.

Anton Ming-Zhi Gao, "Energy Transition Scam in Taiwan: Wrong Legal Strategy?," in: Rose-Liza Eisma-Osorio & Linda Yanti Sulistiawati (eds.), *Environmental Rule of Law in Asia*, published by: Published and distributed by Konrad-Adenauer- Stiftung, Ltd. (KAS), August 2019 (ISBN: 978-621-96185-0-2), pp. 67–86.

Selected Bibliography

Selected Legislation

Acts

Act on Promotion of Private Participation in Infrastructure Projects of 2001
Act of the Organization of the Bureau of Energy
Act on Facilitating the Upgrade of Traditional Industries
Act on Innovative Industries
Act on Monitoring Private-Owned Utilities (Act for Regulating Privately Run Utilities)
Act on Sites for Establishment of Low Level Radioactive Waste Final Disposal Facility
Act on State-Owned Enterprises
Act on the EEZ and Continental Shelf of ROC
Air Pollution Control Act
Atomic Energy Act
Electricity Business Act
Energy Management Act
Environmental Basic Act
Environmental Impact Assessment Act
Governmental Reorganization Act
Ionizing Radiation Protection Act
Marine Pollution Act
Mining Act
Natural Gas Business Act
Nuclear Damage Compensation Act
Nuclear Emergency Response Act
Nuclear Materials and Radioactive Waste Management Act
Nuclear Reactor Facilities Regulation Act
Organization Act of the Atomic Energy Council of the Executive Yuan
Petroleum Management Act
Renewable Energy Act
Water Pollution Control Act

Ordinance

Biogas Electricity Feed-in Tariff Ordinance (enacted on January 22, 2003; last revised October 13, 2009).

Selected Legislation

CHP Ordinance II (enacted on September 4, 2002; last revised December 27, 2010). EIA Operation Ordinance for Development Projects
Mandatory Mixture Ordinance of 2008, July 4, 2008.
Mandatory Mixture Ordinance of 2010. (June 10, 2010). MOEABOE, Notification of Payment for Petroleum Fund Ordinance for GHG Measuring and Verification Ordinance on Accounting Rules for Utilities
Ordinance on Annual Energy Data Submission
Ordinance on Application for Exploration and Exploitation Subsidy Ordinance on Auto Fuel Usage Fees
Ordinance on Comprehensive Measures of Energy Conservation and Emission Reduction of the Government and Schools
Ordinance on Defining Shortage of Supply or Price-hike, Limitation, and Measures Ordinance on Demonstration Investment Subsidy of PV Plants (May 31, 2000). Ordinance on Energy Performance for New Building Construction
Ordinance on Energy Performance of Centralized Air Conditioning for New Building Construction
Ordinance on Environmental Impact Assessment
Ordinance on Environmental Impact Assessment of Governmental Policy Ordinance on Exploration Subsidy Program for Geothermal Power Generation and Demonstration.
Ordinance on Governmental Information Disclosure of the AEC, May 18, 2010. Ordinance on Demonstration Investment Subsidy of Wind Power Plants (March 22, 2000)
Ordinance on Investment Subsidy and Implementation Guide for Solar Water Heaters of 2003, February 6, 2003.
Ordinance on Investment Subsidy for LPG Filling Stations
Ordinance on Investment Subsidy for Renewable Heating Use, April 2010 Ordinance on Investment Tax Credit for Companies Installing Energy Saving or New and Clean Energy Facilities of 1995.
Ordinance on Loan Guarantees of the Credit Guarantee Fund for Small and Medium Enterprises.
Ordinance on Management of Gas Pipeline Contractor Businesses Ordinance on Managing Coal Gas Businesses
Ordinance on Mineral Right Fees Ordinance on Mineral Royalty
Ordinance on Policy of Compulsory SEA
Ordinance on Priority Purchasing of Environmentally Friendly Products by the Government.
Ordinance on Public Liability and Accidental Pollution Insurance for Petroleum Business Ordinance on the Authorization for Laying, Maintaining, Changing Seabed Cable and Pipeline
Ordinance on Quality of Petroleum Products
Ordinance on the Energy Performance Guarantee Program Ordinance on the Energy-Saving Mark.
Ordinance on the Format for Fuel Economy of Vehicles and Motor Bikes Ordinance on the Grant for Purchasing Energy-Saving Labeled Products. Ordinance on the Insured Amount of Public Liability Insurance of Gas Business Ordinance on the Management of Coal Gas Business

Ordinance on the Management of the Governmental Oil Stockpile Ordinance on the Promotion of CHP of 1988
Ordinance on the Promotion of CHP of 1988
Ordinance on the Standard for Calculating Oil Security Stockpile for Oil Refiner and Importer
Ordinance" on the Purchase of Renewable Electricity by Tai-Power on November 4, 2003. Ordinance on Special Levy for Air Pollution Prevention
Soft Loan Ordinance for Buying Energy-Saving Installations of 2009
Soft Loan Ordinance on Buying Energy-Saving Installations (Second Phase) of 2002
Soft Loan Ordinance on Buying Energy-Saving Installations of 1999 Subsidy Ordinance for Ethanol in Taipei and Kaushiun City (July 2, 2009). The Ordinance on Managing Coal Gas Businesses

Bill

Bill on Early Phase-out of Nuclear Power Plants
Electricity Business Bill (liberalization version)
Emission Reduction Bill (GHG Reduction Bill)
Energy Taxation Bill
Gas Utility Bill (Bill on Gas Fuel Utilities)
Nuclear-Free Homeland Bill
Sustainable Energy Basic Bill

Index

The numbers here refer to paragraph numbers.

Index

Index

www.ingramcontent.com/pod-product-compliance
Ingram Content Group UK Ltd.
Pitfield, Milton Keynes, MK11 3LW, UK
UKHW020133290926
15471UKWH00003B/460